Psychology in the Real World:

Community-based groupwork

GUY HOLMES

with

Mandy Barratt, Jo Clare, Ken Davies,
Nicki Evans, Lucy Gahan, Marese Hudson,
Anna Hughes, Carol Johnson, Zounish Rafique,
Carole Stone, John Upton, Elisabeth X

First published in 2010

PCCS BOOKS Ltd
2 Cropper Row
Alton Road
Ross-on-Wye
Herefordshire
HR9 5LA
UK
Tel +44 (0)1989 763 900
www.pccs-books.co.uk

Psychology in the Real World: Community-based groupwork

A CIP catalogue record for this book is available from the British Library

ISBN 978 1 906254 13 1

Cover design in the UK by Old Dog Graphics
Cover artwork by Julie Forshaw, Littlefish Online Studio
Typeset in the UK by The Old Dog's Missus
Printed in the UK by Ashford Colour Press, Gosport, UK

CONTENTS

Dedication

To all the people who have come to, and otherwise been involved with, *Psychology in the Real World* groups.

Acknowledgements

I would like to thank the hundreds of people from various backgrounds who have shaped the way I work (and in doing so shaped this book). There are too many to list, especially as they include everyone who has come to a *Psychology in the Real World* group. I want to specifically mention a few: Jim Kelman who taught me to think clearly about what to say after you say hello; Craig Newnes who helped me develop my ideas and supported the groups that were born out of them; clinicians and trainees I met whilst receiving excellent training from Group Analysis North, the Philadelphia Association and the West Midlands course in clinical psychology; Joe Kiff who helped me come up with the name 'Psychology in the Real World' and, along with Marilyn Owens, Cai Dunn and Anna Perrin, has provided supervision on the groups over many years; Penny Priest and Mark Doel who helped clarify many references; Helen Jones who (often in her own time) has put up flyers and articles about the groups on www.shropsych.org; her partner Martin Hansen who created the node diagrams which represent the matrix; Emma Wallace and Jo Watson who produced computerised versions of my scribbled diagrams; Tim Cooke for his help with the cover design; Maggie, Pete and Heather from PCCS Books for their support and encouragement, and Sandy Green for her kind words and proofreading. I am also grateful to all the contributors for their patience regarding my editing of their work, and for their helpful comments and editing of the chapters that I have contributed. I would also like to thank people who read and commented on earlier drafts: Rae Cox, Cai Dunn, Biza Kroese, Paul Moloney, Joanna Moncrieff, Penny Priest, David Smail and Penny Woolcock.

Permissions

The quotes on 'What is Psychology' in Chapter 2 are reproduced from the website www.bps.org.uk with permission from The British Psychological Society. The Division of Clinical Psychology of the BPS have kindly given permission for two lengthy quotes and one article to be reproduced from their journal *Clinical Psychology Forum*: Chapter 33 is largely reproduced from a paper that appeared in *Clinical Psychology Forum, 164*; Jim Orford's quote on community psychology in Chapter 34 is from a paper published in *Clinical Psychology Forum, 122*; David Smail's quote on the profession of clinical psychology in Chapter 5 is from *Clinical Psychology Forum, 93*. I am also grateful to Jim and David for their personal permission to use these quotes, and for David's permission to reproduce diagrams from his work *Power, Interest and Psychology*. The article 'Coming off Medication' in Chapter 41 is reprinted with permission from *OpenMind*. My thanks also to Phil Barker and Poppy Buchanan-Barker for permission to use quotes from their work and website www.tidal-model.com and the Vipassana Trust Outreach Committee for permission to use a lengthy quote from their website www.dhamma.org in Box 4.

I am also thankful for the permission given by participants in the groups to cite their anonymous feedback which is included throughout the book, often in the form of direct quotations from evaluations of the groups. I am especially grateful to members of the 2006 *Thinking about Medication* group who, after reading the chapters in this section and giving consent for these to be included, also gave me updates of their experiences in terms of taking and coming off medication since the group ended. In addition I would like to thank group members who form central characters in the 'in vivo' descriptions of actual group sessions, who read the chapters and gave their express approval for these accounts to be included; to retain anonymity some details and all names have been changed in these descriptions. I would also like to thank those people who provided me with personal quotations relevant to their experiences of the groups and gave their consent to be quoted by name.

Foreword

Who is the book written for?

I hope that anyone with an interest in human beings will find something in the book that helps them think about what makes people tick. Most people nowadays work in groups, and the book should help people understand group processes a bit better. Primarily the book is written for people interested in group and community work, whatever their background or profession. Although the groups it describes come under the broad umbrella known as 'mental health', the ideas in it are hopefully just as relevant to other services (such as learning disabilities). Many people who set up and facilitate groups seem to do so with little (usually no) training in groupwork – there is a dearth of training available in Britain outside the narrow confines of group psychoanalytic psychotherapy. Similarly, people running groups often have little supervision or help to plan and think through how to structure and run their groups. I hope that this book will act as a guide for people who have done no previous groupwork, whether they see themselves as coming from a professional or service user background, as well as be thought-provoking and helpful for people already engaged in group or community work. People interested in critical and community psychology (whatever their profession or background) have remarked to me that they feel very well informed in terms of deconstructing and critiquing existing practice but often flounder when trying to work in ways that reflect these critiques. Hopefully this book will assist and encourage people to set up their own projects and ventures, which may vary greatly from the ones described here, but do not have to be constrained by some of the constricting ideologies and practices that currently dominate many professions and organisations.

A note on referencing style

When relating *Psychology in the Real World* philosophies to other people's work, particularly well-known quotes or broad descriptions of people's theories, I have not formally referenced this in the text in the traditional Harvard style that I have used throughout my academic and professional life. I was influenced by a conversation I had with Dorothy Rowe who felt psychologists' use of references and other trappings of the scientific research paper style of writing often made their work unreadable for the general public. Like Oscar Wilde, I believe every author is the child of someone else; all that we have read and experienced runs through us and nothing that is written can be said to be truly original. It is impossible to be consciously aware of all these influences, and clumsy to try and formally reference them all.

Having said this, many concepts referred to in the book that I have discovered through the reading of other people's work do name those people and a full reference should be discoverable by following the subject and author indexes and tracking it to the reference section. Alternatively of course there is the Internet – anyone able to use Google can quickly obtain summaries, direct quotations and even whole research papers relating to people or ideas cited in this book. In the 1980s I was trained to reference virtually every sentence apart from those that were original. This was in an era when academic writing was terribly difficult to locate, traceable only through arcane indexing systems in university libraries, or occasionally stumbled on in second-hand bookshops. Since then, people's theories and ideas have been mass published, are orderable with a few clicks on a computer and are easily discoverable in summarised form (often written by well-known academics) on the Internet, usually alongside critiques of those ideas. Academics and clinicians can quickly track original research through use of Athens and other clinical database search engines, but many use Google as a first point of call. Wikipedia (or Psychology Wiki – a Wiki solely for psychological work) represents a democratisation of knowledge that overlaps with some *Psychology in the Real World* philosophies and provides information about the majority of ideas and most of the people cited in this book.

I have endeavoured to write something that is methodologically rigorous and as true a reflection of my experiences of this type of work as I am capable. However, the book is not a research paper or an academic literature review; it is about ideas, and in my opinion ideas do not need referencing as if they are something concrete because ideas convey different meanings to different readers. As such, quotes, philosophies and ideas do not need to be checked up on by going back to the first source in the same way as one might want to look up original research data (which for clarity has been more formally referenced in some sections of the book). If, however, anyone is desperate to read an original source of something referred to in the text and is unable to trace it through the reference section or Internet, I would be happy to be contacted to assist with this at guy.holmes@nhs.net.

INTRODUCTION
Chapter 1

Community-based groupwork and psychology in the real world

Never doubt that a small group of thoughtful, committed citizens can change the world; indeed, it's the only thing that ever does.
   Margaret Mead

This is a book about psychology in the broadest sense of the word; about groups, groupwork and community work; about doing ordinary things; and about doing revolutionary things in ordinary ways. It is written for people who are interested in the diverse ways we can be affected (and psychologically infected) by what happens to us during our lives and the great variety of ways in which we might be helped. It is a book about doing things *with*, rather than *to* or *for*, other people.

Psychology in the Real World is an umbrella term under which, with the support and involvement of many other people, some of whom have written chapters in this book, I have set up a number of groups, courses and ventures in Shropshire since the late 1990s. Rather than bringing people together because they have a shared problem or diagnosis, *Psychology in the Real World* brings people together who have a shared interest. For example:

- *Understanding Ourselves and Others* provides people with opportunities to explore a range of theories that might help us understand various aspects of our lives (e.g. What leads us to be angry; violent; depressed? What helps people feel safe and secure? Why are we so afraid of mental illness?)

- *The Black Dog* enables people to collectively critique the concept of depression and explore a wide variety of theories and research on what leads us to become depressed (e.g. look at whether depression might be one way we react to oppression)

- *Toxic Mental Environments* provides people with opportunities to analyse aspects of the world we live in that might be detrimental to our wellbeing, and link up with others with the aim of bringing about some changes in these environments

- *Thinking about Medication* enables wide-ranging discussions between people who take psychiatric drugs and various professionals who prescribe and help people come off medication

- *Out of the Box* helps people trying to come off psychiatric drugs to support each other during this process

- *Walk and Talk* assists people who have an interest in walking along the riverside to connect with nature and connect with others in their locality

- *The Writing Group* helps those of us who feel we gain much from writing about personal experiences to meet up and share our written work

These groups are described in this book. Although each group is different they share some characteristics, such as:

- They occur in non-mental health settings, such as arts and education centres, libraries, along river paths and in local pubs.

- People are not formally referred to the groups – the groups are open to all and are advertised locally in non-mental health settings as well as within services. When advertising the groups, attempts are made to get as broad a mix of people as possible in terms of age, class, gender, sexuality, race and, particularly, mental health service involvement. Roughly a third of participants tend to be accessing secondary services such as community mental health or assertive outreach teams, a third have had some primary care service (e.g. taken psychiatric drugs prescribed by a GP or received counselling) and a third have had no previous mental health service involvement. The age of participants has ranged from 4 to 84 – from a young child who regularly joined in *Walk and Talk* alongside his parents to an octogenarian who, during *Thinking about Medication,* described herself as a 'carer and psychiatric system survivor who was damaged by ECT over 30 years ago'. This mix of participants contrasts sharply with most mental health services which tend to categorise people in terms of some attribute or presenting problem and exclude people who do not fit certain criteria.

- They are often inspired, planned and co-facilitated by people who have previously attended other *Psychology in the Real World* courses, and are frequently based on ideas that came out of these groups. For example, *Toxic Mental Environments* and *Thinking about Medication* led to explorations of the importance of accessing the countryside as a way of people detoxifying reactions to contemporary culture and as an alternative to taking psychiatric drugs. This led to Anna

Hughes and me setting up *Walk and Talk*. Anna, as well as being a mum and a marathon runner, describes herself as a mental health service user. *Walk and Talk* has subsequently been run and organised by a collective of people, some of whom have a history of mental health service involvement, some of whom do not, but all of whom initially came along as members of the group.

- They are not 'skills for ills' groups – they respect the fact that, as one participant put it, 'there are as many recoveries as there are people'. There is a recognition that each person's reactions to their life experiences are unique and complex, there are a myriad of causes of distress, and sharing our experiences and thoughts with others enables a collective wisdom to arise that often outweighs the wisdom of any expert. Participants are not seen as empty vessels needing to be filled up with knowledge passed on by the group leader, but rather as people who can develop their own ways of critiquing the world that they live in and its impacts on them and others. Group members may learn *how to think* but are not taught *what to think*. As one participant put it, 'I expected to be told the answers, but this is much more liberating!'

- Research findings are discussed and critiqued (e.g. What lessons might we learn from the Milgram and Stanford Prison experiments? Might the validity of research conducted by organisations that have a financial interest in obtaining positive results be sometimes compromised?). However, unlike the National Institute of Health and Clinical Excellence (NICE) guidelines, the evidence of group members' lived experiences, and reflections on those experiences, are given just as much weight as findings from 'the evidence base'. These are also held up for critique (e.g. To what extent are insights gained from our own personal experience applicable to others?).

- We explore theories and research relating to the causes of people's distress, but look beyond immediate factors to the *causes of causes,* for example, aspects of 21st century consumer capitalism that perhaps damage us all.

- Participants are encouraged and assisted to move from critique and analysis to social action during and on ending the groups.

The groups have been evaluated in a range of ways and have been shown to have impacts on various aspects of people's lives and the communities they inhabit. For example, some people's health and wellbeing has improved (e.g. group members have reduced and come off psychiatric medication); others have recognised changes in what David Smail has called *proximal powers* (e.g. by coming to a non-stigmatising and valued group, rather than attending a mental health unit as a 'patient' or 'service user', and going on to attain skills and status as a group co-facilitator, people have taken on roles that accord them greater power); there appears to have been some lessening of stigmatising and prejudiced attitudes in the area of mental health (e.g. people who have never had any involvement with mental health services have commented on having less fear and greater understanding of people who have been in the local psychiatric hospital, or been diagnosed with schizophrenia, having got to know fellow group members who have had such experiences); and people have brought about some modest changes in various systems and environments (e.g. by coming together to improve, protect and increase access to the river paths used on *Walk and Talk*).

A loose nexus of people associated with *Psychology in the Real World* continue to link up with and support other. Some have set up their own projects; others have inspired and assisted the setting up of similar groups. For example, group members, many with considerable histories of psychiatric service involvement, have described the groups at conferences and training events, gone to other parts of Britain to provide advice and assistance to people setting up medication groups, and have initiated eco-projects to help people access the benefits of being in the countryside. Many have re-acquainted themselves with old skills and others have developed new ones. In doing so, many people have escaped being positioned as a passive patient, taking on roles such as researcher, group facilitator, staff trainer, consultant, and campaigner. Those who write well have written about their experiences and their views, for example, in chapters in this book. Just as over the years I have benefited from spending time with and receiving guidance and training from people with skills in groupwork, I have endeavoured to provide support (aimed at being the minimum necessary) to some group members long after the groups have ended as they have tried to bring about some change in a world that they see as flawed or unjust. This has involved help to publicise groups they have set up; assistance to learn and apply research skills; support with giving a presentation at a conference; and the editing of written work for a more academic audience. One-to-one therapeutic interventions have come to dominate practice in the NHS, Social Services and increasingly the voluntary sector, but this book describes a wide range of ways that psychologists and others can utilise skills over and above those associated with the provision of individual therapy.

Evaluations have indicated that, although *Psychology in the Real World* groups are not set up as therapy groups, a significant number of people report benefits that mirror the therapeutic gains people obtain from individual and group therapy. The benefits people describe, however, go beyond those of self-understanding. For example, expressing one's views and being listened to and respected in a group tends to bolster people's self-esteem in a more powerful way than occurs in one-to-one therapy. And if this takes place in a large group in a socially valued setting, such as at a conference, the impacts are even more dramatic. But not all feedback about the groups is positive and not everything is a success. Although drop-out rates tend to be low, people do leave the groups before the end, and certainly not everyone who comes to a *Psychology in the Real World* venture becomes an activist. Although the chapter writers in this book describe some dramatic and long-lasting beneficial impacts following their involvement in the groups (e.g. some no longer conceptualise themselves, or are conceptualised by others, as psychiatric patients, have come off psychiatric drugs after decades of use and have become paid employees in the NHS), for the majority of group members any gains have been relatively modest (e.g. some previously lonely and isolated people have made friends). No group can meet all the needs of everyone who gets involved and all groups have the capacity to harm as well as help. Yet I remain convinced that the kinds of projects described in this book offer opportunities to individuals and communities that other mental health service endeavours often neglect.

The groups inevitably reflect my own interests and beliefs in what helps people. These partly draw upon personal experience. Whilst not wanting to dismiss published psychological research, I have long felt that the 'evidence base' as conceptualised and referred to by some managers and professionals is a very constricted view of what assists people. In the 1990s Craig

Newnes and I regularly ran sessions entitled *Using Common Sense and Personal Experience to Help People*. Members of the public, many of whom had attended mental health services, joined various mental health professionals in order to pool experiences about *what helps us in crisis* and *what helps us maintain our mental health*. These sessions made me aware that many things people identify as helpful (e.g. being with animals) are given scant regard in what is often referred to as the evidence base. Like many who came to these sessions, I too found that spending time in the countryside had a healing and detoxifying effect at times of my life when I felt I was 'going mad' or spiralling into depression, and writing poetry eased distress through enabling me to express things I often found difficult to say in conversation.

My training in clinical psychology and groupwork in the 1990s had led me to feel that the knowledge acquired about various psychological theories, especially when we were given opportunities in small, intimate groups to relate this to our own personal experiences, often felt just as helpful and healing as the individual and group therapy that I had received. When I began working as a psychologist, and tentatively started to bring people together in groups, I found that being open about my life experiences and difficulties seemed to be appreciated by others who, like me, came to feel they benefited from sharing experiences in group settings. My own mental health also seemed to be being helped by having a valued role and a sense of helping others. Local research on service users' views (and *Using Common Sense and Personal Experience to Help People* sessions) kept identifying the importance of things such as: having opportunities to make sense of difficulties; meeting up with like-minded people and discussing common experiences; being in the countryside and other healing environments; discussing the pros and cons of psychiatric drugs; helping people as well as being helped; being listened to and respected; and being involved in 'trying to make a difference'. This research, much of which I had been involved in, had led to very few changes in services. *Thinking about Medication, Walk and Talk, The Writing Group, Understanding Ourselves and Others, The Black Dog* and *Toxic Mental Environments* were therefore attempts to respond to local people's expressed needs and what they identified as being potentially helpful as well as being projects that felt commensurate with my own experiences.

Psychology in the Real World groups also reflect the interests and passions of the co-facilitators: Marese Hudson's sense of having been helped by attending a coming-off medication group and determination to enable others to benefit from a similar experience; Anna Hughes' love of the countryside and of the healing that is brought to the fore when experiences are shared; Nicki Evans' wish to create an arena where people can share and discuss their writing. This book has been inspired by people who have engaged in such ventures and people from around Britain who have shown an interest in them and a wish to find out more about how to set up something similar. The book includes a lot of practical information about how to do this, but it is important that whatever ventures people set up are commensurate with their own interests and passions and their own deeply held beliefs, as well as responding to expressed needs and requests from the people the groups are aimed at helping.

The book can be read from start to finish, but is also written so that people can select a chapter at random and read something that is hopefully coherent in its own right. Some parts of the chapters, particularly the 'Boxes', include the type of information we often provide for people attending *Psychology in the Real World* groups. Such summaries are not intended to be a review of all knowledge about a subject but rather a way of presenting interesting information about a topic aimed at kick-starting a debate. The book can be dipped into and, as with J.G. Ballard's *Atrocity Exhibition,* readers may want to just pick bits that grab their attention. As such it is written to reflect the ways most of us access information nowadays. Because of this, some points made in one section are sometimes repeated in others.

Kierkegaard said: 'The tragedy of life is that it can only be understood looking backwards but has to be experienced going forwards.' Reading this book will make *Psychology in the Real World* ventures seem more coherently thought through than actually they were. On writing the book I have related more theory to each venture than I consciously brought when planning and running the groups, and to some extent I have only come to fully grasp what I have been doing by writing about it. I have tried to be as honest as I can – books that give fictitious accounts of gloriously successful psychological interventions in my view do more harm than good, leaving clinicians despondent when their attempts do not match up to the ones described (and probably embellished) in the texts. The accounts of group sessions in this book tend to focus on things that to some extent went wrong. As Dave Harper and others have pointed out, it is incumbent on psychologists and other members of the helping professions to talk about failure as well as success, and whilst most *Psychology in the Real World* ventures have overall gone well, like any group-based activity there have been many ups and downs.

SECTION 1

Some philosophies and principles underlying
Psychology in the Real World

Box 1   What's in a name?

You can't hear a word and just hear it as a raw sound; it always evokes an associated meaning and emotion in the brain.
   Steven Pinker

As a young boy I enjoyed watching Crewe Alexandra football club. But I recall a discomfort when saying I supported Crewe to my friends, most of whom supported Liverpool and Manchester United. In the 1970s Crewe was associated with finishing in the bottom three of the bottom football division virtually every year and played in a dilapidated stadium where fans stood on crushed cinders from the emptied railway engines. We seem to find it easier to have pride in our group (and consequently pride in ourselves) when we are part of a group associated with excellence or high status, and when we are a member of a group that lots of people want to join. I wince when football clubs are now described as 'brands', but there is something in this. As a fan of Naomi Klein's book *No Logo,* I really winced when community psychologist Bob Diamond described *Psychology in the Real World* as a brand. But he correctly identified that this umbrella term, under which many of the groups sit, has come to convey a lot of information in a short phrase (some of which is elucidated in this section).

Branding and stigma have a long history of association. In Greco-Roman antiquity people deemed 'morally polluted' were tattooed and branded to publicly signify their defectiveness. Whilst people are no longer physically marked, the equivalent in 21st century mental health services is the assignment of people to groups that brand and stigmatise them: MIND have shown that it is easier to get a job having been in prison than having been in psychiatric hospital, and even the most paternalistic or liberal employer balks on discovering a candidate has been diagnosed as 'schizophrenic' or 'personality disordered'.

Labels (and the power of the labellers) are thus important. Many clinicians spend considerable time planning a group but pay little attention to the group's name. This contrasts sharply with business practice where it is accepted that the most important marketing decision is what to name the product and, although a good name is not a guarantee of success, a bad name guarantees failure. It is hard to find a good name, and I often mull it over for longer than any other aspect of the initial group planning. It can be helpful to check out ideas with others. Paul Grantham, as part of the Skills Development Service, does a witty talk about group names he has come across in the NHS. If you take a tour around services you will find names such as 'The Wednesday Group' – not stigmatising but hardly enticing. Still, better than the 'Memory Loss Group', 'Depressed Women's Group' or 'Men's Impotency Group'. All participants instinctively know that membership of groups brands us and, as with the actual branding of people in the past, the effects of this are difficult to erase, yet groupworkers frequently get puzzled when take-up of their carefully prepared but appallingly named group is poor.

Group facilitators often make a fundamental error by asking themselves the question: 'Do I want to run this group?' 'Would I, or someone I respect and care about, want to be *a member* of this group?' is the question that really needs to be asked.

2

What is meant by *psychology*?

The unexamined life is not worth living.
    Socrates

This quote, from the 5th century BC, marks an expansion of interest in philosophical enquiry into the natural world (primarily of physics and cosmology) to one of greater enquiry into people's lives: *How should one live? What does it mean to live a good life? What makes life worth living? Why do people do things?* Socrates believed that rational self-critique could free the mind from what he called the bondage of false opinion. In terms of *Psychology in the Real World* ventures, the quote represents a core ethos: examining our lives, in order to understand ourselves, others and factors in our society that shape people's behaviour, is an important endeavour. As Socrates himself discovered, conclusive answers to such questions are hard to arrive at. The oracle at Delphi had declared that no man was wiser than Socrates, and Socrates himself, typically questioning this, came to the conclusion that he may indeed be wiser than others because he was one of the few people who recognised and fully appreciated their ignorance. This informed sense of ignorance, and resulting humility, resides at the core of *Psychology in the Real World* – people, including myself, often feel they lack knowledge and are terribly confused when trying to understand themselves, others and the world they live in, but what better place is there from which to start? Of course, if we spent 24 hours of every day doing this we would drive ourselves and our friends mad; as George

Eliot said: 'The over-examined life is also not worth living.' But to set aside time each week to critically reflect on life, to question and explore, to engage in the *Socratic method*, seems an important endeavour to undertake.

The British Psychological Society defines psychology as:

The scientific study of human mind and behaviour: how we think, how we act, react and interact individually and in groups. Psychology is concerned with all aspects of behaviour and the thoughts, feelings and motivations underlying such behaviour.

On its website (www.bps.org.uk) the society goes on to say:

Psychology is based in science *and psychologists learn the scientific basis of human behaviour by observing, measuring, testing, and using statistics to show that what they find is reliable evidence and not just down to chance. The* **scientific knowledge** *gained by this research is then used by applied/practising psychologists (those dealing with clients) and other professionals in almost every setting.*

The scientific method – the generation of testable hypotheses, the experimental gathering of analysable data that might support or refute these hypotheses, the refinement of theories and further generation of testable hypotheses – can be a powerful way of making sense of the world. Experimental psychology has revealed that common-sense predictions and explanations of people's behaviour are often inaccurate and the determinants of human behaviour are frequently more complex than is commonly supposed. How people say they will behave in certain situations often differs from their actual behaviour once they are in those environments. Human beings (including psychologists and psychiatrists) are notoriously poor at predicting human behaviour. For example, psychiatrists predicted 1% – 'the proportion of psychopaths in the population' – would electrocute people in the scenario used in the Milgram experiment; experimentally Milgram produced data which showed 67% of test subjects electrocuted people to a point of apparent unconsciousness. Yet the scientific method also has its weaknesses. For example, aggregated data (data pooled from a large number of people studied) is not very good at enabling us to predict an individual person's behaviour. In *Psychology in the Real World* groups we have often debated how we might know whether we, or the people we sit alongside, are one of the few people who delivered no shocks or one of the majority who delivered life-threatening electric shocks in the Milgram experiment scenario.

Many people mistakenly think science is about certainty. Science values accuracy (for example, of things measured) but philosophically it is underpinned by uncertainty – science cannot prove things, just generate theories that best explain the data, with its theories ready to be overturned and replaced by others should future data warrant this. In this book, as in the courses the book describes, I have endeavoured to be accurate. I have not wished to provide a biased impression of the groups, or consciously selected data that only supports my interests. Yet I am just as prone to unconscious biases and distorting influences as any other person. For example, the descriptions in the book of in vivo group sessions (e.g.

Chapters 17, 25 and 51) are not 'the truth' of what happened but a representation of my memories; others would probably remember and describe the experiences very differently.

Bertrand Russell, one of the most eminent British philosophers of the 20th century, was aware of the power of the scientific method in terms of discovering and evaluating insights about human behaviour. Yet Russell also said: 'Science cannot answer the most interesting questions.' The profession of clinical psychology emphasises the scientist-practitioner and (like Freud) recognises the status that comes from being allied to a powerful body of knowledge and method of enquiry. Yet as Peter Chadwick eloquently illustrates in his book *Personality as Art,* the scientific method is limited in terms of helping us understand people, and Art reveals much that the scientific eye misses. Something is captured in *Birthday Letters* that is far too subtle to be picked up by the scientific method, yet reveals much about Sylvia Plath, Ted Hughes and their relationship. Would a personality test reveal more about Van Gogh than his self-portraits? Could psychology ever generate and test theories that encapsulated the complexities of moral behaviour illustrated in Albert Camus' *The Fall*?

Psychology in the Real World ventures have a core ideology that we are all psychologists. George Kelly conceptualised people as formulating theories about the world and testing them against the evidence – in a sense being what we now call scientist-practitioners. *Psychology in the Real World* participants are invited to consider adopting this way of making sense of things, but are also encouraged to consider being 'artist-practitioners'. Psychology is taken not as a narrow discipline that positions itself as only of relevance in narrow arenas of knowledge, but rather as a broad church that incorporates insights into human behaviour that have come from philosophy, sociology, art, biography, novels, poetry and psychotherapy. Indeed, psychotherapy has been called an art just as often as it has been claimed to be a science. Poetry and psychotherapy can both be thought of as engaging in a process of finding words for things that are very difficult to express. We also heed David Smail's warning that, whilst one of the main endeavours of the profession of clinical psychology is to make sense of individual, subjective experience, we must be cautious not to make the error of failing to look beyond the individual in our search for explanations. When trying to understand ourselves, others and the world that we inhabit during *Psychology in the Real World* ventures, we therefore draw upon a wide range of information that goes beyond the somewhat dull boundaries that academic psychology has often drawn around itself. The only thing that is discouraged is analysis of celebrities, as the information we have on celebrities is grossly twisted by their sophisticated PR and the media, so that we can end up debating a brand rather than a person that we know.

On evidence

Psychologists, and increasingly health services in general, emphasise evidence-based practice. *Psychology in the Real World* courses help people to access *and* critique some of this evidence. We give great weight to the evidence of group members' lived experience. We acknowledge that this is open to bias and distortion – any basic psychology textbook emphasises this and in a sense the whole endeavour of psychology is aimed at getting closer to some kind of objective truth whilst recognising and minimising the barriers to this. Unlike the National Institute of Health and Clinical Excellence (NICE), we do not devalue evidence based on introspection and accounts of personal experience in comparison to large-scale research projects such as randomised controlled trials (RCTs). This is

because RCTs, the 'gold standard' of evidence according to NICE, are also open to bias and distortion, most notably the pecuniary interests of the people with sufficient funds to conduct such research (e.g. pharmaceutical companies). Thus when one person on a *Psychology in the Real World* course says they experience withdrawal effects when they stop taking a psychiatric drug (e.g. headaches and electrical shocks in their head), we do not dismiss this on the basis that the pharmaceutical company-sponsored research revealed no discontinuation effects, but rather explore the complexity of this given the myriad of possible causes of any particular problem (such as headaches) and fact that research into medication rarely involves people taking a drug for more than a couple of months whereas many people who come on the courses have taken psychiatric drugs for years.

The evidence that we draw upon during *Psychology in the Real World* courses is therefore wide and diverse, but in many ways we do not seem to get much further than Socrates' position of recognising how little we can confidently assert about our own and others' behaviour. In comparison, clinicians and NHS managers sometimes talk of 'the evidence base' as if most things are known and proven (rather than it being an ever-changing body of knowledge which is open to both minor adjustments and radical overhaul). They seem unaware that even Michael Rawlins, the chair of NICE, has said: 'I mightily dislike hierarchies of evidence.' The belief that there is a lot more that we do not know than we do know seems to be more widely accepted by philosophers than mental health professionals. For example, A.C. Grayling described philosophy (and much of psychology) as primarily focused on two basic areas: the idea of meaning in the universe and the idea that reality has an ultimate nature. After appraising thousands of years of human endeavour aimed at moving along understanding in these areas, he concluded that 'there is still only night at the end of the tunnel'.

In *Psychology in the Real World* ventures we respect the evidence that the wisdom of groups can often outweigh the wisdom of experts. For example, in his book *The Wisdom of Crowds: Why the many are smarter than the few,* James Surowiecki revealed that a group of lay people who seriously debate a problem are often better at making predictions and coming up with solutions than an individual expert. This should not be news to psychologists – one of the founding fathers of the profession, Francis Galton, demonstrated this over a century ago. Healthy groups, where people feel safe enough to 'think aloud' and where differences of opinion are accepted and welcomed can lead to exchanges of ideas and experiences which perhaps get closer to objective reality. Each *Psychology in the Real World* group has revealed wisdom that seems far in excess of any psychology book or lecture that I have come across. In the groups we try and find the balance

that Carl Sagan alluded to when he said: 'It seems to me what is called for is an exquisite balance between two conflicting needs: the most sceptical scrutiny of all hypotheses that are served up to us and at the same time a great openness to new ideas.' We know that human beings are very reluctant to radically overhaul their ways of understanding the world: Leon Festinger's work on cognitive dissonance led him to conclude that: 'We spend our lives paying attention only to information consonant with our beliefs.' But if someone is open to the point of easily being persuaded without critiquing what is said, they are open to absorbing warped ways of understanding the world and ill-equipped to distinguish ideas with validity from those without. Evaluations of *Psychology in the Real World* indicate that many people have left these groups feeling more open to new ideas and more able to critique the world they inhabit – as Sagan put it, the groups appear to have enabled participants (including facilitators) at times to 'winnow deep thoughts from deep nonsense'.

3

What is meant by the *real world*?

Nothing that happens in here is normal; not one thing occurs like it does in your own home.
 Olive Bucknall

Without wanting to get bogged down in a philosophical analysis of whether anything is 'real', *Psychology in the Real World* takes its title from an acknowledgement that mental health services tend to be provided in very odd ways and in very odd environments. Community Mental Health Teams (CMHTs) do not tend to feel like they are part of a wider community, just as psychiatric hospitals have never been envisaged by patients, staff or local people as part of the local community. In many ways CMHTs and other mental health services seem indistinguishable from inpatient facilities with their strange and bureaucratic procedures, overt and covert ways of monitoring people and locked doors with codes for entry. The quote at the beginning of this chapter is from the psychiatric system survivor and activist Olive Bucknall and was said to me during a visit to our local psychiatric hospital when we were members of the Patients' Council. In comparison, *Psychology in the Real World* courses endeavour to be 'normal' or part of the 'real world' in three main areas: the venues, the mix of participants and the language used.

Venues

The venues for the courses, in comparison to mental health services, do feel like they are part of the local community. They are free of signs blaring out 'Mental Health Trust', 'Child and Adolescent Mental Health Service' or 'Early Intervention in Psychosis' that instantly label people as ill or defective no matter what the attitudes or practices of the staff. Unlike our local psychiatric hospital, they are not surrounded by road signs warning car users to look out for hunched people with walking sticks. They do not have locked doors or intercom systems where you have to announce your arrival and in doing so accept your stamp of being ill and in need of help.

Venues used for *Psychology in the Real World* groups include:

- CHEC, a community health and education centre, which was situated on a high street amidst a number of housing estates with high levels of social deprivation. CHEC is staffed by local people, has information about local services, events and resources and hosts a wide variety of courses and drop-in clinics (e.g. the Citizens' Advice Bureau) which are of general interest and open to anyone living locally.

- The Gateway, an arts and education centre in a town centre location in close proximity to the train and bus station. It puts on courses such as computer skills, art, pottery and modern languages for people with differing levels of skills – from introductory courses to modules for degrees.

- The Lantern, an outreach library project in a

deprived part of town with rooms to rent as well as a well-resourced library (which includes sections on mental health).

- The Severn Way, a path along the River Severn with local pubs on route. This 'venue' for *Walk and Talk* is conceptually and physically a long way from the environment of the clinic.

The first three venues named above have proven good places in terms of hosting *Understanding Ourselves and Others, The Black Dog, Toxic Mental Environments* and *The Writing Group*, with cosy cafés allowing people to mix informally before and after the groups as well as during breaks. People often stay for lunch and chat with each other and with the course facilitators. These venues are full of people attending a variety of courses who (like the *Psychology in the Real World* attendees) have not come because they were referred or because they are ill or needing treatment/therapy but because they are interested in something. People mill around in the reception areas, looking at information about local events, and come together in a spirit of learning – this contrasts sharply with mental health clinic waiting rooms where people often sit with their heads bowed, looking deeply uncomfortable about being there and appearing to not want to connect with others in the room.

Some venues have provided free crèche facilities, which has helped people come who otherwise might not have been able to attend (e.g. teenage single mothers). Participants usually sign up for *Psychology in the Real World* courses in the same way as they sign up for other courses at these venues, which helps to create a sense of them as not being part of mental health services. The venues have tended to have friendly reception staff that are keen (or I have helped to be keen) to lessen the anxiety that

people have about coming to the courses. Some venues have employed specialist staff who help people interested in any course on offer to overcome physical and psychological difficulties that can impede access, e.g. they will meet people before the group starts to show them around the building and room to be used; discuss and try and alleviate anxieties about attending; allow supportive friends or family to attend alongside them free of charge.

Many attendees have subsequently signed up for other courses run by these venues on completing a *Psychology in the Real World* course. This differs significantly from my attempts to get people I have seen on a one-to-one basis to sign up for adult education or other courses – such people often leave the sessions apparently keen to do such a thing but their apparent intentions rarely materialise into action. Attending a *Psychology in the Real World* course at a particular venue seems to help people overcome the barriers to signing up for and going on other courses. Links I have made with other tutors at these venues have also been helpful as I have been able to alleviate fears tutors have about mental health matters (for example, having people who hear voices attending their class); discuss with them how to accommodate people's idiosyncrasies; link people who attend mental health services into events and courses going on in community venues by putting up adverts in waiting rooms; and calming the anxieties people attending the CMHT have about signing up for various courses by saying I know the tutor and something about how they work. As mental health workers we tend to automatically think of 'services' when encouraging people to join things, but having links in community education or art settings opens up other avenues.

People get into habits in venues that they have frequently been at and group cultures build up that spill over into new ventures at those venues. This can have a positive influence when the group culture is healthy (see above) but negative group cultures spill over into new ventures in similar ways. This is another reason for getting out of the clinic. Someone who attends a clinic and is given (and accepts) a psychiatric diagnosis is less likely to question the validity of diagnoses at that venue compared to a different venue (especially one that is associated with learning rather than treatment). *Psychology in the Real World* is about opening up new possibilities of seeing the world and this works best at venues that are not associated with entrenched ideologies and practices.

The mix of participants

Fortunately we had a wonderful group of mixed ages and backgrounds. I don't know how well this particular course would run if otherwise.

> Participant on an *Understanding Ourselves and Others* course

Unlike mental health services, there are no referral or entry criteria for *Psychology in the Real World* groups. Such criteria generally serve to exclude one set of people (often in discriminatory ways, e.g. on the basis of age or IQ) and stigmatise another (e.g. label and record them as mentally ill). Having no inclusion/ exclusion criteria brings many benefits. For example, older people mix with younger people in a way that breaks down stereotypes, prejudices and helps both parties. Older members of the group often find themselves occupying a valued role, for example, passing on what they have learned about the death of loved ones, redundancy and retirement to people yet to encounter such experiences. Younger people can forge respectful relationships with older people who act differently from their parents (thus lessening maladaptive transference reactions) or who act differently from the prejudiced view of 'the elderly' that they might

have absorbed via the media. It is not surprising that people fear teenage boys when an Echo Research survey into the most common words associated with them in the media in 2008 were 'yobs', 'thugs', 'sick', 'feral', 'hoodie', 'louts', 'heartless', 'evil', 'frightening' and 'scum', and when 90% of stories in the sample showed them in a bad light. On the courses we try and cite research that contradicts such stereotypes, but prejudice is more effectively countered through personal contact than evidence (see handout Some Thoughts on Prejudice, p. 244). For prejudice to lessen, people need to meet together in conditions that facilitate mutual understanding – according to Gordon Allport, ones of interdependence, where there is equal status of group members, social norms in place that promote equality and where people are working towards a common goal. *Psychology in the Real World* groups try and create such conditions.

People attend the groups as students or participants not patients or clients. Being seen (and seeing oneself) as a student helps people feel better than being seen (and seeing oneself) as mentally ill or in need of psychological help. As well as lessening stigma, having a mixed group also enables the ventures to potentially challenge stigma associated with mental illness. For example, many group members who have attended psychiatric services disclose this fact at some point during *Psychology in the Real World* ventures. Group members who have not had this experience are often surprised to discover that people they have got to know as people have been in the local psychiatric hospital, hear voices or have been diagnosed as schizophrenic, and as a consequence have some of their stereotypes and prejudices challenged. This is taken up further in Chapter 52.

It is not easy to get a group that mirrors the local population and many *Psychology in the Real World* groups have not succeeded in getting as great a mix in terms of some attributes of participants as the facilitators hoped. Several groups have failed to attract people from ethnic backgrounds that are different from the local white cultures that predominate in this part of Britain, even though some of the philosophies of the groups overlap more with non-Western cultures than many mainstream services. For example, Suman Fernando's recent research in Sri Lanka looked at people's ideas of wellbeing and found that wellbeing was conceptualised in terms of communities, and communities in relation to one another (rather than the more Western concept of individual happiness and mental health); many *Psychology in the Real World* groups encompass collective and communal concepts of this type. However, perhaps this has not been apparent in the flyers advertising the groups, or this is insufficient to enable people to overcome other hurdles to attending. Under-represented groups may need more targeted advertising, active encouragement to attend from people who are members of those groups or formats that are more attractive to them. For example, personal disclosure in a mixed group of people who are initially strangers (a key part of several *Psychology in the Real World* groups) goes against the cultural norms of some ethnic groups and this might need some adjustment if under-represented groups are to be helped to overcome anxieties and barriers to attending (see Chapter 53).

We have endeavoured to get an even gender split in the groups ever since feedback from the evaluation of the second *Understanding Ourselves and Others* course included 'the hope that future groups might have a greater mix of men and women'. Yet research has revealed that only 26% of participants who came to six subsequent runnings of this course were men. The 2006 *Thinking about Medication* course consisted of thirteen women and only one man. *Psychology in the Real World* groups that focus on talking and

thinking appear to be less attractive to men (especially working-class men) compared to women. *Toxic Mental Environments*, *The Writing Group* and *Walk and Talk*, which are more activity based, have attracted a more even mix in terms of gender. Men on *Walk and Talk*, for example, have commented that they find it easier to talk whilst walking beside someone or in the pub over a pint of beer than in a group where people sit across from each – where eye contact is unavoidable and having nothing else to do other than talk can create feelings of awkwardness.

During one running of *Understanding Ourselves and Others* we all filled in the Keirsey Temperament Questionnaire and this indicated that, compared to the general population, a disproportionate number of people on the course were classed as *Idealists* in terms of their underlying temperament, and a low number *Artisans*. Although numbers involved were clearly very small, this does fit with other research that suggests people with an identity-seeking personality might be more attracted to groups of this type than more hedonistic people who are drawn to athletic or artistic pursuits.

No small group where people sign up on a first-come, first-served basis can ensure that it is representative of the wider population. However, one of my main aims each time a group is run is that there might be a wide mix in terms of people's previous involvement in mental health services. It is difficult to measure this precisely because data is not gathered on this for every group, people are not referred and participants do not necessarily disclose the level of their previous involvement with mental health services during the group sessions. However, my own estimation is that 30–40% of people coming to *Understanding Ourselves and Others* groups have had involvement with services aimed at people with 'severe and enduring mental health problems' (e.g. CMHTs, inpatient services, residential services), 30–40% have had involvement with primary care services (e.g. been taking psychiatric drugs prescribed by a GP or received counselling) and 30–40% have had no involvement with mental health services. *The Black Dog*, *Thinking about Medication*, *The Writing Group* and *Walk and Talk* have had a higher proportion of people from the first group but have still retained a mix in terms of mental health service involvement.

How to get the mix …

We produce flyers advertising the groups that provide people with information about what the group will be like and how to join. Examples of these can be found in subsequent chapters. The flyers follow some basic guidelines regarding advertising and marketing, i.e. are designed to attract attention, stimulate interest, create a desire and bring about action. They do not oversell the groups but are aimed at providing sufficient information to encourage and enable people who might benefit and contribute to a group to get involved. They clearly state that the groups are open to anyone. As there are no inclusion or exclusion criteria, or pre-group meetings, it is important that the flyers provide as clear and comprehensive an indication of what being involved in the groups might be like, and facilitators are able to provide interested people with more information if needs be, in order that people whom the group would not suit (in terms of it being unable to meet their needs) do not sign up.

Publicity for the groups is achieved in the following ways:

1. Flyers are put up on notice boards of mental health settings in primary and secondary care, in GP clinics, in cafés and shops, in resource and community centres, in the venue in which the group will take place and any other appropriate setting, e.g. *Walk and Talk* is advertised in the Guildhall opposite the meeting place and in the pub where we meet after the walk – members of the local council and staff at the Guildhall are thus encouraged to come and benefit from the experience (and enable people who often have little access to power to informally meet their elected representatives) as are residents and locals who frequent the pub.

2. The groups are advertised on www.shropsych.org which is the website of the Department of Psychological Therapies in Shropshire. Lovingly developed by Helen Jones, this site not only advertises events of interest to local people but is a treasure-trove of information about the department, community-based groupwork and mental health in general.

3. The groups are advertised on www.well-scrambled.co.uk which is the website for local service user and carer involvement. Having people co-facilitate the groups who are current or ex-service users has led to good contacts with the website and has allowed the courses to be advertised by word of mouth at service user forums and meetings.

4. Steps are taken wherever possible to enable people to overcome some practical difficulties in attending. For example, all locations are within walking distance of town centres and local bus and train routes; CHEC put on a free crèche to assist mothers to attend; The Gateway has loop systems to help people with hearing difficulties and has good access for people with physical disabilities. Local NHS premises compare poorly in terms of its facilities.

5. I have accumulated a long list of addresses of people who have come on previous courses and who have expressed an interest in coming on something similar in the future,

and I try and let these people know about forthcoming projects. Thus a wide, loose group or nexus has built up under the *Psychology in the Real World* umbrella. Of course the development of such a nexus is only possible if one stays in the same area for a considerable time. I have met many people who have wanted to practise community psychology but have also wanted the freedom to change jobs when it suits them. Clinicians have often not been able to get promotion without changing jobs (and often workplace area). To practise community psychology one needs to work, and I would argue live, in the same area for a considerable time in order to become known in and part of a wider community; this needs a long-term commitment from both individual workers and their employing agencies.

Language
Everything should be made as simple as possible, but not simpler.
    Albert Einstein

Psychology in the Real World ventures do not present a 'dumbed-down' version of psychology: complex theories are discussed but the facilitators use everyday language and encourage participants to do likewise. Socrates (and many philosophers subsequently) believed that words can distort and deceive, giving the impression of truth but moving people away from it. We live in a society drenched in words spun by politicians, PR workers, management consultants and people in marketing and advertising, all of whom specialise in distortion and creating lands of make-believe. But words are our basic building blocks for understanding the world and communicating with each other. Einstein said: 'It is not enough for a handful of experts to attempt the solution of a problem, to solve it and then to apply it; the restriction of

knowledge to an elite group destroys the spirit of society and leads to its intellectual impoverishment.' Community psychologists such as Bob Diamond have similarly argued for a 'democratisation of truth' and to do this we need to use words that are comprehensible to all and guide us towards real meaning and shared understanding.

On the courses we collectively search for truth. As Chapter 55 shows, this is not done in ignorance of psychoanalytic, social constructionist and postmodern critiques of such endeavours. George Orwell said that 'just to see what's in front of one's nose needs a constant struggle.' Similarly, Noam Chomsky's research into the media led him to conclude that we are mostly fed emotionally potent, over-simplistic explanations of current affairs and these frequently come to dominate public debate. Chomsky feels that each of us needs to develop an independent mind, which is very difficult to do alone and cannot be achieved through the adoption of misleading and bamboozling language. *Psychology in the Real World* groups have tried to get beyond the mystification, jargon, spin and unnecessary intellectualisation that can characterise many debates in the 21st century by using words that we can all understand, explaining concepts by use of illustrative examples, working together to create an environment where people feel safe enough to say that they have not understood something, and engaging in collaborative conversations (see next chapter).

The NHS seems to be drowning in managerialism influenced by outside consultants with no long-term commitment to the NHS and wave after wave of reforms and top-down objectives, each of which add to an ever-increasing lexicon that resembles 1984's Newspeak. Its 60th anniversary was accompanied by an announcement by the Secretary of State for Health of yet another review which would 'chart a path towards achievement', 'improve the Quality and Outcomes Framework' by establishing a 'new evidence service that would ensure best practice flows readily to the frontline' with 'frontline teams supported by a new set of graphically illustrated quality measures known as a clinical dashboard'. 'Frontline staff', meanwhile, have lost the energy to continue mocking such statements: shoulders sag and heads droop when language of this type is used. NHS staff are being ground down not by their work (which can be exhausting enough) but by a system that proves unable to use plain language and chronically wastes money and resources generating data to illustrate a world of make-believe that the general public finds increasingly implausible. There is a need to engage in protest against such developments, and this has to involve resistance to such language and a utilisation of the three quarters of a million words that make up the English language in order to make things as simple as possible, but not simpler.

4

Collaborative conversation

Collaborative conversation is a form of non-adversarial decision making which assumes that (i) no one person can formulate anywhere near an adequate representation of the truth (ii) groups of people if they pool their perspectives in collaborative fashion formulate increasingly accurate but never foolproof approximations to the truth (iii) today's formulations, no matter how useful, may be out of date tomorrow.

    Peter Hulme

Conversation has been described as an encounter where each person takes turns to exercise their own ego. In everyday life, at work or at home, when disagreements occur, whether they be minor or major, most of the time we try and make the other person agree with our view, almost try and place (and, when angry, force) our view inside their head. Throughout all *Psychology in the Real World* sessions participants are encouraged to engage in a different kind of encounter, a form of collaborative conversation, sometimes in pairs, sometimes in small groups but mostly in the whole group. In collaborative conversation knowledge is not 'out there' waiting to be discovered, a fixed thing or commodity to be learned, grasped or memorised. Rather, it is a process; it arises out of interactions between human beings. The object in collaborative conversation is not to win the argument but to bring about mutual understanding whilst exploring ideas and the way we think. As a result of engaging in this process, individual, group and wider social wellbeing may be enhanced. My interpretation

of collaborative conversation relates it to various ideas in different cultures, including Western scientific thinking, Paulo Freire's theories of critical pedagogy in education, the Bahá'í concept of consultation, Bohm Dialogue, and free-floating discussion in psychoanalytic groups as elucidated by S.H. Foulkes.

Carl Sagan said that science is a way of thinking much more than it is a body of knowledge. It involves a recognition that our ideas about the world are theories not truths, that these theories lead to hypotheses – tentative predictions that may well turn out to have been mistaken, necessitating minor and sometimes major overhaul of our theories. We cannot prove a theory, only maintain a position that a theory holds up to scrutiny under what is accepted as the current evidence. Science has increasingly been associated with the scientific method and scientific evidence base; many people purporting to be scientists (or, in the mental health field, scientist-practitioners) do not seem to *think* scientifically. Even those of us, such as psychologists, who are trained in science find it uncomfortably difficult to let go of long-held beliefs when presented with contradictory evidence, disproportionately focus on evidence that supports our entrenched views, rely on the word of experts rather than testing out what we have been told and fall into the trap of seeing our opinions on human behaviour as *the* truth. Collaborative conversation can help us avoid these traps.

Many of the concepts underpinning collaborative conversation are better known in education than mental health, although moves in psychology towards the reflective practitioner have tried to take some of this thinking on board. Some *Psychology in the Real World* ventures have been compared to the revolutionary application of critical pedagogy as described by Paulo Freire (see Chapter 21). Peter Hulme's angle on collaborative conversation (as elucidated in the quote at the beginning of this chapter) is influenced by the Bahá'í idea of consultation. During consultation everyone who might be affected by any decision taken participates in the discussions and decision making, and full and frank debate is encouraged, with the group acting as 'one mind' so that the ideas generated are not conceptualised as belonging to the speaker (therefore no one offends and no one takes offence when differences are expressed). This overlaps with the concept of Dialogue as described by David Bohm (see below). The idea of free-floating discussion in psychoanalytic psychotherapy has also influenced my interpretation of collaborative conversation – like Bohm Dialogue this needs honesty and transparency on behalf of a group of participants who have not met with a set purpose in mind but aim to suspend their usual ways of judging the world in order to collectively explore the ways they make sense of themselves, others and the world they inhabit. Research on forgiveness, reconciliation, anger and compassion (see, for example, *The Compassionate Mind* by Paul Gilbert and the research page on *The Forgiveness Web*) all point to the importance of understanding the ways other people see and experience the world – a key aspect of collaborative conversation.

The physicist David Bohm has set out guidance about how Dialogue can be helped to occur. *Psychology in the Real World* groups try to create similar environments, where:

1. *Participants are encouraged to suspend their assumptions* – The spirit of Dialogue needs participants to have (or develop) an ability to hold many points of view in suspension alongside an overall interest in the creation of common meaning. Suspending an assumption involves 'holding it in front of us' ready for exploration and critique from others and ourselves.

2. *Participants view each other as colleagues or peers* – Dialogue occurs when people appreciate that they are involved in a mutual quest for understanding and insight. A Dialogue is essentially a conversation between equals. It is not an encounter between someone identified as ignorant or lacking in knowledge and someone identified as an expert who is there to teach them. Any facilitator involved in the group does so with an expectation of learning just as much from the conversation as anyone else in the group.

3. *The group benefits from having a facilitator, particularly in the early stages* – The facilitator's role should be to gently and unobtrusively point out when conversations have gone off track and are not following the Dialogue process. Rather than leading from the front, the facilitator leads from behind, hoping to be needed as little as possible and to eventually become redundant.

We each bring our own ways of pre-judging and interpreting the information taken in by our senses. Any standard psychology textbook is full of experimental research evidence that shows that even when people witness the same event they describe and remember what they witnessed in subtly and sometimes radically different ways. Research on perception reveals that we do not see the world, we create an image of it, and that image can be grossly distorted. We have transference reactions – encounters with significant others in the past distort our interpretations of what is going on in current encounters. We feel convinced that our view, or memory, is correct and statements from others that contradict this must be wrong. A bit of us might want to try and understand how another person sees things so differently, but this can get swamped in irritation, frustration and confusion when they do not bend to our take on it, especially if we feel passionately about something. We can use subtle and brutal ways of exerting power to get people to agree with us – Philip Gourevitch defined power as 'the ability to make others inhabit our story of their reality'. It is hard to understand others who are different from us; David Keirsey's influential book on temperament was given the pleading title *Please Understand Me*. It is difficult to be truly open to what others are saying and to see things from their standpoint – not having to agree with them, but not quickly dismissing what they say (and in effect them) without being open to the possibility that there might be something to learn from what they are saying. Through engaging in such a process we might get closer to really understanding others, including people who initially seem so different (and consequently so distant), truly relating and connecting with them.

In *Psychology in the Real World* groups I try and describe some of these concepts in the first session. I encourage everyone to offer ideas, thoughts, reflections and personal stories 'out to the group' where we might each hold them 'suspended in front of us'; where we can 'play' with and critique ideas (not critique the person who offered them); where we can see how they interact with and perhaps challenge some of our own beliefs and ways of seeing ourselves and the world. And at some point (perhaps during or at the end of the session) we might allow ourselves to absorb some of these new ideas. I intervene when one person seems to be trying to force his or her ideas onto (or into) others. I welcome ideas that may be challenging to my (and

perhaps others') long-held and perhaps long-cherished beliefs (trying to model the philosophies underpinning collaborative conversation). At times I try and lessen the emotional temperature in the room so that we can reflect on things said without feeling threatened by new ideas. I normalise the process of feeling a bit shook up when something grates with our established ways of looking at the world (akin to our reactions when a psychological defence is challenged). I tell stories about how my own beliefs about mental health in general, and myself in particular, have changed, often radically, over the years (for example, from seeing my own experiences of depression as a genetic illness to seeing depressive feelings as powerful yet normal reactions to things that happen in my life). I put forward the view that we all need an ongoing sense of humility as it is very easy to think that our way of seeing the world is right – how it must have seemed so obvious to people for centuries that the world is flat. I encourage us all to see ourselves as partners engaged in a joint endeavour of discovery.

Peter Hulme, after decades of working with people who have been diagnosed as psychotic, schizophrenic and delusional, found that collaborative conversation helped people have less 'fixity' about their views and ways of thinking in general – helped people develop 'an ability for reflection and relativism rather than dogmatism and a sense of drowning in their ideas' – and this had profound effects on their wellbeing. Each *Psychology in the Real World* group tends to have a significant number of participants who have attracted such diagnoses, but the collaborative conversation approach is seen as something that might benefit any individual and, if we can foster this way of being outside the groups, might benefit the wider social groups we belong to and society in general.

5

Access to psychology I

Right now we are going through a tunnel of economic gloom. When global problems begin to affect us, community groups are vital means of communication and encouragement, especially when some members of these groups are suffering. No longer can psychologists' work relate only to the mentally suffering in hospitals and after-care – there are implications and healing needs for all sufferers everywhere.

Don Harris, poet and member of
The Writing Group, 2008

For twenty years psychologists in Shropshire, alongside local service users, have been collecting data on what local people want from services and presenting this locally (e.g. to mental health staff, commissioners, service user groups) and nationally (e.g. through publications and at conferences). The vast majority of these requests (e.g. for more say in how services are run) do not in themselves need more psychologists – a range of different professional and non-professional people could meet such requests. But consistently people have said they wanted *greater access to psychologists*. It is not entirely clear what underlies this request, but I would suggest the following:

1. In comparison to other mental health professionals relatively few psychologists are employed and those that are tend to be in specialist services (secondary or tertiary care) that are normally inaccessible to the majority of the population and often have long waiting lists.

2. It takes on average ten years for someone to qualify as a clinical psychologist – from day one of a psychology degree through several years of relevant work experience to completion of a three-year post-doctorate training course in clinical psychology; people recognise that psychologists have picked up some knowledge that might be relevant.

3. People have come to trust psychologists because, until very recently, we have not been associated with the Mental Health Act and compulsory treatments, or as David Smail put it in a seminal article in *Clinical Psychology Forum* in 1993:

    What makes us different from other professionals in the field is ... the position we find ourselves in ... It is ironic that the one thing we have chafed about professionally most consistently over the years has been our relative lack of power, when, paradoxical though it may seem, this has been our greatest strength – in the sense that it has made it possible for us to develop an approach to clinical understanding and care which really is unique. For we are helpful to our patients precisely in not having power over them. We can't lock them up; we can't drug them or stun them with electricity; we can't take their children away from them. The only power we have is the power of persuasion and this ... more or less forces us into an attitude of respect towards our clients. The achievement of that independence without powers of that kind really is an achievement of which we should be proud. It's certainly an achievement which we should jealously guard.

Psychology in the Real World ventures provide an alternative route for people to access psychology and meet a psychologist to being referred to a mental health service. Not only does this mean a greater *number* of people get to meet with me (and other psychologists who co-facilitate the courses), but also a greater *range* of people than otherwise would be the case. In Shropshire adult mental health psychologists are based in CMHTs that, like all services, have tight inclusion/exclusion criteria and exclude people who are over 65 or under 18, people who do not have 'severe and enduring mental health problems' (whatever that means – no one has ever given me an operationalised definition), people with learning difficulties, people who have severe difficulties but steadfastly refuse to be registered with mental health services, and so on. It is not that meeting a psychologist is always going to be helpful; rather, if greater access has been a consistent request from local people then we should try and do something to meet this request.

People are not referred onto the courses – anyone who finds out about them can book a place on a first-come, first served basis. Psychologists and other professionals have traditionally aped systems of referral used in general medicine which, with their use of letters detailing presenting problems and associated specialist reports, and their utilisation of formal inclusion/exclusion criteria, perhaps suit general practitioners and specialist consultants in the physical health arena. However, this is not necessarily the most appropriate, ethical or effective way for other professionals to try and improve the mental health of people in a local community. Referral systems necessarily individualise people's problems and lend

themselves to an expectation of specialist opinion and treatment. This creates in the referred person, referrer and mental health 'expert' what I have called *the tyranny of the expectation of cure*, which can be counter-productive to any therapeutic endeavour and certainly runs counter to the ideologies and aims of much community-based groupwork. When not so actively pursued, we have found that therapeutic benefits can ensue from *Psychology in the Real World* groups, but improving mental health ought to encompass much wider aims than purely symptom relief for people diagnosed as mentally ill.

On access to research
The handing over of research skills by community psychologists provides ordinary people with (i) tools to diagnose what is wrong with their world, instead of the other way around, and (ii) encouragement to find ways of putting that diagnosis to use – as the basis for an attempt to make their world a better place in which to live.
    Paul Moloney

Clinical psychology job descriptions in Shropshire historically delineated five areas in which clinicians have been expected to proportionately split their time: therapeutic interventions, supervision, training, consultation and research. My own view is that clinical psychologists have become too aligned with the provision of therapy (especially cognitive-behavioural therapy, the skills and techniques of which do not need ten years of training to be equipped in) and too little involved in the more general yet core business of applied psychology. With current NHS contracts being signed by people who are often unaware of the range of ways psychology can be used in applied settings and focusing solely on payment for a fixed number of one-to-one interventions, there is a danger of the NHS losing out in terms of the ways psychologists can help a wide range of people benefit from their (very expensive) training.

Psychology in the Real World ventures have had impacts that have resulted from skills that I have acquired over and above those that relate to the therapy room. For example, in the area of research, through:

1. Publishing research about the groups with co-authors, mostly current and ex-psychiatric service users, who have come to acquire research and publishing skills. As chapters in this book indicate, this can have a significant impact on people's self-esteem, often far greater than the impacts of individual therapy. Hopefully it has done more than this, however, and has also equipped some people with skills to engage in the kinds of processes community psychologist Paul Moloney describes in the quote above. Feedback has indicated that this research has been of great interest and relevance to service users and clinicians locally and nationally, many of whom access it via the department website as well as through journals.

2. Providing literature reviews for people setting up their own projects. Mike Evans (who came to two *Psychology in the Real World* groups), with some support from other group members, has been trying to set up an eco-project in South Shropshire. Mike asked for my help in accessing research that indicates eco-projects have beneficial effects on people's mental health in order to obtain funding and Local Authority support for the project.

3. Combating stigma and prejudice. The project referred to above provoked an outcry from some local people during the application for planning permission. Outrageous claims were made about the risks to people, including children, and to

property prices (!) if 'the mentally ill' were 'allowed' to visit the proposed project. I have been able to write to the planning department providing them with research evidence that counteracts some of the prejudiced claims made by people objecting to this development (see Box 2, p. 28).

4. Making psychological research public knowledge. The evidence base is very wide and although Google searches can enable access to a wide range of psychological ideas and theories, academic research is often only available through searching databases that the general public does not have access to. John Sweeny said good journalism enables people without power to discover what the people with power know; Bob Diamond has said similar things about community psychology. Psychologists can never know all of the published literature, but they do know how to quickly access it. Also they are like walking psychology libraries. A solicitor will not know every bit of law and will have to look up cases and statutes but will carry in their head a lot of legal knowledge relevant to any particular legal question; psychologists similarly have access to their own knowledge base in their memory and could make this more widely available to more people than is frequently the case. In many discussions in *Psychology in the Real World* groups I do not offer my own opinion on what is being discussed but instead try and relate discussions to interesting and hopefully relevant pieces of psychological research or theory. Different psychologists will have different knowledge bases but all can help a greater range of people have access to some of this knowledge than by solely providing one-to-one therapy (the protocols of which often discourage such sharing of information, interpreting it as 'intellectual-ising' a problem).

Box 2   Countering prejudice by citing research

Extracts from a letter (sent to a planning department) that was written to counteract prejudiced claims about people with a mental illness diagnosis:

1. The definitive research study on homicides and community care revealed that there was no significant rise in the number of homicides by people with mental illness diagnoses in the period 1970–1995 (when community care replaced predominantly hospital-based care). On the contrary, the figures showed that the numbers *and* proportion of homicides by people with a mental illness diagnosis reduced over that period. The authors concluded: *There is no evidence that it is anything but stigmatising to claim that living in the community is a dangerous experiment that should be reversed* (Taylor & Gunn, 1999).

2. Once alcohol and substance misuse are controlled for, the evidence does not indicate that people with a mental illness diagnosis such as schizophrenia are significantly more likely to commit violent crimes i.e. the evidence reveals that it is alcohol and substance misuse that are associated with significantly higher rates of harm to others, irrespective of whether someone has a mental illness diagnosis or not (see research papers by Fazel et al, 2009).

3. Contrary to public perception, people with mental illness diagnoses are much more likely to be victims of violent assault than be perpetrators of violent assault, are more likely to have suffered physical and sexual abuse in childhood and have suffered violent and sexual assault in adulthood compared to other people in society (Read, Mosher & Bentall, 2004).

4. I have facilitated *Walk and Talk* during the period 2007–2009 which encourages people with mental health diagnoses (including schizophrenia and manic depression) to join with others (the supposedly 'sane') on a weekly walk along the Severn Way. We have not had one incident of anyone being unpleasant to another person let alone harming or disturbing someone else in the group or people we meet on the path or in the pub afterwards.

5. The Disability Discrimination Act (1995) states that it is unlawful to discriminate against people with a mental impairment.

6

Understanding Ourselves and Others; *The Black Dog*; *Walk and Talk*: Reflections on having attended all three

ELISABETH X

I belong to a choir. Sopranos, basses, altos and tenors. For the most part we stay in our individual groups, hearing our own tune. Comfortable, confident and safe. One conductor I worked with would, on occasion, like to mix things up a bit. Once he gained our trust he liked to challenge us. Sometimes he would rearrange the seating so that each choir member was seated next to someone singing a different tune and then go on to rehearse a complicated harmony. The level of concentration increased: we focused, we listened to one another, we altered our volume so that all the harmonies could be heard. We were patient when others struggled. We learned that listening to someone else's notes helped us pick up our own. At other times he would have us sitting in groups opposite one another, tenors and sopranos facing basses and altos, a few feet apart singing the same piece but hearing it differently. Another ploy was to make us learn each other's harmonies – an appreciation of what it feels like to be in someone else's shoes, to understand the difficulties they had. He would encourage us to be bold and sing out, even if we were not sure and got it wrong: the only way he could help us correct our mistakes was to hear them and work on them. Another musical director would teach us a simple four-line song, ask us to close our eyes and then together 'play' with the sound. Sometimes it sounded terrible, sometimes funny and sometimes beautiful. With our eyes closed the awkwardness decreased, and our sense of hearing was heightened to pick out all the different sounds, even the quietest.

This process of listening, focusing, risking and learning is something similar to how it feels on one of the *Psychology in the Real World* courses. You have some idea of what you are getting into but don't know how it will turn out. The effect we have on others. How we feel. Stepping outside our comfort zone to be with people who challenge us. Seeing where we fit in and where we do not. Having a go at something new. Seeing things from a new angle, hearing other people's stories and, maybe, if we are brave enough, helping and being helped. Being vulnerable and surviving. Learning to listen for the unfamiliar voice to see how it blends or clashes with our own … to listen for the 'unexpected song'.

Why it works (most of the time) …
Keeping things simple and stating clearly what is on offer is the initial attraction. No strings. No hoops to jump through. Very ordinary. Some of the most powerful moments have been the most basic … a loaned book, a cup of coffee, acknowledgement of your presence or absence. Remembering your name. Concern without intrusion. For the most part a gentle determination to include you in what is going on. Therapeutic? Yes, but not in the obvious way. Not always in an easy way. Simply there, honestly there, compassionately there.

It has been helpful having something at different times throughout the year, a rolling programme to access independently and use for time out, advice and reflection. A process that does not end when the courses do, but the ideas and experiences weave themselves sometimes obviously, sometimes unexpectedly, but slowly and definitely into lives as patterns change. The topics covered have explored different ways of understanding mental distress. What impact our past and social circumstances have on our mental health. There have been no 'light bulb', 'penny dropping' moments when everything becomes clear but there can be a shift in what we believe about ourselves and others and how we have learned to see the world. When I was small I loved to write, to make up little stories or poems until people told me, as I got older, that my handwriting was terrible, my grammar and spelling atrocious, I couldn't even learn the alphabet, the style of my written work would never get me an 'A'. So I stopped writing, until now. Until I re-learned the power of the pen and the experience of being heard … in the *real world*.

When it might not …

It takes a degree of motivation and commitment to access and attend any *Psychology in the Real World* event. But it makes great sense to be able to get to most, if not all, of the sessions even when the topics or the discussions touch on sensitive or difficult subjects. This on the whole does not seem to be an issue with the current courses – the ones I have been on have always been oversubscribed and well-attended, with the drop-out rate low. *Walk and Talk* is the only one where a longer-term commitment is not needed – people can come and go as many or as few times as they choose. Maybe only do half the walk, maybe stay for a drink and pub meal, maybe just walk and not talk that much at all. To those expecting these courses to be therapy groups there may be disappointment; to those not wanting this, relief. The groups seem to be mostly made up of people who have had some contact with or

are currently accessing community mental health services. Maybe if more staff from services were to come there would be a different dimension to the groups. Sometimes the groups have felt too big and somewhat intimidating, with maybe one or two people dominating the conversation. Sometimes quite intense and emotive. There appeared to be an issue of not being able to please everyone at the same time and of trying to compromise. It can be stressful. The dreaded invitation for comments working the way around everyone in the room – the feeling of being nine years old and the teacher asking me what seven eights are. There have also been times when I have been more aware of being 'observed' by the course leaders who are sat discreetly in a corner of the room during small group work, writing – you can't help imagining what they are taking notes on.

Psychology in the Real World compared to a CMHT

Community mental health seems to have expanded and contracted at the same time. There is an explosion of 'specialties' and 'expertise' offering programmes and treatments that work if you 'try hard enough and are committed to change'. They can be complex and difficult to access and have long waiting lists. If you don't fit into one of the services on offer or if you fail the assessment you get lost. You get confused. A square peg in a round hole is still a square peg, just a bit more battered, bruised, fragile and stuck. The pressures of time, demand and measurable results shape the services on offer, as might value for money – not an unreasonable objective. But value depends on whether you are the deliverer or recipient of the service, looking in the short term or long term and on how you measure or define success. Positive experiences of community mental health services and *Psychology in the Real World* ventures have for me been when people have taken time to get to know me – my love of music, gift wrapping and rain; my fear of snails, the dark and flying (more accurately, crashing); seemingly irrelevant things but a gateway to trust. We have shared books, cookery tips and jokes. We have shared grief, pain and sadness. When professionals seemed to realise that I am more than my problems, that my problems do not define me. When they did not rush me; did not blame me for not asking for or accepting help in a fashion that is comfortable and familiar to them; did not believe that I am unreachable, boring or hostile. When they did not say that I try too hard or not hard enough. In *The Noonday Demon* Andrew Solomon wrote about how to help people with depression: 'Blunt their isolation. Do it with cups of tea or long walks or by sitting in a room nearby and staying silent or in whatever way suits the circumstances, but do it. And do it willingly.' Basically, when you are feeling vulnerable and sad, what makes you feel better? What makes you feel heard? What makes you feel more powerful? What makes you feel safe? Shape the services and your practice around this and you will begin to understand that the client/patient/service user or person you see in front of you is not so different from yourself. I have come to realise that there are no experts with all the answers. As in the Jon Bon Jovi lyric: 'It's OK to be a little broken, everybody's broken, it's just life.' I've learned that we *all* have difficulties, *all* need a break, a helping hand, time, and that if you are struggling you are probably running just about average.

The Black Dog – three years on …

The black dog has not grown over the years. He is still around though and will not be forgotten. She still fears him, but he is better understood now. She has learned about him. He makes his presence felt when he needs to. He warns. He guards. He even protects. He allows his owner to make different decisions. To rest. To recognise danger. When they first met they were strangers. Now she knows his name. She knows what feeds him, what makes him stronger. She continues to learn what tames him. Sometimes she sees him ahead in the distance, just over the brow of the hill. Sometimes he lingers behind and she hears his footsteps. Sometimes he is so close she feels his breath on her face and his weight. They share an unspoken understanding. Respect. They learn to live together.

SECTION 2

On groupwork I: *Beginnings*

7

What is a group and what is groupwork?

[A group is] a number of people or things located, gathered, or classed together for some purpose.
Oxford English Dictionary

In evolutionary terms Paul Gilbert has described us as pack animals, 'a species that searches for individuality but also connectedness and belonging'. Certainly we have congregated in groups and gathered for communal benefit from before the time we evolved into *Homo sapiens*. S.H. Foulkes, one of the founding fathers of group analysis, regarded groups as basic to human existence – all of us are born into social groups (families, neighbourhoods, societies, cultures) that, consciously and unconsciously, continuously shape our lives.

Being in groups brings many benefits. Groups allow us to connect with and learn from each other. They enable us to work together for mutual benefit and achieve tasks that would be impossible to achieve individually in isolation. Groups can foster interdependence and enable people to gain support and help at times of need. They help us attain a sense of 'we-ness', a sense of belonging, which Maslow identified as a basic human need. And yet being in groups is an experience many of us struggle with. It can be experienced as constraining, oppressive and limiting of individual liberty. Cruelty, sadism and scapegoating can flourish within groups. Individual judgement can be warped by pressures to conform and by what Janis termed 'groupthink'. Powerful dynamics can operate in groups, for example, inducing unhelpful

dependence on group leaders. Being in groups can lead to an overemphasis on the similarities between group members and an overemphasis on the differences between group members and outsiders, creating conflicts with people (and groups) seen as 'other'. As discussed earlier, groups brand us, and the branding can be difficult to shake off. Groucho Marx said: 'I'd never belong to a club that would have me as a member.' It is not surprising that being in groups, and groupwork in mental health settings, is approached with great trepidation by people who have had bad experiences of previous groups (family groups, school groups, work groups or friendship groups).

The definition at the beginning of this chapter emphasises the importance of people coming together for a purpose. I have spent the last fifteen years working in community mental health teams where the team is envisaged as a group but the purpose of the group is never collectively understood and made clear. For example, there has never been clarity about whether the purpose of CMHTs is to assist people to be admitted to hospital or to keep people out of there; to care for people deemed ill and unable to consequently make rational decisions or to take a stance where all people are responsible for decisions they make about their life; to focus on treating individual people's problems (or brains) or focus on the wider (and social) causes of their difficulties; to persuade people to take medication and do what is deemed to be in their best interests or to enable people to make their own informed choices about how to live their lives; to protect the public or to provide a confidential service to individuals. Many groups in mental health services suffer from such lack of clarity, whether they are work groups or therapy groups. At the centre of any type of groupwork there needs to be a shared understanding relating to a common purpose or set of shared aims.

According to Toseland and Rivas, groups can be thought of as needing to achieve two main aims: (i) to achieve the tasks the group sets out to achieve and (ii) to meet group members' socio-emotional needs (for example, the need to feel valued and valuable, build and maintain relationships, help and be helped, and have a sense of belonging as opposed to aloneness). Members may contribute in different ways and take up different roles in order to help the group reach a common goal. At times the group may need to compromise some individual member's socio-emotional needs in order to achieve its tasks. Powerful dynamics can pull a group off course.

Because we all find being in groups challenging and know that they can result in destructive experiences for members (and non-members) as well as be constructive influences on our lives and wider society, it can be helpful to have someone facilitate a group. In terms of therapeutic groups, Dorothy Stock Whitaker states that the groupworker's main task is 'to enable and assist each person in a group to achieve personal benefit through making as full use as possible of the potentials of the group as a medium of help'. Social worker Allan Brown has linked groupwork to a slightly wider remit, suggesting that facilitators enable an environment to develop in which individuals help each other (form a support group/mutual aid system) whilst assisting the group as a whole to develop in ways that benefit both individual members *and* the wider community. The groupworker needs to be able to keep one eye on individual members and one on group processes, dynamics and cultures in order that individual, group and wider community needs might best be met. In youth work and education groupwork has been extensively written about. In contrast, although groupwork forms a core part of adult mental health services, comparatively little has been researched and written about it and there is very little training and supervision available in the NHS, social services and voluntary sector.

8

On the effectiveness and efficiency of groupwork

Do groups 'work'? When reviewing the literature the short answer must be 'in the main, yes'. The research indicates that most types of groups are at least as effective, and sometimes more effective, than one-to-one interventions.

Paul Grantham

It is beyond the scope of this book to provide a comprehensive literature review of the effectiveness of all types of groupwork, however it is important to point out that psychiatric drugs and cognitive-behaviour therapy (CBT) are not the only interventions with an evidence base to justify their use, and there is a large body of research that indicates groupwork is both an effective and efficient way of helping people. Readers that want to explore the literature on groupwork are pointed towards Mark Macgowan's book *A Guide to Evidence-Based Group Work* and the website www.evidencebasedgroupwork.com which assists people to conduct literature searches on all aspects of groupwork. There is considerable research that indicates groupwork can be helpful for: people with specific diagnoses such as manic-depression, bulimia, post-traumatic stress, depression, and schizophrenia; people suffering the effects of traumas such as sexual abuse; people with drug and alcohol problems; and people who are struggling with certain roles such as being a parent or caring for ill people. Whilst the majority of this research is on groups that differ from the type of community-based groupwork described in this book, it does reveal

the effectiveness of groupwork in a range of settings and with people with a range of difficulties.

There is some research that indicates groups are not particularly helpful in some contexts. For example, Hodgkinson et al (2000) found that psycho-educational medication groups did not lead to compliance when the aim was to ensure patients took medication professionals had deemed was good for them. However, published studies, including controlled trials and meta-analyses, have frequently indicated that groupwork is effective. Burlingame et al (2003) conducted a meta-analysis of 111 experimental studies that compared various group therapies with control groups and found substantial evidence to indicate the benefits of groupwork. For example, the overall group therapy versus control group effect size of 0.58 indicated that the average person attending a group was better off than 72% of people who received no group intervention (e.g. remained on a waiting list). A meta-analysis by Tillitski (1990) combined results from nine studies that incorporated 75 outcome measures taken from 349 group members. Only studies that contrasted group, individual, and control conditions with a pretest-posttest design were selected. Results indicated that both group and individual therapies (of various models) had a measurable effect that was consistently greater than that of controls. McRoberts et al (1998) conducted a meta-analysis of 23 outcome studies that directly compared the effectiveness of individual and group therapy formats when they were used within the same study. Their results matched previous reports that indicated group and individual interventions are equally effective. Some studies have specifically compared group and individual interventions in terms of cost-effectiveness and found groups to be more cost and resource efficient than providing individual therapy for the same number of people (e.g. McCrone et al, 2005). There is less empirical research on support groups compared to what are often termed therapy or treatment groups but those that have appeared in the literature (e.g. Gitterman, 2004, on mutual aid systems) also indicate the effectiveness of this type of group.

In short, reviews of the literature point to two basic conclusions:

- There is considerable research evidence to indicate that various types of groupwork are effective with a variety of populations in a variety of ways, but particularly in the areas of education, personal growth, therapeutic change and support.

- Groupwork is usually as effective (and occasionally more effective in terms of some benefits) as one-to-one interventions in comparison studies.

The modern NHS often appears to be obsessed with value for money and evidence-based practice. With such support in the literature one would expect more groupwork in state services. It seems effective, evidence-based and time and resource efficient. However, a whole host of factors often come together to prevent even well-motivated clinicians from conducting groups in the state sector. In this chapter we concentrate on one: insufficient time.

Some service contracts based on client contacts do not recognise the amount of time needed to set up and run groups. On top of this they often misunderstand the therapeutics of groups, measuring 20 hours of groupwork with 10 people in the group and one clinician as the equivalent of 2 hours of individual therapy for each. With ever-increasing pressure in the NHS for Trusts to be paid solely for clinicians' time in terms of face-to-face contacts, and the introduction of 'payment by results' with even more convoluted means of contracting, there is a risk of there being little incentive or even opportunity for clinicians to engage in groupwork. As this book reveals, groupwork in community settings involves considerable time spent outside the sessions, e.g. meeting a range of people beforehand to plan the group, preparing and distributing flyers advertising the group, organising the venue, preparing individual sessions, meeting with co-facilitators, setting up the room, debriefing after sessions, evaluating the groups, and engaging and supporting people in follow-up projects. Many of the core philosophies that underpin the groups also need time: for example, running them in community settings, and planning, facilitating and evaluating them with local people who have often been service users and may be learning groupwork or research skills for the first time.

Managers and commissioners, when they hear about *Psychology in the Real World* groups, welcome them as they quickly become aware of the wide range of benefits that flow from them. However, compared to their awareness of other types of intervention, such people are often less knowledgeable about groupwork and less aware of the time needed to set up, run and evaluate such groups. When agreeing contracts and setting priorities in the organisation, senior managers and commissioners usually have other things on their minds. But in an NHS that seems to be pressurising its staff to meet the ever-increasing demands of people diagnosed (by themselves and others) as in need of psychological help, see more and more people with a greater and greater range of problems, and fill in more and more forms for auditing, contractual and risk assessment purposes, there is a risk that only the most determined clinician in the future, who is prepared to work outside the constraints of work hours, will be able to do any type of groupwork.

9

The difficulties of being in groups

JOHN UPTON

When I was a child our family started going on trips to visit relations. I enjoyed the trip out to the countryside but with one of our relations the actual walk from the car along the driveway to the front door presented problems for me. I could be standing at the front to begin with but would somehow manage to conjure up a means whereby I would be at the back by the time we were greeted by my auntie, uncle and cousin. It presented fear to me – it could have been the fear of a kiss from my auntie or the fear of not knowing what to say to them, even though they were lovely people. Once I had passed that ordeal the rest of the day was always enjoyable.

I was painfully shy as a child. Whilst at primary school my mum encouraged me to join the youth club, but I did not want to go and would not go: I just wanted to be by myself. Whilst the other kids were messing about in the street I was tending to elderly people's gardens. I liked to help. In juniors I took a football to school. I recall the kids saying the only reason they played football with me was because I brought the ball in with me. My reaction? None. I remember one ball getting spiked on the school railings. No problem – I brought another ball in. Why did I do that? Was I that desperate to be liked? Why had I got into such an awful plight at such an early age?

I enjoyed playing football. One time during lessons a big match was arranged. Two captains were selected who then picked the teams, best players first and so on until there were two lads left: one who was overweight and not interested

in football and me. I must be picked ... but no. One of the teachers suggested a lad from a lower year who was rather good. So the two of us left were sent over to play on the climbing frame. The other lad was happy doing this and tried to reassure me, but I was inconsolable. I wanted to play and was deeply hurt. I remember this episode like it was yesterday.

It appears as though what I really wanted was to be included. At that time I found it difficult talking to anybody, therefore the idea of being in groups was a really frightening prospect. I was really pleased when the day came that I could leave school behind and start earning a living. During this period I would go on holidays, by myself to begin with. I quickly came to the conclusion that I did not want to be a loner. But I was to discover that, unfortunately, the 'seeds had already been sown'. As the years rolled by I appeared to be less shy but inside I was probably as shy as ever.

During the course of my work as a full-time union representative I attended many meetings. At one point the branch secretary labelled me a professional meeting attender, which still brings a smile to my face whenever I think of it. I expect the 'meeting experience' helped me tremendously in coping with group situations. At one point I did the previously unthinkable: addressed a meeting of about forty union members, where I spoke on a campaign and put forward two propositions (motions). I was as nervous as could be when I got up, but I could feel my confidence growing and by the time of the propositions I could not wait to get up to speak on them. When I am faced with a difficult (to me) group situation I often look back to that time, one of my proudest moments, to give me the strength to get through it.

When my dad died twenty-five years ago I found it difficult to cope. I opted for the one-to-one approach rather than group therapy, which I could not face. I found it difficult to reveal things to one person let alone a whole group and feared, although things are meant to be kept confidential, personal details might slip out in conversations people might have down the pub. In recent times I have attended various courses to help with my personal development. I now prefer to attend group sessions. Having gained a wealth of knowledge through my union work, therapy sessions and participation in groups, I would rather pass it on if I feel that it may be of benefit to others rather than keep it to myself.

I attended three *Psychology in the Real World: Toxic Mental Environments* sessions several years ago which I found interesting and inspirational. I found myself in the company of like-minded people. My only regret is that we did not exchange contact details in order to meet up to discuss any issues currently on our minds and 'to put the world to rights!' I have been attending *Walk and Talk* on a regular basis over the past two years and helped organise it in 2008. As I have been at various levels of depression during that time I have not participated in it as much as I could have although I can appreciate the delights of a walk along the River Severn.

I often wonder what benefit the courses are in finding a way out of the wilderness of my everyday life. Much that I try to help others when I can, I have often felt that I do not 'connect' with others. I think that this has a lot to do with spending far too much time not being in group situations, particularly during my formative years when a whole raft of skills could have been acquired, some of which I am only discovering now. Recently, I have found that I am beginning to connect with other people. This has occurred during a personal development course, a Relate course and a weeklong Fit Club. The latter included taking part in various keep-fit exercises, sporting activities and even belly dancing; I cannot believe I did it but I did. It is like going back to my formative years and learning again from the beginning; the difference being most of it is exciting, enjoyable and good for me.

10

What discourages people from joining or running groups?

Hell is other people.
  Jean-Paul Sartre

Many things that put people off joining groups, whether they be therapy, social, political or *Psychology in the Real World* groups, mirror factors that discourage people from running groups. These include:

1. *Being outnumbered* – As Paul Grantham describes, this is inherently anxiety provoking, especially in situations where the other members of the group are strangers to you.

2. *The unpredictability of groups* – We have many more models to help us understand one-to-one encounters and more quickly become comfortable in one-to-one situations (for example, because there is only one person we have to learn to trust and their behaviour more readily comes to feel predictable).

3. *Previous experiences of having been hurt in group situations* – Gregory Bateson felt that scapegoating was one of the key processes that lead to people being diagnosed as mentally ill (e.g. all the madness in a family is projected by the majority of family members onto one family member, who is seen as the only one who is ill and is viewed as responsible for causing all the disturbance in the group). Many people involved in psychiatric services have had such

experiences and subsequently view any group situation with trepidation. All of us know what it is like to be humiliated in front of others (some school teachers and most bullies are very skilled in public humiliation). Even in less toxic circumstances people talk of feeling 'mortally' embarrassed when all that has happened is that they have made a mistake in front of a group of people. Shame is very powerful and can create severe discomfort in us; this inevitably makes us wary of situations in which such feelings may re-occur. Difficult experiences in groups can leave us longing to be included but at the same time avoidant of the very thing we crave. Fears of rejection and a sense of not being wanted are very powerful in group situations and people protect themselves from re-experiencing such pain – it often feels safer to choose isolation than risk such hurt.

4. *Hell is other people* – Sartre's quote is, I believe, often misunderstood. I think he meant that if we spend time with people who are cruel to us it is like a living hell as we see ourselves through others' eyes – we inevitably take on board their view of us and life becomes hellish in such situations. People fear this will occur in groups, especially when they initially do not know the other people in the group. In groups it can take considerable time to get to know the other

group members, so for some people sticking in a group takes great bravery and commitment as it can take a long time to attain a sense of safety.

5. *Groups are public environments where we are 'on show'* – This makes groups attractive to more extrovert people but feared by people who are more introverted or shy. Some people in *Psychology in the Real World* groups have fed back how much they feared being put on the spot (e.g. when asked direct questions or during a round robin). Performance anxiety tends to be far higher in groups than in one-to-one situations.

6. *Fears of intimacy* – People are drawn to others, perhaps because we are pack animals and interdependence has such a long history in human groups. Adam Phillips believes that because we are of the same kind it is relatively easy for us to identify with and empathise with others. Being with people connects us, and giving and receiving acts of kindness brings us close. However, it also disturbs us – intimacy is what we crave but also what we struggle with. There is often an upsurge in fears – fears of closeness, merging, loss of individuality and control, and ultimately rejection – that push us in the opposite direction: to be separate and safe from such experiences and feelings. Genuine contact with others, especially in group situations, is much more frightening than counting the number of hits one gets on one's website.

7. *The absorption of other people's pain* – John Donne said 'no man is an island', but it can be difficult being with people as when hearing of their disquiet we often experience a sense of absorbing their pain. If we feel overwhelmed by our own struggles we may feel we have little capacity to bear the pain of others. People who have taken a martyr or rescuer role with others sometimes fear hearing about difficulties other group members have experienced, fearing the experience of feeling further burdened. As such, many of us at times choose to limit our contact with needy others, whilst some try and stay completely isolated on their island.

8. *Loss of individuality* – We can feel submerged by a group, or feel our individuality is merging into or becoming lost in the group experience. The name of the group brands us and defines us in the eyes of others. We take on some of the group's identity, which is not always experienced as positive. Groups inevitably have rules or norms that inhibit some expressions of individuality. It can feel frightening to disagree with what the rest of the group think or to break established group norms. The pressures regarding this can feel very inhibiting and are not attractive to people who fear their individuality being constrained.

9. *Reduced access to, and perceived battles for, resources* – In groups there is inevitably competition for resources (for example, time to speak and attention from people perceived as high status). This can lead to re-enactments of past hurts and bring up aspects of our character that are uncomfortable for us – feelings such as anger, frustration, envy and pain associated with not being noticed, not being given opportunities to flourish, being silenced or spoken over, being relegated to perceived low status in the hierarchy and so on. Compared to one-to-one situations, such as a counselling relationship, comparatively little of the focus is on us as an individual (which might be what we crave or need).

10. *Difficulties disclosing private details* – When talking about very personal matters, especially where there is considerable shame

(e.g. regarding sexual matters), most of us, especially if we have never previously told anyone, find it much more difficult to speak of such things in a group compared to a one-to-one situation.

11. *Powerful feelings brought up when people drop out of a group* – Being part of a group where people have not turned up, especially when they have not given advance warning of this and where others previously have dropped out, tends to provoke uncomfortable feelings of being associated with something that one fears is failing. We can construe this as relating to some failure of our own which adds to the drive within us to 'bail out' too.

In a nationwide survey of state and voluntary sector services Mark Doel and Catherine Sawdon asked clinicians of various professions the question: *What makes for successful groupwork?* The answers they got focused on the following factors: adequate resources, especially time; recognition and support from the employing agency, especially senior managers; support from stakeholders (e.g. relatives of people in the group); the commitment of group members; the group worker's skills, knowledge base and professional values; and the ability of the group to meet the members' aims and objectives. People working in services do not often feel well trained in groupwork, where there is little training both during and post-qualification in most professions, there is hardly anyone offering supervision and few books providing clear guidance compared to the resources available for people providing one-to-one interventions.

11

Setting up groups and avoiding common pitfalls

Give me six hours to chop down a tree and I will spend the first four sharpening the axe.

Abraham Lincoln

The lack of preparation for groupwork I have encountered in Health and Social Services, and in the voluntary sector, has at times been breathtaking. Staff are busy and good intentions to meet co-facilitators beforehand and carefully plan a group can get so squeezed that I have heard of people meeting for the first time just an hour before the first session to decide what type of group to run and what to do. Community-based groupwork often needs more hours spent meeting and preparing before the opening session of the group than the actual time spent in the group sessions. One co-facilitator, Lucy Gahan, said: 'I've come to realise that groupwork in community settings is 70% logistics.' As Box 3 indicates, there are a lot of things to think through when considering running any kind of group.

Box 3   Questions to ask when setting up a group

What needs have you identified that are not being met in the local community?
What benefits do you hope participants and the wider community might get?
Why a group?
What are your aims?
What are you going to call the group?
Who are you hoping will join? What mix of participants are you looking for and how might you try and get that mix? Are there going to be any inclusion and exclusion criteria?
How are you going to get people to join the group?
Are you going to meet potential group members before starting the group?
How are you going to discover people's personal aims for participating in the group?
Where are you going to meet? What do you want the physical environment to be like?
How long will the group run for? How regularly are you going to meet?
Is it going to be an open or closed group? Is it going to have a fixed end date?
What might be the advantages and disadvantages of having co-facilitators? What roles and tasks will each facilitator take?
Are there going to be any group rules? How will these be discussed? What norms and group cultures are you hoping might develop? How are you going to assist this?
How will participants be helped to feel safe enough to fully participate and take personal risks?
In what ways might the group be a harmful experience for participants or the wider community? How might you reduce the risks of this?

The risk assessment is for the activity (just as schools do when children engage in activities outside school premises) rather than a set of individual assessments of individual group members (that attach themselves to each individual and go in their health file – as if 'risk' is something that can be formally established rather than something that fluctuates second to second as people react to ever-changing environments). The risk assessment for the activity should go beyond an analysis of risks balanced against benefits for people who come to the group. For example, one risk to consider regarding the wider community is the deleterious impact a state-funded group might have on local community activism (see Makkawi, 2009).

Risk in mental health services has at times been enveloped by hysterical environments where frightened clinicians and managers imagine worst-case scenarios and intervene in ways that may reduce risks of physical harm but, in Wolfensberger's phrase, contribute to a process of 'death-making', where the people supposedly being helped are constrained and treated in ways that lead them to eventually lose the will to live. If human beings are not trusted, they may never learn to trust themselves; if not behaved to in ordinary ways, may never see themselves as ordinary; if not given roles with status, may never see themselves as competent or worthwhile; and if not given responsibility, may never see themselves as responsible. If people are viewed and treated as dangerous ('a risk') they are likely to conceptualise themselves as dangerous (and a risk to themselves or others). We should not then be surprised when people behave in ways that reflect these fears, 'act irresponsibly' (despite clinicians' impeachments for them not to) and act out beliefs in their entrenched oddness, madness and dangerousness.

Over the past decade in the NHS, performance management, audited record-keeping and the creation of hierarchical systems aimed at monitoring professionals have replaced trust in professional judgement. Ultra-defensive practice, 'in order to avoid being blamed should anything go wrong', and monumental amounts of record-keeping, however, cannot enable clinicians to escape the fact that they still have to make moment-to-moment decisions in ever-changing and highly complex situations. And all of this ignores the fact that people only learn by taking risks: as Jan Waterson, author on risk, has stated, taking risks is part of everyday life, and risk taking is as much about opportunities as about threats – achieving maximum independence may involve risk taking where potential losses are great, but potential gains are greater.

Creating a healthy group environment

Many of us who have had to endure therapy groups have an inbuilt dread of entering empty rooms and seeing chairs arranged in a circle.
　Marese Hudson

Many *Psychology in the Real World* groups involve us sitting around a table. It is not quite King Arthur's round table but we do try and create an atmosphere of equality. Given the constraints of having to use what is available at each venue we usually make do with an oval, oblong or square arrangement of tables pushed together. Marese Hudson, who co-facilitated the *Thinking about Medication* groups, helped me realise that sitting around a table is more normal and comfortable for many people compared to other seating arrangements, especially when people are in highly anxious states. The table provides something to hide behind rather than the feeling of exposure chairs arranged in a circle creates, which is particularly helpful in the awkward moments when we wait for people to arrive and the session to start. It is not reminiscent of therapy groups that participants may have previously experienced and therefore does not create expectations of therapy and lessens transference reactions onto us as facilitators that might relate to previous therapy encounters. The set-up is not like school (no rows with the teacher in front) but is more like a meeting room or pub which fits better with the core philosophy of encouraging the sharing of thoughts, feelings, ideas and theories. Having tables enables us to have water readily available for those who might have dry mouths caused by psychiatric medication, and handouts and books for people to look at and take away, as well as a surface for people to write on should they wish to make any notes. Having said this, some people have fed back that the arrangement of tables felt a little stuffy at first, a bit like a board room, and a large number of people sitting alongside each other can create difficulties in terms of people being able to see each other. There are pros and cons to any layout or environment.

One disadvantage of hiring rooms in community settings is that you have little control over the set-up of the room, furniture or general décor and are limited as to how much you can alter this. Cosy rooms work better than cavernous ones where it is difficult to create an intimate atmosphere, but it is helpful to have some space for participants to go into smaller groups without inducing a cacophony of sound where no one can hear themselves think. On the other hand, rooms in community settings are often better equipped than many health service venues, e.g. many have hearing loops and better soundproofing than health service buildings, and they often have more appropriate lighting (bright strip lights are useful for physical examinations but are not great in terms of creating a homely, relaxed atmosphere). The Gateway Arts and Education Centre has rooms that overlook a field and a café that overlooks the river which people have remarked on in terms of this helping to create a calm and

pleasant atmosphere.

Paul Grantham's training sessions on groupwork emphasise the importance of the physical environment in terms of enabling creative, lively debate, and the importance of changing the physical environment (e.g. how people are seated) if the group is not functioning well. It is the facilitator's task to make sure energy levels in the group, which naturally fluctuate, do not drop too low and if they do to change things, e.g. have a break, set up a different type of task, split into smaller groups. Facilitators will find this much harder in a room with very comfy chairs for people to lounge in, that is warm and stuffy, especially if people attending are quick to enter into drowsy states (e.g. through medical problems such as head injury or through impacts of medication). One of the first things I do when going into a room to be used for groups is to open the windows, even in the winter. It is better to get a couple of questioning looks from people who feel a little cold than have a room full of people perpetually on the edge of unconsciousness.

Avoiding and addressing some maladaptive group processes

Melanie Klein believed that we oscillate between two states of mind – the paranoid-schizoid and the depressive position. In the paranoid-schizoid state we split things into black and white, good and bad, and can therefore become somewhat paranoid fearing the bad that we see in (or project onto) others. In the depressive position we view everything and everyone as a mix of good and bad. Groups can similarly oscillate between these ways of thinking. When dominated by paranoid-schizoid thinking there can be extreme splits: 'either you're with us or against us' leads to splits between the group and outsiders, or splits within the group leading ultimately to some people leaving or being expelled. There is a tendency for such groups to be dominated by fear, blaming, and even hating and aggression towards perceived wrongdoers who are seen as threatening the group – this can be in the form of infighting or aggression towards outsiders. This is the ultimate 'four legs good, two legs bad' thinking that runs the risk of being perverted into yet another split ('four legs good, two legs better'). In Monty Python's *Life of Brian* it is exemplified by the People's Front of Judea:

Reg: The only people we hate more than the Romans are the Judean People's Front.

Members of the People's Front of Judea (PFJ): Yeah … splitters!

Francis: And the Judean Popular People's Front.

PFJ: Yeah. Oh, yeah. Splitters. Splitters …

As the number of groups listed as despicable splitters grows, one member states how much they hate the People's Front of Judea, before they all eventually realise that they are talking about themselves! ('*Oh, I thought we were the Popular Front!*').

In contrast, when operating in the depressive position people are aware of the middle ground, the complexity of things and the advantages of considering matters from differing standpoints. There is an acceptance of individual and group fallibilities and the emotional temperature is less stirred up (or manic) as people accept and work towards compromises and realistically appraise what can be achieved.

Many groups suffer when the pressure for homogeneity and conformity overwhelms the ability of group members to think rationally and accept a wide variety of individual differences. Groups can enter states of what Irving Janis called groupthink, a mode of thinking that people engage in when they are deeply involved in a cohesive group and when the members' strivings for unanimity override their motivation to realistically appraise alternative courses of action. Group members can experience a loss of individuality and capacity in the group to think independently. Dissenting views become hard to conceptualise or express, are sometimes seen as unwelcome and can provoke aggressive responses from other group members. Speaking our minds in any group takes courage, but in groups that are tending towards groupthink it needs great levels of bravery and fortitude.

In *Psychology in the Real World* ventures we try as much as possible to avoid groupthink and paranoid-schizoid states. Conceptualising the groups as courses and running them for a time-limited period seems to help. The groups are projects to temporarily engage in rather than something more permanent that might become part of a participant's core identity. We try and preserve individuality and autonomy of thinking and action as much as possible rather than allow a group to become dominated by an insistence on one way of seeing things or doing things. Apart from *Walk and Talk* the groups are not slow-open groups where pressures to fit in with an established group culture can be very difficult to overcome. Most people have opportunities to shape each group as equal members at the start of any venture. Even in *Walk and Talk,* with its ever-changing clientele, we are open to modification of what we do depending on what anyone attending one week might say.

We work hard before a group is set up to try and get as great a mix of people as possible. Homogenised groups in terms of, for example, racial background, age, gender, sexuality and mental health service involvement have a greater tendency to confirm and reinforce their own established views (some might say prejudices). On the courses we reinforce the idea of having humility regarding the ways we see ourselves, others and the world and accept that these should always be open to change. Differences of opinion are valued and splitting questioned. We try and nip in the bud sentiments such as 'psychology good, psychiatry bad', 'service users good, staff bad', 'talking therapies good, medication bad', 'this group good, other groups bad', which do surface from time to time. We do this by: enabling people who see things differently to be respectfully heard; providing evidence that counteracts such thinking; encouraging exploration of our own fallibilities; inviting in members of the 'out-groups'; and discussing group processes that can lead to such thinking. We also try and keep the emotional temperature high enough for the group to be engaging but not too high that it prevents reflection. Some of this is taken up in Chapter 31, particularly the section on Bion's basic assumption states.

Battles for resources can induce unhealthy within-group (and between-group) competition. The powerful emotional states this can induce can be noticed in everyday situations such as waiting alongside others on a crowded platform for a busy train to pull in. Knowledge of this kind of effect helps us understand otherwise seemingly mad events such as the crushing to death of people who have been queuing for the doors to open in a store having a cut-price sale. Group effects of this type can be eased by people in positions of authority providing information that resources will be available for all (or shared fairly), by group members knowing and having a commitment to each other, and by small acts of kindness and consideration (e.g. letting someone go first). In *Psychology in the Real World* groups we try and ensure that everyone has ample opportunities to contribute to the group and for those who want to access the facilitators as a resource this is made available both during the group sessions and after they end (e.g. in the café afterwards).

Groups are also prone to the process known as scapegoating. This term historically refers to the practice of spiritual leaders ceremonially putting all the evil in a community into an animal that was then driven out (and usually killed). Animals in the wild sometimes pick on one member and violently hound it out of the group and as humans we may have primitive tendencies in us that make us prone to this. Certainly we have much to fear from being a scapegoat in any group, where members of the group project onto us aspects of their character that they are uncomfortable with and perhaps blame us for failings in the group as a whole. Gregory Bateson has likened this process to family systems that lead one person in a family to be viewed as the 'mad one' – a process that often ends up with the person being perceived, treated and behaving in a 'mad' way.

Once the scapegoating process has started many of us seem to find it very difficult to intervene and protect that person (perhaps for fear of receiving similar treatment). It is crucial that facilitators exert their power to nip such behaviour in the bud. In *Psychology in the Real World* ventures we see this phenomenon arise more often in less structured groups (such as *Out of the Box*) rather than more structured situations that characterise many groups/courses (such as *Understanding Ourselves and Others*). For example, people have felt picked on for not speaking enough, holding back the group or failing to get as much from the group as others deem they should. Structure seems to be one way of keeping this in check, as does valuing difference, allying oneself with the scapegoated person (in the above example reiterating that it is alright to be quiet and people can learn as much from listening as speaking), and returning the group as a whole (and individual members) to depressive-position thinking. We thus try and establish the conditions for people to be able to 'think aloud' whilst at the same time counteracting forces that lead groups to silence outspoken dissenters.

Box 4   On charging for courses

Donations regarding Vipassana Meditation as taught by S.N. Goenka are accepted only from those who have completed at least one ten-day course. Someone taking the course for the first time may give a donation on the last day of the course or any time thereafter. In this way courses are supported by those who have realised for themselves the benefits of the practice. Wishing to share these benefits with others, one gives a donation according to one's means and volition. Whether a donation is large or small, it should be given with the wish to help others:

The course I have taken has been paid for through the generosity of past students; now let me give something towards the cost of a future course, so that others may also benefit by this technique.

www.dhamma.org

Many *Psychology in the Real World* courses have been free. This allows all people to attend, irrespective of income. Courses that have been run as part of the adult education curriculum at the local arts and education centre have charged participants the going rate for courses of this type. One benefit of this is that the course is advertised alongside other courses at the centre (e.g. learning Italian, painting, computer skills) in a glossy booklet that the centre sends out to local households and organisations, and this has helped to ensure that some people with no previous involvement with mental health services have come on the course. In addition, everyone who signs up for the course does so in the same way they sign up for other adult education courses – there is no stamp of it 'being for the mentally ill'. One disadvantage is that adult education courses have dramatically risen in cost over the past decade. After having the equivalent of OFSTED inspections, charges for *Understanding Ourselves and Others* at this venue rose from £28 to £72 for a 12-week course. Although we were able to negotiate that people on benefits would only pay £5 for the whole course, it was felt that a price hike of this magnitude meant that the courses had become socially exclusive. Ironically one aim of the Government's interventions was to make adult education centres more socially inclusive, but the effects of the increase in bureaucratic and training requirements on the centre and tutors meant that prices had to be raised to cover the increased costs and the people that the centre was being instructed to target were being excluded through price.

Some *Psychology in the Real World* courses where people paid in advance have had reduced (and sometimes no) dropouts prior to the first session or during the course compared to free courses I have facilitated, although this effect has not been universal. *The Writing Groups* have been free but over a third of the people who signed up dropped out each time and members commented that commitment might have been higher if people had paid to join. On the other hand, *Thinking about Medication* was also free yet only one person left before the end of the course. There may be benefits of having a small charge in terms of reduced dropouts, but it is important that poor people in and out of work are not prevented from coming, as they are frequently the people with the most needs and fewest resources. In addition, NHS Trusts seem to be increasingly looking to generate income; those who object to creeping privatisation may view charging for courses or groups that NHS staff are involved in running as unpalatable.

An alternative to charged or free courses might be to follow the principle used on some meditation courses, for example, Vipassana meditation as taught by S.N. Goenka, which run solely on a donation basis (see quote above). In addition to participants who complete the

Vipassana course making financial donations (as fit their means) so that others in the future may similarly benefit, everyone involved, from the management to the teachers to the kitchen staff, serve as unpaid volunteers operating on the same principle – repaying the gift they have received through the generosity of others. Our mental health can be improved as much by altruism as by receiving, and income generated in this way could be used to book rooms and cover costs of future community-based groups.

Community workers operating outside state services often apply for grants to fund their projects and salaries. Ibrahim Makkawi has analysed the impacts of bidding for grants on community psychology in Palestine. He highlights the benefits of grass-roots voluntary groups that are truly independent – of the state; charities; NGOs; and the distracting, corrupting and de-politicising impacts of bidding for grants to set up and run community projects. Grass-roots voluntary groups can retain an independence of thought and action that groups run by paid workers lack. Such groups not only provide support to oppressed people but they have greater freedom to develop ideologically driven political resistance to oppression.

12

Beginnings I

[Early in a group's development] an approach-avoidant conflict becomes evident ... members approach each other in their striving to connect with one another, but avoid getting too close because they fear the vulnerability that such intimacy implies.
> Toseland & Rivas

The opening session of an *Understanding Ourselves and Others* course and of a *Black Dog: Understanding Depression* course are described in Chapters 15 and 25. It might be helpful for readers to look at these in conjunction with the following as they reveal some of my thinking during the first session of a group.

The facilitator's tasks or aims in the first meeting of a group

The following is a list of things facilitators might aim to achieve in the first session of a group. It is loosely based on the work of Allan Brown and is broadly applicable to most types of groupwork:

1. Enable members to reduce and contain their initial anxieties about coming for the first time, and perhaps being in a venue they have not visited before, so that they are able to participate as fully as possible in the first session.

2. Facilitate introductions and help the members to start to join together to form a group which feels safe, is attractive to them and to which they feel some commitment (and in doing so start to facilitate the creation of the matrix, see next page).

3. Achieve clarity within the group about why the group has formed.

4. Clear expectations with members about why they have come and what they hope to gain from being part of the group.

5. Negotiate and agree the group contract, including the ways in which group members will work together and any group rules (e.g. confidentiality, time-keeping).

6. Indicate the way the facilitators hope to work with the group and what their roles will be.

7. Discuss the group programme and methods to be used, and consider what is planned for the next meeting.

8. Help members feel part of the group, facilitate their motivation to 'work' in the group, address any ambivalence and resistance, and begin to establish a helpful group culture.

9. Throughout the process try and balance the task and socio-emotional aspects of the group process (e.g. given expected anxieties about meeting people for the first time, help to reduce anxiety levels to the point where people can think and express themselves as honestly and clearly as possible, and might remember what is discussed, before agreeing the programme/plan for the group).

10. Ensure as far as possible that the experience is positive enough for each person to come to the second and subsequent sessions (unless there are insurmountable impediments to this, in which case talk through with that person the option of them not being part of the current group and discuss alternative ways they might get their needs met).

The matrix and round robin

As well as attending to the list above, my main aim in the first session is to start to build the matrix. The matrix can be envisaged as a mandala-like representation of an interconnected group where every person is connected to each other whilst being held in the boundary of the group as a whole.

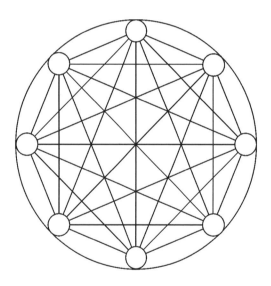

Fig. 1   The matrix

Although I chat with people as they arrive, trying to put people at ease in various ways, I do not normally envisage the building of the matrix until the group officially starts. After talking for about ten minutes, giving (usually flustered) late-comers time to arrive and a period for people's anxiety levels to die down a little (and the atmosphere in the room to calm), I normally initiate a round robin whereby I ask people in turn to introduce themselves and say something about why they have come along and what they want to get from being part of the group. The Asch experiment (see Chapter 13) provides powerful evidence that the first people to speak in a round robin scenario set a norm that others will tend to follow (and struggle to break even if the norm is maladaptive). For this reason I tend to try and pick someone to start us off who has given an indication of being calm and eloquent enough to say something in response to me putting them on the spot and gently probing them about their wishes for coming. I go around the group in turn and in doing so inevitably build part of the matrix, somewhat akin to the creation of a wagon wheel where I am positioned as the axis from which the spokes emanate:

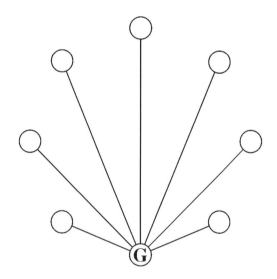

Fig. 2   The wagon wheel

Speaking to the person; getting a reply; having some eye contact; showing an interest in what the person has said; saying something appreciative about what the person has revealed; saying something empathic – all these build a connection between the facilitator and that person (of varying degrees of strength). Rogers' core conditions – *genuineness* (on behalf of the therapist/facilitator), *unconditional positive regard* towards the other person and *empathy* – provide a good guide to the approach a facilitator might take in these one-to-one encounters as the round robin progresses. At the same time I want to attend to the group as a whole so I make occasional comments about the developing group, again somewhat influenced by Rogers' core conditions. For example, I might say something like: 'The ways people are taking a chance and revealing things about themselves, apparently talking very honestly and openly about how they would like the group to be, bodes well for the group … it feels like we might well be able to develop something good here.' It is important that such statements are genuine and come naturally – crass and inauthentic positive statements tend to grate with people and be counter productive.

Statements to the whole group can be helpful in creating the sense of a group. But what is really needed for this is interconnectedness between group members. *Psychology in the Real World* groups are not psycho-education or skills groups focusing on the imparting of information to a set of individuals by the expert group leader. Rather, they are environments which hope to maximise learning, healing and social action through people getting together to exchange ideas with each other. It is therefore crucial to enable interactions and connections between group members as much as possible and important not to establish a permanent wagon-wheel norm where the majority of interactions occur between individual group members and the facilitator. To assist this process, I try and link what people say to things people have said earlier in the round robin. It might be that people have expressed similar aims or revealed similar fears about what the group might be like. As I do this, I repeat people's names to help the whole group remember each other's names and to cement such links.

People can also be linked by difference. I try to counteract strong forces that lead people to distance themselves from those who express views that differ from their own or what they conceptualise as the views or wishes of the whole group. These forces can be powerful in the formation stages of any group. For example, in the opening session of *Thinking about Medication* participants expressed a wide variety of aims regarding what they wanted from joining the group, some of which were contradictory. But, by making comments that did not shy away from these differences and linking people who expressed differing opinions (e.g. 'John wants us to invite psychiatrists, but Janet, interestingly, has a different take on that, thinking it will quell open debate'); using body language that links people (e.g. stretching one hand towards John and one towards Janet whilst saying the above); and enabling people to look at and acknowledge each other, a norm accommodating and welcoming difference started to form. In this instance the group was tasked with coming up with a solution that accommodated the differing wishes and someone suggested the first part of each meeting could involve talks and questions and answers (Q&A) with invited speakers (including psychiatrists) whilst the second part after a break could be reserved solely for group members. The expression of difference enabled us to therefore devise a group which probably worked better than the formats that had initially been envisaged, and a norm of welcoming and valuing difference (when respectfully expressed), essential in a group that is going to discuss highly emotive issues about medication, was nurtured.

Thus, as we progress around the round robin, I try and comment on links between people based on similarity and difference. If someone says something that I cannot link to anything said previously I note this and keep an eye out for future comments from people yet to speak that I can link back to that person. This is especially important for people who may feel like the 'only one' during an initial meeting, perhaps, for example, on the basis of race, age, or background. I also look out for people who might, through body language, be showing agreement or disagreement with something someone says, and might take time out from the round robin process to link them in … 'You seemed to be nodding whilst Joyce spoke of that … was that something you can relate to, Graham?' Of course many connections that people are making with each other will be unknown to a facilitator – the matrix will be developing in ways that are beyond the facilitator's ability to notice. All one can do is try to help this process occur.

The round robin tends to be rather frightening, especially for the more quiet and shy members, yet the benefits of it described above I believe outweigh the discomfort some people feel when waiting for their turn to speak, and it does prevent people from being perceived and treated as outside the group perhaps because they have not spoken in the initial meetings. The round robin also provides opportunities to explicitly discuss 'group rules' without necessarily calling them this. Rules, for me, are too reminiscent of school, and by calling them rules and discussing them in an authoritarian way there is a risk of triggering dynamics of obedience and rebellion that in a time-limited group can be unproductive (as they have to be managed rather than worked through). I tend to think about norms rather than rules (see Chapter 31), and if I refer to them call them 'guidelines to help the group work well'. Sometimes this is relatively straightforward – invariably someone will talk over someone else and I usually intervene to say *I cannot hear what*

people are saying when two people speak at the same time so perhaps we can try our best to avoid this.

Other guidelines involve greater complexity. For example, during the initial meeting people will often reveal something very personal about themselves, perhaps following my example (in the opening introduction before starting the round robin I often recount relevant stories about my own experiences and those of family members, conveying I trust the group members with personal information). Perhaps caught up in a rapidly developing atmosphere of trust and cohesion, one person will frequently indicate that they fear that they have 'revealed too much'. This enables us to discuss group boundaries, confidentiality, privacy, anonymity and respect regarding what is discussed both in and out of the group. I tend to suggest we do not adopt a stance of absolute confidentiality, where nothing discussed in the group is mentioned outside, as the group is not a therapy group and such a stance would invariably weaken the power of the group to have impacts that go beyond those on individual members. In discussing the issue the group as a whole normally come to adopt a position of treating what we learn about each other, especially very personal information, with respect and a degree of anonymity. For example, if people do refer to members of the group by name to non-members then we only use first names; that we would not like people to gossip about very personal aspects of our own life (and many of us might have been hurt by such experiences in the past) so we can perhaps commit to not engaging in such behaviours and keep such information within the group. Together we normally come to some sort of shared beliefs about such things (in subsequent sessions this is often referred back to and shaped as new experiences in the group occur). A list of rules set out on a flip chart cannot accommodate the flexibility and complexity of such norms, and in any case many can often be reduced down to two rules: the ethic of reciprocity, 'the golden rule' – *Do to others what you would like done to you, and do not do to others what you would not like done to you,* and Popper's 'platinum rule' – *Do unto others as they want to be done by.*

Once the round robin is finished there is scope to facilitate more free-floating discussions, with greater interaction between group members, thus the wagon-wheel effect gets less pronounced and the matrix becomes more fully established. Within any group certain people are going to feel closer and more connected to some members than others, but the greater a communal sense of matrix, the more cohesive a group will feel, and the more likely people's individual and group aims will be met. In relatively short-term groups it helps to generate this sense of cohesion as quickly as possible.

13

The Asch experiment and its relevance to groupwork

The individual has always had to struggle to keep from being overwhelmed by the tribe. If you try it, you will often be lonely, and sometimes frightened. But no price is too high to pay for the privilege of owning yourself.

Friedrich Nietzsche

… You walk into the room and nod to the other people sitting around the table. You presume that, like you, they are here to take part in an investigation into perception. Some smile, others ignore you. You take a seat. The man conducting the research experiment comes in and describes the task. All participants in the group are to look at a series of lines and estimate which corresponding line looks closest in length. You glance at others in the group as you are shown an example – it looks straightforward enough. The first set comes up (see below). The answer is obviously B.

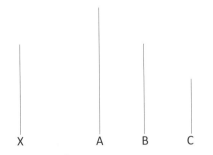

The man in charge asks the person next to him:
   'Which line is the same length as the example line X?'
   'C', he replies.

He moves on to the next person, a smiling, friendly looking woman: *'C',* she responds.

You feel confused … it's clearly B. What are they going on about?

The next person is asked: *'C'.*

The man turns to you. Anxiously you stare at the picture. You look down, then back at the picture. At last you speak: *'It's obvious, isn't it? … C.'*

In the Asch experiment the first three people to respond in the above scenario are stooges – people helping the experimenter in his experiment (not about perception but about group pressure) and primed to give the answer 'C'. In previous tests, without the stooges, the correct answer, B, is given virtually 100% of the time. But when asked to respond after the stooges have given a consistently wrong answer 75% of unwitting participants in the experiment agree with the stooges on at least one presentation of the lines. It seems that group pressures exert such a force that many of us will conform even when 'reality' is so obviously skewed. The pressure to fit in, not rock the boat, to not stand out appears to have a profound effect.

Such pressure to conform clearly has the potential to be a malign influence in terms of groupwork. Norms can quickly be created that lead to groupthink and this exerts significant pressure on group members to conform to what others think and say even when this is clearly a gross distortion of reality. Groupthink is the dark side of a highly cohesive group, when members' drive for unanimity appears to override their ability to rationally weigh up alternatives to those the group is intent on pursuing.

Any pressure to conform and restrict individuality has to be balanced against the need for people to come together with sufficient overlap and compromise to achieve the group's main tasks and for individual and group aims to be met. There is inevitably conflict between these factors, which the facilitator and group as a whole have to manage and work through, trying to create a group that avoids the types of pathological conformity as evidenced in groupthink.

The Asch experiment shows that the effects of pressure to conform can be significant even at the start of a new group. This has important implications for the initial meeting of groups and for the start of each session. If the facilitator starts the session with a round robin it is important, as far as is practicable, to ensure that the first couple of people set a norm that is going to be helpful to the group as a whole. The facilitator may have to intervene significantly if (i) an unhelpful norm is developing (e.g. people just say their name and make no other comment – see Chapter 25) or (ii) an unhealthy or harmful norm is developing (e.g. one where difference does not seem to be expressed or accepted).

SECTION 3

Understanding Ourselves and Others

14

Understanding ourselves *and* others

The illiterate of the 21st century will not be those who cannot read and write but those who cannot learn, unlearn and relearn.

    Alvin Toffler

Psychology in the Real World: Understanding Ourselves and Others is the title of a course that I have regularly facilitated, sometimes with other psychologists or social workers, since the late 1990s. The idea for this course came out of a wish to do something to bring people together in a community where people lived on estates that had been rated amongst the most socially deprived in Britain and where many people felt isolated, afraid, hurt, alienated and depressed. It was also born out of a sense that solely meeting people from this locality on a one-to-one basis at the CMHT base was not meeting many of their needs. For example, when discussing people's paranoia it became clear that there were few places nearby where people felt genuinely safe from physical intimidation or assault. Similarly, when meeting people interested in exploring the roots of their difficulties, it became clear that encouraging them to talk with friends or relatives was often ineffectual as they either had no contact with people outside mental health services or each time they opened up exploratory or intimate conversations with people they lived with these were at best closed down and at worst used as ammunition to be fired back at them at a later date. Quick-fix, one-to-one therapies were becoming increasingly fashionable but were not proving to be very effective with many

people I saw, and I was increasingly finding myself in long-term, supportive relationships with people who did not have other means of regular support outside the therapeutic encounter. I sensed that there were many local people who might have an interest in 'understanding themselves and others'; accessing this through the very narrow and pathologising entry criteria of a CMHT and then being put on a waiting list for one-to-one therapy with the sole psychologist was not perhaps the best way of enabling this.

When a community health and education centre was opened nearby I met with the people working there and started to devise a group that might (i) utilise some of my skills (I did not feel highly skilled in group or community work but did feel I knew how to help people discuss psychological issues), and (ii) meet some of the aims of the centre (which were about having a friendly, respectful place open to all local people who might come in and access information about local services and events, attend courses and connect with other people in their locality).

Sometimes the groups have been entitled understanding *yourself* and others but understanding *ourselves* and others captures the fact that the facilitators usually learn as much about themselves and other people as any other participant. From the very first running of the course they have been pitched as opportunities for people from all walks of life to come together to collectively analyse and discuss aspects of life that tend to affect us all. For example: *What makes us frightened, violent, depressed or full of shame and guilt? What helps us feel safe and secure? How might childhood experiences shape us?* More formal aspects of mental health are also analysed, e.g. *Why are people so afraid of mental illness? Are symptoms of mental illness better thought of as some people's best ways of coping? Why do psychiatric treatments seem so cruel?* The courses focus on *why* questions (rather than coping strategies) and, in attempting to understand the complexities of human behaviour, draw upon a wide range of theories and evidence – sociological, philosophical and autobiographical as well as psychological. The flyers used to advertise the courses have tried to capture the ethos that we are all psychologists and there is as much to be learned in the group from reflections on our own lives as from any text or expert. A black and white copy of one of the original (colour) flyers is included on the next page.

In order to get a mix of participants, flyers for these courses are usually put up in the venue where they take place, local community centres, libraries and cafés as well as GP practices, mental health clinics and in the local CMHTs. People usually book a place on a first-come, first-served basis at the venues. In order to ensure that a number of people from the CMHTs get a chance to attend I encourage key workers to forward the flyer to people they think might enjoy and benefit from the course and I am always keen to ensure at least a third of participants come from the local CMHTs. NHS, social services and voluntary sector workers have attended and joined in the group in the same way as other members. Over the years the reputation of the courses has spread by word of mouth so friends, relatives and colleagues of previous participants often come and people reserve places for courses yet to be planned. Like other *Psychology in the Real World* groups, they have always been fully booked.

The courses have tended to run on a weekly basis for between 12 and 16 weeks and have had between 10 and 14 members. This has usually enabled a sufficiently diverse group with rich differences of experiences and views to come together and feel safe and cohesive enough for people to trust each other with very intimate descriptions and analyses of their life experiences. As a result this has enabled the groups to generate various ways of understanding the often complex and diverse impacts on people of various life events. The psychology aspect of the course means we have an interest in the causes of human behaviour, but we normally also look beyond this, to the causes of causes – the wider aspects of society that impact on us in perhaps less direct or less obvious ways.

Why understand ourselves *and* others?

In my opinion, Western consumer capitalist societies bombard people with overt and covert messages that promote and foster individualism and narcissism. Jean Twenge has reviewed research evidence that indicates both anxiety levels and narcissism (or 'threatened egotism' – a puffed up form of self-esteem) have risen over the past 25 years. Some one-to-one therapies purport to 'treat' narcissism but all primarily focus on individuals talking about and thinking about themselves. *Understanding Ourselves and Others* involves this to some extent, but this takes part in a group situation where people reflect on things that might help everyone in the group to individually and collectively understand themselves and each other. Participants are also encouraged to relate ideas we discuss to other people in their life – family members, friends, neighbours, work colleagues, etc. The idea that one of the main social problems of the 20th century was people had insufficient self-understanding grew exponentially through that period. Some psychoanalysts genuinely believed that more

Psychology in the real world

Understanding ourselves and others

Why are we so afraid of mental illness?

In what ways might our experiences during childhood affect us?

How come so many people don't like the way they look?

What makes people violent, angry, depressed?

How come so many people are taking psychiatric and other drugs?

What is the point of being alive?

What helps us feel safe?

What is it like to be listened to?

Venue: CHEC, Madeley High Street
Dates: Wednesdays 3.00–5.00pm
Sept 16th – Dec 16th

This course will be organised by Guy Holmes. Guy is a local clinical psychologist and honorary lecturer at Birmingham University.

The course will involve short talks and group discussion and will be run very informally.

There is no need to have any previous knowledge of psychology or any qualifications – things will be talked about in everyday language. Participants will be encouraged to draw upon their own experiences and express and exchange their own ideas when discussing the topics.

In the first session there will be a chance to say which topics people are most interested in, as well as suggesting others that are not on the above list.

psychoanalysis and greater knowledge of psychoanalytic ideas would lead to less oppression, cruelty and war as fewer people would project their anger and destructiveness onto others. But as the title of Hillman and Ventura's book boldly states: *We've Had 100 Years of Psychotherapy – and the World's Getting Worse!* A century that saw more people killed by war than any other, and a new war breaking out every year since the end of the First World War ('the war to end all wars') might better have been served by a greater understanding of others.

Some people have found the courses very helpful in terms of understanding family members and have reported shifts in significant relationships following the sessions (although others have stated in evaluations that it would have been better if family members had been present to hear all the group discussion as taking up some of the themes with them did not work as well as they had hoped). Some people have reported less tension and conflict in relationships with friends and family following insights gleaned on the course. Others have come to see themselves as being involved in relationships that are too damaging and have left their partners (see Box 5).

Course structure

Box 6 (p. 64) shows topics that have been included in *Understanding Ourselves and Others* courses. The original list of ten topics initially reflected what I thought were common themes in discussions I have had with people referred to me over the years coupled to some topics I would have wanted to think more about at undergraduate or postgraduate level but were rarely part of the syllabus or taught in a way that helped me make sense of my own experiences. The original list has grown in length as different groups and different co-facilitators have suggested other areas to explore. The opening and closing

---

Box 5   Feedback regarding impacts of the groups on relationships

'The course made an important contribution to enabling me to get out of the rut I was in and to move on with my life by leaving a long-term unhappy marriage, in enabling me to accept and value myself and to sense the care and support of others in the group.'

'As a result of coming on the course I was able to make a decision to end a relationship which was causing me a great amount of mental anguish and illness. I am now recovering well, and beginning a new life, despite a brief period when I was hospitalised due to stress.'

As a facilitator I do not advise people how to conduct their relationships. Neither of the two people above let me know at the time anything about the relationships they describe, or spoke of them in the formal part of the sessions – these quotes were written many months after the end of the course when I contacted people who had previously come on these courses asking for anonymous feedback. None of the sessions were geared to help people leave harmful relationships (although there were sessions such as *Why do people get depressed?* and *Why are people violent?* which may have been relevant). Yet something clearly happened that helped this process. This contrasts sharply with my frequent ineffectiveness during the provision of individual therapy to have similar impacts on people struggling in abusive and very damaging relationships.

Box 6 *Understanding Ourselves and Others* **potential topic list**

- Introductory session. Beginnings: What is it like at the start of things? What is psychology? What is psychology in the real world? What are people's hopes and aims for coming on the course?
- Why are we so afraid of mental illness?
- In what kinds of ways do our experiences during childhood affect us?
- Why are there so many people who don't like the way they look?
- Why are people violent?
- How can we make major decisions and help others to make life-changing decisions?
- What makes us depressed?
- Why are so many people taking psychiatric and other drugs?
- Why do people get angry?
- What is the point of being alive?
- What helps us feel safe and secure?
- What helps at times of crisis?
- Should we 'be careful who we pretend to be because we are who we pretend to be'?
- In what ways is our environment psychologically toxic?

- Is there more to be learned from *The Simpsons* than self-help books?
- To what extent does our personality (underlying temperament) affect how we behave?
- How sane is it to be well-adapted to a sick society?
- Are symptoms of mental illness more accurately thought of as people's best ways of coping?
- Food: Friend or enemy? Why do we have such a difficult relationship with food?
- Why are people deeply troubled by feelings of shame and guilt?
- Are we the authors of our own lives?·
- Why are we so afraid?
- Why are we so conforming?
- Why do psychiatric treatments seem so cruel?
- What is it like to be listened to?
- Ending session.
  What is it like when things come to an end?
  Reflections on the course, evaluation and thoughts about the future.

sessions have been gradually refined but have remained fairly constant due to the importance of beginnings and endings to any group.

In the first meeting participants select from this menu those topics that they are most interested in exploring and are encouraged to suggest other areas that, given sufficient interest from the group, can be included. In subsequent weeks each topic is looked at from a wide set of angles utilising a variety of teaching and facilitating styles, including: short lectures from the facilitators; paired, small group and whole group discussion; and experiential investigation. Crucially, although some of the topics have quite provocative titles, each is explored in a spirit of collaborative conversation (see Chapter 4).

It is not possible to describe each session in detail, however I have tried to give a flavour of how different sessions have utilised different approaches below. Subsequent chapters describe a couple of sessions in greater detail:

- *Why are we so afraid of mental illness?* involves a lecture and discussion on the history of the concept of mental illness, and draws upon historical accounts (e.g. Roy Porter's *Madness: A brief history*) as well as following Foucault's genealogical investigations into the social construction of knowledge. It provides information about the history of people designated as mentally ill being given stigmatising labels (e.g. people with 'insufficient mental hygiene'); being excluded (e.g. put on ships and given food at ports and sent away – the ship of fools; being incarcerated in institutions outside towns); and being grouped alongside other stigmatised groups (e.g. being put in hospitals previously used for people with leprosy). It explores how modern day processes mirror such treatment and degrade and devalue people in their own and other people's minds (see Chapter 52 and the work of Wolf Wolfensberger). It invites discussion about the ways that group processes lead to the scapegoating of people who are different, and how group processes lead people to over-emphasise the sameness of members of the in-group and overemphasise difference in comparison to members of out-groups, and how members of both the 'sane' and 'insane' groups engage in these processes. Opportunities are given to group members to individually and collectively relate discussions of these concepts to their own experiences of, and attitudes to, mental illness and the mental health system.

- *In what kinds of ways do our experiences during childhood affect us?* involves participants listening to a recording of *95 Theses 95* by Garrison Keillor, a (fictional) monologue of a man's childhood experiences and early adulthood. The participants, as a group, produce a psychological formulation – a theoretical map, based on the information we have, of why he is like he is. This tends to include illustrations of various psychological (particularly psychodynamic) theories. It is emphasised that these ideas apply to all of us – they are not just ways of explaining 'psychopathology', but are means of understanding the ways in which childhood experiences stay with and shape us all.

- *Food: Friend or enemy?* involves all members of the group (including facilitators) selecting an item of food from the table (e.g. chocolate, fruit) and reflecting on the kinds of thoughts and feelings associated with making that choice, followed by similar reflections on eating the food.

- *Why are we so conforming?* involves in-depth descriptions of the experience of being a participant in the Milgram Experiment (see p. 12 and p. 132) and Stanford Prison Experiment, and group reflections on how social roles and certain contexts might affect our behaviour far more than we realise. We describe the experiments as they unfolded for actual participants, encouraging group members to put themselves in the shoes of, for example, a guard or prisoner in Zimbardo's mock prison at Stanford University, enabling group members to explore the extent to which roles that we have in life (e.g. parent, patient, psychologist) shape how we behave. Most people are initially sceptical that they might act like an authoritarian guard or passively compliant prisoner, but these experiments help us to question our belief that we are as autonomous and ethical in our decision making as we imagine.

- *Why are there so many people who don't like the way they look?* takes a social-materialist stance by looking at the role of consumer capitalism in influencing people's thoughts, feelings and behaviour. Material used to convey this (a spoof edition of a women's magazine) was co-written with Tina Jarvis who wanted to broaden the debate about the causes of people's discomfort with their bodies (see www.shropsych.org/image.pdf). The session raises discussion about the ways that all of us are bombarded with messages from the fashion and media industries that can lead all of us (not just people diagnosed as anorexic, bulimic or body dysmorphic) to be uncomfortable with our bodies.

- *What helps us feel safe and secure?* starts with an invitation for the whole group to think about this question themselves, and involves free association to the word 'insecure' and participants being given pens and paper to draw the concept 'safe'. The session generates material that tends to be illustrative of various psychological theories (e.g. attachment theory), with participants often moving from individual explanations to an analysis of wider environments that induce fear or help people feel psychologically and physically secure. This session sometimes overlaps with themes included in *Why are we so afraid?* For example, group members have remarked on the irony of some people's attempts to make themselves feel safe (e.g. by driving tank-like 4x4 vehicles) actually making other people (small car users, cyclists and pedestrians) feel, and be, even less safe. This fits with Wilkinson and Pickett's observation that, rather than working together to generate community safety, we sometimes enter into the equivalent of an arms race for individual safety. Others have raised questions about the effects of cultures that seem obsessed with risk and queried whether the state might be intentionally inducing fear in us (e.g. of being killed by terrorists) in order to achieve certain aims (e.g. greater state control of citizens' lives).

- *What is it like to be listened to?* involves paired listening (which we liken to co-counselling) as well as reflection on whether people have ever felt listened to outside the group, whether people feel they have been listened to in the group, and other group reflections.

15

Beginnings II: Opening sessions

The first session of *Understanding Ourselves and Others* courses mirrors those of other *Psychology in the Real World* courses such as *The Writing Group* and *Black Dog*. Below is an example of how I try to facilitate opening sessions, which illustrates the kinds of things that go through my mind during the first meeting of groups. Unlike some of the other descriptions of particular sessions (e.g. Chapter 25), the description below is a composite of events that occurred in several opening sessions of *Understanding Ourselves and Others* groups:

… I arrive three quarters of an hour early and check that the reception staff know about our course and have signs up showing people where to go. I brief them that some participants may be very nervous and it would be helpful if they would look out for anyone looking a bit lost. I pin a poster for the group on the door of the room we are to use. Going in I check out what might be participants' first impressions … too bright … a bit impersonal … too warm and stuffy? I notice a whole wall of health and safety decrees including notices saying not to tamper with any signs and a notice saying not to use pins or blue tack on any part of the premises except the notice boards – which are jammed full of health and safety notices! I take down some of these and make a mental note to ask the staff at the centre whether some new health and safety regime has been introduced and whether they have considered the impact on people of such signs – how it gives an immediate message

of being bossed around. I am doing my best to ensure people feel safe and comfortable in a community-based environment that feels like it is being turned into the type of institution we are trying to escape!

I rearrange the furniture so that there is an oblong set of tables and casually set out the chairs trying to ensure that people have enough personal space whilst hoping to create as cosy a feel to the room as possible. I ask the women in the adjoining café for two jugs of water and some glasses, and when given a somewhat quizzical look explain that people get thirsty during the sessions. I reassure them that we will be coming into the canteen in the break, I will be encouraging participants to stay afterwards for some lunch, and we will bring back the jugs and glasses at the end. In a new venue it is important to build up good rapport with all the staff – being friendly to them means they are more likely to be friendly to the entire group each week, which is crucial in trying to create a psychologically safe environment for the group to take place. I don't let on the real reason behind my request – some participants are likely to be taking medication that makes their mouths so dry that without ready access to water they will be unable to participate in group discussions.

Back in the room, with dead leaves of potted plants removed, water and glasses at both ends of the table, handouts with information about the course laid out, and the window slightly open to get some fresh air (having checked this doesn't sacrifice privacy or quietness), I wait and mentally rehearse the plan for the session. I check my quotes from Socrates and others which are ready on the flip chart. An image of someone shouting out 'Oh no … not the flippin' chart!', as occurred during one group, pops into my head. I'm anxious. Knowing that anxiety induces catastrophising thoughts doesn't seem to be stopping this from happening so I focus on my breathing, using it as an anchor to prevent my fears from flipping out.

Someone tentatively comes through the door.

'Hello. Come in.' I get out of my seat and shake their hand. 'I'm Guy Holmes … you've come for the Psychology in the Real World course?'

'I'm in the right place then. Hi, I'm Emily.' I suggest she takes a seat. We do small talk: 'Have you been here before … do you know where the café and toilets are … you might want to get a drink but are welcome to sit here and wait for others to arrive … yes, it's OK to come early – I'll be here each week at least half an hour before the group starts, getting things ready … yes, when you're nervous and you've not been somewhere before it can make sense to give yourself plenty of time – I expect most of us will be a bit anxious as people tend to be when meeting people they haven't met before.'

There's a bit of me that knows that whilst engaging in such talk I'm missing out on the time I had hoped to use to gather and prepare myself for the session; I'm distracted from what the whole group might need. But *sometimes the needs of the one outweigh the needs of the many*. Whilst listening to the clearly anxious Emily I try and remember the therapist who said this, then track it back to *Star Trek III: The Search for Spock*! In a quiet moment my mind's eye pictures psychoanalytically run groups that I have attended, where the group analyst arrived precisely on the start time, not a second before or a second after, without saying hello – even in

the opening session, leading to a guessing game amongst participants which I christened *Which one of us is the analyst?* This might be a good way of inducing regression in the participants and transference reactions to the analyst, but anxiety levels tend to go through the roof, and although I can see benefits in it for the group leader it doesn't seem an appropriate model for community-based groupwork. My attention is pulled back to the present as more people come in. More hellos; more small talk. Emily introduces herself to some people, others introduce themselves, some start to chat with each other, some sit quiet, others look at the handouts about the course. Eventually it's 11 o'clock. I'm pleased everyone is here, and say: 'OK … let's start.'

I take the opportunity to thank everyone for getting here on time and say it will help me if we can start on time each week. Hopefully, without coming over too bossy and talking about rules, I'm reinforcing a norm that will help the group to function well. I say I'll make sure that we finish on time each week, but I'll be around at the end for anyone who wants to stay for lunch or talk after the end of the session. I let them know something about the plan for today's meeting, including the intention to go around asking people to introduce themselves and say something about what led them to come on the course. I can see this induces panic in a couple of people's faces but at least I've pre-warned them that they will be expected to say something in due course. I know most people are too anxious to talk right now (some may be too anxious to even listen by the look of them) and start to talk generally about the course, why it is called 'psychology in the real world', why 'understanding ourselves and others', and how I hope things might go. A couple of people ask questions and the atmosphere starts to calm. I try and say something positive back, thanking the questioner for raising that point, behaviourally reinforcing the behaviour (inquisitiveness) and hopefully helping to create a group norm of open enquiry and freedom to ask questions and clarify things not understood. Irvin Yalom's assertion that the opening session is not one for the therapist to take a back seat pops into my mind. The questions give me a chance to start to build the matrix.

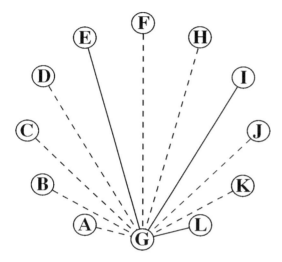

Fig. 3   Stage 1 of matrix creation
Speaking to the whole group, hoping to create some connections between the facilitator and group members, responding to questions and comments, and building the matrix via the wagon wheel

'OK. Now I'm going to go around asking you each in turn to let us know your name and to say what brought you along today. I'd also like you to say something about what you hope to get from coming on this course. I'm going to keep a note of these aims – so that together we can try and create a group where as much as possible the aims of everyone can be met. During the last session of the group I'll refer back to them and get you to rate whether individually, and as a group, you feel these aims have been met. I know going around asking you questions in turn can feel a bit like being put on the spot, being brought under the headlights,

but I have found it works quite well in terms of us getting to know each other and finding out what people want from the group.'

I turn to my left. 'Perhaps you might start us off ...?'

Sitting immediately to my left is Ann. Ann seemed quite talkative before the group started and I'm hoping that she will be able to say something on these themes. The Asch experiment taught me that what the first person says is critical in setting a template for what others subsequently say. If the first person only says their name (and nothing else), especially if this is copied by the second person, then the likelihood is that all others will follow. But Ann helps us avoid such a scenario. She talks about how she found out about the course (from a friend who had found it really helpful – a stroke of luck, such comments help to calm anxieties and inculcate a positive attitude towards a group). Ann says that some of the topics look really interesting and goes on to tentatively make a comment about being quite lonely, even though she enjoys company, so her aims include learning more about psychology and what makes people tick but she also harbours hopes that the course will help her get out of a bit of a rut she's been in since her children left home.

I smile (hopefully appreciatively, not cheesily – I really do appreciate Ann being so honest) and say 'It's great that you have been so open … not an easy thing when we are just getting to know each other.' I take the opportunity to highlight and reinforce some norms I hope will develop: 'Other people might not feel quite so ready to talk so openly, but I do hope that together we will be able to create a group where people feel able to *think aloud*.' I explain what I mean by this, discussing Paul Gordon's work on helping people feel secure enough to, in an exploratory way, try and find words to express complex things relating to the way we feel and experience the world.

We pass on to the next person. Brian says he is also interested in some of the topics listed in the flyer and they seemed very relevant to many things that have happened in his life. I don't push him on what these are (the round robin can feel like being put on the hot spot and I don't want shy, nervous and very private people who are yet to speak to sit in fear of being pushed to reveal things they are not ready to say), but take the opportunity to help the formation of a matrix that I hope will be indicative of a group of interlinked participants. It is relatively straightforward, especially when doing a round robin, to create a wagon-wheel effect (see Chapter 12); the trick is to help forge links between participants:

'Both you, Brian, and Ann said the topics look interesting, and relevant … we will look more closely at these later and people will be able to select ones they are keen on as well as suggest topics not listed.' I use their names – to help me and other group members to remember them, but also to hopefully cement any budding connection between Ann and Brian. My comment hopefully might also help settle nerves about what is coming up later in the session – having a mental map of what to expect helps reduce tension in a group.

We move on to each participant in turn. Christine talks about coming to a previous *Psychology in the Real World* group, *The Black Dog*, and says she got a lot out of it. Again a plus in helping to create a positive vibe, but I'm careful not to let the praise go to my head and am keen to ensure that she forges a link with others in the group (not just me) to prevent the connection between us appearing special to people coming to their first *Psychology in the Real World* venture. She makes this easy by saying that, like Ann, her children have also left home and she wants to 'use her brain a bit more, stop it stagnating'. David reveals that a therapist at a mental health centre recommended he came

along. I ask what interested *him* in the course: I don't want David to position himself as coming on sufferance. He says he's not sure. I'm also not keen for him to be identified as the 'mentally ill person', and I take a chance and ask whether he has ever read anything about psychology. He says he hopes to do an A-level in it sometime, and that a few years ago he read a book called *I'm Okay, You're Okay*. It's hard to link him with what others have said so far, but I hope that these things will link him with group members yet to speak who might have read some psychology texts or might have experienced mental health services. I respond that, if he liked that book, he might be interested in the session *In what kinds of ways do our experiences in childhood affect us?*

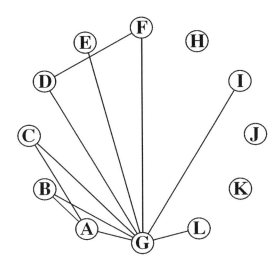

Fig. 4   Stage 2 of matrix creation
Half-way through the round robin the matrix starts to develop

With each person's comments I'm trying to illustrate something about the course, clarify and reinforce group norms, alleviate anxiety, link people with myself (the wagon-wheel part of the matrix) by engaging them in conversation (this will help them feel connected and help them come back next week) and, more importantly, link them with others (this will help create a cohesive group and a sense of belonging). Empathic comments help create very quick and powerful links in the matrix: later Freda will say she never normally tells people she gets help from the local CMHT but David saying what he did has made her think they have nothing to be ashamed of and perhaps have learned things that will be relevant to the course.

I'm trying hard to highlight connections between people, including people who are connected by difference: Harriet says she does not want to study anything where she has to write essays and be assessed. I confirm that the course is designed to be thought provoking and will be academically rigorous – it is not a dumbed-down version of psychology – but it will cover a different curriculum to A-level or degree-level psychology and has no assessment. I also comment on how Harriet's attitude differs from a couple of other people who want to use it as a springboard into more academic study, and this is great as I hope that the group will be a 'broad church' accompanying lots of different views. I explain Peter Hulme's ideas about collaborative conversation.

The round robin goes quite well although I am concerned by John who comes across as a brooding presence – he revealed little about himself and is sitting very stiffly, occasionally looking as if he is glaring at me. He may be suffering parkinsonian side effects of medication. On the other hand, he may be angry about something or be feeling very anxious. When Kelvin rather supportively said, 'Like John, I'm not that clear what I want to get from coming', John did not respond in terms of body language but just stared ahead. I'm keen (if possible) to ease whatever it is that is affecting him in this way, both for his own sake and for the sake of the group dynamics, but am not sure what it is at the moment.

It is time for a break. I make sure everyone knows where the café and toilets are and join people in the queue for coffee. Whilst some people stand quietly, the more sociable members start conversations. Kelvin seems keen to connect with the other men and in the break sits with David talking about Eric Berne's *Games People Play;* John sits nearby but doesn't join in the conversation. Fifteen minutes later I suggest we return to the room. I try and chat with John as we walk back but the conversation feels awkward.

The second half of the group involves discussions about potential topics. No one feels up to leading a session but we manage to agree on which topics to focus on. I spend a little time referring to the psychology and psychotherapy literature on 'beginnings' and say that the last session to some extent will mirror today's in that it will involve some discussion of the literature on 'endings' but will also involve people hopefully discussing their own experiences of endings, including what it might feel like for this group to come to an end. A couple of people reflect on how they have felt coming to the group for the first time and we broaden the discussion to how all of us tend to feel at the start of something new.

With ten minutes to go I begin to bring things to a close, confirm the topic we will cover next time, say that I will draw up a timetable and bring it next week, and suggest another round robin to end the session. I ask people to repeat their names, acknowledging how tricky it can be to learn so many new names, and suggest we do a thought experiment: *imagine you are on the journey home, perhaps on the bus or in a car … what might be going through your mind about having been here today?* I'm asking them to do something quite challenging – rather than be polite and say what they think I want them to say, I'm actively encouraging people to share thoughts that we normally experience in private

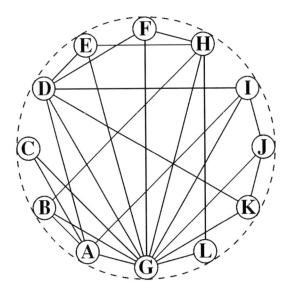

Fig. 5   Stage 3 of matrix creation
The matrix develops: connections I am
aware of by the end of the first session

and usually keep to ourselves. It goes well. Some of the people who came across as confident speak of being initially nervous which I can see registers with the more anxious and shy members. John's tense body appears to soften. His statement 'It's been alright … I'm glad I'm not the only man' comes across as rather begrudging and a bit attacking, but I nod and welcome his honesty. Most people are fairly positive. A couple of constructively critical comments are made which I welcome – I take the opportunity to again reinforce the norm of people feeling confident and safe enough to speak their mind and the importance of us being able to express views and feelings that differ from other members of the group (including mine). Compared to the initial round robin I link people's comments to those made by others in less overt ways, but mentally note how the matrix is continuing to develop, having a

particular lookout for anyone who seems to be becoming separated from others in the group.

By the end of the group I am aware of at least one connection between each member of the group and one other person apart from myself. Of course many other connections I am unaware of might have been made as group members silently relate to things people have said. This is especially true for the quieter members of the group. I take a deep breath – I seem full of a mix of exhilaration, trepidation and relief. I wonder how much of this relates to my own feelings and how much I might be picking up from the group as a whole.

As the clock ticks around to 1.00 p.m. I do my best to convey some sense of this, draw the group to an end, and say how much I'm looking forward to seeing people again next week. I genuinely am.

16

Understanding Ourselves and Others: A participant's account

JO CLARE

Although I have my community mental health nurse to thank for informing me about the course, this is where any involvement from the CMHT stopped. The course was held in an education centre open to the general public, therefore anyone was allowed access. This point is crucial since being involved in the mental health system often makes me perceive that I live in an abnormal and isolated world. To be able to access the course in a non-mental health setting allowed some aspect of normality back into my life (obviously what is normal and abnormal is very subjective so I use the terms loosely!). I appreciate that being with other mental health suffers can be reassuring and useful but I feel it is just as valuable and perhaps less constrictive to have the opportunity to attend a course as a member of the public without a label. I was able to attend the course not as a sufferer but because of who I am and what I am interested in. I personally am not suggesting that a course of this kind could replace individual therapy for the majority since I believe certain experiences to be intensely private, perhaps traumatic, and in need of the security of one-to-one professional support. However, I have no doubt that the course I attended enhanced the confidence of individual members of the group, which can only be of benefit to anybody going through individual therapy. In addition, alternative ideas and views expressed by the participants may also have been of help. Also, interestingly, Feifel and Eells (1963) found that clients receiving individual therapy rated success in terms of

better insight and understanding of themselves, qualities that the course may well have improved upon.

The people in the group very quickly relaxed in each other's company, became very supportive of each other and the environment was considered safe to talk. This I believe was aided by the fact that Guy, aside from sharing his knowledge, was upfront and honest about his own feelings and experiences which broke down barriers straight away. People chose to talk as little or as much as they felt able – there was no pressure either way. Also because the weekly activities varied those who found it too daunting to address the whole group were given opportunities to talk in twos or threes. As the course progressed people opened up and relayed quite personal experiences. I was humbled by this and felt privileged to be part of the group. This affected me to the extent that during the last session I was able to share something personal to me, not because I felt I had to but because I wanted to – I wanted to give something back!

The topics were by no means 'easy' topics to discuss, many of which would be deemed to be socially sensitive such as *What is the point of being alive?* and *Why are people violent?* However, I do not believe that hiding from these issues is the answer, especially as it would be going against the whole ethos of the course. In fact, it is these controversial issues that are more likely to spark off discussion and help to bridge the gap between any inequalities that these issues may create. Also, as mentioned earlier, the topics were discussed in a supportive and safe environment and anybody was free to leave if they needed time out. In addition, it could be questioned whether any topics are guaranteed to be non-sensitive.

The topics were diverse and interesting and it was intriguing to hear people's views, especially since culture and religion were often involved in the equation. Even though Guy had an agenda, it was flexible, particularly since there was no restricting syllabus to follow. This allowed us to go off on tangents and follow some fascinating lines of thought. Frequently we were limited by lack of time not lack of ideas. Often Guy would give out and recommend reading material and inspired by what I had heard during the sessions I would be eager to follow up these recommendations. One such book is *Opening Skinner's Box* by Lauren Slater that looks at the untold stories behind key psychological experiments of the twentieth century. In my opinion the book is written in a highly readable manner and not only did it add to Guy's explanations during the sessions but it made me want to find out more.

Right from the beginning of the course we were encouraged in the belief that we are all psychologists and that we all have the right to question the world around us. This fits with Socrates' statement that 'the unexamined life is not worth living'. Socrates maintained that public discussion of the great issues of life is vital for the justification of human existence. This philosophy was a common thread that lasted throughout the course and I frequently went home stimulated by what had been discussed and mulled the themes over in my head. It could be proposed that each session created its own set of what Richard Dawkins has termed *memes* – ideas that can be thought of as contagious thoughts that sculpt our minds (Blackmore, 2000).

The group became quite social and due to the bonus of a pleasant coffee shop within the same building discussions were continued before each session, during the break and even after over lunch! In fact the social aspect has continued beyond the ending of the course as I still meet regularly with two members of the group.

17

Middles: An account of the session
What is the point of being alive?

… I'm early. Waiting for people to come. It's week eight of the *Psychology in the Real World: Understanding Ourselves and Others* course. I want to think through the session but everything's blank. Liz comes in first. She sits down without saying hello, head bowed, staring through the wooden table to her shoes. I sit quietly looking at her then look away. I think of Rupert Sheldrake's experiments into the capacity of people to know they are being stared at. Liz, me, the room itself – everything seems to be becoming fuzzy. I try to focus on the tasks in hand.

'Are you OK?'

I'm never sure what to do in these pre-group encounters. My group analysis training taught me to have no contact and not to speak to group members apart from during the 90 minutes of the group. But that seems plain odd in this situation.

Eventually the silence is broken.

'This is the one I've been dreading.'

My heart sinks. What am I doing? At this point in my life I'm very happy to be alive, love and am loved by my partner and child, and feel joy on a daily basis. But what about the other members of the group? Can a group like this manage the emotional impact of discussing *what is the point of being alive?* Is the topic just too raw?

People start to file in. There are a few friendly hellos. Some people are quiet. None as quiet as Liz. Some don't notice her, but Martin anxiously grimaces when he does.

'OK. Welcome back. It's eleven o'clock. Shall we start? Today we are going to explore the topic *What is the point of being alive?* Two things have led me to conclude that it's important to explore this. In my work a great number of people seeking help have said this to me; although when they've said it it's been more of a statement than a question … they haven't expected us to discuss it. Whenever they've said "What's the point of being alive?" to other mental health workers it has led to risk assessments, crisis team involvement, hospitalisation, even ECT. But I have always felt it's an important question to think about. And when I read Camus I discovered a renowned philosopher who said that not only was it an important question, it was *the fundamental question* in philosophy. Camus said that all other philosophical questions come afterwards.'

I look around. Everyone now seems to be doing an impression of Liz, all staring, eyes wide but glazed, through the table.

'Err … because it's quite a tricky topic I've brought some notes … some things to read, about … it.'

I nervously look in my bag for the handouts. At least people will be able to stare down at these. This should bring some containment; allow the emotional temperature to come down a bit; enable us to look at things a bit dispassionately. Yes, there are those great quotes by Sartre, Camus, Buber and Frankl. And then we can get into our own experiences later, when things have lightened up a bit.

I rummage around. The handouts are not in the bag. I look on the table. Look in the bag again. I know that when you panic it's easy to look for something and not see it.

I look in the bag again.

They are not there.

'I seem to have left the handouts at home,' I meekly announce.

My heart sinks fast. I know it's the adrenalin making me nauseous but knowing that doesn't seem to help. I know it's the fight/flight response preventing me from remembering any of the quotes on the handout. In my mind's eye I can picture the handout but there are just vague black squiggles – I'm not even sure if they are letters – on the imagined sheets of paper.

My training kicks in. Jim Kelman is dead, but I hear his voice as clearly as the day he supervised my first venture into groupwork: *Trust the group. You might panic, but things are rarely as bad as they seem. Trust the group.*

'Perhaps we could go around and people could just say something, anything, that came into their mind when they saw this topic title?'

Silence. Then June – June the extrovert, June the person who doesn't like silence, June the one who likes to rescue and help out – helps out. Psychotherapists might have pathologised these aspects of her character, but all groups need a June. And I am truly grateful for her today. She talks of her initial dread on seeing the topic on the list at the first meeting and how she did not feel confident enough to say anything then. She talks about a time in her life when she lost her religious convictions and spiralled out of control. She talks. And as she does the atmosphere begins to change. People's heads are coming up. Her story triggers some sympathetic comments from Martin. Emily speaks about the importance of faith, her relationship with God and a sense of being guided to help others in terms of helping her to not sink into a sense of life having no meaning. This is really helpful but

I don't want the session to be dominated by religion. Suddenly I can remember the handouts … *if meanings are not divinely ordained – if they do not exist 'out there' – how does a being that needs meaning find meaning in a universe that has no meaning? Camus and Sartre believed that the world is indifferent to us and that it is absurd that we, as meaning-making beings, have to live in, and therefore struggle to find overarching meaning in a world that has no meaning.* A conversation starts about existential views. This triggers more thoughts from the group as people grapple with how close we can be to existential crises throughout our lives. There is an energy here. I take a risk and talk about how my early twenties were characterised by 'long dark nights of the soul', often punctuated by repetitive playing of Joy Division's *Atmosphere* and Mahler's *Songs on the Death of Children*, of cold days spent wandering graveyards troubled by a heavy wish not to be here and to fade away.

The atmosphere changes. Quietness enters the room again. Liz's head remains bowed but others look at me … with shock … intrigue … care?

'That surprises me. I've never thought of psychologists as being like that,' says Martin.

The energy returns and people recount personal stories – of the impacts of sudden traumatic experiences and the loss of comforting beliefs that there is an overarching purpose and sense to what happens in the world; of the effects of loneliness and disconnectedness from people; of unemployment and the absence of having a meaningful role to play in life: a variety of stories that help make sense of how life at times can feel like it has no meaning. Someone virtually paraphrases Sartre's view that we have to discover things that provide us with personal meaning – often small, achievable things – as on a grander scale *all existing things are born for no reason, continue through weakness and die by accident … It is meaningless that we are born; it is meaningless that we die.* I'm relieved: it's going well. Better than that – it's amazing. Stuff the handouts, this is great!

Liz gets up suddenly and leaves the room.

What now? Do *I* leave? Everyone's quiet and looking at me. Is it more important to look after a distressed individual or look after the group and the group process? What should I do?

'Perhaps you could carry on exploring this for a while? I think I'll just go and check on Liz. I'll be back in a minute.' I try to speak with some calm authority but realise I'm mumbling a bit.

Outside the door I find her. It's as if she's been pinned to the wall.

'Are you alright?'

'I knew this would be the one. I knew I wouldn't be able to cope with today. This is my problem.'

'What, you can't cope with the group?' I clumsily spurt out.

'No. *This* is my problem … I don't want to be alive.'

We talk for a couple of minutes. Liz says she's all right; she will just have a bit of time out and rejoin us after the break.

I re-enter the room and reassure people, saying that Liz is taking an early break. The conversation becomes a bit stilted and we too decide to break.

We walk into the cafeteria area and I flounder again. Liz is sitting alone. Do I go over, or let her be? If I go will that break the ice and other group members might join us, or will that put them off and they will leave it to the expert psychologist to 'sort her out'. I'm not sure I know what to say to her even if I do go over.

Whilst I dither, Ann goes straight to Liz, puts an arm around her, and starts talking. In a couple of minutes Liz is talking, even smiling. I am reminded yet again that psychologists are not the best healers – many people are natural healers, yet I would only give that sobriquet to a

few psychologists. And not to myself. Other group members join their table and at the end of the break Liz returns with us all to the room.

The talk becomes animated again. Liz doesn't speak but she does hold her head up, make eye contact and is clearly engaged and interested. We end the session with a 'round robin' where we each say one thing that at some period of our lives has formed part of an answer to the question 'What is the point of being alive?' Faith and family are the most common answers. 'My god-daughter,' answers Liz.

I end the session and experience a sense of relief – I had planned the handout to spark various discussions but we seemed to have broached most of these anyway as well as going into areas I had not envisaged.

Liz hangs back. Others respectfully leave. The group knows I'm happy to stay behind to talk to people in the room at the end of each session and several often do. This time they all say their goodbyes and give Liz some space.

'I wasn't sure what to say at the end … I guess I just felt I had to say something.'

'That's OK.'

'I'm sorry I left earlier.'

'It's OK. It's OK to leave. For all of us things get too much at times. I'm glad that you were able to come back though – I'd have been worried if you had just disappeared.'

'I'm glad too. And, although I dreaded today, and at times it was awful, I'm pleased I came. Also, I think I would like to see those handouts you prepared … I'm not guaranteeing I'll read them though!'

I make a mental note to remember to bring the handouts next week. And to compile a handout generated from today's session to give to the group.

Liz reassures me. She has felt like this for years. Others, including mental health professionals, know this. She does not feel any worse now than she normally feels. She knows she has to find something to make her life meaningful but since leaving her job on the grounds of ill health that has proven impossible. It seems a long road to getting work or finding something special that provides that sense of meaning. Like Sisyphus – who rolled the boulder up the hill, day after day, and at the top, completely drained and exhausted, watched it roll back down to the bottom, only to return to the bottom to start the process again, knowing he would do this forever – the task seems daunting.

But at least there is no pretence it is otherwise.

18

Examples of materials used:
On advice and making difficult decisions
and
What is the point of being alive?

Box 7   The decision-making matrix

Making difficult decisions

Sometimes it can be very difficult to make decisions, whether they are life-changing decisions or comparatively small decisions. We sometimes lie awake at night, get pulled this way and that, find our mind racing from one thing to another, go over the same issues time and time again, receive conflicting advice from friends, or find ourselves thinking only of the negatives (or positives) regarding a decision. Even when we make a decision, we can be deeply troubled that we have made the wrong decision, or feel very differently once we have made the decision. People have found filling in the the decision-making matrix and using the following technique helpful:

1. In your own words, write *the changed situation* (e.g. 'leaving home'; 'drinking less alcohol'; 'going to college') and what *carrying on the same* would involve (e.g. 'living at home'; 'drinking lots'; 'being at home on benefits').

2. Brainstorm the good things about the changed situation, e.g. write down as many things as you can think of that would be good about 'leaving home'. Write them as they occur to you in your own words.

3. Then brainstorm the bad things about that decision (e.g. 'leaving home'). Follow this by brainstorming the good and bad about carrying on the same (e.g. the good things about carrying on 'living at home', followed by the bad things about 'living at home').

4. If you think of something that goes in another category (e.g. a bad thing about leaving home whilst writing a list of the good things about leaving) write that down in the other column, but then return to your original list until you can think of no more things.

5. At the end, read through your lists and add anything that comes to mind.

6. If appropriate, talk it through with people you trust and who do not have a vested interest in what you decide, and modify your lists if you need to.

7. Try and weigh up whether the good things/advantages of, for example, leaving home outweigh the bad things/disadvantages, and whether the bad things/disadvantages about living at home outweigh the good things/advantages. If so, on balance, it indicates that you want to leave. If not, on balance, it indicates that you do not want to leave.

8. Before going ahead with any decision, try to reduce any bad things about this decision, if at all possible.

9. Realise that you have to live with the consequences of any decision, and that if that was easy then you would not be so troubled by the dilemma that faces you. Also, once a decision is made the feelings about it and salience of some of the factors listed can shift. The process can be gone through many times as our feelings and thoughts about dilemmas regularly change.

Box 7   The decision-making matrix, contd.

The changed situation:

Good things/Advantages   Bad things/Disadvantages

Carrying on the same:

Good things/Advantages   Bad things/Disadvantages

The only thing to do with good advice is to pass it on.
    Oscar Wilde

To give or withhold advice is quite a dilemma in individual therapy, with most theoreticians advising against it, most therapists denying they give advice, and some people in therapy reporting being confused by the lack of response to questions such as 'What would you do?' How much advice is actually given behind the closed doors of counselling rooms is unknown. In groupwork on the other hand, advice and guidance are identified as therapeutic factors (see Chapter 30). Of course, the richness of a group means that advice and guidance can be varied and multifaceted and is not just dependent on the (comparatively narrow) experiences of the therapist. Evaluations of *Psychology in the Real World* groups have indicated that the offering and receiving of advice from group members, in the sessions and during the breaks, has been experienced as helpful.

I have found the decision-making matrix (see Box 7) more useful than advice in terms of helping people think through and make decisions regarding important dilemmas in their lives. Feedback has been positive when this has been incorporated into *Understanding Ourselves and Others* courses, where people pair up to discuss and talk through their dilemmas in a process similar to co-counselling. It forms a core part of the session *How can we make major decisions, and help others to make life-changing decisions?* It also forms part of *Thinking about Medication* (see Chapter 41) when people use this process to weigh up the pros and cons of coming off against the pros and cons of staying on medication.

Handouts
Most handouts used in *Psychology in the Real World* courses are prepared beforehand and brought to the relevant session, but we also produce handouts based on the discussions and debates that occur during sessions. These can be used as reminders for group members and used as a resource in other groups or services. The handout on next page is of this ilk, being written after the session described in Chapter 17. It incorporates a list of the things that people on a *Psychology in the Real World: Understanding Ourselves and Others* course discussed during a session entitled *What is the point of being alive?* It cannot convey the richness of the discussion, but is an interesting list of the very varied kinds of things that make life meaningful for people:

What makes our lives meaningful?

Religious meaning e.g. faith; finding and doing God's will; not seeing death as an end

Viewing life as a gift (from God); we have a duty to make the best of it

Love; both receiving and giving love

Family, e.g. a wish to protect and not hurt family members; enacting maternal instinct; 'family just is meaningful'

Providing a service to the world; helping to make the world a better place

Political action (although it doesn't have to be action, e.g. 'I shall not cease from mental fight')

Working for a good cause that you feel strongly about, e.g. justice

Changing things in a way that might 'live on' after we die

Having hope that the world will change

Helping and educating others

Nurturing development in others

Pursuing a philosophical interest in life

Finding something unique and innate in ourselves; finding something beyond ourselves

Individual contentment; joie de vivre

Self-actualisation/fulfilling our potential – possible after having other things in Maslow's hierarchy of needs met, e.g. basic survival needs (air,

food, water, shelter, protection from threats) and higher needs (love, security, belongingness, identity, self-esteem)

Materialism is alienating and money does not lead to happiness, so it is important to find what does

Meaningful work

To obtain more power and be able to make choices

Escaping systems that create meaninglessness, e.g. bureaucracy often kills meaningfulness

Having an uncomplicated vision of life

Creativity, e.g. art, music

Nature, e.g. an appreciation of the beauty of the snowflake/universe

To be moved and affected deeply, e.g. whilst holding a baby

Laughter

Relating to people

Friends; supporting one another

Seeing the good in people

Being with animals; walking the dog

Having a meaningful role (in life and as regards other people)

We also asked: *What kind of democratic system might enable people to live meaningful lives?*

The list overlaps with Irvin Yalom's categorisation of activities that provide people with a sense of life purpose referred to in his book *Existential Psychotherapy*, which include *finding a purpose through religious and spiritual beliefs,* and secular activities such as *altruism, dedication to a cause, creativity, hedonism, self-actualisation* and *self-transcendence*. It also overlaps with the work of Erich Fromm who put forward the idea (in *Science and Human Responsibility*) that we have five basic needs: *relatedness* – relationships with others which tend to involve care and respect; *rootedness* – having a feeling of belonging (in groups and with nature); *sense of identity* – seeing ourselves as both unique and part of a social group; *a frame of orientation* – a way of meeting our need to understand our world and place in it; and *transcendence* – which includes creativity and opportunity to develop a loving and interesting life.

19

Evaluations of *Understanding Ourselves and Others*

*We were led through a long path to acceptance –
accepting others and who we are, not what the
breakfast ads indicate we have to be like.*

> Participant on an *Understanding Ourselves
> and Others* course

*Psychology in the Real World: Understanding
Ourselves and Others* has been run six times, twice
in Telford and four times in Shrewsbury. The
courses ran on average for 14 weeks (range 10 –
16). Reports and evaluations of the courses can be
found on www.shropsych.org/
psychologyintherealworld.htm – these include
descriptions of methodology, data analysis and
results. The evaluations mostly took the form of
anonymous questionnaires to be returned in the
final session. One retrospective evaluation sent
out postal questionnaires between six and
eighteen months after people had completed a
course. Questions included invitations to write
about general experiences and express general
views of the course, requests for specific feedback
about individual sessions, and closed questions
regarding some of the aims of the course. Various
types of content and thematic analyses have been
used and, when the data was rich enough, a
grounded theory analysis, with some evaluations
being published in peer reviewed journals (e.g.
Holmes & Gahan, 2007).

The participants
On average 12 people (range 10 – 14) signed up
for each course, each of which has been fully
booked. Drop-out rates in groupwork are
frequently high, often up to a third of group
members, but comparatively few people
dropped out of these courses – on average just
under two per course (range 0 – 5). As people
are not referred to the course and detailed
demographic data is not recorded on
participants it is impossible to report the precise
percentage of people who attended these courses
who had had contact with mental health
services, but from disclosures made by people
during participation in the courses it is
estimated that this is over 60%, ranging from
people in primary care services (e.g. taking
psychiatric drugs prescribed by a GP or people
who have seen an NHS counsellor) to people
who had had multiple admissions to psychiatric
hospital and were taking antipsychotic
medication. Approximately one third of people
on each course were concurrently attending local
CMHT services (which cater for people with
severe and enduring problems who have been in,
or are at risk of, admission to psychiatric
hospital). The age of participants ranged from
16 – 77; 74% of attendees were women. Just
under 10% of participants worked in mental
health services.

Feedback
Evaluation data on *Understanding Ourselves and
Others* and other *Psychology in the Real World*
groups, including descriptions of positive and
negative impacts (and ways that the groups have
struggled to have any impact) are included
throughout the book. Those interested in the

data for each course evaluation are referred to the original reports; extracts below have been taken from these to highlight various points whilst endeavouring not to misrepresent the original data. The evaluations indicated participants benefited in the following ways (those listed first being reported by the majority, those listed towards the end by a minority, of participants):

- *greater understanding of self,* e.g. 'Having the opportunity of sharing openly and honestly in such a group seems to be the most effective way of understanding myself better'

- *greater understanding of others,* e.g. 'Learning through contact with 'strangers' (course members) that apparently well-balanced persons can have deep-seated concerns resulting from earlier experiences in life'

- *greater understanding of the impacts of a wide variety of factors that affect people,* e.g. 'Being more aware of things, for example, big companies and advertising, drug companies, mental hospitals; to see therapies as a help, a way of coping with something, not a cure all'

- *increased confidence, knowledge and skills,* e.g. 'Knowledge is power; I was also able to confront my fear of talking publicly'

- *increased psychological wellbeing,* e.g. 'Helped me to come to terms better with my thoughts and feelings by seeing them in a clearer perspective'

- *increased self-esteem,* e.g. 'Helped me to face deep feelings of guilt and shame by enabling me to accept myself better and not be so self-condemning'

- *feeling a greater part of a community or group,* e.g. 'I feel I have a greater affinity with other members of the human race'

- *joining other groups and enrolling on educational courses,* e.g. 'I was viewed (and viewed myself) as a voice hearer who'd done nothing for years … and now I've signed up to do a module of a degree'

- *developing different (e.g. less stigmatising) views about 'mental illness' and 'the mentally ill',* e.g. 'I feel a lot less fearful of people with mental health problems. I see mental health now as a scale that we are all on somewhere rather than "them and us"'

- *enhanced employment prospects,* e.g. 'Helped encourage me to change my job after nine years which has increased my confidence'

- *less loneliness,* e.g. 'While on the course it was nice to be around intelligent people and this has now made me seek intelligent conversation with friends'

On mental health promotion

Hanson, McHoul and Rapley have asked whether, in today's society, anyone is *Beyond Help?* They cogently argue that over the past 30 years there has been a mass marketing campaign for us all to be labelled, and to label ourselves, as psychologically ill or defective in some way. The 'Defeat Depression' campaign in the 1990s was primarily aimed at members of the public reclassifying their problems as symptoms of depression. The recommendations of leaflets that accompanied the campaign did not refer to antidepressants but did (as many Internet questionnaires currently do) recommend a visit to people's local GP. Sponsored by pharmaceutical companies, the leaflets did not mention the fact that prior to the campaign these companies had blitzed GPs with gifts, meals and summaries of research that promulgated the view that there was significant under-diagnosis of clinical depression in the general population and SSRI medication was virtually risk free and very potent in terms of its antidepressant effect – claims which have been shown subsequently not borne out by the evidence, including evidence that the original drug trials revealed that SSRIs were not more effective than older antidepressants and could induce suicidality in people (see Healy, 2001). In short, there is a propensity for things done in the name of mental health promotion to be in effect mental illness promotion that leads to more people being involved with psychiatric services and receiving treatments for their problems. Evaluations of *Understanding Ourselves and Others* courses have indicated that, in contrast to such scenarios, they do not act as an encouragement for people to attend mental health services. If anything they do the opposite: one evaluation based on three runnings of the group revealed that 13% of participants had less contact with services after doing the course and no one reported having more contact.

20

Reflections on attending
Understanding Ourselves and Others 2008

ELISABETH X

Aged about four or five, sitting cross-legged on the school gym floor, forefinger of my right hand pressed tightly to my lips, I hold my breath. I do not move. I want to be chosen. As a class we had been collecting money for the 'starving children' in Africa and now two children were to be chosen to present a cheque. Confused I thought the starving children would probably prefer my marmite sandwiches. However I sit perfectly still and wait to see if I would be good enough to take the cheque to Africa and be home in time for tea … my first group experience?

We all have an understanding of what it is to be in a group. Our families, friends or social class. Our education, faith and political associations. Hobbies, clubs or star signs. Some memberships are life long, others transient. Some we can never change and others are formed out of a need to change. We participate in some because of our abilities and are placed in others, by default, by our disabilities. This brings to mind the idea that being in a group can be a positive and powerful experience, however being put into a group to which you do not want to belong or being excluded from a group for whatever reason, especially one in which you would like to belong, can be damaging and isolating.

My most recent group experience has been the *Psychology in the Real World: Understanding Ourselves and Others* course and this has been the second time that I have participated in such a group. This course has allowed me to reflect on how we all are in groups. A chance to step outside of the roles imposed or created by the other groups to which I belong. To think about how we are understood. What can we learn about ourselves when we are still? What shapes our personalities? Is stubbornness really determination? Does hostility disguise fear? What makes us laugh or cry? What makes us hide? In the confines of the group, how we hope and fear, trust and risk, irritate and entertain. To reflect on how, as Hemingway put it, we are 'strong in the broken places'. The group experience helps to highlight our differences, but more commonly, our similarities – the same in our uniqueness.

So what is different about this course and mental health-related therapy groups? The balance of power is central to the outcome. From the moment of first contact and referral from a GP the balance shifts from client to health professional. As clients we wait for an appointment, we come to your workplace, we wait until you are ready. We hope you don't cancel or are late. We know nothing about you, but you already know something personal about us. We retell our story again and again until it is watered down to a couple of sentences on a page and lost. We hear your reassurances about confidentiality and your apologies when records go missing. We are assessed, discussed, judged and allocated. Some of us are told 'we don't fit the criteria for the help on offer'. Our choices diminish as our part in the process becomes less relevant. As Geneen Roth put it, we 'drown when no one is looking, not wanting to bother anyone'. We are discharged.

Psychology in the Real World courses demand that we are and remain proactive from the beginning. We choose. We apply and turn up to a venue that is new to all of us, both facilitators and participants. We are all nervous. Some of us have met before. We are remembered. We are not defined by our problems, diagnoses or hang-ups. We have coffee breaks together. It is almost impossible to leave one of these community groups without some new insight into ourselves and others, either because of, or in spite of, who we are or who we pretend to be. Maybe one of the most hopeful things that can be heard during an exchange of ideas is 'I never thought of it like that before'. The belief that there is no such thing as fate, knowledge is power and a chat over a cappuccino can change your mind.

SECTION 4

Is this community psychology?

21

Is this education?
Is this community psychology?

I thought I would be told all the answers, but this is much more liberating.

> Participant on an *Understanding Ourselves and Others* course

Is this education?

Psychology in the Real World courses are not educational in the sense that the Labour government pursued its mantra of 'education, education, education'. Participants are not treated as empty vessels waiting to be filled with knowledge conveyed by an expert psychologist. One of the main aims of *Psychology in the Real World* is to bring people together in a joint endeavour where we critically reflect on areas of life that hold resonance for us, and where we are all open to having our established beliefs and knowledge base challenged, modified and expanded. The courses concentrate on *Why* rather than *How* questions and actively encourage participants to generate and formulate their own ideas and theories in response to questions about our psychosocial environment and how it affects us. The courses reflect contemporary interest in social intelligence and the wisdom of groups rather than the wisdom of experts (see Daniel Goleman's book *Social Intelligence* and James Surowiecki on *The Wisdom of Crowds*). Victor Frankl said 'happiness ensues, it cannot be pursued', and wisdom is perhaps similar. The evidence we look at and critique includes research from quantitative and qualitative studies. Lauren Slater's book *Opening Skinner's*

Box and Eliot Aronson's *The Social Animal* are popular texts with participants as they are so readable, whereas many academic psychology research papers need translating by the facilitators into everyday language before participants can engage with what they reveal about human behaviour. We do not confine ourselves to psychology texts however, seeing merit in sociological, political, philosophical and psychological perspectives that lie outside academic psychology (from documentary films such as *The Corporation* to Albert Camus' essay *The Myth of Sisyphus*). We weigh all this against another kind of evidence – the evidence of our own lives. No one text or type of evidence is seen as containing 'the truth' – all are critiqued and seen as potentially flawed and open to bias. So we try and access as wide a range of evidence as possible and encourage each other to search for 'truths' that help each of us to make sense of the world we each inhabit.

Are these *psycho-education (skills-for-ills)* courses?

Psychology in the Real World courses are very different from psycho-education courses. NHS services commonly provide Anxiety Management, Coping with Depression, CBT Skills, and many other *Skills for Ills* groups. *Strategies for Living* adult education courses have tried to help people learn self-help strategies to cope with what are deemed to be common psychological difficulties; these have been run in both NHS and non-NHS settings.

Community-based courses, for example, on stress management utilising cognitive-behavioural and other coping strategies, have been shown to be an effective and economical way of reducing stress and anxiety in people who use and do not use mental health services (although some feedback has suggested that programmes offering fewer methods and more time to explore things, including opportunities to collectively discuss problems, may be more effective – see Brown et al, 2000). Such groups have their place and undoubtedly many people have found them helpful. However, *Psychology in the Real World* ventures are not psycho-educational courses where participants with identified problems are taught about what is wrong with them and how to put it right. The ventures focus on things that affect us all and give weight to the social and distal causes of distress. They are more about understanding and analysing things than learning coping strategies.

Psychology in the Real World philosophies overlap with some aspects of what the Brazilian educator and theorist Paulo Freire called 'critical pedagogy'. Freire critiqued the 'banking' approach to education, where students rather passively absorb 'deposits' made by the teacher. He believed that there is no such thing as a neutral education process: it either operates to integrate people into the logic of the current social system, and trains people to conform to that system, or it becomes the 'practice of freedom', the means by which people critique their world and discover how to participate in its transformation. This process involves unlearning as much as learning. It was only through this process that Freire believed we become 'fully human'. Like Freire, *Psychology in the Real World* ventures take a broad view of what education is, which includes engaging people in processes that might assist their psychological and social development as well as equip them with skills to critique their own and other's views of the world they live in. However, the facilitators have not tended to see themselves as consciousness-raising social educators of the type Freire's work has often inspired – rather as the creators of environments in which all kinds of personal, social and political development might occur. Like Patrick Casement's view of therapy providing an encounter where therapists learn just as much as their clients, *Psychology in the Real World* facilitators envisaged learning just as much from the debates and experience of doing the courses as the other participants, and this has proven to be the case. This mirrors Freire's concept of education being a two-way process.

Sometimes I wonder whether someone like Noam Chomsky sitting in on a group might call it anarcho-syndicalism whereas my daughter's teacher Mr Jones might see it as not dissimilar to many of the exploratory class discussions he facilitates in their primary school. It is not very original to suggest that (good) education is helpful and therapeutic for individuals and of benefit to wider society. Such an idea tracks back at least as far as Plato and the origins of the university. People involved in informal education are very aware of the breadth of benefits adult education outside mainstream settings can bring (see www.infed.org). The WEA (Workers' Educational Association) has amongst its stated aims and values: changing and enriching lives through learning, at individual and community levels; creating equality and opportunity and challenging discrimination; believing in people, communities and their potential to change through education; challenging and questioning ourselves. Evidence from evaluations suggests that *Psychology in the Real World* courses can make a modest contribution in these areas.

Is this community psychology?

There will always be some patients for whom clinical guidelines' recommendations are not appropriate and situations in which the recommendations are not applicable.

National Institute of Health and Clinical Excellence (NICE) Guidelines on Depression

Community psychology, perhaps because ideologically it encompasses a broad church of ideas, is not easy to define. In many ways it sits very much on the margin of mainstream psychology. However, as David Fryer has pointed out, in the UK there are moves to create a community psychology section of the British Psychological Society, there is a journal entitled *The Journal of Community Psychology and Applied Social Psychology*, a discussion list with over 200 members (COMMUNITYPSYCHUK) and its practices and ideas have become increasingly elucidated at conferences and on training courses over the past decade. The ideas and interventions that underpin community psychology have often been inspired by the work of activists overseas, particularly in the Americas, for example, the liberation social psychology theories and practices of Ignacio Martín-Baró. It is beyond the capacity of this chapter to provide an adequate résumé of this area but the interested reader might consult Reich et al (2007), Cox et al (2010) and the special edition of the *Journal of Critical Psychology, Counselling and Psychotherapy* (2009) *9*(2).

In the UK community psychology has come to encompass many of the following ideas:

- Placing people in their social contexts, focusing analysis and interventions on the social causes of distress and correcting the individualistic bias in psychology

- Sharing ideas and valuing diversity of knowledge

- Learning from and working collaboratively alongside (rather than doing things to) others

- Analysing the impacts of power and disempowerment

- Questioning whose interests are served by various theories, policies and practices

- Focusing help on people in society who have been marginalised and oppressed

- Creating and nurturing self-supporting systems or communities

- Resisting oppression, silencing and social injustice

- Promoting social change

- Engaging in participatory and action research that takes its lead from others and encompasses qualitative methods (rather than research that tests theories devised by experts)

Psychology in the Real World ventures were not consciously set up with such a coherent list of aims at their onset, but they have come to incorporate such ideas not least because, as the people involved (both members and facilitators) have reflected on what has been discussed on the courses, they have come to see such things as important. As Augusto Boal discovered when practising the *Theatre of the Oppressed* around the world, the cops are not as violent in Europe as in many South American countries, but the 'cops in our head' are often so oppressive that comparatively large numbers of people commit suicide and community interventions are needed just as much in socially fragmented Western countries as in other parts of the world.

The questioning approach that runs through all *Psychology in the Real World* and community psychology ventures can be seen as revolutionary by people in positions of power who have a vested interest in maintaining the status quo.

Whilst Joaquim Coimbra and Isabel Menezes have described community psychology as 'the craft of making politics by other means', others have wanted to avoid being labelled 'political' due to associations that go with such labels. As the Brazilian archbishop Hélder Câmara said: 'When I give food to the poor they call me a saint; when I ask why the poor have no food they call me a communist.'

Whilst we are sold the idea that Western medicine is at the cutting edge of treatments for mental health problems, comparative studies have for a long time revealed that countries where people are not admitted into specialist centres, automatically medicated or given therapies by experts but instead remain in supportive communities have better outcomes even for diagnoses such as schizophrenia. For example, Jablensky et al's WHO study revealed significantly better prognoses for people diagnosed with schizophrenia in India and Nigeria compared to Western countries. It seems that there may be more to learn from studying the kinds of communities that enable people to recover from serious breakdowns than from listening to drug reps who ply us with free food and present research conducted by companies who have a pecuniary interest in obtaining outcomes that show their products in the best possible light.

On operating at the margins

Psychology in the Real World ventures, like all community psychology endeavours, operate very much at the margins of mainstream mental health services. Some would say this is necessarily so. The NHS and Social Services in many parts of the UK have funded community mental health teams but these have focused on monitoring, treating and reducing risk associated with individuals who are deemed to have severe and enduring problems that fit certain psychiatric diagnostic categories. They have had little to do

with people's community. The quote above from NICE offers the slightest of get-out clauses for people who are sceptical of the individualistic, medically dominated, cost-reducing NICE regime and who want to work in ways that reflect their training and acquired experience of what might meet some of the needs of the communities they are employed to help. Mental Health Trusts in the future may only be paid for a fixed number of sessions of therapies decided by NICE to be cost effective for people with certain diagnoses. An NHS that is bringing in a system of payment by results and being stealthily privatised appears ill-suited to community interventions. Richard Layard has written an influential book and produced reports for government that recognise the damaging impacts on people of poverty, inequality and social deprivation, but this has transmogrified into funding a massive increase in individual cognitive-behaviour therapy (CBT). When we ask whose interests such policies serve the answer might not be the interests of the large numbers of people damaged in a sick society. Certainly they seem to suit the interests of governments that have little appetite for addressing the social causes of distress but great appetite for getting people off sickness benefits and into poorly paid jobs, and of private health care companies who make billions of pounds in other countries and want to sell their wares (individual treatments for individual problems) in the lucrative UK market.

As David Fryer has pointed out, community psychology is increasingly describing itself as *critical community psychology*, influenced by Foucault who said being critical does not consist of saying 'things aren't good the way they are': it consists of showing that things are not as straightforward or obvious as people believe. Foucault said that 'to do criticism is to make harder those acts which are now too easy'. Fryer and other critical theorists, such as Ian Parker, have called for community psychology to bring its critical analysis onto itself, raising the possibility that processes that lead us to pathologise individuals are now leading us to pathologise 'the community', and questioning whether 'the community' is being positioned as yet another market for the psy-complex to penetrate and exploit. These questions, and indeed the whole questioning approach, are important, and the kinds of things we try and engage in during *Psychology in the Real World* groups.

It is increasingly hard to envisage community psychologists (or any person trying to work with communities rather than individuals) being valued in the current state and voluntary sectors. The people working in these sectors (both managers and frontline staff) appear to be run ragged by demands to increase the number of individual treatments delivered, comply with performance management agendas, and fill in convoluted forms as part of bidding processes for funding that both exhaust and pervert any ideological impulses. Organisations such as NHS Foundation Trusts and charities appear to have become just as sensitive as private businesses to having any of their practices critiqued for fear of losing reputation and consequently income. Community psychologists may have to work

extremely hard in the foreseeable future to have the legitimacy of their work accepted and funded (this is taken up in Chapter 63). Critical community psychologists may find all ideology corrupted. Ibrahim Makkawi has written a brilliant paper on the destructive effects of community ventures bidding for money and the impacts of NGOs in Palestine on grass-roots organisations that made the First Intifada a successful community endeavour. He likens funded community psychology to an invasion, associating it with a breakdown in support for voluntary political action groups, and views this as actively harmful in that it has brought about a modern day form of colonialisation. For example, bids are made by community psychologists to gain grants to set up schemes to assess and treat people's post-traumatic stress, which diverts energy and attention away from the setting up and maintenance of the types of self-sustaining, mentally healing, politically engaged grass-roots groups that previously ran with no official funding or state provided professional involvement, and were instrumental in bringing about diverse and effective forms of non-violent political resistance.

22

On power and empowerment

Mao Tse Tung said Change must come ...
Mao Tse Tung said Change must come ...
Mao Tse Tung said Change must come ...
Change must come through the barrel of a gun.
   Alabama 3

In the 1990s Wolf Wolfensberger said he thought the phrase *empowerment* had 'high craze value'. By this he meant it was being used by lots of people, especially people in the helping professions, as if there was agreement as to what it meant, but in reality empowerment had come to mean many different things to many different people; few of these meanings had much to do with people attaining more power; many were contradictory; and all could be phrased more

sensibly. Over the past decade *recovery* has probably replaced empowerment as the phrase used in services that has the highest craze value. Whilst we might not agree with Mao, Alabama 3's lyrics highlight the difficulties faced by people with little power to exert change on their lives and the society they live in and the naivety of some people's purported attempts at empowerment.

I was once asked to do some training for CMHT staff on empowerment. I asked each member of staff to think of one person they knew whom they considered powerful. I then got them to generate a list of the things that gave that person power. We then made a pooled, collective list. It included things like money,

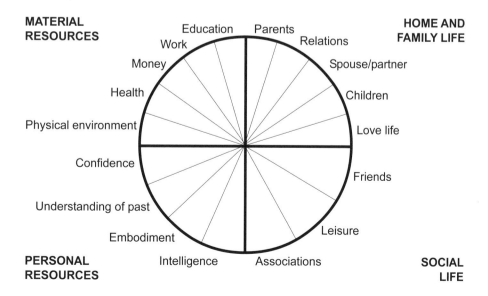

Fig. 6   **Terrain of proximal powers/power map (from Hagan and Smail, 1997)**

wealth, high status in work, qualifications, high educational achievement, connections with very powerful people, and physical threat. I then asked the staff to think of things that they did in their daily work that helped the people they were paid to help get more of these factors. At this point several people left and many of the remaining people argued that I had tricked them. We never got on to the final part of the session – how they could change their jobs in ways that might actually help people attain more power.

The list generated overlapped with what Teresa Hagan and David Smail have called proximal powers (see Fig. 6). Most psychologists invest considerable hope that areas of the power map that they focus on (e.g. understanding of the past) will have beneficial effects on other proximal powers. My own experience is that for individual therapy this is only rarely the case, especially for people who live in what I have termed socially and psychologically toxic environments (for data on this see Holmes, 2003). Years of providing one-to-one interventions with people whose difficulties relate to the impacts of poverty, the lack of opportunities to gain meaningful and decently paid employment, terrible loneliness, poor accommodation in depressing and frightening neighbourhoods and multiple psychosocial wounds on the basis of being treated appallingly as a result of their class, racial background, gender, sexuality and mental health diagnosis lead one to conclude that one-to-one therapies have only a modest impact on the majority of such people. In addition, the benefits people experience often do not carry on once the therapy ends if they remain in environments that are toxic to their wellbeing (these people are often re-referred to the same or a different part of the mental health service). This fits with the research into who benefits most from psychotherapy (e.g. Roth and Fonagy's *What*

Works for Whom?) and with Maslow's work on the hierarchy of needs: once people's physiological needs are met the next important needs relate to safety and security, love and belonging, and engagement in activities that bring sustained self-esteem and a positive sense of identity, and if these are not met then any talking therapies aimed at self-actualisation or improved self-worth are likely to fall short in terms of bringing about the aimed-for changes. One of the main motivations for setting up *Psychology in the Real World* ventures has been the hope that, compared to one-to-one therapy, the groups might provide some avenues for helping people attain more power and for areas of their lives illustrated in the power map in Fig. 6 to provide them with more support and less harm. *Psychology in the Real World* ventures do appear to have had modest but beneficial effects in some parts of the power map.

Prior to setting up community-based groups I was not aware of one person that I saw for one-to-one therapy at the CMHT, despite my encouragement, signing up for a course at CHEC or The Gateway. People who are involved with the CMHT who have come to *Psychology in the Real World* courses have, however, subsequently signed up for other courses at these venues. By meeting at a place where people can see others signing up for courses, and by having overcome barriers to going through the doors of the venue, people seem to have been helped to get into further education. For example, one person with a long history of hearing voices and psychiatric service involvement enrolled on a university language degree module. Tracey Austin has written of the need for psychological ramps to enable some people to access educational establishments (in a similar way that other people might need physical ramps to enable access) and *Psychology in the Real World* groups appear to have provided a ramp for some people.

Other participants have made progress in terms of the power map by subsequently setting up their own groups or courses. For example, one person on a *Black Dog* course subsequently set up a *Changes* group under the auspices of this service user-led charitable organisation, the initial members of which had also been on that *Black Dog* course, which grew into a self-sustaining group that ran for many years. Authors contributing to this book provide vivid illustrations of how various aspects of their lives pertinent to the power map have changed after getting involved, as members or facilitators, in *Psychology in the Real World* ventures.

Many evaluations of the groups have shown that participants have reported beneficial impacts of attending the groups in each of the four quadrants of the power map:

Home and Family Life, e.g. people have reported improvements in relationships with family and friends which have become less stressful and more mutually supportive; left abusive partners; carried on debates initiated in the group in other environments with beneficial consequences; moved house to a neighbourhood and environment that was perceived as better for their wellbeing.

Social Life, e.g. people have reported making friends with others in the group; signed up for other courses; joined other groups and associations; joined together to lobby for changes in systems they disagree with.

Personal Resources, e.g. people have said they have come to recognise their intelligence; realise they have something to contribute to public debate; become more confident in terms of speaking their mind; felt less troubled about what other people think of them (including their appearance); taken on roles that have led to greater confidence and wellbeing (e.g. trained staff, given presentations at conferences, published accounts of their experiences).

Material Resources, e.g. people have enrolled on other courses that led to qualifications; applied for and got jobs that interested them; become paid service user consultants regarding *Psychology in the Real World* groups and elsewhere in the NHS Trust; have gone on to work for the Trust (see next chapter).

In 2008 Lucy Gahan carried out a piece of research where participants on an *Understanding Ourselves and Others* course were specifically asked to assess whether the course had made an impact (positive, negative or no impact) in each the 17 areas of the power map (see www.shrop sych.org/psychologyintherealworld.htm for a report on this research). Despite the numbers involved being very small and feedback indicating that a questionnaire format to assess this was confusing and not the best way to assess these things, and despite the fact that the course only ran for 12 weeks, positive effects were identified by at least one respondent in 15 of the 17 areas of the power map and positive impacts outweighed negative impacts by 33 to 4. The areas that most people felt they gained some benefit in were: Education (*'This inspired me to seek similar groups/courses should they become available'*); Understanding of the past (*'Some previous behaviours made more sense after looking at the psychology behind them'*); Confidence (*'My confidence levels varied week to week, but overall there was a boost to my confidence as I felt listened to'*); and Associations (*'Groups of people brought together due to similar interests inspire confidence and encourage me to seek more of the same'*). Other areas of the power map seemed to have been little affected by this particular group experience. For example, in terms of Relationships with spouse or partner, the majority felt the course had had no impact, with one participant commenting: *'It was difficult sometimes to share thoughts and ideas covered on the course without my husband having experienced the discussion'*. This contrasts with evaluations of some other runnings of the course where significant changes have come about in this area (see Box 5, p. 63).

It would be ludicrous to claim that short-term courses can have radical and immediate impacts on entrenched areas of people's lives where change is difficult and relates to many factors outside the locus of control of individuals coming on the courses. Getting a job, for instance, is more affected by government and multinational companies' policies than one's own skills or confidence regarding applying for posts. Such distal powers are even harder to have an impact on than the proximal powers identified in the power map (although members of *Psychology in the Real World* groups have

wanted to try – see the section on *Thinking about Medication,* p. 159). However, my conclusions from evaluating both my own one-to-one therapeutic work and *Psychology in the Real World* groups over the past twelve years are that, although both can be helpful, the groups seem to have greater impacts on some of the areas of the power map that one-to-one therapy struggles to impact on. If we feel these are important (in John O'Brien's words 'something that is worth working for') then community-based groupwork of this type ought to have its place alongside more fashionable one-to-one interventions that are coming to dominate mental health and other services.

23

The journey from service user to paid employee

KEN DAVIES

In 2008 I attended a *Psychology in the Real World: Understanding Ourselves and Others* course that was recommended to me by a friend who had attended an earlier course run by Guy. My interest stemmed from my lifelong personal experience of depression and anxiety. I have to admit that yet again I was searching for answers – *What makes us ill? What is the route to recovery? How can I use my experiences of mental illness in some positive way?*

When the course started I was going through a low point in my life, a period of deep debilitating depression that had caused me to lose my job and had impacted on virtually all areas of my life. My comfort zone was the sofa, a blanket and the company of my cat, Gracie. But somehow I found the wherewithal to attend. I noticed that other mental health service users were on the course and that they still turned up even when they were clearly struggling with their symptoms. The session on the variety of possible causes of mental illness sparked a lot of interest and good-natured debate, with people variously identifying with the nature and nurture theories and many others besides – I found the idea of 'being dealt a hand of cards' gave me much food for thought. On the subject of food, we did a session on people's attitudes towards eating and drinking, a fairly innocuous and benign subject you might think. But I was astounded to see the reaction of some people for whom the very mention of it stirred deep emotions, upset and tears. This brought home to me the fact that mental illness presents itself in many different

guises which has stayed with me as I have gone on to try and help others who struggle with mental health problems. Not everything on the course went so well for me – some of the debates and questions I found very uncomfortable, to the point where I was unable to respond fully to them in a group environment. They touched raw nerves, sometimes felt too close for comfort, and I did not always feel able to explore such personal things in a public arena.

The unique approach of this course, however, contrasted sharply with my experiences of 'formal' treatment within mental health services. Some of my treatment has been good, but some has been truly awful – even damaging to my health at times. But I found the *Psychology in the Real World* course really helpful. During the course and after it finished interesting things started to happen. Very gradually, almost imperceptibly, I started to make a recovery. I began to feel stronger. And I recalled the peer feedback I had received on the course, which had often been along the lines that I was supportive to others and showed good insight into their situation. I started to work as a service user consultant in the NHS Trust. I sat on interview panels for jobs in local services. Then one day I found myself, quite unexpectedly, applying for a post as a part-time, paid STR (Support, Time and Recovery) worker in the local mental health crisis team. The job required that applicants have either experience of mental illness or of working in a mental health role – and boy did I have bags of the former! I was successful and have been in the job for almost a year. I often think back to the course, how it helped me back into employment and how hearing and witnessing the experiences of other people who attended has made me a lot more sensitive and vigilant in my work.

SECTION 5

The Black Dog: Understanding depression

24

The Black Dog

Our generation has had no Great War, no Great Depression. Our war is spiritual. Our depression is our lives.

    Chuck Palahniuk

It's a recession when your neighbour loses his job; it's a depression when you lose yours.

    Harry S. Truman

The term clinical depression finds its way into too many conversations these days. One has a sense that a catastrophe has occurred in the psychic landscape.

    Leonard Cohen

The course has reinforced the idea that depression must never be seen as one entity since everyone's experience of depression is individual with similarities interwoven amongst the uniqueness.

    Black Dog participant

We have run several *Black Dog: Understanding Depression* courses at The Gateway, a local arts and education centre, as part of their normal curriculum over the past decade. People sign up for *The Black Dog* in the same way as they sign up for other courses at the centre (e.g. on art, modern languages, local history) – by phoning the reception and booking a place. The flyers advertising the course try to give a flavour of what it will be like:

*What is depression? What kinds of things lead us to describe ourselves (or be labelled by others) as depressed ... loneliness, negative critical thoughts, powerlessness, hurtful life events, brain biochemical imbalances, meaninglessness, the repression of difficult emotional states, the inequalities of modern society? Might **de**pression be a reaction to **op**pression? Come along and explore ideas about the roots of depressive feelings and experiences. The topics will be discussed in everyday language and are open to all. More information can be found on www.shropsych.org where there are short reports of previous* Black Dog *courses.*

I have jointly facilitated *Black Dog* courses with other psychologists (usually people in training, e.g. on specialist groupwork placements). Like myself, where appropriate, co-facilitators have not only utilised knowledge gained from training in psychology but have been able and willing to draw upon their own experiences of depression (and taking antidepressants). Feedback has indicated that such personal ways of interacting and discussing things has helped to create a healthy group atmosphere, where personal disclosure and self-analysis become the norm. Different co-facilitators bring different knowledge bases and skills in helping people explore things. For example, Cai Dunn's interest in art and humanistic approaches led us to design the topics *How might I draw depression?* and *How can I get my experience across to others?* Bringing in paper and art materials and creating an environment where people felt safe enough to 'give it a go' enabled group members and facilitators to try out different ways of expressing and representing our experiences of depression.

People who find it particularly difficult to express things in words and join in group discussions were thus given greater scope to participate and express themselves through different channels.

We have tended to limit the groups to a maximum of 12 people although the first course worked well with 14. We run them on a weekly basis for eight weeks with each session lasting 2 hours with a 20 minute break in the middle. Each week different theoretical approaches to depression are presented and discussed, giving participants opportunities to think together about how each approach might fit with their experiences, and whether it generates any ideas about what might be helpful for them. Everyday language is used throughout and people are free to talk as much or as little as they like. As the quotes at the beginning of this chapter and the topics outlined on the next page indicate, a key philosophy of the course is that there is not one idea of what depression 'is' or one key theory of what underlies people's experiences of depression. The facilitators have not wanted to promulgate or align themselves with a particular theory (indeed, have differed in the extent to which different theories hold relevance for them). Rather, we wanted to bring people together to collectively explore and critique various ways of conceptualising and understanding depression and to create an environment where people could individually make sense of their own and other people's experiences. The groups have embraced the philosophy that we are all psychologists and experts regarding our own experience, and the wisdom and knowledge of the people in the group might hold as much relevance as knowledge gleaned from outside sources (such as researchers and writers on depression).

Black Dog participants and course curriculum

As with other *Psychology in the Real World* groups, we present a list of possible areas to explore in the first session, to which participants can add, and then get people to say which ones they are most interested in. Box 8 (p. 102) provides examples of topics covered in *Black Dog* groups.

The curriculum offers the facilitators opportunities to bring in theories and ideas from the broad church of psychology. A glance down the topic list in Box 8 shows the relevance of the work of, amongst others, Martin Seligman, David Smail, Paul Gilbert, John Bowlby, Jacques Lacan, Sigmund Freud, Joanna Moncrieff, Aaron Beck, Dorothy Rowe and Jean-Paul Sartre. We also cite classic pieces of research into depression, such as Brown and Harris' 1978 study of depressed women on a housing estate and the epidemiological research of Richard Wilkinson.

The course is open to all. Some attendees live with people who have been diagnosed as depressed. NHS, Social Services and voluntary sector staff sometimes attend. These people quickly find ways of participating that involve applying the ideas discussed in the course to their own experiences as well as to the experiences of people they have contact with through work. A mix of participants is achieved, although compared to other *Psychology in the Real World* groups there tends to be less divergence in terms of the ways that people experience suffering. Because The Gateway advertises the groups to the general population, people who have never had any contact with mental health services come and participate alongside people who have been frequently hospitalised and had a vast array of psychiatric and psychological interventions. This can lead to fascinating exchanges between people and challenges to long-held beliefs. For example,

Box 8 – **A *Black Dog* curriculum**

Opening session. Introductions. Why have people come on the course?

What is it like to feel or be depressed? What does it mean to me to say 'I am depressed'?

Is everybody's experience unique? Are there similarities between our experiences of depression?

How might I draw 'depression'? How can I get my experience across to others?

Why do I keep my depressive side secret? Is it helpful to be able to describe and talk about being depressed?

What life experiences lead people to feel depressed and get stuck in depressive feelings?

Is depression a natural reaction to oppression?

Is depression the normal state to be in at times of our life when we have very little power to escape from difficult life experiences?

How can we map and increase the power we have in our lives?

Why do threats to our social status affect us so profoundly? Might the biological symptoms of depression relate to evolutionary adaptive factors that evolved to protect us after physical trauma and challenge to our status in the pack, but in modern societies 'kick in' as a result of a great variety of perceived risks to our status?

How does depression relate to loneliness and the sense of aloneness? How lonely are we, in terms of numbers of people we know and how close we feel to them? In what ways does modern society lead to such loneliness?

How does depression relate to separations and losses?

Do we suffer the ultimate separation at birth and then feel the 'lack' forever?

What are the similarities between grief and depression – between 'mourning and melancholia'?

Is depression an illness? Is it an illness caused by brain biochemical imbalances? What is a diagnosis? Can doctors measure serotonin in my brain? What do antidepressants actually do?

Is depression caused or made more unmanageable by negative thinking patterns? How does cognitive therapy help?

What is the relationship between repression and depression?

Are depressed people a bit 'Jeckyll and Hyde'?

Is depression something we experience as a defence or (unconscious) coping strategy against feeling an uncomfortable or threatening emotion, such as anger?

Is depression something we feel when we are overwhelmed by a sense of meaninglessness?

Do some aspects of 21st century Western culture induce depression? Are societies with gross inequality of income, wealth and opportunity more likely to induce depression in its citizens?

Concluding session. Review and evaluation. What have we got from being on the course? What are our 'top tips' for living with depression? What plans have we got for the future? If people have found it helpful being together on the course, how are people going to keep in touch with each other?

some people with long histories of mental health service involvement (and mental health service staff) hold a belief that people who have received psychiatric interventions ('the clinically depressed') are fundamentally different from people who have not ('the worried well'); in the group this has been challenged by such people spending time with group members who seem to get just as severely depressed as hospitalised patients but who have never had any involvement with psychiatric services. Such encounters can open up new ways of thinking about and responding to experiences of depression, which is one of the main aims of running the groups.

Presentation styles for different topics

Just as differing theories are presented and explored, based on the idea that different people will identify with some more than others, various presentation styles are used in order to enable the group to make best use of the variety of skills group members have and differing ways that they might contribute. The topics *Is depression the normal state to be in at times of our life when we have very little power to escape from difficult life experiences?* and *Is depression a natural reaction to oppression?* usually involve a lecture about Martin Seligman's theories of learned helplessness and research into the reaction of dogs given inescapable shocks: how their reactions mirror those of humans in a depressed state (they 'curl up and give up'), and how dogs able to predict and escape shocks do not react in this way. Research about adverse life events and depression can be linked to this. Participants are encouraged to discuss these concepts in small groups of three or four. *How*

can we map and increase the power we have in our lives? involves people individually working on their own power map (see Chapters 22 and 26), applying David Smail's ideas about the need to be able to increase our power over what impinges on us in damaging ways. *What are the similarities between grief and depression?* revolves around Freud's paper *Mourning and Melancholia*. In the session they pair up to discuss the ideas in this paper and are encouraged to look at their own experiences of grief and whether these overlap with what they (or others) call depression. Many sessions start with whole group discussion of the topic with the facilitators bringing in relevant theories or research that they are acquainted with as and when it seems relevant. Experience has revealed that it is important to do this in as impartial a way as possible. Clearly, the particular interests of any facilitator are likely to skew which pieces of research are cited. But taking a polemical stance on any particular theory has tended to have a deleterious impact on the group experience. For example, pointing out that doctors cannot measure and do not know the healthy level of serotonin in their patients' brains has sometimes had a dramatic effect on group members' ways of understanding their experience of depression. In contrast, repeating Peter Breggin's quip that 'mental illness is the only illness that can be passed on by word of mouth' has sometimes raised a laugh but has been interpreted by some people as a side-swipe at a model that holds relevance to them, leading to a fracture in the group norm of respectful and open exploration of ideas, and greater entrenchment of views in some people.

25

Beginnings III
The first session of the first *Black Dog* course

… Cai is a little worried about how things will go as this is the first time she has co-facilitated a group like this. I reassure her: things normally go well in the first session of *Psychology in the Real World* groups. We sit at opposite ends of a long table hoping this will enable us to interact more easily with group members at both ends of the table. People come into the room. There are a lot. Fifteen people booked but I had expected a few 'no-shows'. However, it is time to start and everyone is here bar one. No one has said anything apart from a few hellos. Cai, sitting at the opposite end of the room, has tried to introduce herself without much response. People sit in silence. Most stare straight down.

I take the lead, start us off, outline the course, and talk about why we wanted to get people together to explore different ideas about depression. I can tell people are finding it really difficult to be here and remind myself that if Cai and I are nervous then the other participants are likely to be even more so. I know some people are not relaxed enough to speak yet and decide to talk on, hoping for a lowering of the emotional temperature.

I talk about my grandfather's experiences. How he stopped going to work, refused to get out of bed and became virtually mute, not even talking to his family. How these radical changes in him dramatically reversed after he was given electro-convulsive therapy (ECT). How this can be thought of as fitting with a medical model explanation of depression. And yet there are different ways of understanding his story. Prior

to his breakdown, he had tried to cover up the fact that at the Railway Works where he was employed as a foreman there was insufficient work repairing the trains to maintain the work force. Scarred by his experiences during the 1930s' economic depression, he assigned people to certain jobs then stayed behind every evening, working through the night undoing much of their work, before catching a few hours sleep then assigning people different tasks the following morning. He kept this hidden as long as he could before burning out, and like most men of his generation found himself unable to speak of his dilemma, or the pressures on him, even to trusted members of his family.

I talk about my own experiences. I try to show that my own ideas about depression have changed and evolved over the past 25 years. From seeing my own depressions as something out of my control, that felt like a malevolent possession each time they occurred, that seemed to come and pass when they liked, probably being the result of a genetic illness; to seeing such experiences as reactions to life events, something difficult yet normal, that relate to impacts on me of past experiences and the ways I respond to pressures and conflicts. I also remark that, as the material and social circumstances of my life (and the coping strategies I employ) have changed, depression has frightened and troubled me less, not sticking to me as it seemed to in the past.

I can see people have listened quite closely, but nobody has commented as people usually do when I recount personal stories that illustrate different models or theories that can help us understand experiences like depression. Cai talks a little about herself and her interest in depression and this course. Again, nobody comments.

It is time for the round robin – the opportunity for people in turn to say who they are, say something about themselves, talk about why they have come on the course and what they hope to get from participating in it. There are 40 minutes to go to the time for our proposed break – it should fit in nicely to our plans for this opening session.

Three minutes later the round robin has been completed. No one has said anything apart from their name and how long they have been depressed for. The first person to speak in a round robin invariably sets the norm that most people will follow. The norm that has arisen here is: 'My name is Joe. I have been depressed since 1992.' A quick calculation reveals to me that the average length of time people are saying they have been depressed for is 15 years. One person did not even say their name, saying they found it easier to speak when not asked a question or put on the spot. The matrix is a wagon wheel without spokes of any substance. Cai has tried to respond to a couple of people's comments but with little impact. Silence reigns. A sense of awkwardness and hopelessness weighs down on us all. I look to Cai who had been worried that we had not prepared enough to do in this opening session (I had reassured her that initial round robins can often take up to an hour). I see pure panic in her eyes.

My mind is racing. What were we thinking of, bringing so many people with the same way of experiencing the world together? One of the first lessons in my group therapy training was how it can be unhelpful to have groups where everyone utilises the same defence … and this is what we have done!

I start to blame Cai – why did she go along with my mad idea? Of course a group of depressed people are going to depress each other, confirm each other's stuckness, be devoured by the black dog.

'Let's have a break,' I mutter.

In the break people sit uncomfortably together, or go off for a smoke. Nobody in the group seems to want to be here. One look at Cai's contorted features tells me she doesn't want to be here. I don't want to be here either! I can't think of anything to say but eventually force something out of my mouth, rambling inanely about the venue and the virtues of camomile tea. Camomile tea! I feel so unauthentic. What I really want is alcohol. I'm scared to say what is actually going through my mind and the words coming out don't seem to be mine.

I try and gather myself. A bit of me realises I'm getting overwhelmed by powerful emotions, some of which relate to the group. Bion's ideas on fight/flight come to mind and I try and hold on to his advice about being able to think under fire.

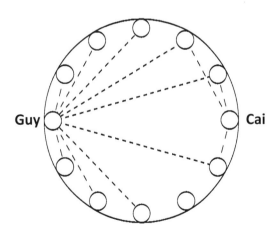

Fig. 7   The apparent lack of development of a matrix after the initial round robin

After the break we gather again. I notice one person has not returned. We wait. And wait.

'I think I saw him walking quickly off towards the bus station when I was outside having a fag,' says one member whose name I can't remember.

My heart sinks further. I panic that a norm of leaving the group without letting anyone know is being created, alongside other maladaptive norms – silence, lack of disclosure of any feelings or thoughts, passivity, dependency … too many to counteract. It feels overwhelming.

Suddenly there is a knock at the door. A middle-aged woman bursts in, all fluster, all energy, saying hello to everyone as she explains why she is late. She rattles off a string of sentences like a gatling gun.

'I'm often down but today I'm buzzing. Sorry I'm late. I'm Nadine. Got caught up with stuff, knowwhatimean? What have I missed then? What did you all talk about?'

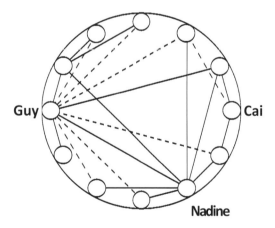

Fig. 8   Apparent connections shortly after Nadine joins the group

I try and fill her in, but there is not much to say. I try and connect her to the matrix and try and connect the others by something other than their shared despondency.

But Nadine does not need this – she's a one-person-auto-connector.

'Really? That's interesting, I'm often like that.'

'I knowhatyoumean. I have days like that but today I feel *so* different."

'I'm really looking forward to this group. I hardly go out during the day. Just stay in going over stuff in my head – are you like that?'

Some people might call Nadine manic. She describes herself as 'a manic-depressive'. I just marvel at the gift of energy and life she has brought to us. The heads of the people in the group are rising. An idea has been raised about whether depression is 'all bad' and we have gone on to consider whether human beings might have evolved to become depressed in certain circumstances – this is a new idea to most people. It puts a different slant on what gets called the biological symptoms of depression. I had planned to introduce this idea much later in the course, but abandon this and go with the flow. I explain a bit about Paul Gilbert's ideas: how evolutionary pressures have perhaps meant that humans and other pack animals are driven to try and move up the hierarchy in their pack (and get better access to mates and food) and how there needs to be powerful inhibitory states to counteract this drive otherwise there would be continual fighting for dominance within the pack. Perhaps depression (induced by defeat in a personal battle or some other loss of status) is the mechanism that achieves this. We discuss how depression tends to be experienced as an overwhelming drive to not engage with people, to avoid eye contact, to hover at the edge of the group, with a reduction in heart rate, sex drive and appetite – all factors that mean a defeated and damaged animal might be more likely to survive and avoid further conflict. This is crucial for an animal that is at high risk of attack from others in its pack that see an opportunity to move it further down the hierarchy and elevate themselves.

This theory makes sense to people. They question Cai and I, and each other, as they chew it over – how it makes sense of experiencing depression after losing one's status (e.g. job) or after being humiliated, bullied or put down by others. And it helps some people make sense of why depression is experienced very physically – how it can feel impossible to get out of bed, be assertive or even look someone in the eye when you feel depressed. How it sheds light on why depression leads us to shun contact with others. Why we feel physiologically shut down – necessary in a wounded animal to avoid bleeding to death but perhaps unhelpful in a modern world where most injuries are psychological.

The interactions are starting to become free flowing. The matrix feels like it is forming. Suddenly I notice the clock. The session is nearly over. I quickly wrap things up, saying that the kind of debate we have just had will hopefully mirror discussions we might have about other theories of depression and we can sort out a timetable next time. The second half has felt like a blur. My mind feels like it is blurred. People leave, some chatting, some with heads bowed again as they retreat into their shells, ready to face a world they don't feel part of, or find hostile and frightening, or only feel safe in when they are on its borders. Paul's ideas have hopefully helped them make some sense of this.

'Does it normally go like that?' asks Cai,

once everyone has gone.

'You're kidding!'

At the beginning of Session 2 I feedback that the man who left has let us know that he will not be coming again. He feels it is not for him. I am amazed that anyone has come back – although the second part of the first session had been interactive, the uncomfortable feelings generated by the opening hour had stuck with Cai and I and we had feared that most people would not want to encounter that type of experience again. But everyone bar him is here, and on time. We do another round robin – Cai asks what people made of last week, asking members to share if possible their thoughts on what it was like for them. Virtually everyone is positive:

'It was great to be somewhere where I did not have to pretend.'

'It really helped being with people who felt similar to me.'

'It's so important to be accepted for who you are, not who you're expected to be.'

The only person not to speak is the woman who said she did not want to be put on the spot or asked questions – I assure her that that is fine and pass on to the next person. But later she joins in, saying: 'People here seem OK. I feel safe, which is unusual.'

By the end of the session the matrix feels more complete. Nadine is much quieter but others have started to speak, ask questions and comment on things said in the group. We are starting to feel like a group of interconnected people. It is hard to know if there will ever be a truly interconnected matrix but that no longer seems impossible.

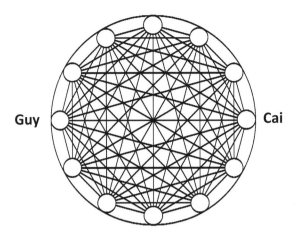

Guy   **Cai**

Fig. 9   Diagram of a complete matrix with both facilitators

26

Example sessions

Depression is rage spread thin.
    George Santayana

Is depression something we experience as a defence against feeling an uncomfortable or threatening emotion, such as anger?
This session explores a psychodynamic view of depression. First we raise the possibility that depression might relate to difficulties people have connecting with and expressing anger. Normally this gets quite a sceptical response, although occasionally a few people nod or

express some agreement with this idea. Next we explain some concepts that underlie psychodynamic theories, in particular the way of formulating people's problems in terms of defences against hidden feelings that characterise David Malan's work (often know as *Malan's Triangles*). As a group we complete a triangle of conflict regarding a hypothetical person who might feel troubled by the feeling of anger. The whole group is invited to generate anxieties people (including ourselves) have regarding feeling and expressing anger (see Fig. 10). Then

Defences

Repression
Suppression
Denial
Numbness of all feeling
Anxiety/fear
Avoidance ... of conflict, intimacy, people
Unassertive; appeasing
Put others' needs first
Avoid eye contact
Harm self rather than others
Cut (to let feelings out)
Guilt and shame
Loss of energy and drive

Anxieties (about feeling or expressing anger)

'If I got angry I'd completely *lose it* like last
   time'
'I can't bear the idea of losing control'
'I'd go mad if I got angry'
'I'm nasty when I'm angry'
'I would be just like my dad'
'If I got angry I might hurt someone'
'I made a vow never to be like my violent
   Mum'
'I'd explode'

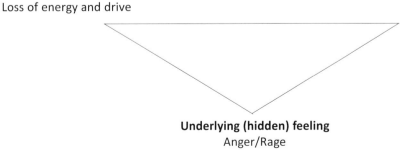

Underlying (hidden) feeling
Anger/Rage

Fig. 10   *Triangle of Conflict* regarding anger (generated during a *Black Dog* course)

we hypothesise how a person with such fears might react to such anxieties – internally (perhaps unconsciously) and in terms of how they live their life (see the list of defences in Fig. 10). By the end many people can see something of themselves or people they know in this 'hypothetical person' and can see that what get called the symptoms of depression overlap closely with psychological defences or ways of avoiding the experience of anger.

Not everything goes well

The goal of psychoanalysis is to turn neurotic misery into everyday unhappiness.
    Sigmund Freud

Some people when they leave *Black Dog* sessions are extremely quiet and appear far from happy. Although the group is not a psychoanalytic group it can lead people to confront defences that make them prone to getting stuck in certain states and at the same time connect people with the depressing nature of their lives. Whilst being on *The Black Dog* some people have reported a loss of the comfort of believing they are ill, with its accompanying hope of a quick or eventual techno-cure. As facilitators we are well aware that people might have suffered a lot of criticism in their lives and, as a consequence, can quickly slip into self-criticism during or after a *Black Dog* session. We have witnessed group members blame themselves for factors that seem largely out of their control, such as the lack of opportunities to get meaningful work, be less lonely, or escape constant criticism from family members. Many people caught up in the benefits system are repeatedly treated as if they are a case to be processed, whose time does not matter, who foolishly do not understand the myriad of forms and procedures needed to obtain benefits; group members often interpret such treatment as being provoked by their own inadequacies (rather than being indicative of a problem with the system). It is important to not let such people sink into self-oppression because factors outside themselves that might be inducing depression seem so difficult to change. However, this is not the same message as peddled in many self-help books, which tend to sell hope: *You can do it if you put enough effort in – here's the proof … I did!* Whilst hope is crucial in warding off depression (especially if one gives weight to the evidence that depression relates to inescapable pain and a sense of there being no light at the end of the tunnel), the reality of many people's lives cannot be countered with a bit of cognitive restructuring and some simple quick fixes. *Black Dog* sessions, like Freud's famous quote on psychoanalysis, can lead people, for better or worse, to be very connected to their everyday unhappiness.

An account of a session on power mapping

The following is an 'in vivo' representation of a session where we looked at the relationship between depression and power regarding aspects of our lives that provide us with support or distress as envisaged in the power map/terrain of proximal powers identified by Hagan and Smail. To make sense of this it might help to have looked at the diagrammatic representation of the power map in Chapter 22, p. 93

… Time is ticking on and I have now explained how to fill in the power map three times. I wonder whether there is a group block on understanding how to complete the maps. As facilitators we circle the group and respond to the continual comments that people cannot work out how to fill in each section. It feels like we are teachers … actually it feels worse than that – like we are vultures. *Black Dog* sessions, once people have got into the course, normally have a flow to them, a group atmosphere of exploration and participation, but not today. It feels all wrong. Every group member seems uncomfortable. People fill in aspects of the map in red if that aspect of their life is having a negative impact on them, in black if the impact is positive. As I circle I realise that virtually no segments are being filled in black. No wonder there is a reluctance to do it! The brutality of getting people to do this themselves (David Smail does not advocate this) and in a public arena (although people are reassured they won't have to share their maps with others, just discuss the process) suddenly seems deeply questionable. It reminds me of the session on loneliness where we asked people to list people whom they felt close to and then draw connections between themselves and those people, putting people they trusted and felt close to near them, others further away. My heart had sunk when I noticed that one man had only listed two people and put them on the extreme edge of the paper.

At the end of the power mapping process the whole room is quiet. Then one man blurts out: *'Clearly I feel shit because my life is shit.'*

It feels like the group are all going to turn on us and shout in unison: *'Thanks for pointing out the obvious!'*

I make some clarifications – about how difficult it is to bring about changes in areas of the power map and how this can take years not days. But I feel distanced from the group. When doing the exercise myself, filling in much of the map in black, I came to understand how far I had come in terms of acquiring power that means I no longer get stuck in depressive states (compared to periods of my life when I too filled in much of the map in red).

People are being confronted by the fact that there is no quick fix. I grasp for the first time why Melanie Klein called seeing things closer to reality the 'depressive position'. The alternative (what she called the paranoid-schizoid position) has its attractions, as does seeing depression as something purely internal – it can seem easier to change internal factors (thoughts; feelings; brain biochemicals) compared to external ones (the way people treat us; our lack of helpful friends and family; roles in life that might give us status or a sense of meaning; poverty traps). When depressed we are robbed of energy, and increasing our power (e.g. acquiring the means to escape depressing aspects of our life) requires concerted effort and is usually a long haul, with aspects of our society often making it almost impossible to achieve.

As people leave I blurt out: 'Don't feel too down … next week we are looking at cognitions and you will get to learn about cognitive therapy – a therapy with a large evidence base in terms of treating depression.' Half an hour later I can't believe I said this – it did not even seem like me saying the words. On reflection, I come to wonder whether cognitive therapy provides therapists such as myself just as much (potentially delusional) hope in a quick fix as the depressed people we sometimes try it with.

27

Black Dog evaluations and tips for living with depression

I have been fascinated at the many ways in which people adapt and cope. They seem to have an innate survival mechanism. These strategies can be interpreted and treated by professionals in many ways. However unhealthy they may be they must be given respect because they have allowed someone to survive to a point on their life's journey where change is possible. So what helps? Having a safe place to fall.

Participant on a *Black Dog* course

Evaluation forms, filled in anonymously at the end of each *Black Dog* group, have indicated that people completing the course have been satisfied with the content and the facilitators' efforts to help people achieve their individual goals for coming to the group (see www.shropsych.org/psychologyintherealworld.htm for full evaluation reports). However, not everybody completed the courses: although drop-out rates were lower than expected (range 1 – 4 in groups of 12 – 15 people) despite our efforts we were unable to obtain feedback from people who only came to a few sessions – a clear weakness when evaluating the courses in this way. It is also known that people can express very positive views about a course (or individual or group therapy) but there may be very little long-term change in their problems or lives. Nevertheless, the feedback indicated that many people felt that they benefited from: being with other people who had experienced something similar; being able to talk about their experiences and ideas about depression in a safe, supportive environment; and from the theoretical content of the course (that

they found interesting and relevant). Some participants (including people who described finding friendship difficult) became quite friendly with one another and arranged to meet up after the end of the course. The courses also spawned a couple of self-help groups that members went on to organise and facilitate.

Feedback referring to wider impacts on people's lives included:

'I've talked with people in my family about things we discussed here and that has been helpful.'

'I have been looking at other courses on offer – to help find a new meaning to life (my job used to give my life meaning).'

'I decided to join the library.'

'I made a decision to move closer to my children.'

'For years I took pills. I have come off some now and only take one.'

Comments on the facilitation style of the course included:

'It has felt safe to talk and to not talk, to sit and be quiet.'

'It was helpful to say I didn't like being put on the spot when asked to talk.'

People who did not speak much in the sessions appeared to still find it helpful:

'I haven't felt able to contribute much to the course but I have found both the material from Guy and Laura and the participants' viewpoints very interesting. Plus I have found it reassuring to hear about people's experiences that I can relate

to. This reassurance allows me to feel that I am not alone.'

This sense of 'we-ness', or belonging, where people feel safe enough to express their thoughts and feelings in an honest and straightforward way, seems a gap in the lives of many people who come on *The Black Dog*, and whilst the courses ran, and at follow-up sessions where we met several months later, people did express a sense of how therapeutic they felt this was:

'Talking with people who have had a similar experience made it easier to explain how I felt.'

'I found a release; I spoke about certain things for the first time.'

The following quote indicates such groups are worth trying, especially with people who find trust difficult:

'I found trust and openness within the group of people. At the first session I worried it might be just a group of depressed people depressing each other even more, but it wasn't.'

Black Dog participants' 'tips for living with depression'
'There is a lot of wisdom in this room; it's a shame we can't get it across to more people.'

The Black Dog course explicitly sets out not to be a coping with depression course. Feedback indicates that some people find the experience, in the short and long term, helpful, but the group's primary aim is to explore different ideas about depression rather than provide treatment or therapy. However, in the last session of each course, we do ask people for their own 'top tips for living with depression'. We generate these through doing a round robin, debating and discussing people's suggestions, recording them, and then later we send out a list of these to people who complete the course along with a report of

the course incorporating participants' feedback. No one pretends that these are quick fixes; they are just some things that some people have found somewhat helpful. Of course, what one person finds helpful another finds unhelpful or even harmful. One woman described cognitive therapy (the 'C' in CBT) as a 'life-saver'. But another person has likened it to 'spending time with an evangelical – if you believe in an afterlife your fear of death recedes, and if you persuade yourself that your problem is not your depressing life but your thoughts you can talk yourself into feeling better – but if you can't you end up even more despondent having spent a year on a waiting list to learn how to delude yourself.'

In order to respond to the request made by one participant during an evaluation session (see the quote on wisdom) I collated each group's lists and have used these as a resource. Rather than self-help books which are often based on one person's experiences or views and theories, this list encompasses the lived experiences of over 30 people. Not everything will be relevant to everyone's experience of depression, but there is an increased chance that something might. This list of what helps is available in our local CMHT waiting rooms for people to take away and can be downloaded from the department's website. I have also put it on tapes for people who have not attended a course but are searching for ideas for what might help when they feel depressed and who like to listen to things rather than read. In these ways the collective expertise that we generated in the groups gets spread even wider. In a sense we are producing a living and ever-evolving self-help body of knowledge. Of course it reflects things of relevance to people living in the Shrewsbury area – if we had run the course in the most deprived estates of Telford (or London) it would have incorporated different themes and suggestions. But this very local research project avoids the mistake of trying to apply ideas or research findings from places and cultures that are very different from our own and may not generalise to different environments.

Just as the course encompasses many ideas about the experience and causes of depression, the list encompasses a wide variety of things that can be helpful. This is in contrast to a Health Service that is increasingly dominated by pressure to follow NICE guidelines which have a much narrower conception of what constitutes and effectively 'treats' depression. In *The Black Dog* we have described the NICE doctrine as a 'cook book' approach where one recipe is meant to suit all. Many participants feel this approach has failed them or, even if they benefited from CBT and medication, feel such narrowly defined forms of help would be unlikely to assist all people as there is a failure to recognise the diversity of underlying causes and ways of easing depression that are collectively identified on *Black Dog* courses.

The list is updated when people contact us to add their own views and each time we run the course. In 2009 it encompassed the following:

Box 9   'What helps you when you're feeling depressed? What are your top tips for living with depression?'

Nature
Being in the countryside – nature is the soul's place
Being near running water, e.g. a waterfall
Getting to a high place, e.g. going up the Long Mynd mountain
Walking

Making sense of what is going on
Noticing anger in myself
Recognising symptoms/underlying causes, e.g. fear of death
Recognising that there are lots of different theories and ideas about why we feel depressed, lots of different ways of dealing with things, and lots of different things to draw on
When I feel depressed or think of depression I also try to think of repression and oppression: What am I repressing? Who or what is oppressing me? Am I oppressing myself? How have I been oppressed in the past and how is this affecting me now?

Getting away
It's important to find an escape route from people or things that are hurting you
Getting some personal space
Escaping from pressure
Taking a day off
Having time and space for me
'Recognising that you don't have to put yourself through it'

Being with people; communicating and expressing things
Getting out and mixing with people
Being needed
Being with my son
Helping someone else; doing something with others for others
Family and friends and being with like-minded people
Talking to my mental health nurse
Going to church

Trying to communicate
Expressing anger

Activities
Planning the week ahead
It is helpful to have something planned and something to look forward to
Having at least one thing to do every day – trying not to have a blank day in my diary
Having a routine
Re-engaging in activities you once enjoyed, e.g. music and theatre; this allows you to hope
Trying something new
Swimming
Cycling or doing something that has a simple rhythm – you do something requiring energy, get
    hungry, eat, rest, and then cycle again
Baking
Spoiling myself

Helpful self-talk
Reminding myself that *I will get over it*
Every time I spiral down I now remind myself that *it is a spiral, not the same pit I always fall into –*
    time moves on and so do I
Being gentle with myself and reminding myself that *I have value in 'being' not 'doing' – you are*
    what you are, not what you do
I try to get a wider perspective, by drawing a dot in the middle of a piece of paper and imagining
I'm looking down on my head
Trying to think positively
I've found it helpful to not put myself under too much pressure, and be able to say no or to cancel
    things without feeling overwhelmingly guilty
Saying '*I didn't ask for this*'
Positive thinking and challenging negative thoughts
Challenging thoughts containing the words 'should' 'ought to' 'must' 'have to' etc. and recognising
    you have choices. It's OK to take time out and just *be*
Saying to myself *it will pass*

Therapies
Alternative therapies, e.g. aromatherapy, massage, reflexology, and other physical and non-
    physical therapies
Medication
One-to-one and group therapies, such as CBT (cognitive-behavior therapy)
Relaxation and visualisation
'Outlook' organisation (self-help for depression)

Miscellaneous
Not feeling oppressed by *having to work*
Chocolate
Playing, e.g. with a remote control tractor, *Hide and Seek*
Books
Wisdom cards
Improved physical health (e.g. through diet; better pain relief)
Pets
Finding somewhere where you fit in, that sustains self-worth and is meaningful

SECTION 6

On groupwork II: *Middles*

28

The facilitator's tasks during the middle sessions of a group

Individuality is an illusion created by skin.
    Albert Einstein

When a group has met several times and started to settle into a pattern, when the initial anxieties experienced by both members and facilitators during the opening sessions have eased, and when the connections between people have begun to form a matrix there can be a great up-swell of positive feelings in a facilitator towards the group. A cohesive group that has developed healthy norms and a group culture that enables people to have many of their socio-emotional needs and individual aims met creates a warm atmosphere that both members and facilitators experience. This is to be enjoyed – groupwork can leave facilitators tired and drained even when sessions have gone well. But positive feelings can be seductive and lead the facilitator to taking his or her eye off group processes that need regular attention. Each session has its own rhythm, its own beginning, middle and end, with each phase triggering differing emotional reactions in participants and facilitators. Each session has times when the group is on task and times when it is pulled off task, and this needs to be constantly attended to.

Psychology in the Real World facilitators work hard in early sessions (see the chapters on *Beginnings*) to help a group generate healthy norms and function effectively, i.e. to get a group *on course*. Fewer interventions are needed to keep groups on course. Like piloting a ship, the group can feel like it is sailing itself.

However, it is easy to go off course, especially when concentration is lost. An unnoticed slight deviation can mean a ship ends up miles away from its destination, despite there being no obvious calamitous event, and it is the same for groups. It then takes a great deal of intervention to bring the ship or group back on course. Maladaptive norms once established, even when tackled in middle sessions of groups, frequently resurface in subsequent sessions, like the spontaneous recovery of learned individual behaviours. The main tasks of the facilitator in the middle sessions of a group then are to observe, monitor and reflect on various processes to see that a group continues to be 'on course' and to gently intervene as and when in order to avoid the need for major interventions later in the journey. Such reflection needs to take place during each session, afterwards in discussion with any co-facilitator and in supervision.

On the importance of being able to *think group*

Fiona McDermott felt that the capacity to 'think group' is the most important skill for groupworkers to learn. People well-versed in one-to-one work often need help to avoid the wagon-wheel mode of facilitation, where they work with each individual in turn providing similar interventions to those they use in individual therapy. Instead, they need to see that individual growth and development is something that emerges out of group interactions and group life. Training in

Box 10   Some questions facilitators might reflect on during the middle sessions

Are we on task (e.g. are people developing and deepening their psychological knowledge and applying this to themselves and others)?

Are we utilising the experiences of the group members or have things become too dry, abstract or academic?

Is the emotional temperature at this moment appropriate for the tasks we are currently engaged in?

Are we avoiding anything that needs to be brought in (for example, avoiding disagreement, or difficult, emotionally painful areas that would be helpful to explore)?

Are the less vocal members being excluded from opportunities to contribute? Is it best to invite them to say something or change the group task to enable this without them feeling put on the spot (e.g. get people to pair up or discuss things in small groups)?

Am I listening too attentively to each person whilst they speak in the group and neglecting the majority (that are not speaking at any one time)? For example: Who looks bored or disengaged? Who wants to speak but isn't getting a chance? Who might be irritated because X always goes on a bit? Is anyone distressed?

Have the interactions in the group become more wagon wheel than matrix?

Do I need to create space for group members to take up certain roles (e.g. provide comfort and psychological healing for people who have been deeply moved after revealing something very personal)?

Am I intervening too much – do I need to trust the group, say less and see where things go?

Am I (perhaps subtly but nonetheless powerfully) backing a particular opinion on this subject in a way that closes down exploration of this area and silences people who hold different views to my own?

Am I preventing or enabling the group to develop as a mutual aid or self-support system?

Am I spending too much time thinking about individual group members and their individual needs? Have I taken my eye off the group as a whole? Do I need to attend more to the norms and group culture? Do I need to remind myself to think group?

Are we going too far off course, developing a maladaptive norm, or avoiding something that needs addressing?

Are members getting Yalom's therapeutic benefits from being in the group? Which are being neglected? What opportunities are there to enable some to occur?

What are my feelings and what is at the root of these? Are they reactions to group processes or do they relate to things outside the group? Do they provide me with trustworthy information that might guide an intervention?

What group boundaries do I need to attend to and what is needed to balance today's session? For example: Is it time for a break or better to allow this discussion to continue? Is it important to finish what I am saying or is that all in my own head – in reality have people lost concentration and stopped listening? Is it time to move on to another area we planned to cover?

How am I dovetailing with any co-facilitator? Am I preventing or enabling the group to make the most of having two facilitators? Am I undermining or being too deferential to the co-facilitator?

counselling or clinical psychology leads people to focus very much on individual needs as currently training in these professions is almost 100% focused on one-to-one encounters. This creates habits in workers that are hard to undo in groupwork, and can lead facilitators to engage in a disproportionate number of one-to-one exchanges with group members. Listening skills acquired on these courses (e.g. leaning forward, appropriate eye contact, nodding, conveying a sense of the person being listened to) in group situations can lead to individual members being encouraged to talk for longer than is optimal. In such scenarios one person might feel attended to but thirteen might feel ignored. Rather than say something empathetic, the group as a whole (and the individual who has perhaps just disclosed something very personal) may be better served by the facilitator inviting other members of the group to respond. In any group situation there is often a range of responses people make to the disclosure of some very personal information: one group member may be empathetic to someone's plight and emotional state; another might encourage stoicism; another relate a similar experience so the person no longer feels they are 'the only one'; another may give the person a hug; another might challenge that person's interpretation of events and encourage them to see things from a different point of view. In short, the variability in the group leads to a whole range of responses which may be of help to the individual in different ways; some might be taken board, others not. But the group provides a rich resource from which the groupworker can enable an individual to be assisted (see Section 9, pp. 191–212).

29

Phases of group development

We can never understand the total situation without taking into account the evolving situation.
  Mary Parker Follett

Groups have beginnings, middles and ends and everything within this overall structure can be thought of as going through various phases of development. Bruce Tuckman proposed that most groups go through five stages. Initially they *Form* (a process whereby members are trying to get to know each other and attempting – Tuckman suggested pretending – to get on and get along). This is followed by three stages that are not necessarily proceeded through sequentially – groups can oscillate between each of these stages. They include *Storm* (where members let down the 'politeness barrier' as they try to get down to the work in hand and are perhaps confronted by the challenge of the task – tempers can flare up in this stage); *Norm* (where people get used to each other and a settled pattern and way of doing things emerges in the group); and *Perform* (where members efficiently work towards a common goal on a cooperative basis). When the group comes to an end, whether the group task is accomplished or not, there is then a stage when members *Mourn* the loss of the group.

Fig. 11 includes Tuckman's model and concepts that other theorists, particularly those who have run and researched psychotherapy groups, have put forward as relevant at different stages of group development. Some of these ideas are taken up in other chapters (e.g. Bion's work on dynamics, see Chapter 31). Each horizontal band incorporates a different way of describing what is happening in a group's life, from its beginning to its end. Some movements between stages are progressive, others cyclical.

Stages	Beginnings	Middles	Middles	Middles	Endings
Tuckman	Form	Storm	Norm	Perform	Mourn
Focus	Leader	Group	Group	Group	Group + Leader
Defences	Projection Regression	More mature defences and ego growth Here-and-now defences, e.g. suppression			Denial Regression
Transferences	Powerful	Negative	Positive	Diminishing	Resurfacing
Dynamics	Dependency	Fight/Flight	Work Group	Work Group	Pairing Fight/Flight

Fig. 11   Phases of development

In the first phase group members tend to be fairly passive, projections are happening, the instinct to fit in predominates and there is usually dependency on the group leader. Most facilitators will allow and cater for this, accepting it as a necessary phase and, having a developmental model of group progress in mind, will look for ways to gently help the group go through this phase. After this orienting period, dissatisfaction often sets in. This can be difficult for group facilitators who have invested considerable effort and energy in setting up a group, but in terms of group development this can be conceptualised as healthy progression. At this stage group members with an idealised view of the potential of the group, or the skill of the group facilitator, may drop out. Others may realise a need for some other kind of help or recognise a wish to take part in a different kind of group. The facilitator needs to be able to contain the feelings that people dropping out bring up in remaining group members. For example, hostility to people who leave; anger towards the group facilitator for failing to prevent this; sadness and disappointment regarding the departures; feelings of being abandoned. Depending on the type of group, such feelings might be openly discussed and, where they perhaps mirror past hurts, linked to previous experiences. The facilitator has to ensure that these feelings do not prevent the group from achieving its aims and should seek to allow the creative potential of the group to come through.

It is not possible for a group facilitator to know each individual's problems, history or what might be 'going on' for each person during every minute of the session. Rather the focus should be on creating healthy group norms that will help a group achieve its aims. As things settle down the group facilitator needs to pull back so that the group can begin to 'work'. If a group remains facilitator-dominated there is a

loss of potential for members to take various roles and a risk of unhelpful dependence on the group leader. Most groups benefit from the facilitator's ability to move the group from one of dependency on the facilitator to one of working in an interdependent group culture where members of the group themselves are collaborating and achieving the group's tasks.

One belongs to a group but is different from it. There is oscillation in each individual between self and group; between being focused on the task and being disinterested, disengaged or disturbed by powerful emotional states; between feeling part of the group and enjoying the sessions to feeling isolated, constrained, irritated with members and the facilitator and having impulses to leave. Group facilitators need to 'think group' and watch for group currents as well as respond to individuals who are being pulled (or serving to pull the group) off course. If a group is in 'work group mode' the facilitator may say very little (perhaps just as much as the average group member). At other times more interventions might be necessary to get a group back on course and help people not be pulled into emotional states that interfere too strongly with the group achieving its aims. This is covered in Chapter 31 (pp. 128–35).

When a group nears its end there tends to be an increase in anxiety which often leads to regression. Group analysts speak of the group having been internalised as a healthy vital structure and when members face the fact that this has to be given up there is a process of mourning. During this stage there may be denial of the importance of the group or of any sadness or anger associated with the ending, and what Bion called 'pairing' and sexual liaison can arise as an antidote or manic defence against feelings associated with the ending. Most therapists believe that feelings triggered by the 'bereavement' need to be felt, expressed and 'let go of' in order for group members to manage the ending and be ready for the future, a future where they will not be a member of this group but will be a member of many other groups.

Psychology in the Real World groups are not psychotherapy groups. Nevertheless, some of the above ideas are useful to hold in mind when facilitating any group. Unlike psychoanalytic groups, it would be inappropriate to divert the group into collective analysis of all the individual and whole group defences illustrated in Fig 11. However, these feeling states need to be managed in individual members and in the facilitators in order for any group to not lose its way. Having some group psychotherapy training can be helpful for group facilitators whatever type of group they run as it can help facilitators recognise and have some ways of understanding and mapping various emotional states and dynamics that can come to the fore in any group situation.

Although each group is unique, stage models can help facilitators map out group processes. For example, *Walk and Talk* has a different membership each time people meet. Some people attend regularly, others sporadically, some every now and again, others only once. Reviewing the literature on stages of group development, Toseland and Rivas concluded that groups with high degrees of openness such as this only rarely proceed beyond the Beginnings stage of development. Compared to other *Psychology in the Real World* groups, such as *The Writing Group* where high levels of cohesion, intimacy and powerful inter-group feelings can occur very early on in the group, facilitators need to accept that, no matter how hard they try, the *Walk and Talk* group is always going to some extent to be in the dynamics and experiences that characterise the 'form' stage of development. Nevertheless, in the last meeting of *Walk and Talk* each autumn, people who have

become very attached to the *Walk and Talk* experience often speak of how much they will miss the group, how they don't want it to end, and (sometimes with encouragement from facilitators) express other feelings common to endings. This can seem strange as there might also be people who are attending that week for the very first time.

Whilst in *Psychology in the Real World* groups facilitators mostly try and manage the powerful emotional states that relate to group stages of development, we occasionally highlight these in order that members might learn something about group processes. The beginnings and endings of groups always offer opportunities to help people notice, speak of and reflect on their own reactions to such events and see how these might mirror other beginning and ending experiences in their lives. Group discussions of this ilk also provide opportunities for people to realise that to some extent our reactions are universal, e.g. we all have our unique reactions to the beginnings of new ventures but everyone is responding to the inevitable anxieties people feel when going to a place for the first time and meeting new people. In *Understanding Ourselves and Others* courses the last session is usually entitled 'What is it like when things come to an end?' which tends to involve looking at the literature on endings (e.g. on grief reactions when people die, facing our own death, reactions to the loss of a job or retirement) and on separations (e.g. reactions in children and parents when separated). As well as discussing Bowlby's work on attachment theory, group members are given opportunities to reflect on their own reactions to various endings and separations in their life, and encouraged to speak about their reactions to the group coming to an end. Group processes thus generate material that group members can productively learn from.

30

Yalom's therapeutic factors in groupwork

I am a part of all that I have met.
  Alfred Lord Tennyson

One inspiration for the *Psychology in the Real World* groups was a realisation that therapeutic factors that research has indicated operate in psychotherapy groups can also operate in groups where there is a task over and above (or alongside) therapy or personal development. I have facilitated many psychotherapy groups where the analysis is, as S.H. Foulkes advocated, *of the group by the group,* and where the group engages in *free-floating discussion* (no tasks or topics are introduced by the therapist – rather the members generate the material to be analysed by talking about anything that comes to mind). Such psychotherapy groups have been experienced as helpful by many participants but have not been popular – there is a great reluctance on behalf of many people to sign up for them, and the anxiety about being in such groups can take many weeks to subside (which is one reason for running psychotherapy groups for at least 40 sessions). People seem keener to come to the *Psychology in the Real World* groups (which have always been fully booked and usually over-subscribed), where topics are known about to some extent in advance and people's anxieties about 'being analysed' are far less.

S.H. Foulkes identified three types of what he called treatment groups:

1. *Activity Groups* – groups whose activities have a specific aim that is deemed to have therapeutic effects, e.g. *Skills for Ills* groups such as relaxation for anxiety, cognitive therapy for depression.

2. *Therapeutic Groups* – groups that are organised around a specific activity (e.g. dance, drama, rambling) but the activity may be of secondary importance – the group experience itself leads to the majority of therapeutic gains.

3. *Group Psychotherapy* – distinguished from other types of groupwork in that the group relies solely on verbal communication, the individual members are the 'object of treatment', and the group itself is accepted as the main therapeutic agent. The group is facilitated for the personal development of its individual members and for no other reason.

Psychology in the Real World ventures encompass aspects of all three types, but might best be placed in the second category. Participants are usually inspired to come by the activity, but the facilitators' focus is often just as much on creating a group culture where therapeutic group factors, such as those identified by Irvin Yalom, can materialise.

Yalom's eleven therapeutic factors are derived from comprehensive self-report research with a large number of people who have experienced interpersonal group therapy (see Yalom, 2005). In 2008 Lucy Gahan researched which of

Yalom's factors members of an *Understanding Ourselves and Others* group rated as having occurred in a group they attended. Although the sample size was very small and the methodology open to criticism, the results matched my own observations and interpretations of feedback provided on many *Psychology in the Real World* groups. The following is a list of Yalom's eleven therapeutic factors, with factors that Lucy's research and previous evaluations of other groups indicate have been the most pertinent and therapeutic for group members listed first:

Universality

People come to realise that they are not the 'only one' with a particular life experience or problem; nor are they the only person who thinks or feels a particular way. Some things they may share with just one or a few members of the group, other things come to be seen as universal and common to all. This helps people feel less isolated from others, provides a sense of relief, and leads to a connection with other members of the group and to the human race in general. One participant on an *Understanding Ourselves and Others* course commented: 'I feel less isolated and reassured that I'm not the only one who feels like this! I think one of the hardest things about mental illness is that unless you have been there yourself you just cannot fully understand how it feels, but being with others in a similar situation can be a real relief because no explanations are necessary.' On completing *Thinking about Medication* one person commented: 'The group has been very helpful and inspiring. I have felt I am not on my own trying to reduce or come off medication.'

The development of socialising techniques

Psychology in the Real World groups provide a safe and supportive environment for members to take risks and build up their social skills. If they were called social skills groups it is unlikely

many people would attend. Yet feedback indicates that people gained confidence and developed new skills through being in the groups, e.g. 'I feel I can join in groups more – before I felt rather hesitant and felt I shouldn't – that perhaps I wasn't wanted (pathetic but true).'

Imparting information

Members often report that it has been helpful to learn factual information from the content of the sessions and from comments made by other group members and the facilitators, e.g. (from *Thinking about Medication)* 'Availability of books to borrow [was] much better than just having a reading list which I might or might not have got around to investigating'; 'I have a greater understanding of pharmaceutical drugs and have recognised side effects that I have suffered that have been overlooked by hospital staff.'

Cohesiveness

A cohesive group allows members to feel the warmth and comfort of being part of a group; feel like they belong; feel that they value the group and are valued by other group members; feel accepted. Yalom believes cohesiveness is the primary curative factor in group therapy and cites research that cohesive groups have been shown to have better outcomes. Clearly a large proportion of people in mental health services have not had many experiences of feeling they belong – in family, work or friendship groups. Many do not feel a sense of belonging in their wider community or indeed the human race, an experience that can lead many people I have worked with to express ideas that get labelled psychotic. The evaluations of the groups generate many comments indicating the importance of this to people, e.g. 'The interesting discussions led to self-disclosure that brought the group close together'; 'I found the group bonded well and this in itself to me is supportive and gives me that bit more determination to safely reduce my meds as in the past I have just stopped taking everything with disastrous results.'

Interpersonal learning

A group member can achieve a greater level of self-awareness through the process of interacting with others in the group, who can also give helpful feedback on the member's behaviour (and its impact on others). Evaluations of the initial *Understanding Yourself and Others* courses indicated that the most frequent feedback was that people benefited from 'hearing and learning from others' stories and experiences'; one person said: 'It was interesting to see how people behaved in the group – nice to see people express what perhaps were more contentious opinions and not just following like sheep.'

Altruism

Helping others (providing it is not driven by martyring) boosts our self-esteem and provides us with a sense of purpose. Therapists know that much of their own self-esteem derives from altruism in and out of work, and yet most mental health services and therapies are one to one where the dyad and imposition of boundaries mean the people with the biggest need of boosts to their self-esteem are denied opportunities to get it through acts of altruism in that service. This is not true in *Psychology in the Real World* ventures where there is an expectation that group members will look out for and help and comfort each other. As one participant put it: 'Some group members appeared very vulnerable at times and others, including myself, recognised this and were very supportive. I certainly felt motivated to help in any way.' In *Walk and Talk* several people who attended initially as participants have subsequently taken leading roles in organising the group. One commented: 'I have always just

received services. What I really get out of this is a sense of being involved in something that others benefit from too – I don't want to be paid, I like doing it on a voluntary basis, doing something for local people.'

Instillation of hope

Participants often appear to absorb the (real, not manufactured or pretend) enthusiasm of a group facilitator for the group, and can be inspired and encouraged by other members who have overcome problems that they are still struggling with – whether that be escaping services they feel are detrimental, coming off medication, getting a job, managing difficult feelings, surviving abuse experiences, or escaping from violent relationships (participants have mentioned all of these and many more).

Imitative behaviour

One way in which group members can develop social skills is through a modelling process, observing and imitating the therapist and other group members. Bandura has shown this can be a very rapid and powerful form of learning where people overcome problems by witnessing others do the same and by modelling themselves on that person. For example, several people on *The Black Dog* courses have been surprised by people who seem to experience equally severe depressions as themselves yet do not go into the psychiatric hospital, have ECT or take psychiatric drugs; their previous view that their own depressive experiences were much more severe than those of other people who do not go into hospital has been therefore questioned, and they often start to envisage and put in place steps to become more like group members who experience overwhelming states of depression but live with these by means other than psychiatric interventions.

Existential factors

Existential factors include concepts such as: every group, like every aspect of life, and life itself, has a beginning, middle and an end and can be perceived as a journey with many ups and downs along the way, no life can be free of pain and suffering, and issues of responsibility and freedom are complex and challenging. One *Thinking about Medication* participant said: 'I have learned to take absolute responsibility for my health and wellbeing', comparing this with previous oscillation between unquestioned acceptance and angry rejection of advice from her psychiatrist (the 'responsible medical officer').

Catharsis

Catharsis occurs when people express deep emotional feelings and experience a sense of release and of healing. When *Psychology in the Real World* group members tell their story to a supportive audience they often report a feeling of relief from chronic feelings of shame and guilt. Both during group sessions and in evaluations members have remarked that it has been helpful to get something 'off their chest', or as one *Black Dog* participant put it: 'I found a release – spoke about certain things for the first time.'

Corrective recapitulation of the primary family experience

Groupwork offers people opportunities to gain understandings of the impacts of childhood experiences on their personality and ways of coping, and can help people learn to avoid repeating unhelpful past interactive patterns in present-day relationships. Sometimes members can unconsciously identify the group therapist and other group members with their own parents and siblings and learning can occur when this becomes consciously apparent to that person. Several members of *The Writing Groups* have remarked on how it has helped to feel accepted for whom they are in the groups, having revealed through their writings how this had not been the case during their childhood.

31

Group dynamics

Insanity in individuals is rare – but in groups, parties, nations and epochs it is the rule.
  Friedrich Nietzsche

The phrase *group dynamics* probably has what Wolfensberger calls 'hi-craze value' – it has become a phrase that is often used but which has an ill-defined meaning and can operate as a catch-all concept. This chapter looks at group dynamics from two models: (i) Toseland and Rivas (2005) who have a broad conceptualisation of dynamics as group processes – the ways members react to the ever-changing group experience and act towards each other; and (ii) Bion (1961) who used the phrase in a more psychoanalytical way (akin to the phrase *psychodynamics*), referring to whole-group processes that may be outside conscious awareness but have a great impact on members and pull the group off task. Bion felt, like Nietzsche, that groups could enter into mad states, but like me did not feel this is the 'rule': it is inevitable that this will happen sometimes, but if groups can be helped to enter such states for as little time as possible they perhaps offer opportunities for individuals to spend more time being 'sane' than if people live a purely isolated existence (which induces its own forms of madness).

1. Toseland and Rivas' four dimensions of group dynamics

Toseland and Rivas conceptualise group dynamics as processes that limit members' freedom, individuality and independence but stabilise and regulate the way a group operates and help people feel comfortable and secure in their positions in a group. The facilitator's tasks in terms of dynamics are to balance the needs of the individuals, including their wish to have their individual socio-emotional needs met via group participation, with the needs of the group as a whole; assist the creation of a healthily cohesive group; and seek communication patterns, norms, roles, status hierarchies and cultures that benefit rather than harm or hinder individuals and the group as a whole.

Communication and interaction patterns

The patterns of communication and interaction between group members include things such as: the ways members talk and respond to each other and the facilitator; non-verbal communications; particular styles of interaction that arise, e.g. wagon wheel (maypole), round robin, hot seat, and free-floating. These are affected by factors such as the physical environment, size of the group, subgroups, what types of interactions are reinforced in the group and the power and status of members and the facilitators.

In *Psychology in the Real World* groups we tend to start off the first session with the round robin style but attempt to move quickly into free-floating interactions (see the chapters on *Beginnings*). At the end of the first session and beginning of the next two we tend to do a round robin where people repeat their names and are asked to reflect on what it has been like to come along, what they think of the sessions so far, whether they have any thoughts from the previous week's session, and so on. This helps to link people with each other, link each week's sessions, and develop interaction patterns where everyone's contributions, no matter how small, are seen as important. It helps to build the matrix. Although people can feel put on the hot seat and in evaluations sometimes report that they dreaded being first (or last as the pressure grows), the round robin method does ensure that everyone gets to speak and say something early in the group.

After a few sessions we drop the round robins, but bring them back (i) in the middle session when we informally review the group and want to hear each person's reflections on how things have gone so far, what they feel they have been getting from coming to the group and any suggestions for changes; and (ii) in the last session when we are keen to hear each member's reflections on what they feel they have got from the group and their thoughts and feelings on it coming to an end.

As the chapters on *Beginnings* indicate, although we describe part of this format as round robin, as facilitators we often respond to what people say (creating the wagon wheel) and are interested in any other comments other group members make in response, before waiting for a lull and then asking the next person in turn to give their thoughts. Restricting group size to no more than 14 means that the round robin process is manageable in terms of how long this process takes. Even so, a round robin will take half an hour if each person's comments and any reactions from the facilitators or other group members take just two minutes each, and frequently it has taken up to an hour at key stages in a group (e.g. during a review when the group has not been going particularly well).

Group cohesion

Leon Festinger defined group cohesion as 'the result of all forces acting on members to remain in the group'. One of the most consistent findings in the research into what makes groups effective is that cohesiveness is positively correlated with beneficial outcomes (see Toseland and Rivas (2005) and Yalom (2005) for a review of this literature). In *Psychology in the Real World* we try to create as cohesive a group as quickly as possible by:

- Promoting and reinforcing open interaction

- Helping individual and overall group aims to be identified and clarified

- Trying to ensure some individual and group aims are met as quickly as possible, highlighting this as it occurs, and remarking on aims that we hope will be met in subsequent sessions

- Enabling all to feel they are contributing

- Creating an environment where people can feel pride in being part of the group

Some of these factors can be worked on before the group starts. Names and locations are important in enabling people to have pride in being part of a group. Although people frequently get benefits from therapeutic groups run in services, it seems unlikely that people will easily feel pride in being a member of The Self-Harm Group run at the Personality Disorders Clinic in the Mental Health Trust – the stigma associated with mental health serves to counteract what might otherwise be positive feelings about being a member of such a group. The flyers that advertise *Psychology in the Real World* groups sometimes give great clarity about the group's aims (see the *Thinking about Medication* flyer, pp. 166–7; in other ventures the aims indicated in the flyer are more fuzzy but are clearly there to be worked out once the group starts (for example, in *The Writing Group*).

In the first session people are asked why they came and what they hope to get from the course. In most groups a record is kept and these individual aims are pooled and become a core part of the group's overall aims (see Chapter 38). In my opinion many groups fail because of lack of clarity about the aims – psychotherapy groups and personal awareness groups for clinical psychology trainees seem to regularly turn into difficult experiences for members and facilitators because of insufficient clarity about what the members and facilitator hope people will get from the group. This can lead to unhealthy group dynamics with lots of acting out towards the facilitator.

Psychology in the Real World facilitators try and emphasise the positives of any group experience early on in a group whilst at the same time remaining genuine – false praise always tends to grate. People are often highly tuned, perhaps by evolutionary forces, perhaps as a result of daily experiences of being manipulated and exploited in marketing cultures that infuse everything, to be on the look out for the 'inauthentic stranger' and do not react well to false platitudes from a facilitator. The loss of trust that this generates is hard to recapture. Genuine positive comments about the group might involve observations on how quickly people seem to have started to trust each other, how interesting the debates have been, that it feels like it is going to be a 'good group'. It is obviously easiest to do this when things are going well – an upward spiral/feel-good factor develops which is easy to observe, comment on and reinforce. Healthy norms start to develop.

Cohesiveness, however, can occur through mechanisms that run counter to the overall aims and philosophies of *Psychology in the Real World* groups and can have maladaptive impacts. Festinger's own work was inspired by his research into a small religious group who met to make plans for a forthcoming cataclysmic flood and alien invasion that would wipe out all human beings apart from those who believed in the God Sananda (see Lauren Slater's *Opening Skinner's Box* for a beautiful description of this research, or Festinger, Riecken and Schacter (1957) for the original report). The group was so cohesive it was able to continue meeting even after the date specified by the group for the end of the world had passed! Groups can become cohesive whilst operating in what Bion called fight/flight mode, even though they are not 'on task'. In mental health services a sense of cohesion can sometimes be created by overemphasis on similarity within a group and overemphasis on difference between the group and other groups. Mental health service staff groups sometimes do this by overemphasising their 'saneness' compared to their patients' 'madness'. Service user groups sometimes do this by overemphasising their 'difference' compared to staff 'who can never know what it's like to be us'. *Psychology in the Real World* ventures often question and challenge divisions of this type so that a type of cohesiveness that enables people to question fundamental beliefs and engage in collaborative conversations can be achieved.

Social integration: Norms, roles and status

Toseland and Rivas focus on norms, roles and status regarding the ways people become socially integrated in a group. *Norms* are shared expectations and beliefs about appropriate ways to behave in groups. They stabilise and regulate behaviour and help to encourage organised and coordinated action to achieve goals. However, they can be dysfunctional and hold a group back. They sometimes need unfreezing, for example, by discussing how they came about and whether they are helpful.

Psychology in the Real World facilitators try and quickly reinforce what we view as helpful group norms, especially in the first few sessions.

This tends to include comments and observations such as the fact that everyone arrived on time, and how starting and ending on time helps groups to work well; the helpfulness of the fact that people are not talking over each other; how great (and unusual) it is to be with people who seem to genuinely respect each other's views, even though we don't have to agree with everything each one of us says; how it appears that people seem to have an open mind and a respect for and interest in difference; how some people seem to have taken a risk and revealed some personal things; and so on.

Irvin Yalom said that the early sessions are not ones for the therapist to be quiet. Most participants at the outset are looking for guidance or subtle indications on how to be in the group and commenting positively on observed norms that one is keen to establish reinforces these in a process akin to positive reinforcement in behavioural theory. Some behaviours that are not sought can be ignored (e.g. not reinforced by eye contact or nodding from the facilitator who then shifts attention to something else, thus lessening the likelihood of them occurring again compared to reinforced behaviours). Others, for example, a person disrespectfully dismissing or belittling something another group member has said, in my opinion need a clear response – not just to counteract any damaging effect on the recipient, but to prevent a maladaptive group norm from taking root. In such circumstances we normally make a comment about how all of us at some time will have had experiences of feeling our ideas have been dismissed and how unpleasant a feeling that can be. In such scenarios we are normally covertly speaking to both the belittling and belittled person – most people who frequently dismiss others have had damaging experiences of having their own views dismissed, often in childhood. We might follow this up with a comment about how it will probably help us all

if we can create a group where people feel safe enough to speak their mind whilst at the same time being respectful to other people and acknowledging the possibility that others may have very different views to our own. We then look for opportunities to reinforce examples of such behaviour later in the session (e.g. by nodding, enthusiastically following up something someone has said, keeping eye contact and smiling). Some therapists are uncomfortable consciously utilising reinforcement in such ways (although undoubtedly they unconsciously do this). But groupworkers have to 'think group' – a facilitator needs to be constantly reflecting on and attending to the needs of the group as a whole and unhealthy group norms can be very damaging to individuals as well as the group process. They are also notoriously difficult to shift once they take hold.

Unhealthy norms need to be unfrozen once they have taken root, by open discussion and exploration of how they might be hindering the group. Hoping they will go away rarely works although crises can sometimes arise that provoke avoided discussion. More common than crises, however, is a steady increase in the number of people who remain silent in a group, followed by a steady reduction in the overall number of group members as these people stop coming.

Different individuals take different *roles* in groups, some of which they may not be consciously aware of. Roles allow division of labour and certain people to take care of particular group functions. We tend to accept the fact that most people in short-term groups such as *Psychology in the Real World* will take up roles that they are used to and comfortable with, but often make a comment that the start of any new group is like a new chapter in one's life and this gives one the chance to not automatically take up a role that is normally taken, but to try out new roles if people are so inclined. Group members have reported that they have enjoyed not having to be 'the one who always looks after everyone else' or 'the one that makes things work'. People with long histories of involvement with mental health services frequently remark on the benefits of having opportunities to 'be a person who helps others rather than the ill person who is there to just passively receive help'.

Toseland and Rivas refer to *status* in terms of the ways that each member of a group evaluates and ranks their own and other members' positions in terms of hierarchies in the group. This might relate to factors such as perceived expertise, popularity and social status – the factors vary between members and between different groups in terms of what is given prominence – and these in turn influence group behaviour. They cite social psychology experimental evidence that indicates individuals who perceive themselves as low status in terms of the group hierarchy are sometimes less likely to conform to group norms because they see themselves as having little to lose by deviating and such people can therefore be 'disruptive influences'. This risk can be minimised if they have hope of attaining higher status. Individuals perceived as high-status also tend to deviate from group norms more than middle ranking members but this is normally interpreted differently by facilitators and other group members who tend to give them more slack.

Whilst accepting any group will be working out and reacting to status hierarchies, we work hard in *Psychology in the Real World* groups to flatten as much as possible power hierarchies within the group. Stanley Milgram's experiments showed that when the experimenter dressed in a white coat and stated he was from a prestigious university participants in the experiment were more likely to obey and electrically shock people who incorrectly answered questions in a supposed test of memory than when the

experimenter was scruffy and not from a prestigious institution. Although I refer to aspects of my professional status in the flyers advertising courses (e.g. being an honorary lecturer at local universities) this to help people see the course as high status and to enable pride in being part of the group. Once a group starts, however, I and any other facilitators try not to emphasise things that elevate or accentuate our own (or any other member's) status. It is crass to blithely imply that everyone in a group is of equal status or has equal power. Our society is structured on the basis of hierarchies that cause massive inequalities in terms of wealth and power and which greatly shape our thinking and behaviour. However, in some fundamental ways we are all equal. I find myself guided by a family maxim passed on by my grandfather, an orphan, welsh miner and private in the First World War, who was told by his adoptive parents: 'No one is better than you. At the same time, you are better than no one.' We try and create a group culture where, as much as possible, people can gain a sense of such equality, for example, by trying to treat everyone's comments as of equal value to the group. That is not to say that every comment is of equal validity as an explanation of human behaviour or all group members' comments are of moral equivalence. Rather, they all add to the melting pot of ideas to be discussed and reflected upon – what is important is what is said, not who said it.

Group culture

A group culture emerges from the mix of values individuals bring to the group and the values of the agency and wider society from which the group emanates. Group cultures have the potential to provide helpful contrasts with the values of the cultures that have previously shaped individual members.

As the principle facilitator in most groups it is likely that *Psychology in the Real World* group cultures will be influenced (consciously and unconsciously) by many of my own values (which in turn relate to late 20th century Western cultures that have shaped me). Qualitative research on these groups has revealed many comments from group members that overlap with ideas that are important to me, e.g. at a fundamental level all human beings are of equal value; when in healthy environments people tend to make thoughtful and ethical (rather than selfish and harmful) decisions; some aspects of our culture are psychologically harmful and there is therefore a need for constant critique of what we think and what we do; people are responsible for the predictable consequences of their (not others') actions; harm is reduced by creating norms of mutual respect rather than having a minority of people devise rules and laws that purport to govern all people's behaviour; collective action is sometimes needed to bring about change in inequitable systems. Although every group is unique, over the years, partly through some people coming to more than one group, some members becoming facilitators, and flyers attracting people to new ventures reflecting previous groups' values, *Psychology in the Real World* appears to have developed a general culture which probably impacts on each new group that gets set up. Whilst this undoubtedly attracts some people, it may put off others, and is not in itself a necessarily good thing. Yet many evaluations have indicated that where the philosophies and values that characterise *Psychology in the Real World* groups contrast with cultures that attendees are more familiar with this has proven to be of interest and of benefit to some members.

A different facilitator coming from a different cultural background in a different part of the world would influence a series of groups in different ways, which in turn would be attractive or off-putting to people who might sign up for that group. I hope people reading this book will set up their own groups that develop their own unique cultures reflecting the backgrounds and values of the facilitators and of the people who come along. The philosophies and dynamics I describe in this book reflect beliefs and values that have been shaped and informed by doing groupwork of this kind and by closely attending to what people say and do in these groups as well as by wider influences. They are put out for readers to think about and consider, not blindly follow. They are not the only ways to run groups and will not suit all people or types of groups. They are merely what I currently see as helpful when being involved in community-based groupwork.

2. Bion on group dynamics

Bion studied groups through holistic spectacles.
Irvin Yalom

Wilfred Bion is one of the founding fathers of groupwork in Britain. Along with people such as S.H. Foulkes and Tom Main, he worked with groups of soldiers who had been traumatised by their experiences in the Second World War. Through clinical observation in this and subsequent periods of his work, Bion explored why groups frequently get stuck or pulled off course. He felt that the three main reasons for this were:

1. Ambivalence within individual group members between their desire for autonomy and their desire for dependence.

2. Differences between the needs of the group (for the group's sake) and the needs of its individual members.

3. Powerful emotional states that relate to an unconscious assumption held by the group that overwhelms group members and interferes with the functioning of the group.

Bion observed that, although groups are normally set up to pursue sensible and realistic goals, they are often pulled off task and go into a form of collective madness which he called 'basic assumption functioning'. Bion listed three basic assumption states: dependency, pairing and fight-flight. These states involve magical thinking and unconscious wishes to be rescued, and sometimes result in members fighting between themselves, rounding on scapegoats, denigrating or fighting other groups, and splitting (both psychologically – seeing everything in 'black and white', and practically – members separating themselves or others from the group). Bion felt that, when operating in basic assumption states, the group was trying to sort out leadership issues, and said that group leaders need to be able to 'think under fire' in order to help groups return to states where they can make rational, considered decisions.

Dependency groups operate on the assumption that there is a leader (usually, but not necessarily, the therapist or facilitator) who can gratify all the group's needs. When *pairing,* a group operates on the basis that the pairing up of a couple of members will produce something redemptive that will save the group from its present predicament and eventually lead to the group having all its needs met. *Fight-flight* states are highly emotive reactions to the need for protection, and groups in these states often do extreme things to try and attain a sense of safety, e.g. by fighting or running away from something threatening (including the facilitator and the group task). Bion argued that these processes (or dynamics) are mostly unconscious but if noticed by a facilitator or therapist they can be managed and perhaps understood by the group, allowing the group to get back on course and operate again in 'work group mode'.

Psychology in the Real World groups are not therapy groups. Psychoanalytic groups such as Bion's, with very little structure and minimal overt guidance or involvement from the therapist apart from whole-group interpretations of what are considered to be unconscious processes, often induce anxiety states in participants that lead members to behave in odd ways that result in the group going into one of the basic assumption states. This makes sense if the members have come together to learn about such processes. However, members of *Psychology in the Real World* groups come together for different purposes, and whilst learning something about group processes may be of interest and relevance, it is not one of the main individual or group aims. As such, facilitators try to keep the group on task as much as possible and try and manage group dynamics that might take the group off course. Bion's framework regarding what pulls groups out of work-group mode can be helpful to hold in mind regarding this. As facilitators, for example, we try to:

- Help members retain their sense of individuality whilst accepting some constraints on this during the group sessions. Having a time-limited group helps – it can be perceived as a group of individuals collectively engaging in a project rather than acquiring membership of an ongoing group where membership confers some kind of permanent stamp. We encourage members to speak of and accept their ambivalence about being in the group, and try to create a culture where the success of the group is viewed as being dependent on the actions of all of us (rather than primarily on the actions of the group facilitators).

- Avoid hidden agendas and help members attain and retain clarity about their individual aims and the collective group aims. Groups where people do not know why they are meeting quickly fall victim of basic assumption states; indeed, it is not clear whether such groups can ever operate in work-group mode.

- Limit the amount of time a group might operate in terms of basic assumption functioning. For example, we try to manage dependency by emphasising and reinforcing the need for the group to generate material to be discussed and analysed by the group as a whole. We are realistic about what is achievable in order to manage over-the-top expectations that can lead to pairing. We try and reduce fight-flight dynamics by monitoring and managing the group's emotional temperature, and by trying to avoid within-group splitting (e.g. by welcoming difference) and inviting reflections on between-group splitting (e.g. *four legs good, two legs bad* – our group good, other groups bad).

Of course, this is not always successful. A session on shame went badly after we tried to get people to explore their own experiences of shame – in hindsight something that was too ambitious in a group that was still finding its way in terms of safety and personal disclosure. The emotional temperature in the group became too great, people went into fight-flight mode, the task was not accomplished and less threatening attempts to explore shame in that session induced only minimal participation. The facilitators were left with profound feelings of incompetence (and shame) as the group searched for members that would rescue it from its ordeal. It took a couple of sessions to recover healthier group norms and dynamics that involved people sharing personal experiences in ways that they could manage, and to get into work group mode where we all were on task trying to understand ourselves and others.

32

An overarching model of groupwork that incorporates individual and social change

The underpinning philosophy of the project is to see the whole programme of intervention as a dynamic movement from private symptom to public action which engages both the professional and the client/patient alike.

    Sue Holland

Figure 12 is my adaptation of a model first proposed by Sue Holland in the 1990s to describe various interventions that characterised a form of social action therapy that she developed whilst living and working on the White City estate in London. I have adapted it so that it might provide an overarching way of conceptualising various types of groupwork. It incorporates dimensions relating to whether:

- the focus of the group is primarily on individual people or on environments and wider social systems

- the focus of the group is primarily on bringing about some kind of change or is on helping people gain greater understanding of something.

Any group in the voluntary or statutory sectors could be placed in one of the quadrants; some may bridge several. For example, 'skills for ills' groups would mostly be conceptualised as relating to Quadrant 1 as they are aimed at equipping group members with strategies to overcome or bear distressing physical experiences; anxiety management and cognitive therapy for depression would be examples of these types of groups.

Many people who have come on *Psychology in the Real World* ventures have given testimony to how helpful such groups have been to them. Personally, I do not feel that most people's problems and experiences can be categorised as 'ills' or as defined mental illnesses in the way that the *Diagnostic and Statistical Manual of Mental Disorders* (*DSM*) purports to set out. For example, people do not seem to solely experience symptoms of depression without symptoms of other mental illnesses. In my experience, people usually describe a wide range of difficulties that do not cluster in the ways psychiatric diagnoses set out but for each individual combine in a set of unique ways. Because of this, I do not facilitate skills for ills groups and prefer to offer groups in Quadrant 1 that are solely conceptualised as skills groups. For example, I recently co-facilitated a group that taught mindfulness skills to a wide range of people irrespective of their presenting problems (or 'ills'). Groupwork that comes under the rubric of *Psychology in the Real World*, however, is pitched in the other three quadrants.

Quadrant 2 positions participants as people rather than patients (or sufferers) and groups that typify this quadrant tend to be aimed at helping individual group members gain understandings of the root causes of their difficulties. Such groups tend to focus on participants' individual histories, traumas, family experiences, current stressors and so on. They are focused on generating insights and making difficult and confusing experiences meaningful. Psychotherapy or narrative therapy

MAIN FOCUS

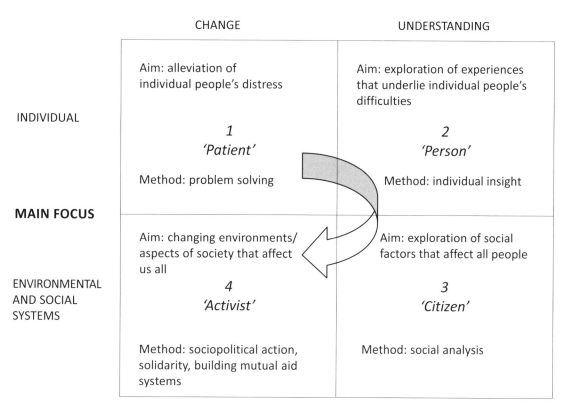

Fig. 12   **A model of groupwork incorporating individual and social change (adapted from Holland, 1992)**

groups are good examples of groups that come into this quadrant as they are primarily aimed at helping people understand their unique history in terms of how that has shaped them and affected the ways that they interpret the world. Most sessions in *Understanding Ourselves and Others*, *The Black Dog* and *The Writing Group* fit this quadrant. However, all these groups also emphasise the importance of understanding others as well as ourselves, and in this sense this leads them to overlap with Quadrant 3.

Groups in Quadrant 3 are more focused on the world outside individual experience, for example, concentrating on the environments we live and work in. They often involve reflection on the ways that aspects of society, such as

inequality and racism, impact on us and others. People in these groups may come to see themselves more as citizens than isolated individuals and, as well as reflecting on social factors that affect us all, groups in this quadrant often enable members to provide each other with a sense of shared experience. The seminar parts of each *Toxic Mental Environments* session encapsulate this type of group. *Thinking about Medication* and *Out of the Box* sessions start off with discussions that fit Quadrant 2 but gradually move into shared understandings of wider social structures (Quadrant 3). For example, participants frequently discuss personal experiences that might be due to adverse drug reactions rather than other factors, discuss how mental health professionals have not given sufficient emphasis (in their opinion) to such reactions, and go on to critique the impacts of business practices and the profit motive on pharmaceutical company research and the modern NHS, including analysis of how this filters down to patient–mental health professional encounters.

Quadrant 3 type groups often generate strong feelings of solidarity and lead people to contemplate ways of improving social systems. The group experience helps members recognise the importance of peer support. Quadrant 4 groups actively encourage people to act on these feelings and set up mutual aid systems. The group members themselves might provide this, or might set up support and political action groups outside the running of the group or after it ends. In Quadrant 4 groups, people can be envisaged as activists. The focus is on the world beyond that of personal experience – the socio-political rather than individual world. The second part of each *Toxic Mental Environments* session, which asks people to think about and start to plan how to bring about changes in environments people feel are toxic to their own and others' wellbeing, provides an example of groupwork that is representative of Quadrant 4. Other examples include members of *Psychology in the Real World* groups being involved in and independently setting up projects aimed at bringing about changes that they hope will improve the lives of others, e.g. by lobbying drug companies; helping people in other areas set up medication groups; improving the condition of the path and campaigning to increase access and prevent building development on the *Walk and Talk* route; developing an eco-project; organising mutual aid systems (e.g. informal groups that run independently of any helping agency); and designing and running *Time to Change* projects aimed at combating stigma in and outside

mental health services.

The model in Fig. 12 does not claim that groupwork that fits one quadrant is better or more effective than groupwork representative of any other. Rather, it provides a map for groupworkers in terms of the range and scope of various groups that can be set up. A disproportionate amount of state-funded mental health groupwork lies in Quadrant 1. In all aspects of healthcare, resources spent on treatment vastly outweigh those spent on prevention or social change, despite the history of success of many public health interventions (e.g. resources spent on ensuring clean water is much more effective than individually treating people for diseases caused by dirty water). Prevention strategies and public healthcare interventions aimed at the causes rather than impacts of distress are in the public interest. However, it can be argued that they are not in the interests of many multinational companies who make enormous profits whilst damaging our psychological and physical environments *and* make enormous profits selling us cures for the impacts of that damage.

Fig. 12 also clarifies that different people might benefit from different types of groups, and some people may benefit from different types of groups at different times of their life. Sometimes people are so crushed and distressed by their life experiences that they might need Quadrant 1 interventions before being able to fully engage in and contribute to groupwork that is representative of the other quadrants. In Sue Holland's original model, interventions that were relevant to Quadrant 1 included ten weeks of focused individual psychotherapy to help people gain some relief from their distress. Similarly, I provide relatively short-term one-to-one interventions for people referred to the CMHT where I am based (these people also have support from their care coordinator and sometimes other people). As well as being aimed at bringing about some relief from distress, these individual sessions offer opportunities for people to make links between their current problems and past and present experiences. Groupwork of any kind rarely enables people to talk in great depth and detail about intensely personal, often abusive experiences with someone whose express purpose is to help them make sense of how these experiences might have shaped them. Some people who engage in one-to-one work with myself later join *Psychology in the Real World* groups. Groups offer people opportunities to share insights they have come to about the impacts on them of hurtful experiences and chances to try out different ways of relating to people or managing reactions and emotions brought up in interactions with people. This is what therapists call 'working through' and community-based groups can provide far richer environments for people to do this than one-to-one therapy.

My experiences have led me to conclude that the need for Quadrant 1 interventions (whether individual or group based) does not relate particularly to psychiatric diagnosis. People with diagnoses of manic depression, schizophrenia, psychotic illness and personality disorder have contributed to and been key members of *Psychology in the Real World* groups operating in Quadrants 2, 3 and 4. In evaluations of these groups, such people have indicated that they attained great benefit from being treated as and taking the roles of 'person', 'citizen' and 'activist' compared to the normal role they are positioned in of 'patient' or 'sufferer'. People with such diagnoses have also been involved in helping organise and facilitate such groups. A more important factor than diagnosis has been the level of current distress and instability in people's lives and their ability to manage this whilst participating in the group.

Sometimes *Psychology in the Real World* experiences move from Quadrant 1 through 2

and 3 to Quadrant 4. For example, one *Black Dog* participant remarked on finding some relief in talking about being depressed with other people whom (she was surprised to discover) really listened to her. In a later session the group explored the impacts of experiences of loss on people and, when another group member spoke of feelings experienced after the death of his wife, she went on to make a link between her own experiences of loss and the sense of emptiness and profound sadness that she had previously labelled depression (the group had moved to Quadrant 2 type analysis). The discussion later became more Quadrant 3 as the group critiqued 20th century Britain in terms of cultures that prevent people from grieving in ways that might be helpful to them. A couple of years later this group member contacted me after the death of another member of her family as she wanted help to publicise a small group that she had set up that met monthly at a local café, where 'anyone can come along and have a cup of coffee with some friendly people who have also experienced bereavement'. This group, an example of Quadrant 4 type groups, continues to meet.

The power horizon

Members of *Psychology in the Real World* groups have found the power horizon diagram in Fig. 13, overleaf, helpful as it shines light on (i) why we are all drawn to focusing on changing aspects of ourselves as individuals (rather than the world we inhabit) and (ii) why personal change is often much more difficult than we (or our therapists) envisage. The power horizon positions aspects of our society and culture that have great influence on us far away from us in terms of the personal contact we have with people who shape and influence these institutions and bodies. For example, a mere 26 companies own 50% of all media in America (the 'land of the free'). As ordinary citizens we do not like to think that the

Fig. 13   The Power Horizon (from Smail, 2005)

media shape what we think, feel and do but owners of those 26 companies do not share that view. As Adam Curtis in *The Century of the Self* illustrates, there is a long history in modern societies of powerful people and organisations using psychology (rather than brute force) to influence and control the majority of us. It can be argued that Edward Bernays has been even more influential than his uncle Sigmund Freud as, in the early part of the 20th century, he successfully pioneered the application of psychoanalytic theories to the manipulation and unconscious influence of large groups and, through use of the mass media, of whole societies. In doing so he can be said to have fathered the public relations industry, provided Goebbels with many of his ideas on state control, and shaped current practices of mass marketing and advertising which are not only used by business to sell us goods but, Curtis argues, are operated by politicians and elites in modern-day society to 'engineer consent'.

As ordinary citizens we have very little influence over the memes projected into us by the media. But such memes perhaps shape the ways we think and react to our world more than we like to think. Because such influences are so distal we tend to not have them in mind when trying to understand our personal everyday experiences. What burn brightest for us are our own emotional experiences, our thoughts and our bodily sensations. These are our lived experience. The ever-burgeoning therapy industry (of which clinical psychology is increasingly a part) offers various one-to-one interventions aimed at modifying our reactions rather than modifying our environments. The key shapers of the environments we experience – the papers and books we read, the programmes we watch on TV, the types of neighbourhoods (and wider society) we live in, the systems we work in – and the dominating explanations 'out there' to draw upon when we try and understand and cope with personal and social difficulties have what David Smail calls *the impress of power* running through them. David has warned that whilst clinical psychologists, and other people committed to helping people in distress, obviously need to pay close attention to people's individual experience, when looking at the causes of their troubling feelings and thoughts clinicians need to be careful not to be drawn into purely focusing on the individual. They ought to look beyond people's thoughts and feelings to other parts of the power horizon when trying to help people understand why they are troubled, but this is not easy as individual experience burns so powerfully in us (making us attend to it) and organisations that are doing well out of the current social system have an interest in making such analysis difficult. Therapists increasingly seem to be telling us that aspects of the power horizon outside individual experience are factors outside our control – 'we have to focus on ourselves as this is what we can change' – but changing our thoughts, feelings and levels of self-esteem may not be that easy when we are exposed to so many messages every day telling us contrary things to those our therapists would like us to hold in mind.

One way we have tried to illustrate some of these ideas and bring them up for discussion in *Psychology in the Real World* groups is by using a different form of laddering from that used in cognitive therapy. Cognitive therapists start with one thought and get people to discover links in the ladder until they arrive at an underlying, often unconscious, internal core belief that they hold about themselves. We try and take the ladder outwards rather than inwards, taking the analysis to outer regions of the power horizon, to things people might be unconscious of in a different way from what therapists usually mean. For example, as an asthmatic I am aware that, whilst wheezing, my attention is drawn to my malfunctioning lungs, and I inevitably focus on these when considering the causes of (and potential treatments for) my problem. But by doing so I neglect the impacts of things that are more distant from me, such as pollution caused by the car and oil industries, and the fact that our government allows multinational companies to pollute our air with their products without having to pay for the costs of this or be held responsible for the death and damage this causes.

Psychology in the Real World groups also utilise social formulations: see Chapter 35 and the spoof women's magazine *Image* on www.shropsych.org/image.pdf that asks *Why are so many people unhappy with the way they look?* This was heavily influenced by *Adbusters: Journal of the Mental Environment* and was co-designed by Tina Jarvis who wanted to highlight the damaging impacts of the fashion, magazine and cosmetics industries on people's self-image.

Psychology in the Real World groups thus create space to explore the roots of our experiences and to move between explanations that incorporate both proximal and distal influences on us. For example, a member may go from the centre of the power horizon (or Quadrant 1 in Fig. 12, p. 137) in terms of understanding depression: *There is something wrong with me – with my brain biochemicals or cognitions*; to aspects of the power horizon within 'touching range' of themselves (or Quadrant 2): *I am suffering as a result of suddenly being made redundant – Martin Seligman's research on learned helplessness fits my experience as unpredictable, hurtful life events from which we cannot escape induce depression*; to the more outer regions of the power horizon (or Quadrant 3): *Whose interest is served by the sudden closing down of factories and the moving of most manufacturing jobs to parts of the world where people are paid low wages with few workers' rights? Who pays for the damage such decisions inflict on people?* It is very difficult to engage in such analyses alone – one of the advantages of *Psychology in the Real World* ventures is that people with a great divergence of opinion and experience are often brought together. This enables a 'democratisation of the truth' as previous chapters have hopefully revealed. It enables, often in quite modest ways compared to some of the examples referred to in Watkins and Shulman's book *Toward Psychologies of Liberation,* 'psychic spaces' to be opened up where we can collectively critique a great range of aspects of the world we inhabit. Discussions in the groups have included, for example, references to the malevolent impacts of poverty, inequality and powerlessness; decision making lying within the remit of the few rather than the many; and the medicalisation of psychosocial insults. It often seems very difficult to change such distal factors that are embedded in our society. But we perhaps need to spend more time, energy and resources on this rather than trying (sometimes valiantly, sometimes vainly) to change our personal reactions to life events that we experience ultimately because of some of the decisions made by organisations and people at the outer reaches of our power horizon. Bringing people together is crucial: as Watkins and Shulman put it: *the liberation of psychic space goes hand in hand with the creation of social spaces that support the development of critical consciousness, the strengthening of dialogue, and the nurturing of imaginative practices of representing history and conceiving the future.*

The enormity of the challenge of bringing about radical change in embedded aspects of our culture and society can overwhelm us and we sometimes need to 'think small' (see Chapter 34), do what we can at any one moment and seek out allies. When I began critiquing pharmaceutical company research over 20 years ago the only people interested were people taking psychiatric drugs (whose experiences had

inspired the critiques). Very few psychologists, even though we are trained in research methodology, seemed to see this as relevant. At times I felt that bringing this up in team meetings, giving lectures, publishing research and running groups that explore the whole power horizon regarding medication was a pointless exercise next to the wealth, power and sophisticated marketing machine of the pharmaceutical industry. But 20 years on things seem to be changing. Service survivor activist Olive Bucknall said to me: 'When it came to psychiatric drugs, in the past we were told nothing and we knew nothing.' But nowadays information is readily available and informed consent is seen as a core part of services that provide medication; conferences which service users attend alongside professionals are full of people who, whilst able to recognise the benefits of medication, are informed and feel confident enough to talk about damaging aspects of these drugs and how the discourse regarding drugs has not given sufficient credence to their toxicity; newspapers print stories of pharmaceutical industry cover-ups akin to those of the tobacco industry; and websites buzz with people exchanging personal experiences whilst campaigning for change – see the Scroxat User Group (www.seroxatusergroup.co.uk) and APRIL (Adverse Psychiatric Reactions Information Links, www.april.org.uk) to name but two. A small number of initially isolated people speaking out about such issues now form part of a loosely connected group that, with powerful allies in the media as well as professional and voluntary sector organisations (such as MIND), have become a formidable force for change in this area.

SECTION 7

Toxic Mental Environments

33

Toxic Mental Environments

David Webster

The handout below was written for people attending the first session of the *Toxic Mental Environments* course in 2006 and for people who did not attend the first session but expressed an interest in coming to subsequent ones. It was written to provoke thought and debate. It is of its time and reflects a manic period a couple of years before the onset of a worldwide economic recession. Clearly any similar course in the future might reflect different socio-economic circumstances and take up different themes as well as include more up-to-date information (such as Wilkinson and Pickett's *The Spirit Level*). The handout has been included here as it gives a flavour of what the course was like as well as providing an example of how one can tailor-make handouts that might be of interest to people who come on courses and others (it has been available to download from www.shropsych.org and was published in *Clinical Psychology Forum, 164* thus enabling a wider group than those who came on the course to engage in debates on its themes):

Toxic Mental Environments

What do we mean by 'toxic mental environments'?

The concept of toxic mental environments has been outlined by Kalle Lasn and others, principally through *Adbusters: Journal of the Mental Environment*: Thirty years ago, people became worried that the physical environment was becoming toxic and making people sick. This anxiety led to the green movement. In the West (but also increasingly globally) we have been able to consume enormous amounts of consumer goods which we were led to believe would make our lives easier and happier, but we live in a time when people are experiencing great levels of dis-ease, describe themselves increasingly as stressed, are diagnosed with mood disorders and mental health problems on unprecedented scales, and are prescribed ever-increasing amounts of psychiatric drugs. Business cultures and the $450 billion a year advertising industry appear to have infiltrated everything, and perhaps infect our thinking and behaviour in ways that human beings might not have evolved to cope with. We are all saturated with advertising stimuli (thousands per day) which continually fight for our attention. The media is owned by a small number of people with agendas to get us think in ways that make corporate profits soar but may not be good for us as human beings. Pharmaceutical companies make billions of pounds selling products that purport to cure mental health problems but the numbers of people being treated for so-called mental illnesses continues to rise and increasing numbers of people report the drugs are making them ill. Is it time to clean up our mental as well as physical environment?

What is going on...?

... 1905: 1 in 100 Americans experienced depression by the age of 75; a century later, 1 in 13 Americans experienced depression in the past year.

... Mexicans have a greater risk of developing mental health problems the longer they live in the USA – being exposed to a place that hundreds of thousands of people are trying to emigrate to appears to be making them ill.

... In the UK Richard Layard reported to Government in 2005 that 16% of working age adults have a mental illness, half of them a serious mental illness. Cost to society: £22 billion.

... In 'developing' countries GDP, incomes, infrastructure, Western health care, Western style education, and access to global media are increasing, as are addictions, suicides and mental health problems. WHO studies indicate that diagnoses of schizophrenia have increased by 45% since 1985 in 'developing' countries. Perhaps these countries are developing in ways that are hazardous to their mental health?

... WHO predicts depression will become the second most common disabling disorder in the world (after heart disease) by 2020.

Can these trends be explained by the dominant theories in late 20th and early 21st century psychiatry ... faulty brain chemistry and genetics? Or are there alternative explanations?

The *Psychology in the Real World: Toxic Mental Environments* **Course**, in 4 parts (can be accessed together or people can come to one or some of the sessions) aims to explore modern environments that might be toxic for us:

1st Feb 10.00AM – 1.00PM
Toxic mental environments and the destructive effects of television and a speeded-up society

10th May 10.00AM – 1.00PM
Making and breaking children's lives (with Craig Newnes)

2nd August 10.00AM – 1.00PM
Everybody must get stoned: why so many people are taking psychiatric and other mood and mind altering drugs, and using food in response to toxic environments

1st November 2006 10.00AM – 1.00PM
Creating healthier work and community environments (with Penny Priest)

All sessions are free, numbers limited to 20. Please book by phoning The Gateway.

The course looks at factors which rarely get mentioned in psychology and psychiatry textbooks, such as poverty. In Western society there is considerable evidence that poor people suffer disproportionately in terms of mental and physical health problems. In short, the people sometimes disparagingly called the *losers* in society lose. But it also increasingly appears that the *winners* lose too.

Richard Wilkinson has looked at different countries in terms of health and social problems and found that countries with the greatest disparities in incomes have the greatest health and social problems, for example, in terms of the proportion of people committing violence, being imprisoned and suffering mental and physical health problems (such as anxiety, obesity and heart attacks). Interestingly it appears that all people in such countries suffer, not just those on the lowest incomes. On the face of this evidence, inequality seems to be bad for us. Oliver James cites evidence that affluent, young British women are increasingly prone to anxiety, depression and eating disorders, with a rise from 6% to 18% suffering from 'serious mental illness' since 1987. What is causing this, given the fact that there appears to be less overt sexism and greater opportunities for young women in the 21st century compared to previous eras?

There is evidence to indicate that people with very materialist values feel neither secure nor good about themselves, have fewer intimate relationships, feel little control over their lives, never feel satisfied and are always looking to the next promotion or purchase rather than enjoying what they have (see Gregg Easterbrook's *The Progress Paradox*). Materialist values are reinforced, sometimes lauded, and are certainly conditioned into us, but is it possible that the more we absorb them the more psychological problems we experience?

Richard Wilkinson's analysis indicates that Western countries with higher rates of inequality of income and wealth also have less social capital – less social interconnectedness between people. Might too little of our contact with others be social (in the natural, intimate sense of the word)? Have we evolved to be suited to a culture very different from our own?

Since 1945 shopping has gone from largely being seen as a chore to being listed as people's favourite hobby. A study in 1997 indicated 57% of women and 42% of men were more interested in the idea of an unlimited shopping spree than the idea of unlimited sex. Compulsive Shopping Disorder is now diagnosed by psychiatrists with a prevalence estimated at 2–8% of people in the 'First World'. It can be successfully treated with psychiatric drugs as shown by a research study sponsored by a pharmaceutical company.

Is it possible that our society first makes us mentally sick and then sells us the cures for such sickness?

Life events and depression ...

There is a large body of evidence regarding recent adverse life events as factors in depression (e.g. Paykel et al, 1969: people diagnosed as depressed reported three times as many harmful life events in the period prior to their depressive episode than non-depressed people). These include redundancy, bereavement, trauma, imprisonment of self or a close family member, debt, loss of home, and separation from or loss of a confidant. Long-term risk factors include abuse and neglect in childhood, death of a mother during childhood, social isolation and loneliness, and suffering prejudice and poverty. Research of this kind is no longer state funded in the USA (since Reagan and the 'decade of the brain') or referred to very much in psychology and psychiatry textbooks.

Why is there a reluctance to look outside ourselves and our individual bodies to our environment when trying to explain human distress?

David Smail refers to the *power horizon* and how things that we notice tend to be things closest to us, e.g. our emotional and physical reactions and people we are in close contact with. Factors that might be more important are less noticed as they are more distant from us, and as a result are less in conscious awareness. Might there be some people and groups in society that share an interest in mystifying us and hindering our attempts to identify the causes (and causes of causes) of our problems, especially when such insights do not suit their interests?

On our speeded up society ...

Exercise: How did you wash your face this morning?

Exercise: How much coffee, tea and high-sugar/high-energy drinks do you have per day?

Exercise: What are you like in queues?

Exercise: What are you like when using a computer that is old and slow?

Exercise: What percentage of books that you buy or start do you finish?

Exercise: How are you affected by there being over 1,000,000 different products in each supermarket store?

Do the exercises indicate you are being affected by our speeded-up society? Are you one of the one in three adults in Britain who say they 'almost always feel rushed'?

Children (and many adults) have learned to multitask – to do homework with the TV on, with music in the background or through headphones, whilst texting or engaging in mobile phone conversations and eating supper. It is amazing, but is it good for people? How might this relate to the rapid rise in children diagnosed with ADHD (Attention Deficit Hyperactivity Disorder)? What is happening to children's brains? Grace Jackson MD, in *Making and Breaking Children's Lives*, cites evidence that such activities are creating structural changes in children's developing brains that might make activities with low sensory input – such as being still or reading – more difficult for children.

We are 'wired' – we are connected to mobile phones, computers, the Internet, interactive TV and video games at home, outside the home, even in cars. But are we 'wired up' for this? Haven't our bodies evolved to go at a slower pace and to spend considerable time periods without much happening?

Richard DeGrandpre believes that human consciousness is being transformed – we have developed a tolerance of speed and bombardment of sensory input but have also become hooked on speed. This might explain the rises in intake of stimulant drugs: caffeine, high energy drinks and foods, cocaine, ecstasy, Ritalin, SSRIs. Also the fact that people spend increasing amounts of time in high sensory environments (e.g. nightclubs, watching TV and playing video games). Low stimulation environments can induce boredom, restlessness, fidgeting, irritation, anxiety, impulsiveness and a need for movement (as a response to and need to bump-up the stimulation). Many children in low stimulation environments (e.g. having to sit still and listen to a teacher talk) cannot manage and may be on the way to being diagnosed with ADHD.

Diane Ackerman has written on how our senses crave novelty. Any change alerts them, which involves a signal being sent to the brain. If there is no change, no novelty, they doze and register very little. A constant state, even of excitement, will eventually trigger very little and be experienced as fading into the background, or when noticed be experienced as tedious, because our senses have evolved to report only changes.

We are being saturated with advertising stimuli which continually fight for our attention. Advertisers spend millions of pounds (including monitoring brain activity) learning how to do this. Men get to read adverts whilst they pee. We have learned how to shut it out but perhaps in doing so we induce in ourselves states akin to depersonalisation or dissociation? Shopping malls bombard us with light, products and mood music. Perhaps this attracts people hooked on our speeded-up society but overwhelms others, who get labelled agoraphobic or are said to suffer panic attacks?

On TV …

The introduction of television into parts of the world where there had previously been no TV has been linked to rises in individual and social problems. Burke and Lotus' critique of TV *Get a Life!* describes Ladakh in the Himalayas, where a very rich culture based on song and dance, which encompassed people creating individual variations of shared songs, became replaced with a culture dominated by the majority of people staying in watching celebrities sing on television. People came to feel inadequate as they tried to replicate the standardised versions of popular songs. Are Western culture and Western problems being exported straight into people's heads?

Advertisers are very aware of what psychologists call classical conditioning: products are paired with beauty, success in business, wealth and success in getting sex. These things have to be perceived as desirable in order that they can be encoded in one image or a 15-second commercial. We are exposed to this message millions of times in our lives. There is often a rational bit of us that knows this is ridiculous, but conditioning works beyond the rational and affects our behaviour. Our brightest psychologists have gone into advertising, not mental health work.

Might TV be warping our view of the world? American television shows 7.5 acts of violence per hour. Might this be connected to people's paranoia and fears about going out, even when they are members of groups with a very low risk of violent assault whilst out of their homes, such as elderly people? Perhaps modern capitalism benefits most from having people at home watching TV/adverts, occasionally reading magazines that reinforce the same messages, and going out only to earn or spend money, on products we have been conditioned to 'need'?

Evolutionary psychology suggests that we are wired up to make comparisons between ourselves and others in our pack. But now we are comparing ourselves against thousands (not dozens) of people that we 'know'. Oliver James has described this in *Britain on the Couch*. We compare ourselves against the rich and successful and the 'celebs' (success now defined as having been on TV). We have constant access to the beautiful and the made beautiful (through cosmetics and surgery and doctored images). We are tricked into thinking we know these people but only have access to their made-up lives (PR people control 'real life' interviews with 'the stars'). James cites research evidence to show we rate the attractiveness of real people (including our partners) lower after exposure to images of TV 'beautiful people', and our mood lowers when exposed to TV 'beautiful people' of the same gender as us.

Exercise: Monitor the time each day you spend in high vs low intensity activities (TV is not low intensity as it bombards our senses).
   Question the thoughts that pop into your head when engaged in slow/low intensity activities (e.g. 'Life is passing me by;' 'I should be …') Where did such ideas come from?

Exercise: List what gives you 'quality of life' and monitor how much time you spend doing those things.

What kinds of activities are people engaged in when they experience sustained periods of contentment? Mihaly Csikszentmihalyi has conducted over 20 years' research into this question and found that these turn out not to be activities characteristic of passive lives of ease and physical comfort (the idea of retirement after most of our life has been spent in physically hard, tedious or stressful labour). Nor are they high sensory input activities that we engage in on a solitary or semi-solitary basis. What brings sustained periods of contentment is 'deep engrossment through involvement in meaningful and challenging projects'.

Have we even discovered which projects each of us might find meaningful, engrossing, captivating and challenging? In the short time we have on this planet, how much time are we going to spend doing these activities?

If you are interested in discussing some of these themes, engaging in open debate, thinking creatively about the environments in which we live and thinking about how to change these in some ways (in Kalle Lasn's words 'clean up our mental environment like we recognise the need to clean up our physical environment') then come along and be part of the *Toxic Mental Environments* course.

34

Bringing about environmental and social change

The question for clinical psychologists and other 'psy' workers is: Do we help to sedate or to activate?

Sue Holland

As the handout in the previous chapter indicates, *Toxic Mental Environments* was more narrow and perhaps more polemical in its themes than most other *Psychology in the Real World* ventures. It not only involved the group putting their minds together to generate formulations (or analyses) of people and the environments they inhabit, but also involved express encouragement to change aspects of environments that people felt were unhealthy. Compared to other *Psychology in the Real World* courses it could be argued that the sessions, in terms of contributions from the facilitators, did not provide a balanced view – the intention to some extent was to stir people up and provide a balancing rather than balanced view, as we hoped to bring the focus of participants' attention to the environment and go beyond the world of individual experience. As such, it broke some of the underlying assumptions of collaborative conversation and Bohm Dialogue (see Chapter 4) as the facilitators did have a purpose over and above that of bringing people together to explore and understand things. It more closely reflected Paulo Freire's belief that education cannot be a neutral process – it either conditions people to accept the status quo or helps them critique the conditions of their life in a way that enables people to participate in the transformation of their world.

Each session followed a similar format and involved:

1. A round robin where people introduced themselves and were encouraged to say anything that came into their minds that was triggered by the day's topic.

2. A usually interactive presentation from myself and invited others that included a critique of Britain and other countries in terms of environments that we felt can have detrimental effects on people's psychological wellbeing.

3. A substantial period for people to express agreement and disagreement with our ideas, express and debate their own ideas, in the whole group and in small groups where appropriate.

4. A break to permit more informal conversation and for people to make connections and network with each other.

5. A final part where people could individually and collectively think through and make plans about how to bring about some changes in their local environments (home, street, school, workplace, town, etc).

When being helped and encouraged to think about changing environments most people feel overwhelmed by the task and often feel quite powerless to bring about change. In such situations we encourage people to *Think Small* and use the overheads shown in Boxes 11 and 12.

Box 11   On Smallness

On Smallness

1. Small is beautiful
2. Small is effective
3. Small is tolerable
4. Small is manageable
5. Small is knowable
6. Small is usual

The bottom line … Small is normalising

From Mosher and Burti's *Community Mental Health*

Box 12   Think Small

What next? *Think Small …*

How can you …
- Spend less time in toxic mental environments and more time in healthy mental environments?
- Help other people do this?
- Reduce environmental toxicity for yourself and others?
- Set up and help others set up a mentally healthy environment?
- Work collaboratively towards changing embedded toxic elements in our society?

'On smallness' often leads to discussions about the advantages small projects can have over large ones. It is also aimed at helping people counteract the negative impacts of feeling helpless triggered by the fact that some social problems seem overwhelming in magnitude. For example, there is considerable evidence that inequality is psychologically and physically unhealthy for people in all strata in society, with people in poverty suffering the most (see Lynne Friedli's WHO report), but how do you bring about change in such an ingrained aspect of society? During *Toxic Mental Environments* people raised the possibility that it suits certain vested interests to ensure that vast numbers of people feel unable to change the status quo. Learned helplessness does ensue when people struggle to change inequitable systems without success. But there is also mystification. When people think of the anti-war protests about Vietnam they tend to envisage students and then the wider population protesting in ever-increasing numbers until the American government pulled out. But if you listen to accounts from people involved in the protests from their inception it is clear that for many years only a small number of people protested, these people were mostly met with indifference and hostility, even on university campuses, and it took years of commitment and resilience to keep protesting until the movement started to grow and eventually snowball. *Mighty oaks from little acorns grow*, but it does take time, and for every acorn that grows into a powerful tree hundreds have a different but not necessarily unimportant history. As the quote at the beginning of this book from Margaret Mead sets out: 'We should never doubt that a small group of thoughtful, committed citizens can change the world; indeed, it is the only thing that ever does.'

Reflections on the *Toxic Mental Environments* course

The task of community clinical psychology is to help people:

1. *Understand the connection between the social and economic reality of their lives and their states of health and wellbeing*
2. *Join with others with similar realities to give voice to this understanding*
3. *Engage in collective action to change these realities.*

Jim Orford (from 'Have we a theory of community psychology?' *Clinical Psychology Forum, 122*)

Most *Psychology in the Real World* ventures have run weekly or fortnightly whereas *Toxic Mental Environments* sessions occurred at three-monthly intervals. It was hoped that a core group of people would come to all four sessions, link up and get engaged in projects outside the sessions. Places were booked by directly contacting the venue and, unbeknown to me, people were prevented from booking more than two sessions ahead. Demand for places was high and once advertised each session was quickly booked up. This resulted in it being more like four one-off sessions and the hoped for continuity did not arise. There are advantages in having a community venue handle the booking arrangements in terms of how the enterprise is experienced (e.g. not as a mental health service but as a community venture) but on this occasion their policies about not allowing sessions to be booked more than 6 months in advance mitigated against some of the aims of the project being met. For data protection reasons I have been unable to access the addresses of people who came along, which has hindered the collection of follow-up data and the creation of a network of activists resulting from the sessions. In hindsight, as a set of 'one-offs' it would have been better to have a full day on each area rather than the half-day sessions that took place. Despite this, however, the series concept, with a couple of months between each meeting for people to work on their ideas, still remains an attractive idea.

The importance of having a mixed group was very apparent during *Toxic Mental Environments*. For example, participants with expertise in a variety of work environments – union reps, 'creatives' in advertising, people who had experienced change in privatised industries, workers in catering and the helping professions – were able to make informed contributions to our attempts to collectively analyse the impacts of aspects of these industries on our mental environment. People spoke eloquently about their current and past work, home and community environments, identifying aspects that were beneficial or toxic to their wellbeing. It is interesting to ask where the mental illnesses – the schizophrenia, the manic depression, the personality disorders and psychoses – were during these discussions? From my involvement with the CMHT I knew that some attendees had attracted these kinds of labels but I would defy any person sitting in on the sessions to have been able to distinguish the people with these diagnoses from the participants who had not accessed mental health services. The diversity of backgrounds of participants and fact that we were able to draw upon experiences beyond those that related to mental distress and mental health service involvement helped ensure that the social formulations and debates we engaged in were rich and broad as well as rooted in people's lived experiences.

In hindsight, having 20 people per session had some disadvantages. Doing a round robin took too long and the matrix could not be adequately established (especially as there was little consistency of attendance over the four sessions). In effectively operating as a series of one-off events it did not immediately lead to community activism in the way I had hoped. Nevertheless, the three main aims of clinical community psychology referred to by Jim Orford were apparently met. People involved in mental health services attended as people interested in the topics (rather than as the mentally ill attending for treatment) and brought as wide a breadth of expertise as any other attendee. Group members collectively analysed aspects of environments that they felt were harmful to psychological wellbeing. The focus of attention, at least for that period, was shifted from the internal to external, from people as individuals to the communities we inhabit, from the apolitical to the socio-political.

And people identified areas that they wanted to focus on in order to bring about some change in the environments they encountered. It is not possible to know how far people's expressed intentions went as no formal follow-up has been done. However, I have subsequently become aware of some things that were inspired by the course, including:

1. Several people got rid of their televisions and stopped buying magazines that they felt 'polluted their mental space', discussing the reasons for this with other friends and family.

2. Several people have told me that following the course they spent more time with friends and family they feel close to rather than, as one person put it, 'racing around doing lots of things I don't need to do'.

3. One person changed the ways he managed a mental health team so that (i) it was better insulated from directives ordered by higher management that were felt to be detrimental to the staff's wellbeing and ability to practise in ways that met the expressed needs of the people the team was set up to help, and (ii) the team could focus more attention on the service users' community rather than solely providing individual sticking plasters for psychological distress caused by the myriad of psychosocial insults that people living in poverty experience.

4. A pub owner committed to not providing children's meals and drinks that were high in additives and sugar that may contribute to behaviours that lead children to be labelled as suffering Attention Deficit Hyperactivity Disorder (ADHD).

5. The session *Everybody Must Get Stoned* led to people requesting more sessions at the local MIND centre about psychiatric drugs. A project group met to discuss how to do this. Eventually this led to Marese Hudson and I

facilitating a *Thinking about Medication* group (see Section 8), which in turn has helped similar groups to set up around the country.

6. The session *Creating Healthier Work and Social Environments* involved much discussion about the detoxifying effects of being in the countryside and was influential in leading to the setting up of *Walk and Talk* (see Section 10). *Toxic Mental Environments* attendees have been involved as part of a collective that now ensures *Walk and Talk* runs throughout the year.

7. Some attendees campaigned both as staff and service users within the local Mental Health Trust to bring what the Trust does under greater democratic control of the people who use the service (rather than people be passive recipients of care deemed by others to be in their best interests – whether it be determined by paternalistic professionals or management decree). They have championed the payment of service users for their time and expertise, not just in terms of sitting on committees, but also in terms of running groups. They have also spoken out about the need for people to have access to healing environments, which often seem in short supply in mental health settings. For example, the local acute wards are viewed as environmentally toxic by some patients in terms of their physical and psychological environment and the fact that staff can be too busy or too stressed to spend significant amounts of time with them. In fact, the wards can be so short-staffed and dominated by risk-averse policies that patients are unable to access the beautiful grounds that surround the hospital. Ex-members of the groups have raised these and many similar points with staff in appropriate forums.

Box 13   On solidarity

First they came for the communists, and I did not speak out because I was not a communist. Then they came for the trade unionists, and I did not speak out because I was not a trade unionist. Next they came for the Jews, and I did not speak out because I was not a Jew. And then they came for me. And there was no one left to speak out for me.
    Pastor Martin Niemöller

Groups offer people opportunities for solidarity. When trying to bring about change in social systems, or resist changes that are perceived as harmful, people often need allies. People who come together and form a resistance group or movement for progressive change can feel, and in reality are, safer than individuals struggling alone (who are more easily ignored, threatened, bullied, picked off and crushed by people in positions of power).

Jacques-Charles Dupont said: 'Any man aspires to liberty, to equality, but he can not achieve it without the assistance of other men, without fraternity.' In our community-based groupwork we try and enable solidarity without the group entering into states of 'groupthink' or oppressively restricting members' sense of their individual identity.

One way we have tried to foster this is by encouraging people to get involved in single-issue campaigns. There are advantages and disadvantages to such groups. Single-issue campaigns often only involve small numbers of people and can lack the power of numbers that large organisations benefit from in terms of resources and lobbying potential. However, small groups enable collaborative conversations both within the group and with out-groups one might want to influence, have greater democracy and enable greater debate about strategy with less pressure to toe the party line. They also have the advantage of people not feeling branded by being part of a group whose policies and actions in other areas a member may fervently disagree with, and are perhaps more attractive to people who have been disenchanted by party politics. Small, single-issue groups can form alliances with other groups and thus increase their power.

Wolf Wolfensberger has said that if you ally yourself with people assigned to socially devalued groups you will eventually come to be treated in similar ways. Che Guevara said: 'Solidarity involves running the same risks.' If you show solidarity with those diagnosed as mentally ill, people may start to call you mad, irresponsible or out of control; you may increasingly have your version of events ignored, dismissed or seen as not based on the real world; you may be at increased risk of being seen as 'needing to be reined in and put in your place'. All of this at times has happened to me. Fortunately many people, especially people from a service-user background, have shown solidarity with me during these times.

35

Examples of materials used: Social formulations and toxic work environments

Social formulations

The object of the therapy should not be to promote acceptance of the status quo, but to put the distressed person in a position where he/she may freely chose between passivity and action in response to his or her social situation.

    Frantz Fanon

Clinical psychologists are trained to work with formulations – maps of how people's life experiences, presenting problems and coping strategies link together. These tend to focus on individuals, particularly intrapsychic factors and personal history (for example, impacts of childhood experiences on thinking patterns and inner conflicts). In *Toxic Mental Environments* we do not discount these, but direct our attention to aspects of our society that affect us all. For example, in terms of modern (or postmodern) society in the formulation in Fig.14 the group explored many things, including:

- The lack of attachments (intimate relationships) many people experience, and how this might relate to: people regularly moving house (e.g. for jobs, or to move up the property ladder) and the subsequent loss of regular contact with friends and family and loss of a sense of a neighbourhood; the increasing fashion to live alone (this suits societies that want to maximise consumption as every household needs its own furnishings, burglar alarms, etc); what psychologist Denis Trent calls 'pseudo-intimacies' (e.g. via the

Internet) replacing real intimacy – being with people we trust and feel close to.

- An increasing culture of narcissism, where people have been conditioned to continually look inwards, make constant comparisons with others, and search for and tend to their inner self (whereas happiness research suggests contentment may be better found by turning consciousness outwards, thinking about and caring for others and spending money on others rather than oneself).

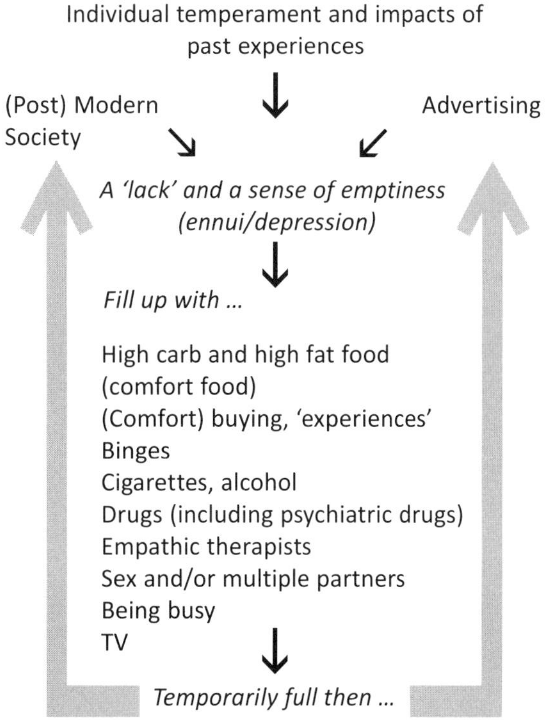

Individual temperament and impacts of
past experiences

(Post) Modern
Society   Advertising

*A 'lack' and a sense of emptiness
(ennui/depression)*

Fill up with ...

High carb and high fat food
(comfort food)
(Comfort) buying, 'experiences'
Binges
Cigarettes, alcohol
Drugs (including psychiatric drugs)
Empathic therapists
Sex and/or multiple partners
Being busy
TV

Temporarily full then ...

Fig. 14   Social formulation of ennui or depression

- The incorporation of highly competitive cultures into every aspect of an increasingly unequal society where 'winning' only produces ephemeral happiness and 'losing' induces more long-lasting depression.

- Employment that provides meaningless or insecure jobs, often on the basis of short-term contracts where commitment to colleagues and joint endeavours is often weakened, and there is little sense of 'we-ness'.

- Impoverished spiritual life and (poorly understood) existential meaninglessness.

- The smothering of desire through the subtle control of what we do and feel by a wide range of state-funded agencies (from teachers to mental health workers).

- An underlying sense that buying non-biodegradable goods that bring only fleeting pleasure might be severely damaging the planet.

- A sense of helplessness and powerlessness to improve the world.

Many of these ideas and observations, generated by group members themselves, match research in these areas. For example, Wilkinson and Pickett revealed that income inequality in Britain is greater than in virtually every other Western country: the top 20% (people on an annual income of £42,000 and above) are seven times richer than the bottom 20%. This is a problem as the greater the income inequality the greater the health and social problems a country experiences. The authors relate this to unequal societies having less 'social capital', i.e. less helpful interconnectedness between members of society. Roseth and colleagues reviewed 148 independent research studies on over 17,000 adolescents conducted over an 80-year period in 11 different countries that compared cooperative with competitive or individualistic behaviour and found cooperativeness was far preferable, for example. leading to higher achievement, more positive peer relationships and better health outcomes. Michel Foucault's *Discipline and Punish* and Augusto Boal's *The Rainbow of Desire* both shine light on how constraints on behaviour in modern Western countries tend to be the 'cops in our head' (which suffocate desire and rebelliousness) rather than external constraints, such as state-sanctioned violence and bodily punishment, that characterised other eras, are still common in many non-Western countries and, although horrific, may not envelop people in the types of depression that characterises 21st century Western countries.

When generating the formulation it was helpful to have a member of the group who had worked in advertising. He gave us insights into how advertisers exploit and indeed create a sense of 'lack' in people that they then promise to fill with their products, and how consumer capitalism needs people to value certain things (e.g. a narrow concept of beauty or cool; success to be signified by money and attractiveness) in order to sell products that are gateways to these desired states (beauty products, clothes, cars, etc). He also helped us analyse TV programmes, including the proportion that could be classed as 'advertainment' compared to the proportion that serve to increase people's awareness and knowledge about the world that they inhabit. All this helped the formulation we generated incorporate a rich analysis of the ways our everyday environment constantly shapes us.

Toxic work environments

The exercise of power in any institutional form – whether economic, political, religious or sexual – brutalises both the wielder of power and the one over whom it is exercised.

Martha Ackelsberg

As Penny Priest and I worked on a literature

review for the session *Creating Healthier Work and Community Environments* (see Box 14, overleaf) we became somewhat despondent. There was all this research data a quarter of a century ago yet, in many ways, things seemed to have got worse since that period. The NHS, for example, with even greater irony regarding mental health services, seems to have become increasingly embroiled in many practices listed in Box 14 that have been shown to make the workforce mentally and physically ill. In short, the published literature on the psychological and physiological damage caused by unhealthy work environments in the 1960s, 70s and 80s appeared to have had little effect. We decided to confine our literature review to the period 1965–1988 for two reasons: (i) these studies are still cited today and little has been subsequently added to the knowledge gleaned from this research, and (ii) we wanted to encourage a debate in the group about why evidence such as this has not led to changes in the workplace. This led to a wide-ranging debate in the group about the factors that might have the greatest impact on work environments, e.g. profit motives; government agendas; health and safety legislation; fears of being sued; union activity; obsessions with new technology; globalisation and the impacts of highly competitive markets. We discussed whether research about what suits people's psychological wellbeing is as powerful a mover for change as some of these other factors, even in organisations such as the NHS with its mantras about 'evidence-based practice'.

Tim Childs, who participated in this session, subsequently made the following comment:

My workplace can often feel like a 'toxic mental environment'. I work as a team manager in a multidisciplinary CMHT. Part of my role is to be responsible for performance management, which involves responding to a continual series of edicts and requests for data passed down a managerial chain accompanied by unrealistic deadlines and what can feel like threatening undertones. I attempt to challenge these when the rationale behind them appears flawed and unhelpful. At other times they require implementation. The effect on me personally can be draining, stressful … toxic. One of the things I have found that helps me cope in this environment is to think back to the session and to focus on why I do the job. Certain ideas and quotes, such as the one below from Lucy Johnstone, can help a detoxification process to take place, one that brings renewed energy and enthusiasm:

> *'Questions about how we respond to human suffering are not simply ones of science or evidence, though that may be a part of it. They are ultimately moral, ethical and political issues on which we all need to take a stand.'*

Box 14   Research on the major sources of stress at work

Kornhauser, A (1965) *Mental Health of the Industrial Worker*. New York: John Wiley.
Poor mental health directly related to unpleasant working conditions, the necessity to work fast, to expend a lot of physical effort and to work excessive and inconvenient hours.

French, J & Caplan, R (1972) In A Marrow (ed) *The Failure of Success.* New York: Amacon.
People who admitted to feeling work pressure were observed to suffer more interruptions from visitors and phone calls.

Cobb, S & Rose, R (1973) Hypertension, peptic ulcer and diabetes in air traffic controllers. *Journal of the Australian Medical Association, 224,* 489–92.
Shift work affects blood pressure, metabolic rate, blood sugar levels, mental efficiency, work motivation, sleep patterns and family/social life. The longer the work shift, the greater the stress, with rotating shifts being the worst, followed closely by night shifts.

Ivancevich, J & Matteson, M (1980) *Stress at Work.* Glenville, IL: Scott, Foresman & Co.
Relationships with colleagues can provide valuable support or, conversely, can be a huge source of stress (e.g. if people are being bullied). They found that the support of colleagues mediated the effects of job strain on cortisone levels, blood pressure, glucose levels and the number of cigarettes smoked. They also analysed stress in the domain of career development – factors such as lack of job security, fear of redundancy, obsolescence or retirement, and numerous performance appraisals, induced stress. People suffering from career stress often showed high dissatisfaction, job mobility, poor work performance and less effective interpersonal relationships at work.

Karasek, R, Baker, D, Marxer, F, Ahlbom, A & Theorell, T (1981) Job decision latitude, job demands and cardiovascular disease. *American Journal of Public Health, 71* (7)*,* 694–705.
Hectic and psychologically demanding jobs increase the risk of developing coronary heart disease (CHD) symptoms and premature CHD death. Low intellectual discretion and low personal schedule freedom was also associated with increased risk of cardiovascular disease.

Karasek, R, Theorell, T, Schwartx, J, Pieper, C & Alfredsson, L (1982) Job psychological factors and coronary heart disease. *Advances in Cardiology, 29,* 62–7.
Proposed four categories: high demands, low control = strain; high demands, high control = active; low demands, low control = passive; low demands, high control = relaxed. They argued that perceived control over one's work environment is crucial, and increasing demands are harmful only when environmental constraints prevent optimal coping and opportunities for personal development.

Sharit, J & Salvendy, G (1982) Occupational stress: Review and reappraisal. *Human Factors, 24,* 129–62.
A large number of factors qualifying as potential sources of occupational stress have been highlighted in the literature. However, if any one variable were to be singled out as a predominant source, they would choose uncertainty.

Cooper, C, Cooper, R & Eaker, L (1988) *Living With Stress.* London: Penguin Books.
Person–environment fit is important. Sources of support can affect people's response to/ perception of stress. Organisational workers sometimes complain they do not have a sense of belonging, lack adequate opportunities to participate, feel their behaviour is unduly restricted and are not included in office communications and consultations.

SECTION 8

Thinking about Medication

36

The need for *Thinking about Medication*

Just knowing the group is running has helped me reduce my olanzapine and I no longer get paranoid. I have been able to go out more. I plan to come off. I used to think of myself as a schizophrenic but this group has really opened my eyes … I now think of myself as a woman.

Participant on *Thinking about Medication* course

My experience in the 1980s and 1990s of being with people who were taking psychiatric drugs, especially antipsychotic drugs, was that these people spent an inordinate amount of time talking about the negative impacts of the medication. When I asked why they spoke so often with me about their medication (rather than their nurse or prescribing doctor) I was frequently told 'because you listen'. The more I learned about side effects the more my job at the time (assistant occupational therapist and education instructor) seemed bizarre: I was expected to play badminton with people who were drugged into exhaustion and indifference; improve the reading skills of people whose vision was so blurred they could not make out the letters; improve the fitness of people who had doubled in weight; hold discussion groups with people who stared blankly ahead; help people develop social skills who were dribbling and slurring their words; and provide relaxation sessions for people who paced up and down and were furious about being kept in a secure unit and medicated against their will.

Such experiences have stayed with me. After

qualifying as a clinical psychologist I started to provide training (usually co-facilitated with a psychiatrist) for qualified clinicians and trainee psychologists about medication, including information on the weaknesses and biases inherent in pharmaceutical industry research, the citing of studies that revealed the extent and severity of adverse drug effects and the problems many people experience when trying to come off psychiatric drugs. Sometimes such topics were met with great interest, at other times with indifference. At the same time people taking the medication and their relatives seemed desperate to access and discuss such information. During the 1990s psychiatrists would often tell me in private that any powerful mind and mood altering drug is likely to create withdrawal problems for some people but the pharmaceutical-company-influenced evidence base only identified minor tranquillisers (such as benzodiazepines) and sleeping pills as creating such problems. It seemed important to try and broaden the public debate about medication as much as possible.

The first *Thinking about Medication* events

In the 1990s Sutton Hill MIND centre in Telford provided the best voluntary sector drop-in I have experienced. Set in the midst of one of the most socially deprived estates in Britain, it was surrounded by boarded-up buildings and a maze of alleyways that social planners thought would lead to an interconnected community but which had contributed to a disparate set of people sharing a communal fear of being mugged. The centre catered for 'paranoid people' yet to walk to it, even from the car park, induced paranoia in even the calmest person. But once inside it had a well-worn comfort and was full of second-hand furniture which, along with the members, helped create a homely atmosphere and degree of warmth that compared favourably with many mental health centres that are much better equipped but where few people feel comfortable due to their bare, clean sterility. It was here that Marese Hudson, an ex-service user who had come off psychiatric drugs and who worked as a MIND volunteer in a neighbouring centre, and I organised the first *Thinking about Medication* events.

These initially involved a series of weekly sessions lasting a couple of hours where a local psychiatrist or mental health nurse was invited to the centre to give a short talk about a particular class of psychiatric drug (antidepressants, mood stabilisers, anxiolytics, antipsychotics) and have an open Q&A session with whoever turned up. Marese and I advertised the sessions locally, introduced the speakers, chaired the debates and in the final week did a similarly structured session on coming off medication – Marese spoke of her experiences of coming off psychiatric drugs and I contributed as someone who had helped people through the withdrawal process. The sessions were always lively, with the audience and speakers, once their nerves had settled, revelling in the opportunities to debate things outside the narrow confines and pressures of clinical consultations. Differences of opinion often meant the discussions were passionate but

only rarely did we have to intervene to emphasise the need to respect such differences or to prevent discussion between a clinician and a patient on their caseload becoming too personal and inappropriate for public debate.

What these meetings lacked, however, was some kind of continuity. The majority of attendees came from the MIND centre that hosted the sessions (being occasionally joined by staff and people who attended local NHS services) yet only a few people came to all the sessions and it always felt like a series of one-off events rather than a cohesive group. Each time we ran these series of sessions we hoped that they might lead to the setting up of a coming-off medication group or a medication action group. For example, a recurrent theme in the discussions was that most people felt they were given inadequate information about adverse effects of medication and an action group could have lobbied for this, perhaps locally and nationally, but follow-up groups never took off. In fact they never got past the stage of Marese and I suggesting them in the final meeting. When setting up the *Thinking about Medication* group in Shrewsbury we bore these things in mind, advertised the group much more widely in order to get a varied mix of people, and asked people to commit to coming to all the sessions rather than just ones that particularly interested them. This appears to be important as it created a group-bonding effect that the Sutton Hill courses never achieved and this seems to have enabled impacts of this group to go beyond those that can be achieved through one-off events.

37

Two accounts of taking and coming off medication

CAROLE STONE and CAROL JOHNSON

Being in control of medication (rather than the other way around) by Carole Stone

Prior to attending the *Thinking about Medication* group in 2006 I had a history of depression lasting for about ten years, including several hospital admissions and two courses of ECT. During this time I had taken about 20 different types of psychiatric medication. By the end of 2005 I was looking for an alternative approach to treating an illness that had been diagnosed at one point as 'treatment resistant'.

Thinking about Medication started me on a path to control my own health. During the course we had the opportunity to meet many different people including three psychiatrists, each with their own views on medication and other treatments for psychiatric problems. I decided I would be less dependent on a doctor's viewpoint and to listen more to my body. By the end of the course I made the decision that the right thing to do would be to remain on medication as I had started seeing a psychologist and learning CBT and felt that I needed to concentrate on that rather than potentially upset it by starting to reduce my medication. However, I knew that, armed with what I had learned while attending the course, I was more able to be in control of my medication rather than the other way around.

While I was on the course I was taking reboxetine 10mg and escitalopram 20mg each day. At the end of 2006 I decided that the time was right to start reducing my medication. I was told that reboxetine was possibly going to be discontinued so, after discussing it with my CMHN (community mental health nurse) who was a nurse prescriber, I decided on reducing this first. It took about 12 months for me to completely stop this medication, despite my psychiatrist's advice of reducing the dose by 2mg every week! I chose the timing of each dose reduction so as not to coincide with anything important or stressful, such as school holidays or starting work, and waited until withdrawal symptoms (e.g. extreme tiredness and a strange whooshing noise/pressure in my ears) had completely disappeared. I took it even more slowly with escitalopram and it took me nearly two years, again carefully choosing when to make each dose reduction and allowing myself plenty of time to adapt to each decrease. During *Thinking about Medication* we had lots of discussions about reducing medication and withdrawal symptoms and this helped me to be confident, to trust myself and above all to take my time.

I am now proudly able to say I am an ex-service user. I no longer take any medication, having finally finished in September 2008, and I haven't seen a nurse or doctor about my mental health for about 12 months. I am about to start a new job working with people with mental health problems and hope to make use of my experiences, as we learned during *Thinking about Medication* that we are all experts by experience. I cannot say that I am 'back to normal' because years of depression and psychiatric treatments have changed me and I can no longer remember the person I was before. But I now view mental and physical health in the same way – we all have times of illness and wellness regardless of it being in our mind or body. It is up to us to find ways of controlling our health: on our own or with help, with or without medication, with or without health professionals. But we need to put ourselves in control as we know ourselves better than anyone else can ever know us.

Difficulties in coming off antidepressants by Carol Johnson

Many years before attending *Thinking about Medication* I was diagnosed by a psychiatrist as having 'reactive depression with endogenous elements'. This was subsequently changed to 'endogenous depression with reactive elements'. The difference seemed pretty meaningless to me, especially as it appeared inconsequential to my treatment. Initially I was very reluctant to take medication but was eventually persuaded that my state was not improving with the mere passage of time. I was prescribed a series of different psychiatric drugs, including several tricyclics and lithium, all with limited benefit. Although I would consider myself reasonably intelligent and articulate, somewhere along the way my resistance to medication slipped into a passive acceptance of the 'need' for medication, and I was deterred from stopping the drugs by warnings that the depression would worsen or return. Following a bereavement, when I was more tearful than usual, I was prescribed venlafaxine. After taking it for six years I began questioning if I needed the drug, what might be any long-term consequences of taking it and whether a doctor should have reviewed it. At this point I had no involvement with any mental health professionals so I discussed the matter with my GP who, to my slight surprise, readily agreed that I could come off, but advised that I do this slowly. Although I had encountered antipathy towards stopping medication, no

doctor ever indicated that there might be any withdrawal problems. As missing only a single dose had previously caused an unpleasant light-headed feeling, I anticipated I might have problems but nothing prepared me for the scale of the difficulties I encountered.

The first reduction, from 225mg to 150mg, made prior to joining the *Thinking about Medication* group, caused no adverse effects and after two months at this dose I reduced to 75mg. Within two days I began feeling light headed and generally lethargic and unwell. This rapidly progressed to strange feelings in my head, which I would describe as a cross between a shiver and an electric shock, followed by a few seconds of disorientation. The frequency of these sensations was completely random and bore no relation to my activity. I could go for a couple of hours without any and then experience them every couple of minutes. They occurred when I was walking, driving or lying completely still in bed. Meanwhile the lethargy and feeling of malaise continued unabated. I was able to sleep at night but my dreams were vivid and disturbing. Emotionally, I felt constantly tense and agitated, with inexplicable bouts of tearfulness. After about ten days of these problems, and with no sign of them diminishing, I admitted defeat and reverted to 150mg. It was disappointing, but the sense of entrapment and anger at the pharmaceutical industry and medical profession fuelled my determination to get off the drug completely. I was unsettled that reducing medication could make me feel so dreadful. Not only was it difficult to stop but also nobody could provide any reassurance about any long-term effects the medication might have if I remained on it. I was no longer convinced by the argument for remaining on medication for life.

I was immensely fortunate that the reduction to 75mg and subsequent reversion to 150mg coincided with attending the *Thinking about*

Medication group. Had this not been the case I would have been completely unprepared for this alarming gamut of sensations and emotions. Attendance at the group also enabled me to feel sufficiently confident and well informed to return to my GP and request a prescription of 37.5mg tablets so that I could reduce more gradually. I successfully reduced my dosage from 150mg to 112.5mg. The next reduction to 75mg also passed without ill effect, only for the same withdrawal effects to recur when I reduced to 37.5mg. By this time the group had ended and I was attending the *Out of the Box* support group whenever possible, although work and personal circumstances made this quite infrequent. Splitting the 37.5mg tablet was difficult and ineffective, so I resorted to opening the venlafaxine capsules and removing the ingredients in weekly increments of 20 'balls'. Despite these tiny reductions I continued to notice withdrawal effects, albeit at a considerably diminished level from those experienced previously. I eventually ceased taking venlafaxine 15 months after I began reducing the dose.

When I was on venlafaxine I had a feeling of detachment from the world and events around me. This was not entirely undesirable as being numbed to the pain made it more bearable, but what I failed to realise when I was on medication was how all my emotions became blunted. Without medication the feeling of detachment went. Instead, for very many months, I found I got easily upset, angry and frustrated. These were not the abnormal reactions that arose without provocation while I was reducing medication, just responses to the stresses and strains of life, but after years unaccustomed to dealing with them, they were disturbing. Personally, this period of adjustment was when I most needed support, but unfortunately the *Out of the Box* group had by then finished and no other relevant support was available.

It is now well over two years since I took venlafaxine. Although I hope to remain medication free, I cannot say that I would never take antidepressants again if in my opinion the circumstances warranted them. I would avoid venlafaxine and any doctor (or mental health professional) that extolled the virtues of medication without giving credence to the potential debilitation caused by them or drug withdrawal.

38

The 2006 *Thinking about Medication* course

GUY HOLMES and MARESE HUDSON

I found the group bonded well and this in itself to me is supportive and gives me that bit more determination to safely reduce my meds as in the past I have just stopped taking everything with disastrous results.

> Participant on the 2006 *Thinking about Medication* course

The course structure

The structure and venue for the group was arrived at after a series of discussions and planning meetings initially between ourselves, people who had come on previous *Psychology in the Real World* groups and identified a need for such a group, and members of the local MIND centre. Later psychiatrist Nick Swift joined this planning group, and we had additional consultations with other local psychiatrists, nurses and service users. After thinking through the pros and cons of different ways of running a group, it was decided that:

- Participants would opt into the group rather than be referred.

- No contact would be made by the facilitators with participants' prescribing clinicians during the running of the group – participants would be left to take up any thoughts or wishes regarding their medication with their GPs or psychiatrists at their usual appointments with these professionals.

- A non-mental health venue would be sought in order to provide distance and 'thinking space' for members who might regularly have clinical consultations in mental health venues.

Compared to other *Psychology in the Real World* ventures, finding a venue proved difficult. No one said 'Are you kidding – we don't want a load of mad people turning up having stopped taking their medication!' but we sensed such thinking might have influenced some venues that turned us down or quoted such a high room rental to make the running of the group prohibitively expensive. Eventually, on the back of previous good connections, The Gateway Arts and Education Centre let us have a room for free (although they declined the opportunity to run the course as part of their usual curriculum). The flyer advertising the course was distributed widely in the town and surrounding areas in GP practices, venues providing mental health services, cafés and various community centres as well as being prominently placed in the venue itself.

A key philosophy of the course was that the participants would generate their own individual aims in the opening couple of meetings and that these collectively would make up the group aims. The black-and-white version of the flyer (on the next two pages) gave an indication of what the group might entail but we were open to it being shaped by the people who came along. The format of the group involved an initial set of two meetings for people to: get to know each other; to express their hopes for what

thinking about medication

How do psychiatric drugs affect people?

Is my experience similar to or different from other people's?

What are the pros and cons of taking psychiatric drugs and pros and cons of reducing or coming off medication?

Informal, friendly, weekly meetings
open to anyone taking psychiatric medication

Venue: Room G11, The Gateway, Chester St, Shrewsbury
Dates: Thursdays 2-4p.m. From January 12th to April 6th 2006
Facilitators: Guy Holmes and Marese Hudson with invited experts

PTO for further information and how to join ...

thinking about medication (p. 2)

Surveys have shown that people frequently want more information about psychiatric drugs and more opportunities to think and talk about wide-ranging issues relating to medication. Despite assurances from the pharmaceutical industry that many drugs do not have withdrawal problems, a lot of people have experienced difficulties when trying to come off their medication.

The *Thinking about Medication* group is being set up to:

- Help people access information about drugs they may be taking and may be considering taking
- Provide a place for people to talk about their experiences, exchange views and get support in a safe and friendly environment where people respect each other's opinions
- Provide people with access to expertise from various sources, e.g. people who have successfully come off psychiatric drugs, consultant psychiatry, community mental health nursing, substance misuse workers, people who offer alternative therapies
- Help people weigh up the pros and cons of taking medication and pros and cons of reducing or coming off medication
- Help people think about and access alternative ways of getting benefits they receive from medication
- Provide advice and support for people who decide to reduce or come off their drugs, including advice and support regarding withdrawal reactions

The group is a follow-on from the highly respected *Thinking about Medication* courses that previously ran at Sutton Hill MIND. This group will run initially for 12 weeks on a weekly basis with an opportunity to review things near the end of this period including the option of extending the end date. The group is **free** to attend.

The group will be facilitated by Guy Holmes and Marese Hudson. Guy is a local clinical psychologist who has a special interest in medication and lectures at Birmingham and Coventry universities on psychiatric drugs; he has helped numerous people to reduce and come off their medication. Marese is a co-founder of Shelton's Patients' Council and volunteer at MIND; she has taken and successfully come off psychiatric drugs in the past.

The format of the group will involve weekly opportunities for members to share their thoughts and experiences and get advice from invited experts in the field. The group is aimed primarily at people who are taking psychiatric medication or considering taking medication, but is also open to anyone interested in medication and mental health.

Venue: The Gateway, Chester Street, Shrewsbury

Dates and times: Thursdays 2.00PM – 4.00PM 12th January – 6th April 2006

If you would like further information or to join the group please contact Guy Holmes, preferably by email at guy.holmes@nhs.net or alternatively by letter at Winston Churchill Building, Radbrook Complex, Radbrook Road, Shrewsbury.

they wanted out of being on the course and therefore generate individual and group aims, and agree on whether they wanted to invite experts to come to the meetings and if so which experts were to be invited to which sessions. From these initial meetings we arrived at a timetable and structure that included an eight-week period where the first part of each session involved short talks and Q&A with invited experts followed by a break and then open discussion which may or may not relate to the themes of that talk. Although the invited speakers were called experts, a key philosophy of the course was that the participants would be experts in their experience and it would be through the sharing and thoughtful consideration of these experiences that individual and group expertise would develop. It was also intended that the invited speakers would hopefully learn from being with the group as well as pass on their own knowledge and experiences. A two-week period at the end was reserved for evaluation, reflection, and future planning.

During each meeting participants sat around a large rectangular table in the middle of which were jugs of water and books and articles about medication for them to look at and borrow for a week. A short break in each two-hour session offered opportunities for people to provide each other with mutual support on a more informal basis, as did the fact that people frequently stayed after the formal ending of the session to carry on discussions about medication with the facilitators and other group members. A key part of the group was the utilisation of the decision-making matrix tool used to weigh up the advantages and disadvantages of coming off medication and advantages and disadvantages of staying on medication as described by Holmes and Hudson (2003) – see Chapter 41. Participants were given time and encouragement to work through this process both during and outside the meetings.

Data from an evaluation of the 2006 *Thinking about Medication* course

The group members

We set a limit of fourteen people for the group and it was quickly booked up. It was difficult to let keen people know that we had reached our limit but places were booked on a first-come, first-served basis. The age range of the attendees was 23 – 84. Of the fourteen people who came, thirteen were women. One person dropped out before the end (citing other commitments) – this person was the sole male participant. The average attendance was eight sessions (range 3 – 11).

Eleven of the fourteen group members were concurrently taking psychiatric drugs. Two of the three not taking medication had successfully come off psychiatric drugs in the past and all three of these stated they were attending due to being in supportive or therapeutic relationships with people currently taking medication. The length of time group members reported having spent in the mental health system ranged from 0–25 years, with the majority of members having taken psychiatric drugs for more than three years. Over half of the group reported having been hospitalised at some point, including some involuntarily under Mental Health Act legislation.

Evaluation data

A two-page feedback form and accompanying letter were given out in the penultimate session. The questionnaire asked closed and open questions about people's medication, their aims for joining the group and whether these aims had been met, with a final question asking for general comments about the group. Participants were free to chose whether to fill in the form or not and the questionnaire was anonymous. Descriptive statistics and content analyses were conducted on the initial questions with a grounded theory analysis of the type described

Box 15   Timetable for *Thinking about Medication* course

1. Introductions, discussion of medication experiences, aims for coming, suggestions for outside speakers

2. Reflections on first meeting, discussion of medication experiences, aims for coming (listed and used as the group aims)

3. *Craig Newnes, Head of Dept of Psychological Therapies*: Psychological therapies and alternatives to medication

4. *Jane Lillington, Head Pharmacist*: Research on different types of psychiatric drugs; beneficial and adverse effects; information leaflets from United Kingdom Psychiatric Pharmacy Group

5. *Monique Scott, Substance Misuse Team*: Techniques for helping people come off and stay off illicit drugs and how these might help people who take psychiatric drugs

6. *Jane Wilkinson, Community Mental Health Nurse*: The benefits of psychiatric drugs; how to get these benefits from other sources; improving mental health by means other than medication; community mental health interventions

7. *Dr Jane Muris, Associate Specialist (Psychiatry)*: The pros and cons of psychiatric drugs; open Q&A re psychiatric practice and mental illness

8. *Geoff Hardy, Natural Health Centre*: Complementary therapies (e.g. massage, herbal remedies, acupuncture) as alternatives to psychiatric drugs and as aids during withdrawal

9. *Dr Anil Kumar, Consultant Psychiatrist*: Open Q&A re all aspects of mental health and psychiatry

10. *Dr Nick Swift, Associate Specialist (Psychiatry):* Antidepressants and coming off antidepressants

11. Penultimate meeting: Reflections on what people have got from the group

12. Final meeting: Evaluation, plans for the future, saying goodbye

by Pidgeon and Henwood carried out on the question that asked for general comments. More detail of the methodology, including a copy of the questionnaire and description of the data analyses, can be found on www.shropsych.org/evaluationmeds.pdf.

Eleven group members completed the questionnaire. The mean number of psychiatric drugs that they listed as having taken in the past was 7.3 (range 1 – 16) – an underestimation as three people stated that they had taken more drugs than they could list. Drugs listed came into all categories of psychiatric medication: antidepressants (tricyclics, MAOIs and SSRIs), mood stabilisers, antipsychotics/neuroleptics, atypical antipsychotics, anxiolytics,

Table 1   List of participants' aims and feedback on whether they were met

Aims	Not met	Met to some extent	Fully met
Learning about medication and how to safely withdraw			
Learn more about coming off medication			+
Distinguishing between withdrawal effects and relapse		+	
Long-term effects of medication	+ (as not known!)		
Learn as much as possible about long-term effects (years)			+
Gain more knowledge of medication and results			+
To get support in reducing or/and coming off medication			+
To get information on reducing/coming off meds		+	
Learn more about SSRIs especialy venlafaxine			+
Info on avoiding/minimising withdrawal (reactions)			+
To become more informed about withdrawal reactions			+
To learn enough to come off medication safely and confidently		+	
To access more info re drugs and side effects etc			+
Information about drugs, effects, long-term effects, safe withdrawal			+
To learn more about the effect of the medication and withdrawal			+
Finding out about alternatives to medication			
Alternatives to medication			+
Finding out more about alternatives		+	
To access other avenues of knowledge		+	
To have an holistic approach		+	
To look at alternative ways of coping with the illness		+	
To debate mental health theories and practices			
Why different doctors differ so much in what they prescribe		+	
To access the knowledge of the speakers			+
Be aware of human rights, particularly mental health law		+	
Gain some insights from professionals and to help them understand the subject better		+	
Knowledge and be able to ask questions of the professionals			+
Sharing experiences and learning from each other			
Hear other people's stories and opinions			+
To learn from each other			+

Aims	Not met	Met to some extent	Fully met
Listen and learn from others			+
To meet like-minded people			+
To listen and learn		+	
Learn from other's experiences			+
Reassurance that there are other people in a similar situation			+
To meet others in a similar position and learn from each other			+
Support with like-minded people			+
Support for the future			+
To meet and support/receive support from other sufferers			+
Miscellaneous			
Self-awareness		+	
To develop empathy and professional development		+	
To enable me to help and support others in a non-judgemental way			+

benzodiazepines, barbiturates, hypnotics and medications prescribed for adverse effects. Nine of the eleven were currently taking medication (mean number of drugs 1.5, range 0 – 4) including eight people taking an antidepressant, one person a mood stabiliser, three people antipsychotics and three people anxiolytics.

The vast majority of participants' expressed aims were met (see Table 1, p. 170).

After starting the group seven of the nine people taking medication who filled in the evaluation reduced their dose/started to come off their medication during the period that the group ran, with one person reporting going back up to their original dose after a period of reduction and increase in distress. The other two people taking medication stated they wished to come off their drugs in the future. Table 2 (p. 171) lists comments made by participants about coming off their drugs during that period. When giving consent for this chapter to be published some members of the group let me know their current situation regarding the taking of medication and consented for this to be included: three years on, four members of the group no longer take any medication; one person stopped taking antipsychotic medication but takes an antidepressant and a minor tranquilliser when needed; one person reduced their antipsychotic medication to a very low dose (below the supposed therapeutic level); two members said they had experienced difficult periods when on lower doses and had returned to a higher dose at certain stressful periods of their lives, but retained a determination to try and lower their dose and perhaps eventually come off at some point in the future.

The grounded theory analysis of the open invitation to make general comments led to four revisions of concepts and definitions of categories relating to 55 data strips. The main themes were characterised as:

Table 2   Participants' feedback on whether they reduced or came off their medication during the group

Participant

A	Reduced chlorpromazine, coming off Depakote.
B	Reduction of olanzapine from 15mg to 10mg with further reduction to 7.5mg planned
C	Reduced (venlafaxine) from 225mg to 150mg prior to group without ill effect. Attempted further 75mg reduction after group started but suffered withdrawal effects. Now OK on 112.5mg.
D	I have started to reduce the escitalopram but I'm in the process of swapping to Prozac in order to come off antidepressants completely.
E	Same dose for carbamazepine and citalopram but hardly ever take lorazepam now.
F	I am now taking 25mg of quetiapine (50% less) and have slept well, even a few nights when I had no medication. I was able to do that because of regular support.
G	(Reduced) but have had to go back to my original dose (venlafaxine).
H	No reduction. I will when I am ready.
I	No reduction. I plan to over several years.

• **Making informed and thoughtful decisions about medication and taking responsibility for decisions about taking, reducing or coming off medication**

Before the group was set up some anxieties were expressed that the group might be 'anti-medication' or lead to people abruptly stopping their medication and rejecting psychiatric staff and their advice. In fact the opposite seemed to happen, with members taking much more care about taking, reducing or coming off their medication, and entering into more collaborative relationships with their prescribers rather than having disagreements that occasionally led to what was perceived by participants as the reckless stopping of medication through anger and frustration with being told they had to take drugs they were very ambivalent about:

'I have learned to take absolute responsibility for my health and wellbeing. It is up to me and no one else, but to recognise when things are unbalanced and take action by seeking help and be open to medication AT A LOW DOSE!'

'Knowledge gained enabled me to restore my medication to a higher level when I experienced difficulties and importantly to speak to my GP about my dosage and get my prescription changed'

'After attending this group I feel more able to go forward with my own recovery and feel more in control of the treatment I am receiving. I am clearer about what I want from the mental health professionals that I receive care from, but also more aware that they do not have all the answers'.

- **Changing relationships with doctors and changing the wider mental health system**

Members of the group expressed a wish to change their relationships with their own doctors (e.g. go from passive recipients to a more collaborative approach) and reported helpful changes to these relationships as a result of attending the group. In addition to this, participants expressed a desire to be part of a movement to change the ways that all patients and doctors interact and to change things in the wider mental health system regarding medication, whether that be in terms of attitudes and practices, or in practical terms, e.g. campaign for medication to be available in small doses to help people who want to reduce their dose slowly. For example, it has been recommended, especially for people suffering withdrawal reactions to reductions in dose, that they reduce their dose in 10% incremental steps. But this is not possible with drugs such as venlafaxine where the smallest dose tablet of Efexor is 37.5mg so reductions in daily dose might start at 17% for someone on a dose of 225mg but end up at 50% as someone tries to reduce down from 75mg. Participants' comments on these themes include:

'It appears unfortunately not the norm but both my GP and psychiatrist have been very supportive with regards to me coming off medication … I think it is important to recognise that some doctors are willing to listen. Hopefully this group will have given people confidence to express their views to those doctors who are currently unwilling to listen'

'If I can find the time I will contact drug companies and request that lower doses are available to be flexible and are available in liquid form so one is able to take responsibility for one's own health and cleverly self-medicate'.

- **Therapeutic effects of a safe and supportive group where people are able to share ideas and experiences with each other**

'The group gelled very quickly and there was an immediate sense of safety (might it have had something to do with the facilitators?!)'

'The group has been very helpful and inspiring … I have felt I am not on my own trying to reduce or come off medication.'

- **Empowerment through information and positive impacts relating to the format of the group**

Complimentary comments were made about all the speakers. Positive comments were also made about having opportunities to discuss things with people (particularly doctors) outside the context of a clinical consultation (such as an outpatient appointment) – how this enabled a more open and free discussion of medication issues:

'Good to be able to quiz psychiatrists. Much easier when well and within the strength of a group than at a vulnerable time during a consultation.'

The most favourable feedback regarding the reading material provided was for the *UK Psychiatric Pharmacy Group's Information Leaflets* about individual medications, *Psychiatric Drugs Explained* (Healy, 2005), *Coming off Medication* (Holmes & Hudson, 2003) and *Coming off Psychiatric Drugs* (Lehmann, 2005). A full bibliography of resources made available can be found on www.shropsych.org/ psychologyintherealworld.htm. Comments made included:

'the reading material (and information available) … has helped me move on as I am familiar now with 'jargon' and language required to get my rights understood'

'I have a greater understanding of pharmaceutical drugs and have recognised side effects that I have suffered that have been overlooked by hospital staff'.

Positive comments were made about the format (e.g. *'The way the hopes/aspirations of everyone were collected and expressed as a formula for the group I found very good')* with recommendations that the group ran for longer than two hours and with more time being spent on alternatives to medication. Several participants expressed a belief that many other people would benefit from a similar group.

Conclusions from the evaluation

The results of the formal evaluation described above matched informal feedback from participants, invited speakers and the group facilitators' impressions that the group was very successful. In our opinion it provided a good example of multidisciplinary work in the area of medication: having an ex-service user as a group facilitator helped participants to feel safe to open up and speak their mind in the group, as did having a co-facilitator trained and experienced in groupwork. The fact that the facilitators did not have a clinical role with individual participants (beyond organising and running the group) and did not have an agenda or aim for individual people to increase, stay on, reduce or come off their medication was also felt to be significant. Speakers, especially psychiatrists, were able to speak in a somewhat different way in the arena of debating things with a group of interested people compared to the confines and pressures of clinical appointments. There was time to debate the benefits and risks of medications, research evidence, drug company profits and marketing strategies, and consent issues without the time pressures and patient and family pressures to come up with cures that can be characteristic of ward rounds, outpatients appointments and other clinical consultations.

Although psychiatrists did not facilitate the group, their input was crucial not just in terms of being invited experts, but also in terms of meeting with the facilitators to plan the group (e.g. recommending that the group have no input regarding prescribing but leave participants to take up any issues with their prescribing doctor). Time pressures did not allow a psychiatrist to co-facilitate the group – a problem that mirrors difficulties for doctors trying to help people think through the complexities of taking, reducing and coming off medication and monitoring people during a process of withdrawal. This group revealed that people can become better at monitoring themselves and engaging the help of other services users, friends and family during a process of reduction and withdrawal from psychiatric drugs, which does not negate the need for medical involvement during withdrawal, but does increase the number of people who can assist and monitor this process.

We feel that the *Thinking about Medication* group model offers an alternative approach to compliance-based strategies whose success is questionable anyway (see Moncrieff, 2009). For group participants, a history of repetitively being told of the reasons why they should take psychiatric drugs had clearly started to grate: many of the participants described previous conflicts with consultant psychiatrists and other professionals regarding medication issues, had had multiple hospital admissions, been on many different medications, and in the past had abruptly stopped medication (in their words) 'with disastrous results'. There are question marks over the generalisability of the findings: the group was relatively small, self-selecting and the only male member dropped out. Yet the group did appear to comprise of people who had experienced great difficulties in coming off medication in the past, during the group and at follow-up, and it did appear that through a process of becoming better informed and encouraged to make up their own minds regarding medication members took greater responsibility for their medication and a significant number were able to reduce and eventually come off their drugs.

39

Some impacts of *Thinking about Medication*

I am taking back some control in my life by communicating my mistreatment from the psychiatric services. I hope to do this by sending a Yellow Card and outline my best course of action and treatment with an Advanced Directive. I hope to earn respect as my self-respect restores. I am living proof that I am recovering and can and will change the system from the inside.

Thinking about Medication participant

Out of the Box

The most immediate impact of the 2006 *Thinking about Medication* course was the setting up of a coming off medication support group. When *Thinking about Medication* came to an end, some members were still weighing up the pros and cons of coming off medication and preparing to start a withdrawal process, whilst others were in the midst of reducing their medication; many of these people expressed a wish to meet up on a regular basis to obtain and provide each other with support. After a couple of meetings of a planning group arranged on the initiative of group members, Marese and I were asked to facilitate *Out of the Box*, a fortnightly support group. Group members took greater responsibility for organising this group, including coming up with the name and finding and booking a venue (a room in the nurse training block of the general hospital). We collectively devised a flyer (see right) that was sent to everyone who had come on the 2006 course. It was agreed that the format would follow the 'model train operator' facilitation style described

Out of the Box

A fortnightly support group for people trying to reduce and come off psychiatric drugs

Come along and ... share your experiences in a respectful and friendly atmosphere ... give and get support, advice and encouragement from people with experience of being on and coming off medication ... explore alternative ways of thinking about mental health and spending the short time we have on this planet

When: Thursdays 2.00 – 3.30p.m.
Where: Room M, School of Health Building, RSH
Contact: Marese Hudson and Guy Holmes guy.holmes@nhs.net

in Chapter 43, whereby each member would be given an opportunity in turn to talk about 'how things were going for them', both generally as well as regarding their medication. The facilitators' main role was to ensure that the discussions that arose stayed 'on track' and the group did not go too far off task. Everyone would have a chance each meeting to give an account of their experiences over the previous couple of weeks, especially regarding any impacts on them of reducing medication, and be able to receive support and advice from other group members. Thus the group would offer opportunities for members to help others as well as receive help. Whilst the facilitators might occasionally provide some particular expertise regarding medication based on their own experiences, they would mostly be focused on assisting the group to, in Sam Kaner's phrase, 'do its best thinking'.

Like many support groups the group was set up with no end date. This was because no one knew how long they might need the group for. *Out of the Box* was a relatively small group; eight people signed up but several were unable to attend as regularly as they had hoped. After nine months some members felt they had got as much as might realistically be expected from the group, others had become interested in seeking alternative means of support, whilst for some the practicalities of attendance had become difficult (e.g. one member had a baby); the decision was then taken to bring the group to a close. Relatively unstructured support groups of this ilk can be quite fragile entities in terms of regularity of attendance and can sometimes feel like they are drifting. When numbers dwindled we often had discussions about whether the group should be opened up to new people who had not come on *Thinking about Medication* and thus become more of a drop-in group, but we never made this step. Support groups of this type can be tricky to facilitate, especially when attendance drops, but even when they involve low numbers they can be experienced as very powerful and helpful for attendees (see Chapter 40).

More general impacts

Much has changed since the first *Thinking about Medication* ventures were set up. For example, from there being little public debate and virtually no information about problems people experience when trying to come off psychiatric drugs such as antidepressants and antipsychotics, there have been books by clinicians (e.g. Breggin and Cohen's *Your Drug May Be Your Problem*), current and ex-service users (e.g. Lehmann's *Coming Off Psychiatric Drugs*) and articles and programmes in the national media (e.g. the BBC's *Secrets of Seroxat*). The SSRIs Seroxat and venlafaxine, originally marketed as creating no problems regarding dependency, have had the highest number of reports of withdrawal syndromes reported to regulators of any drugs in history (Healy, 2005). There has been a groundswell of interest in researching people's experiences of taking and coming off psychiatric drugs. For example, research by MIND involving 204 people found that over half of the sample had difficulties in coming off psychiatric drugs, many withdrawal reactions mirrored psychiatric symptoms/disorders and people who came off against medical advice were just as likely to succeed as those whose doctors agreed they should withdraw. In addition, psychiatrists and general practitioners were identified as less helpful than other professionals and non-professionals in terms of assisting people to withdraw. Recommendations included: people need access to more information on psychiatric drugs and withdrawal effects and access to alternatives to medication; people's wishes to come off drugs should be considered and respected; services are needed to support people through the process of coming off their medication (Read, 2005, 2009).

It is possible that *Thinking about Medication,* as well as meeting such recommendations, has made some modest contributions to the increase in public awareness and debate about medication-related matters. People involved in the groups (as members and facilitators, often jointly) have:

- been involved in local projects aimed at enabling greater access to information about medication in readable formats in inpatient and community settings

- contacted drug companies to campaign for drugs to be available in doses small enough to assist gradual, step-by-step withdrawal

- published articles in national journals and made these available on well-accessed websites; had the work of the group highlighted in other texts (e.g. Jim Read's *Psychiatric Drugs: Key issues and service user perspectives*)

- spoken at national conferences (e.g. MIND's *Coping with Coming Off* conference)

- consulted with and given presentations to clinicians from various professions and voluntary organisations on medication issues and the setting up of medication groups

- provided information and given interviews to people in the media about the experiences of taking and coming off psychiatric drugs

- set up local groups that provide alternatives to medication and help people who are trying to come off medication (e.g. one member set up a number of walking groups, another an ecotherapy project)

- helped other medication groups be set up through: providing advice and encourage-ment; having descriptions of our group on www.shropsych.org; visiting other areas to talk about the group and assist service user-led organisations to set up medication groups.

Whilst the 2006 *Thinking About Medication* course was running, one of the group's participants and myself, at the invite of Network for Change – an East Midlands voluntary sector organisation which promotes and supports user-led groups and activities – gave a talk and Q&A about the group. Over fifty people, the majority taking psychiatric drugs, turned up and this led to interest in starting a similar group in Leicester – the *Living with Psychiatric Medication* group. This group has been meeting since 2006 and in turn has been instrumental in helping another group – the *Mind Medication Group* – take off in Nottingham. Each group consulted with us but has developed its own ethos and ways of doing things. The Leicester group in 2008 set up a psychiatric drug advertising amnesty project aimed at opening up dialogue about the ways that drug companies advertise their products. This has stimulated debate in the local NHS Trusts about their reliance on 'freebies' and the impacts of such merchandising on clinicians and service users. The group involved a local arts-based organisation in redesigning some of the mugs, pens and other drug company advertising paraphernalia that infiltrates many mental health services. Members of both these groups made a presentation about their groups at the 2008 *Psychosis in Context* conference, which was attended by over 150 people. We have also provided consultations to Rufus May regarding medication issues relating to the alternative mental health collective *Evolving Minds*. This group has set up a website that offers information about psychiatric drugs, how they are thought to work and the withdrawal process (www.comingoff.com). Group members have begun to collect stories of people's attempts to come off medication in order to put them on this website. At the time of writing each of these groups are ongoing and open to new members joining.

Things are also changing in the NHS. In 2008 the Department of Health published *Medicines Management: Everybody's Business. A Guide for Service Users, Carers and Health and Social Care Practitioners.* The opening paragraphs of this booklet, which was sent to all Mental Health Trusts' Chief Executives with a directive for implementation, stated: *People's experiences of using medication have often been negative, preventing them from engaging properly in ordinary life activities … service users and carers have been crying out for impartial advice in relation to medicines in order to make an informed choice … medicines management is everybody's business.*

The importance of involving other professions

I have frequently been asked how local clinicians, especially psychiatrists, react to some of the *Psychology in the Real World* projects that can appear quite radical, in particular *Thinking about Medication*. Local clinicians have always been very supportive. I have usually involved them from the beginning, both in terms of planning the groups, developing the ideas and practices, and as invited experts.

My experience is that, when away from the confines and pressures of a clinical consultation, psychiatrists tend to be open about their practice and the pros and cons of psychiatric drugs (see Box 16, p. 179). They are aware of the biases in drug company research, the impacts this industry has on clinical practice (e.g. they have sometimes been the only profession to support my efforts to keep drug reps out of CMHT services) and are happy to discuss such matters in the debating arena of *Thinking about Medication* groups. I remember Gary Hosty saying in the late 1990s during a *Thinking about Medication* session in Telford that the new atypical antipsychotic medications were marketed as being more effective and having fewer side effects than the older drugs, but there

was little evidence to support this claim and they probably had 'different' rather than 'less' adverse effects. Ten years later the editor of the *British Journal of Psychiatry* is finally saying the same (see Tyrer and Kendall's 2009 article *The spurious advance of antipsychotic drug therapy* in *The Lancet*).

Local psychiatrists (and other professionals) have sometimes encouraged people who are ambivalent or antagonistic towards taking medication to attend *Thinking about Medication* as they have discovered that some of these people, when no longer pressured to take drugs, after freely debating issues about medication and weighing up the pros and cons of taking a particular drug, no longer abruptly stop taking medication – with ensuing crises and subsequent periods of resentfully going back on the drugs – and start to take or come off medications more responsibly and carefully.

Psychiatrists have comparatively high caseloads compared to other clinicians, with often over 100 patients seeing them on an outpatient basis. At MIND's *Coping with Coming Off* conference one psychiatrist said that a major problem he has in supporting people who want to come off medication is that he is unable to offer sufficiently regular consultations whilst people go through the potentially long and risky process of withdrawal. *Out of the Box* has been seen by medical practitioners as being of significant assistance regarding the monitoring and support of people during this process.

In short, through involving local clinicians and members of different professions, projects such as *Thinking about Medication* have come to be seen as a form of multidisciplinary work that many people value, with the exchange of ideas and views between people taking psychiatric drugs and members of different professions being experienced as a constructive process that helps all people who engage in it.

Box 16   Psychiatrists on psychiatry

The aims of any medical practitioner? To cure ... sometimes. To relieve ... often. To comfort ... always. We should never let knowledge get in the way of wisdom.

Dr Anil Kumar, consultant psychiatrist (Shrewsbury)

Many psychiatrists feel tension between the duties prescribed for them under the Mental Health Act and their desire to work in a negotiated way with service users. This is particularly so given accumulating evidence that calls into question the benefits of many of the treatments we use.

Professor Pat Bracken, consultant psychiatrist (Cork) and Professor Phil Thomas, consultant psychiatrist (Central Lancashire)

Psychiatric drugs can be of some help to some people with some of their problems some of the time ... but usually at some cost.

Dr Gary Hosty, consultant psychiatrist (Telford)

One history of medicine is of doctors prescribing medicine which is subsequently regarded as useless and often dangerous.

Dr Duncan Double, consultant psychiatrist (Norwich)

Psychiatry is tarnished in the public mind by a difficult history of coercive practice, dubious treatments and the alienation of the unwell. In modern psychiatry we also fall under the pressures imposed by a material culture demanding of labelling, categorisation and cure. On top of this, time limits often put strains on practitioners to rush decision making – particularly regarding prescribing.

Dr Nick Swift, associate specialist psychiatrist (Ludlow)

If professional staff undermine you by continually telling you that coming off medication will fail, you may need to seek help from other service users and organisations with more positive attitudes to stopping medication.

Dr Joanna Moncrieff, consultant psychiatrist (London)

40

Out of the Box

NICKI EVANS

After the *Thinking about Medication* group at The Gateway came to an end it was clear that some people in the group still felt a need for support and that they would benefit from further meeting to discuss medication matters. Some wanted to change, reduce or completely come off their medication and wanted support regarding any problems that might be associated with this. To me the *Thinking about Medication* sessions, although crucial, were quite reserved and formal, and people perhaps held back from expressing some things so there was a need for a more informal, less structured group. Because the support is simply not out there, there appears to be a huge gap between taking medication pushed by the medical profession and struggling alone to come off or reduce medication (which is often met with disapproval from professionals). I have discovered that doctors' views and ideas differ and some are more open about the troublesome side effects of medication and withdrawal than others. However, I am sure I am not alone in experiencing withdrawal reactions being seen by professionals as 'the illness returning or getting worse' and being told 'you're relapsing'. A vicious circle can ensue and a feeling of being unable to stand your ground as your mental state feels worse and you end up being medicated again.

The psychological issues involved in taking illegal and prescribed psychiatric drugs I think can be similar. For example, both can be taken to alleviate the effects of distressing life events –

to feel oblivious or high for a while or to simply numb the pain. The side effects when coming off many illegal drugs are similar yet less severe than for prescribed psychiatric drugs. There is well-established help for people to come off illegal substances and yet, apart from *Out of the Box*, there is no help that I have been aware of for coming off prescribed medication.

The *Out of the Box* group met fortnightly for nine months, in the nurses' training department in the general hospital. There were a smaller number of us than at the *Thinking about Medication* group, usually between about five and eight. I had trouble attending all the sessions of *Out of the Box* due to the fact I was an inpatient at the local psychiatric hospital at the time. Regarding attending the group, I received similar reactions from mental health professionals as I had a few years later when I co-facilitated the first *Writing Group*: comments like, 'What is this group you're doing now?' 'What's been put in your head now?' 'No doubt you're going along to be told to stop taking your medication.' In some people's eyes there was a conflict between being in hospital and attending this group, and when I talked about the group I was faced with direct criticism and sarcasm about Guy and his general attitudes. My response was that the group was about accessing information and general discussion of medication matters, and it might be deemed 'anti-medication' by people who never want to discuss the downsides or see medication from both a negative and positive point of view, but at no point had Guy or Marese (as group facilitators) said people should stop taking their medication. People were attending to discuss their experiences (good and bad) of medication, to think for themselves, make their own minds up and make choices. A lot were reducing or trying to come off their medication, but not all. I made the point that attending the group at least got me out of bed and out of the hospital, which was not usually the case when I'm in hospital.

Eventually the comments stopped. At the end of the day if I'm going to do something I do it; if people try to stop me I make it my mission to defy them further. Not all hospital staff were negative about the group and me attending; I was surprised by some student nurses' comments when I chatted about medication and the group and was met with genuine interest and questions on my thoughts on matters about medication. At the time I put this down to them not having certain ideas drilled into their minds yet, but have since come to wonder whether they were naive or more open to different opinions. Would their attitudes eventually change or are a more open-minded generation of nurses seeing things differently?

Out of the Box was more personal than *Thinking about Medication* due to the more informal nature of the meetings. At each meeting we took turns to describe how we were doing both in terms of medication and in a more general sense. Thus the group operated as a support group, which felt more intimate and meaningful and I found myself able to openly discuss things I would normally not talk of. We discussed a wide range of topics connected with medication. I remember a conversation about painkillers being brought up and speaking about how I felt some of my past problems had been caused by becoming addicted to strong painkillers and the consequences of this.

Discussions in the group were sometimes

profoundly personal and at times people became very emotional, myself included. I was infuriated with my personal situation of being stuck in hospital due to accommodation difficulties. Before the group the very thought of crying in front of people horrified me, but when I got upset I actually felt OK. I knew that I would not be judged for it or secretly deemed unstable or 'a mess'. To be met with reassurance and kindness from all in the room was liberating and touching. To feel no shame for once and to not get hysterical (because getting upset can be uncomfortable for others and ignored resulting in a fuelling of the despair) was important to me. Because you feel alone (maybe you literally are) in psychiatric hospital it is commonplace for people to cry and for it to be ignored. For me this leads to a feeling of hopelessness, which in turn leads to immense negativity. This could easily be prevented given a change of attitudes and practices in mental health settings, but hospital nurses are simply too busy to provide individual attention. I therefore found the group not only a good opportunity for me to get out, but an emotionally supportive experience, as well as it being informative and offering an opportunity to learn from others' experiences. I was also able to make friends, something I've never been good at.

Two years on I still take medication. I no longer take antipsychotic drugs however as they make me feel numb. I lose all creativity and am unable to feel – it's a big shock now to actually feel things. I find that in itself difficult to deal with as it's so alien to me. I don't know what to do with my emotional responses at times. But at least I am able to see things with a little more clarity. Various discussions in the group led me to realise that years of constant swapping and changing of combinations of drugs might have been messing me up – I have sometimes wondered how I could think straight whilst taking antipsychotics, antidepressants and other tranquillisers at the same time. Certainly there were times when I could not think clearly, but I have continued to take medications. The professional staff at the hospital were wrong to worry that I would be told or persuaded to stop taking psychiatric drugs. I continue to think about the prospect of gradually reducing them with the aim of coming off and wonder whether I am avoiding this. If I'm honest, I perhaps take them for the 'wrong' reasons – they are something to lean on, an imaginary crutch that I dare not lose grip of for if I eventually became medication 'free' I would also in a sense be 'alone'.

I found *Out of the Box* unrestrained yet with structure, creating a place where members were able to say exactly what they felt due to the sense of warmth, understanding and compassion in the room. Such experiences often seem lacking in mental health services. The reasons for this are not always to do with negative attitudes: it can be due to staffing levels and paperwork giving insufficient time for clinicians to provide individual attention except at allocated, time-limited periods in hospital or in the community. Sometimes there is a necessity for distance – it does not mean mental health professionals are without humanity. But to go to a group where the overall attitude from all is patience, interest and neither misplaced concern or over-clinical thinking but a happy 'human' medium was, even if it helped just one person, in my eyes a great success. In my opinion this type of group is necessary for so many people, myself included. I have long held a wish for it to run again, not just to get things from attending but to pass on my experience of things: I am as unique as any other that might attend and, although not medically trained, feel I have something to contribute to a support group such as this. I feel the general concept of the group was and still is a necessity for so many people as there is much to be debated and thought about regarding medication.

41

An example of materials used: *Coming off medication*

GUY HOLMES and MARESE HUDSON

The following article is one of many resources available to people attending *Thinking about Medication* ventures. It is an updated version of an article that first appeared in *OpenMind, 123,* 2003.

Some people's recovery from breakdown and mental health problems can be helped by psychiatric medication. But for others it can be a hindrance. Even people who find medication helpful at some point usually give consideration to coming off their drugs, especially when they have come through the worst of a crisis. Mental health professionals have often been reluctant (or have lacked the expertise) to assist people in this process, and have frequently engaged in strategies to persuade people to carry on taking their drugs (this is sometimes called *compliance therapy*). The benefits of drugs have historically often been over-sold, with the risks, especially of long-term use, going unmentioned (Moncrieff, 2009). In our view this is ethically and legally wrong. In the United States many people have successfully sued mental health professionals and authorities for not warning them of the (sometimes irreversible) adverse effects of psychiatric drugs and associated problems in coming off medication, and people in the UK have started to follow suit. There are virtually no designated specialist services to help people come off prescription drugs at a time when we are being swamped with messages of there being a 'pill for every ill'.

Campbell, Cobb and Darton (1998) found that 63% of people who had tried to stop taking their psychiatric medication had experienced problems. Similar figures were found in MIND's survey *Coping with Coming Off* (Read, 2005). People can experience withdrawal or rebound effects, the most common of which include: flu-like symptoms; nausea; sweating; chills; shakes; noise in the ears; dizziness; muscle weakness; spasms; headaches; appetite change; diarrhoea; night sweats; strange and painful sensations (such as electric shock-type feelings and 'weird' sensations in the head). Some withdrawal effects mirror psychiatric symptoms, e.g. mania; hallucinations; agoraphobia; depression; voice hearing; nightmares; panic; extreme tension; insomnia; fatigue; impulsivity; suicidal thoughts; tearfulness; and heightened emotional reactions. These effects can occur within hours, days or weeks of stopping or reducing medication, and may last for hours, weeks, months, or occasionally be permanent (Breggin & Cohen, 1999). It is impossible to predict in advance who might suffer these effects, what the severity of these reactions might be, and who might have no adverse reactions to coming off their medication. However, the longer someone has been taking a drug the more likely the person is to suffer withdrawal reactions, as the body (having adjusted to the daily intake of that drug) reacts to its absence (Moncrieff, 2008).

Other problems with coming off medication include the resurfacing of the original problems and the loss of the benefits of the medication. Although some mental health professionals might call this 'relapse resulting from an untreated illness', people describe benefits from medication even when they do not conceptualise their problems as medical in origin. Psychiatrist David Healy has said that the main effects of psychiatric drugs are the creation of a sense of indifference and a general emotional dampening effect (Healy, 2005). The losing of this, especially if a person is living in a psychologically and socially toxic environment, can be very difficult. People also fear becoming as distressed or disturbed as they were at the height of a previous crisis. Mental health professionals, family and friends can escalate that fear, as they can be worried about how a person might be (and the knock-on effects on their relationship with that person) if they are not 'on' their medication. Prediction of breakdown and threat of compulsion are widely reported by people when they try to have conversations about coming off their medication. Until recently there has been little information on withdrawal reactions and how to go through the withdrawal process. In our experience, many people who have abruptly stopped their medication have probably suffered significant withdrawal reactions which have been interpreted as relapse, with the person then being put back on medication, and with increased fear on all sides of the person ever trying to come off medication again.

Our top tips for coming off psychiatric medication

These are based on the first author's experiences of helping people to come off their medication and the second author's experience of successfully coming off medication.

1. Think through the pros and cons of coming off *and* the pros and cons of staying on your drugs. One of the best ways to do this is to brainstorm four lists (see Fig. 15). Do this individually then talk through the list with someone you trust. Only put down things that you feel are important to you (not what you 'ought' to put down) and write things in your own language – in the way the thoughts come to you. Once the lists are complete you may become aware of the mixed feelings you have about being on drugs, but also be in a position to make a judgement about whether overall you want to stay on or come off your drugs. Where does the balance lie? Do the advantages of coming off medication outweigh the disadvantages? The lists may also identify areas you can start to tackle before starting the withdrawal process.

2. Get as much support as you can, e.g. from family, friends, your doctor, other professionals. Talk over your reasons for coming off your medication with people who are prepared to listen and support you. But be realistic – you may not get the support of all these people. Many people have successfully come off their psychiatric medication against the advice of mental health professionals (see Crepaz-Keay, 1999). It has been suggested that a sceptical and disillusioned attitude to psychiatry can be helpful regarding the withdrawal process (Lehmann, 2001). But if possible, find a doctor or pharmacist who has successfully helped people come off their medication and will help you in doing this. Workers from substance misuse organisations often have experience of helping people come off a wide variety of illicit and prescription drugs, have sometimes come off drugs themselves, and may be able to offer help, advice or set up a support group specifically for this purpose.

3. Talk to people who have gone through the process of coming off their medication. Learn what you can from their experience, although your experience will be unique. If possible, join or set up a 'coming off

Good things/advantages in coming off meds	Bad things/disadvantages in coming off meds
'I won't feel zombied out' *'I'll feel more confident if my weight returns to normal'* *'My creativity and motivation might return'* *'It will confirm I'm better'*	*'I might have another breakdown'* *'I might struggle to get to sleep'* *'My partner might get uptight/get on at me to take them'* *'I had a panic attack when I didn't take them for a couple of days'*
Good things/advantages in staying on meds	**Bad things/disadvantages of staying on meds**
'I don't risk the withdrawal effects' *'I'm quite stable'* *'There's no risk of people getting worried or getting on at me about deciding to come off'*	*'Side effects – lethargy, weight gain'* *'Sex life is affected, which affects my relationship'* *'I don't like doing what others think is best for me rather than what I want'*

Fig. 15   Making the decision to stop or carry on taking medication

medication' group. From a group you might get knowledge and expertise, support and encouragement, positive competitiveness and a reality check that you are not 'going mad'.

4. Read up as much as possible on your drugs, the common withdrawal effects from your drugs, and about how to maximise your chances of doing it successfully. Useful books, including books written by people who have taken medication and which provide many accounts of people's experiences of coming off psychiatric drugs – such as Lehmann (2005) and Read (2009) – are reasonably priced and can be obtained by your local library. Several websites have also recently been set up (e.g. www.comingoff.com) that include advice written as collaborative projects by mental health services users and professionals (e.g. *The Harm Reduction Guide to Coming Off Psychiatric Drugs and Withdrawal* by The Icarus Project, www.theicarusproject.net).

5. Make sure you have alternatives to medication as ways of coping with things. Have strategies to help with the possible increase in emotional sensations and withdrawal reactions. Sometimes you might need to just 'sit things out', but relaxation techniques and doing physically and psychologically soothing things can help.

6. Try to get in as good physical health as possible before starting to come off your drugs. If possible, start the process at a time of relative stability in your life, and be prepared to put other aspects of your life on hold if you have severe withdrawal reactions.

7. View coming off your medication as a journey (it could be a roller coaster ride!).

8. Plan it well and be prepared to possibly do it more slowly than you would ideally want.

9. Withdraw from one drug at a time if you are on more than one drug. Consider leaving withdrawing from 'side-effects medication'

(e.g. procycledine) and, if you have been on them a long time, minor tranquillisers (e.g. benzodiazepines) until last.

10. The longer you have been on a drug, the longer the period you should consider regarding withdrawal. Be prepared to think in terms of months, rather than weeks, if you have been on a drug for over a year. People who have been on psychiatric drugs for many years have often taken over a year to come off.

11. Take a step-by step approach: taper your dosage. Reducing your dosage by 50% is a big step – people do succeed by taking such big steps (or by stopping their drugs altogether in one go), but by doing so you are increasing the risks of having withdrawal reactions to the drugs. Medically trained practitioners more frequently recommend just a 10% reduction each step, with at least a week to ten days between each reduction (longer if you have been taking a drug for more than a year, or if you have severe reactions to reducing your dose). Ask your doctor and pharmacist to supply your drugs in doses that allow you to take incremental steps in your dosage (e.g. a mixture of 2mg, 5mg, 10mg tablets, or if this is not possible consider changing to the same (or a very similar drug) that comes in liquid form). For some drugs (especially the minor tranquillisers) the steps might need to be smaller than others, and the final step might need to be broken down into very small reductions before you finally stop.

12. Try and analyse whether anxiety about recent or future reductions is primarily psychological or physiological, and if the former, try and challenge anxiety-inducing thoughts and get reassurance from others.

13. If you have severe reactions to reducing your dose be prepared to raise the dose again temporarily in order to (i) check that your reaction is a withdrawal/rebound effect (ii) reduce the dose by a smaller amount at the next step.

14. Be flexible – be prepared to change and adapt your plans. You might want to take breathers in between steps, or put things temporarily on hold if things become stressful in your life. It might take time to find a plan that suits you. Everybody's reactions to coming off medication are different, and there are no set rules.

15. Remember that thousands of people have come off their medication and lived lives free of psychiatric services.

42

Being inspired to come off antidepressants after 28 years' use

MANDY BARRATT

Early in 2006 I saw a flyer advertising *Thinking about Medication* which said the meetings were open to anyone taking psychiatric medication and as I had spent the last 28 years taking antidepressants I was interested in what the group may offer. I was particularly attracted by the wording: 'What are the pros and cons of taking psychiatric drugs and the pros and cons of reducing or coming off medication?' These words implied to me that the facilitators acknowledged that coming off medication can indeed be a positive thing and I was surprised to read that an NHS psychologist, along with other invited clinicians, were willing to speak on this. This was something long-awaited and totally new to me.

My history with psychiatric medication began at the age of 14 when I told my GP I cried a lot. He prescribed diazepam, asked nothing about what was making me so upset and quickly ushered me out. The drugs were perceived as something to potentially use in an overdose as much as something to supposedly help. Two years later I returned to my doctor and said I was still crying a lot. I received … a prescription for diazepam.

The following year whilst doing nurse training my feelings of hopelessness became so great I was admitted to a psychiatric hospital. It was here that I was first told I was suffering from a mental illness. I told the staff: 'I've always felt like this, so if I'm ill, I must have always been ill.' For the following 28 years I took various antidepressants, changing them as and when they became ineffective in masking my depression.

The first time I ever felt well was when I was given Prozac. I was able to do things that I had struggled with previously – I could drive a car, talk to people, use the telephone and so on. After some years of being well I decided that I wanted to be free of psychiatric medication; I had heard about St John's wort being used for depression and thought that if I had to take something a herbal remedy would be preferable. My doctors had told me many times that I had a chemical imbalance in my brain and in order to function well I would need to take medication for the rest of my life. I was told to think of it as like a diabetic needing insulin – they know they need it and so they take it. Although I had always hated taking medication I had now come to believe what I was told – after all it was true that each time I tried to stop taking psychiatric drugs I sank into deep depression. Over the next week, after persuading my GP, I reduced my medication whilst increasing the dosage of St John's wort until by the end of the week I was solely on St John's wort. However, two weeks later my mood had dropped so low that I was having suicidal thoughts and so my GP put me back on Prozac – but this time it had no effect at all. I was told this was because I had stopped taking it and that it often does not work second time around. Now I was feeling depressed and guilty that I had inflicted this upon myself by trying to come off medication, especially as I had previously felt so well.

After two hospital admissions my mood stabilised whilst taking venlafaxine and I resigned myself to accepting that if I wanted to be well then I had to take medication for the rest of my life. In January 2006 I began attending the *Thinking about Medication* group. I found the group both supportive and informative. From the visiting speakers I learnt that there are no tests an individual can have that prove mental illness is the result of a chemical imbalance in their brain. I learned that nutrition can make a big difference as can drinking sufficient water. I also learned about the importance of light and of exercise, about how to reduce medication and that what I had been told was relapse could in fact be withdrawal symptoms. This really helped me see that my experiences on stopping medication might be temporary and not proof that I had to be either depressed or on medication. It gave me hope, something very important in recovery. I was also helped by hearing that other people had also experienced difficulties in withdrawing from antidepressants as I had always been told they are not addictive. Another thing that helped me was a comment from Guy when he said: 'Often depression is about feeling trapped.' Looking back on my times of deep depression this does seem to have been the case.

During the time that I was attending the *Thinking about Medication* group I attempted to gradually reduce my high dose of venlafaxine. Unfortunately I found that within weeks of doing this I became extremely distressed with thoughts of suicide. That, and the fact that I was now working within mental health services and needed to be well at work, together with my husband and I planning a mission trip to China in October of that year, resulted in me resuming my regular dose with the intention of trying to reduce again in the future. In July 2006, whilst attending *Out of the Box*, I met a Chinese woman who is a born again Christian like myself. She told me: 'God is going to heal you of depression before He sends you into China. He's not going to tell you to pack up your depression and take it with you.' I was thankful for this but still could not risk coming off at that time and so in October I packed my medication and went off to China.

While in China, working with orphans, my husband and I began thinking about adoption and when we returned home we looked into the requirements for this. We discovered that anyone who has taken psychiatric drugs for a 'serious mental illness' (including depression) in the last two years cannot adopt a child from China. This made me frustrated and angry: here I was having to take medication so that I could function well and have a good life but being discriminated against because I was on medication. I thought about God's promise to me and began to put into practice what I had learnt at the *Thinking about Medication* group. I joined a gym and began using a light box. I started visiting a nutritionist who gave me dietary advice and supplements. She told me that depressed people are usually dehydrated ('causing the brain to shrink like a dry sponge'). I had only ever drunk tea and coffee, never water, and I started drinking water daily and reduced the sugar in my diet (I have since discovered that if I have too much sugar I cannot sleep and have dramatic mood swings).

While I was putting these things in place I intended to take my medication as usual and then gradually reduce it in a step-by-step process (as advocated on the course as the least likely way to induce withdrawal effects). However I realised that, after 28 years of taking medication each morning, I was now forgetting them every now and then, sometimes going a day, sometimes two, without remembering to take them. When I realised that it had been four days since I had last taken any medication I decided to stop them altogether. This was not what we had been advised in the group but it worked for me: I had no withdrawal symptoms, no depression, just wellness.

It has now been just over two years since I came off psychiatric medication and during this time I have experienced some major losses in my life which have been very stressful but I have not become depressed, have not needed to go into hospital and have not needed psychiatric drugs. Instead I have grown stronger and have grown closer to God. So what do I conclude from this? I am grateful to the medication for keeping me alive at times when I wanted to die but I can also feel sadness for what could have been and that I spent 28 years not knowing who I was, only knowing the person the medication enabled me to be. I am a woman who can now feel both the joys and the pains of life without those feelings being numbed by psychiatric drugs. Who has found God *and* found herself.

SECTION 9

On groupwork III: Facilitation

43

Facilitation styles and interventions

Facilitation styles

Values are at least as important as evidence in human affairs. People do not love, or share, or go to war primarily on the basis of evidence.

David Seedhouse

Since White and Lippitt in the 1930s observed the effects of different types of leadership on groups of children engaged in various tasks, facilitation styles have traditionally been conceptualised in three ways: authoritarian, democratic and laissez-faire. Paul Grantham and Yulia Budnik have more recently updated this in terms of the types of groupwork usually done in the modern helping professions, describing a tripartite of directive, facilitative and refereeing styles.

A directive style involves group leaders speaking from an expert knowledge base that they plan to impart to recipients. A facilitative style is more appropriate when there is greater emphasis on process issues in the group – an expectation that members will learn as much (if not more) from being part of the group and from group interactions as from what might be imparted by the person organising the group. A facilitative style mostly employs the use of open questions put to the group which are aimed at stimulating thinking. Most *Psychology in the Real World* groups primarily utilise this kind of facilitation. In training provided by the Skills Development Service, Paul Grantham has argued that such groups require members with high levels of social skills, but we have found

that many people who would not be conceptualised in this way find such a style liberating, useful and enjoyable compared to more authoritarian, directive, controlling styles that they have previously experienced (and often reacted against). If group norms are quickly established that are appropriate to the task and the emotional temperature of the sessions prevented from getting so high that individual members no longer feel safe, facilitative and refereeing styles can work well. Great attention is paid to trying to make the *Psychology in the Real World* group experience feel as safe as possible as quickly as possible – the safer it feels, the less need there is for structure and more authoritarian ways of running a group. The refereeing style is very hands off – we normally use this once a group culture that enables collaborative conversation and free floating discussion has been established. Grantham has argued that this style, where the group is left to get on with the task with only occasional interventions by leaders to prevent conflict or the group getting too far off task, works best when the group is engaged in a task that is familiar to all and where there is a high level of group functioning, but rarely works well with very distressed, vulnerable or poorly boundaried people. The clinical notes of many people who have come to *Psychology in the Real World* groups would include descriptions of participants that included such phrases (as well as referring to 'schizophrenia', 'delusions' and 'personality disorders'). However, possibly because we work hard to enable group cultures that create cohesive groups with high interdependence and a sense of responsibility shared amongst members for seeing that individual and whole group aims are met, we have not found significant difficulties in terms of utilising this style of groupwork. *Walk and Talk* is very much conducted in this style, as are many middle sessions of other groups.

Different group leaders, by virtue of their personalities, will have different levels of comfort with different styles of facilitation. For example, some people are nervous of, or opposed to, being more directive or authoritative, by virtue of past experiences, temperament or ideological values (but see Box 17, p. 194 for clarification about different types of authority). Others fear that chaos might ensue should less control of a group be exercised. As David Seedhouse has pointed out, clinical decisions, like many decisions in society, tend to be heavily influenced by our values base (even though we might not consciously be aware of this at the time). There are advantages in facilitating groups in a style that we feel comfortable with. However, different group tasks require different amounts and types of intervention from a leader. For example, training people in a skill that they have no previous experience of will not readily occur by having a very laissez-faire approach ('any ideas on how to do this?') and is often more suited to the authoritarian or directive style. It is necessary therefore to run groups in styles that best suit the task, and people may need to acquaint themselves with techniques and styles of facilitation that are outside their comfort zone or normal modus operandum. Many groups will benefit from increased intervention from a facilitator as they go off task or when maladaptive norms start to develop, and similarly benefit from a more laissez-faire approach when they are on task and functioning well.

However one might describe the style of

facilitation to be utilised, most groups, once they have started, benefit from a great deal of responsibility for the success of the group being devolved to the group members themselves. The facilitator's job is to provide a framework that helps people feel safe and competent enough to manage this. A sense of how to do this has hopefully been conveyed through the descriptions of group sessions in this book as well as the sections on groupwork and underlying philosophies. Different *Psychology in the Real World* groups, and different sessions within groups, have however utilised different styles, some of which are described below:

Leading a seminar

Alexi Sayle said: 'Anyone who uses the word workshop who isn't connected with light engineering is a wanker' and we have preferred to call many *Psychology in the Real World* sessions 'seminars' even though they involve more experiential learning than the word seminar implies. Groups such as *Understanding Ourselves and Others*, *The Black Dog* and *Toxic Mental Environments* often involve participants discussing topics and talking from their own experience (including their current experience in the group). The facilitators might: outline a theory and perhaps relate ideas pertinent to that theory to their own experiences, before opening up discussion in the whole group; describe an experiment such as the Stanford Prison Experiment as it might have unfolded for participants, with encouragement for group members to imagine that they were one of the people involved (see www.prisonexp.org for materials on how to do this); engage the group in an experiential exercise (e.g. ask them to chose food from a selection including fruit and chocolate and subsequently eat that food in front of people, before reflecting in the group on that experience); or hand over the topic to the group to start exploring from scratch – maybe in

Box 17   On the difference between *having authority* and *being accepted as an authority*

In a group the facilitator, whatever style of facilitation is adopted, is positioned by the group as a person with some authority. This authority relates to the role – it helps to have someone who starts the group off, brings it to an end, intervenes to stop people talking over one another, and so on. This authority is normally accepted by members of a group as necessary for the group to function effectively. The facilitator may be seen as having earned this through experience or perceived competence in the role, or through having taken an organising role in getting the group off the ground. Groups need people to take various roles in order that the group task can be achieved and one role is to facilitate the group process. In *To Have or To Be?* Erich Fromm called this type of authority 'rational authority', and saw it as being based on competence; a form of socially accepted expertise where a person is *accepted as an authority* in some area. He felt this type of authority has been earned and can often 'enable people who lean on it to grow'. He compared this with 'irrational authority', which he saw as predominantly based on power exercised by one person, consciously or unconsciously exploitatively, over another. *Having authority* of this kind relates to a social relationship based on status which is predominantly derived from being situated in a hierarchical position. The person in authority may be competent but the authority comes from and is exercised from the hierarchical position (irrespective of any socially accepted competence).

The exercise of power through irrational authority inevitably disempowers others, with power on the one side and fear on the other (Fromm called these the twin buttresses of irrational authority). People who exercise power from hierarchical positions often fall foul of the maxim *power corrupts, and absolute power corrupts*

absolutely. When having authority of this type over others it can become too easy to just tell people to do something, and often too irritating to converse with them about their objections, especially in pressured situations (such as the NHS). As Stanley Milgram showed, authority figures, once their status is made clear, can get people to conform by initially telling them to do small things they might be uncomfortable with (giving mildly uncomfortable shocks to people making mistakes in a test of memory). This can then progress in incrementally small steps (slight rises in the power of the shocks) until a situation arises where a majority of people will conform to virtually anything, apparently even shocking strangers to death who continue to make mistakes in the experiment. The Milgram experiment reveals that although we tend to perceive ourselves as autonomous, ethical people who make up our minds on each dilemma that faces us, human behaviour is very much conditioned to be obedient to people who are in a hierarchically higher position to us. As Fromm put it, this kind of authority 'is not a quality one person *has*, in the sense that he has property or physical qualities. Authority [here] refers to an interpersonal relationship in which one person looks upon another as somebody superior to him.' People who want to spend time in systems that are not based on irrational authority perhaps need a better understanding of anarchism than the misconstruction that it involves a worship of chaos and rule breaking. Rather, as Bakunin put it: 'Anarchists ask nothing better than to see [others] … exercise over us a natural and legitimate influence, freely accepted, and never imposed … We accept all natural authorities and all influences of fact, but none of right.' These ideas are discussed and further elucidated in *Spunk Library* (www.spunk.org).

small groups, maybe in the group as a whole. For groups to be interesting and to enable each member to contribute as fully as possible, it is best if different sessions are conducted in different ways, with facilitators utilising a range of techniques that are familiar to many people working in education settings (and familiar to those of us who have done training in psychology and other fields where our own training will have been conducted in a variety of styles by different trainers).

These ways of running sessions have more structure than Bohm Dialogue (see Chapter 4), and how the facilitator introduces each topic will steer subsequent conversations, but the spirit of collaborative conversation can be sought, especially once debate broadens out after the initial introduction. The first part of each session is often aimed at calming anxieties and getting conversation going rather than in imparting crucial information that participants need to learn. It is in the ensuing discussions that the group is facilitated to do its 'best thinking'. During such discussions the facilitator may use open questions, short tentative summaries of what is being said to attain clarification of meaning and spark contributions that may differ from those stated, as well as general invitations to people in the group to contribute: *What do other people think? Does this strike a chord in anyone else? You looked like you were nodding, do you see things similarly? Does anyone have a different view on this? For example, I am aware that there is some research that shows some people …*

Chairing

Some *Psychology in the Real World* groups (e.g. *Thinking about Medication*) involve outside speakers giving a talk and Q&A session on different topics that the group have indicated are of interest and relevance to them. Facilitation of such a process is akin to chairing a debate, where

it is important that the facilitator, speaker and group members collaborate to create an environment where all can exchange ideas and learn from each other (rather than try and out-argue each other in a usually fruitless attempt to get others to see the world as we do). This involves, for example, the facilitator ensuring that:

- everyone treats each other's point of view with respect

- the speaker is given enough opportunities to get across his or her point of view and answer questions but the members of the group equally are given sufficient opportunities to speak and develop their ideas (not just ask questions)

- the exchanges, whilst being potentially challenging of each person's point of view, are not dismissive of people who hold minority views

- expertise derived from experience is given weight alongside expert knowledge of clinical practice and the evidence base

A good way of acquiring these and other facilitation skills is to chair meetings or groups in other settings (e.g. team meetings). The chair holds a lot of power and needs to put his or her agenda and wishes on hold. The chair needs to constantly 'think group', focusing on the group task and managing group dynamics that might take the group off course. Other tasks for a chair include:

- Keeping a check on time boundaries to ensure the group gets through the agenda

- Assigning sufficient time for each topic to be discussed, perhaps with negotiation with the whole group as to the importance of each item to be addressed

- Enabling all to participate in discussions who wish to

- Ensuring decisions are made when needed

- Preventing discussions from wandering onto interesting but not currently relevant things if it is at the cost of being unable to complete the current task

People do not innately have these skills; they acquire them through practice. Many work groups I have been part of have shied away from having a chair who is not the manager and who chairs meetings for a considerable period of time (at least six months) thus enabling people to learn these skills and feel confident and competent in this role. Such experiences provide a good grounding for anyone who wants to learn groupwork skills.

Model railway

This has been the predominant style in *The Writing Group* and *Out of the Box*. In *The Writing Group* we want people to feel comfortable enough to describe their poem or piece of writing, read it (or get another group member to read it), and then join with other members of the group in a group discussion about things that the writing brings up. This structure is designed to help people feel more confident about their writing (and more confident in general) as well as provide material whereby people might learn from each other's experiences and from the ensuing group discussion. In essence this is what might be termed the *group task*. The structure of the group is set up for people to initially give some background as to when and why they wrote their piece, and then read it, followed by a period whereby other group members give their reactions to and discuss the themes in the work, relating it to their own experiences as they feel appropriate. The facilitators ensure that everyone gets at least one opportunity each

session to read one piece of work. We came to envisage the facilitation process as somewhat similar to operating the points on a model railway (see Fig.16). What works best is when this appears seamless – the group (train carriage) progresses smoothly around the track, allowing everyone ample time to read something and comment on the themes underlying their own and other's work. The facilitators have to make judgement calls about when discussions might have gone on too long: *Is the person speaking the only person interested in this? Are some people keener to read their work or move on to hear someone else's work than they are to carry on this discussion? Is this a potentially helpful discussion about pertinent psychological issues or have we gone off track? How much time have we got before the break or end of the session?*

In such a group the facilitators have to weigh up and try and balance several factors at once:

1. *Time* – have we got sufficient time for everyone to read their piece? Have we spent a disproportionate amount of time on this one poem and the ensuing discussion?

2. *Dynamics* – although in a group like *The Writing Group* most people are very anxious about reading their work and what others might say about it, there is also likely to be a 'battle for resources' (e.g. a wish to not have your share of the time squeezed out) and powerful emotions that relate to this. It is the group facilitator's job to ensure that previous hurts (e.g. being ignored, forgotten, overlooked, denied resources which are lavished on others, silenced) and corresponding emotions (anger, resentment, envy, jealousy, depression) are manageable for people whilst ensuring the group task is carried out.

3. *Depth of discussion* – does this discussion have meaning for the participants? Are we

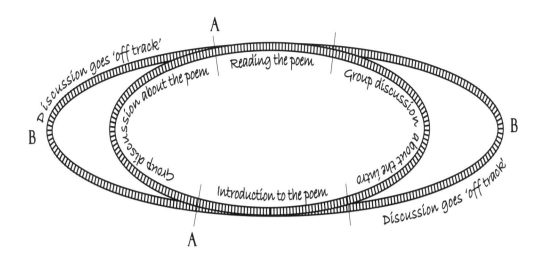

Fig. 16   Diagrammatic representation of model railway operator style of facilitation

glossing over complex or potentially painful or difficult issues? Is this the kind of discussion that these people regularly have or is it touching on areas that for many are often taboo but might be helpful to explore?

We try to allow ample time for discussion without things going off the rails or going on a long track that takes us too far away from the group task. Inexperienced groupworkers, such as psychology trainees, have frequently expressed fears about bringing conversations to an end, especially when this might involve interrupting people who might have been talking at length. Counselling training develops skills that are all about deepening conversations – useful when this might benefit the person talking and the group in general (points A on the diagram); counterproductive when the group would benefit from a particular discussion being closed down and the group returning to the main track/the group task (e.g. at points B).

Unobtrusive shepherding

This is the predominant style of facilitation on *Walk and Talk*. The facilitators (initially two but now we have a small group of us sharing this role) aim to enable each person coming on the walk to maximise what they want to get from coming along whilst maintaining a coherent group experience so that interested people may come again. During the walk people are free to walk as quickly or slowly as they want and to be by themselves or to join in conversations with others. The trick is to continually yet unobtrusively keep an eye out for everyone and assess whether people *are* getting what they want. *Has the person at the back, way behind everyone else, stopped to admire the view; or are they hearing voices and finding it hard to move on; or perhaps they're exhausted? Do the people who are walking on their own want to enjoy a quiet walk where they can connect with nature, or are they feeling chronically shy and ill at ease because no one is talking to them? Has the person who has shot off at the front done so out of social anxiety, and do they know where they are going? Is the person who has come for the first time happy to have listened to that talkative man for the past half an hour or are they wanting opportunities to meet other people as well?* In this sense it can be a bit like having a cocktail party – the trick is not to be like the Alison Steadman character Beverly, the host in *Abigail's Party*. At the end of each *Walk and Talk* we usually go for a drink in a local pub but none of us go around saying 'A little top up, anyone?'

Types of intervention
In groupwork I often feel like I am closing down just as many conversations as I am opening up.
     Rae Cox

Rather than styles of facilitation, John Heron breaks things down further into types of intervention people running therapeutic groups might use. He defines an intervention as an identifiable piece of verbal and/or non-verbal behaviour that is part of the practitioner's service to the client. He categorises interventions as either *facilitative* or *authoritative.* Facilitative interventions are aimed at *enabling people to become more autonomous and take more responsibility for themselves.* Authoritative interventions are where the group leader *takes a more dominant or assertive role, taking responsibility for and on behalf of the people in the group.*

Psychology in the Real World facilitators have utilised all the types of interventions outlined by Heron (see Box 18), but have tended to use more facilitative interventions than authoritative ones. *Catalytic* and *supportive* interventions are utilised throughout the groups. *Cathartic* experiences do occur but, unlike in psychotherapy groups, these are not so actively sought by the facilitators. Rather, participants are encouraged to interact in ways where the support and empathy they provide each other enables people to sometimes be profoundly moved (and in therapeutic language perhaps 'healed').

Informative interventions have not been given in the authoritative style (as 'instruction') that Heron outlines. Rather, information has been offered as ideas, theories or evidence that people are invited to consider, mull over, debate, relate to their own experiences and ultimately reject or take on board. Although the facilitators hold their own personal views about which theories make most sense to them and best fit their own experiences and the experiences of people they know, great effort is made to put each theory out for discussion in as unbiased a way as possible, i.e. provide factual information about a range of theories, not give credence to some and set up straw men regarding others. It is never possible to be completely objective, as subtle and sometimes unconscious biases will be conveyed to the group. The facilitator's perceived opinions will often carry a lot of weight. But it is possible to create group cultures where this power is lessened and people feel free to make up their own mind rather than accept and adopt what the group leader (or other people in the group) think. This may seem naive to people well-versed in postmodern critiques of such endeavors, but we have felt it to be a laudable aim even though we accept much of these critiques' emphasis on issues of power.

Authoritative *prescriptive* and *confronting* interventions have only rarely been used by *Psychology in the Real World* facilitators, usually in situations where the needs of the group warranted directive interventions of these types to preserve the integrity of the group and prevent the creation of norms that might be harmful to group members. For example, where one person wants to skew the group's aims to their own agenda which is not of interest to other group members, or one member dominates all debates and appears to solely use what other's say as invitations to further espouse their own views. As a first point of call there are usually alternatives to directly confronting a person about their behaviour (see Chapter 44) but on occasion we have had to state to individuals that if they want to use the group in this way then the group is probably not the best arena for them. When coupled to the rewarding of behaviour that is less disrespectful of other group members, this has usually sufficed. We have never had to ask someone to leave a group but would be prepared to do this if they repeatedly behaved in ways that prevented the majority of other group members and the group as a whole from having its needs met.

Box 18   Types of intervention in groupwork (adapted from Heron, 2001)

Facilitative

Catalytic Interventions
Help people to reflect, discover and learn. Involve (and encourage) the asking of questions

Supportive Interventions
Build up group members' confidence. Involve positive reinforcement, praise, and the modelling of supportive comments for group members to make to each other

Cathartic Interventions
Empathic. Help people to express and learn to accept or manage powerful emotions and accompanying thoughts

Frequency of use

Authoritative

Informative Interventions
Aimed at providing information, helping people build up knowledge and assisting people find meaning

Prescriptive Interventions
Assist group members by giving advice and providing direction

Confronting Interventions
Challenge the behaviour or attitude of a group member by direct feedback

44

'Difficult' group members

Everything that irritates us about others can lead to an understanding of ourselves.

Carl Jung

Textbooks on groupwork often classify group members that are difficult for facilitators to manage, giving them names such as *the dominator, the free rider, the help-rejecting complainer, the cynic, the silent one, the self-righteous moralist, the brooder, the bore, the saboteur, the narcissist, the joker,* and *the know-it-all*. My own view is that it is often better to think of behaviours that interfere with the group having their individual and collective needs met than to classify people in such disparaging ways. This chapter covers some areas that are broadly applicable to a variety of difficult behaviours, but concentrates on how to manage one particular (and common) problem: the situation where one person is dominating all discussion and appears unaware of the needs of others and the impacts of their behaviour on fellow group members. When training people in groupwork, many people have described instances to me of groups that they have participated in or run that have been unsatisfactory experiences due to one member monopolising most of the time for discussion. This phenomenon has occurred in some *Psychology in the Real World* groups despite our efforts to establish norms that value a rich exchange of ideas and encourage contributions from all members.

It is possible that some people who dominate discussions have deep-rooted and desperate needs for recognition that they feel have never been met. Some might lack understanding and awareness of the impact of their behaviour on others (including difficulties noticing and reacting to other people's non-verbal behaviour). Some might have organic damage, perhaps caused by ECT or other head trauma, which leads to difficulties in finding the right words and making succinct points in conversation. Others may be caught up in emotional overwhelm that leads them to repetitively talk at length about a particular trauma. Facilitators may at times be able to identify such factors and make cautious interpretations or statements that act as a mirror to people about their behaviour and helps them to link such behaviour to underlying causes. This can help people to notice when it occurs and to rein it in. If done gently, sometimes other group members can join the facilitator in acting as a mirror to the person and thus help them spot when they have spoken for too long or not given others a chance – this works well when the dominating person is committed to changing this aspect of their behaviour. However, such comments can fall on deaf ears (or worse provoke irritation) if this is not one of their aims for being in the group, or if it is done in a clumsy or punitive way.

As well as being thought about individually, dominating and other 'difficult' behaviours can be interpreted as group phenomena. Psychoanalytic group therapists often think of the 'troublesome' person as someone who is stating things that others in the group feel but, perhaps because they are uncomfortable with that aspect of their character, have disowned. For example, the dominating person might be expressing repressed drives that all group members have to be in positions of power, influence, authority, importance or domination. All group members might have an unconscious wish to be the centre of attention. As such, the dominating person is thought of as acting out the repressed wishes of the group (but in doing so is resented for it). Alternatively, the dominating person might be provoking transference reactions in other group members, e.g. provoking feelings that relate to previous encounters with dominating people (e.g. parents, teachers, bosses, partners that never listen but solely espouse their views). Psychotherapy groups give facilitators more opportunities to make analytical interpretations of this type, but in any group it is sometimes possible to allude to such things. In *Psychology in the Real Word* groups we have sometimes discussed psychoanalytic ideas, group phenomena and cited Jung's quote at the beginning of this chapter, which has helped people to reflect on their irritation with the troublesome person.

Whatever the underlying causes, dominating and monopolising behaviours, if they continue and are not amenable to the interventions described above, have to be reined in by the facilitator for the sake of the group as a whole. Other interventions a facilitator can use include: clarifying the group rules (e.g. expressing the view that groups like this benefit from ensuring that a diversity of opinion is expressed and emphasising the importance of everybody getting an opportunity to speak) and enforcing them if this does not suffice; behaviourally reinforcing behaviours that run counter to the monopolising behaviour (e.g. commenting on how well the person listens to others) and taking care not to inadvertently reinforce the troubling behaviour (perhaps by maintaining eye contact and nodding whilst the person speaks); using 'punishment' as understood in operant conditioning (e.g. withdrawing attention from the person, or stopping them from making a point – even in mid sentence if needs be – by saying that you want to hear from others in the group who have not had chance to contribute yet); mirroring (e.g. feeding back to the person the impacts of his or her behaviour on the facilitators and others, in the session or outside, perhaps in a break); changing the structure of the session (e.g. having small group exercises or asking people to discuss things in pairs where people have to share the time available in accordance with the task); changing the dynamics in terms of communication patterns (e.g. asking people to contribute in turn through having round robins). No one pretends, however, that any of this is easy to do or instantly effective in all situations. *Psychology in the Real World* groups with members who have needed to be continually managed in this way have felt less cohesive, had less positive feedback that has sometimes referred to the impacts of the dominating behaviour, and had a greater number of dropouts.

Knowing that one person's behaviour is having an impact on others in the group (who are becoming irritated with that person) often induces a wish in facilitators for other group members to challenge that person, but in whole group discussions they rarely do this as they expect the facilitator (who is perceived as having the power and responsibility for such things) to take the lead and deal with the situation. Facilitators schooled in one-to-one therapy have often devised strategies that work in one-to one situations. For example, in an hour's session you can wait 20 minutes for someone to talk incessantly about something – it may even be necessary for them to do this to be calm enough to be able to go on and analyse the situation.

But in a group, where there may be much to cover and 13 other people wanting to contribute, this is not appropriate. Interrupting someone then becomes a skill people have to learn – how to do it in ways that do not seem too harsh both to the interrupted person and to the rest of the group. The facilitator who interrupts someone may feel and be perceived by some group members as rude, authoritarian or even brutal but the facilitator needs to *think group* and this may be less damaging to the group as a whole than allowing (and being perceived as allowing) one group member to monopolise all discussions. Supervision can help facilitators to not get too caught up in their emotional reactions to people who repeatedly dominate discussions, or spend too much energy endlessly speculating about 'pathologies' that drive the individual, and instead focus on strategies that might help the whole group (including the dominating person) get their needs met.

The use of exclusion criteria or de-selection of 'difficult' people prior to commencement of a group

I remember one mental health worker, when seeing an advertisement for a *Psychology in the Real World* group, remarking: 'I know just the person for this group. He speaks all the time, never listens to anything I say, you can never get a word in edgeways – this will be ideal for him'. I explained that the group was open to anyone but that she might consider alternative ways of helping that person to listen and relate to others prior to him joining a group that would be mostly based on group discussion; on the other hand, maybe she'd just like to screw it up! *Psychology in the Real World* groups take a risk in not having explicit inclusion and exclusion criteria and no pre-group selection process, which group theoreticians state enable the careful selection of people who are more likely

to work together to form a successful group. No matter how it is done – by what Gandalf might call 'wormtongue' or by telling it straight, applying the maxim *sometimes the needs of the many outweigh the needs of the one* – people are likely to struggle with feelings of personal rejection after a pre-group meeting where the facilitators have decided the group is not for them. For those people who have had multiple and painful experiences of rejection this can be another wound. Not having inclusion/exclusion criteria or pre-group meetings does mean facilitators, however, take a risk on who will sign up and they often have to work hard to help a cohesive group to develop.

I usually ask mental health workers to encourage people they are supporting to come to the groups. Often I just give the staff copies of the flyers to give out, but sometimes in the community mental health team where I work, especially when the team is under a lot of strain, I make some general comments on who might get most from the group, who might get little, and who might create difficulties for other members and facilitators. For example, workers' attention is often most acutely focused on those people who are in the midst of a severe crisis, but these people may be caught up in repeatedly talking about their current difficulties and traumas and may have little space to contemplate other things; as such, they may dominate discussions, divert the group into trying to meet their pressing needs, and thus block the rest of the group from learning from other avenues. It is helpful to have work colleagues who, even when under strain, are keen to encourage potential attendees who might benefit from *and* contribute to a group, thus helping to create a successful venture (rather than have colleagues who might unconsciously or consciously be trying to sabotage the group – perhaps by giving you a taste of how difficult they find a particular person, or by acting out some envy as regards what might be perceived as your project). When colleagues have come to me to discuss someone they are supporting whom they think might benefit from the group, I have sometimes offered to see that person on a one-to-one basis, or to support the worker through supervision, in order to help the prospective group member have some of their immediate needs met, so that should they subsequently join a group they will be able to get more from the experience and have a less deleterious effect on the group dynamics than if they had joined without such prior input.

45

Applying Carl Rogers' core conditions to community-based groupwork

I was particularly impressed with the way Guy told his own story which removed the 'them and us' feeling. Also the way he is able to listen to the daftest comment as if it is relevant and valid!

Participant on an *Understanding Ourselves and Others* course

Carl Rogers wrote about the core conditions of counselling relationships that lead to people benefiting from that relationship, and the importance of *genuineness* on behalf of the counsellor, the need to have a stance of *unconditional positive regard* to the client and the importance of *empathic understanding* being conveyed to that person. Mark Smith has written a brilliant paper entitled *Carl Rogers and Informal Education*. Influenced by this, I have tried to apply Rogers' core conditions to groupwork of the type described in this book:

Genuineness

Facilitating a group involves taking a role but it is important that the facilitator is genuine in the sense of not pretending to be someone they are not. Rogers would argue for the importance of the facilitator being 'real': being first and foremost a person not a group leader, who enters into relationships with group members without a front or façade. This involves careful attention to, rather than denial or repression of, one's own feelings which can be helpful in terms of understanding individual group members and group processes. It involves entering into direct, personal encounters with people and is about

engaging in warm relationships rather than coldly providing information. Of course the genuineness relates to the role – I do not believe that we have a 'real self' that goes through life in a consistent way irrespective of the environments we encounter or roles we take on. The Guy who is a member of groups (therapy groups, work groups, family groups) is at times radically different from the Guy who facilitates groups. As a non-facilitating member of groups I can be frequently pessimistic (some might say cynical); am much more prone to seeing things in black and white; am less likely to think about how my words or behaviour might impact on others; am less focused on doing things that serve the interests of the group as a whole; am more likely to do things that take the group away from its main task because of my own frustrations or agendas, and so on. At times I am aware that, when caught up in powerful dynamics of groups that I am not facilitating, I have said some very destructive things. People who have only known me through witnessing me facilitate groups would probably be surprised to see 'this other Guy'. But he is just as real and genuine as the Guy who is careful not to do these things and tries to rein in other people doing them when facilitating groups – it is just that being a member of a group and being a facilitator of a group affects people in different ways and brings out different aspects of people.

Prizing and accepting each group member for who they are

Rather than having unconditional positive regard for each group member, Smith uses the term 'prizing' – each member needs to feel prized by the facilitator: prized for who they are, their feelings, their opinions, in fact their 'whole person'. This way of being can be described as *caring about* rather than *caring for* each person in the group, accepting each individual as a separate person who has worth in his or her own right. At a fundamental level, although we all have failings and are imperfect, this involves seeing each group member as 'fundamentally trustworthy'. This is a laudable stance for any groupworker to take but it is, in my opinion, rather idealistic to imagine one can maintain such a stance throughout every encounter in one's life. I am frequently unable to achieve this in my private life or when a member of a group, but holding such a position towards the relatively small number of people one encounters when facilitating a group for the two or three hours a week the group takes place is more feasible, and this certainly helps to create a cohesive group.

Empathic understanding

Rogers felt that in educational settings students learn best when they have a sense of being understood – not evaluated or judged, just simply understood from their *own* point of view rather than the teacher's. To really try and 'put oneself in someone else's shoes', to feel what they feel and see things through their eyes, and to somehow get this sense across to people requires great effort, concentration and openness. Whether we can truly empathise with another person in the way Rogers implies is open to question. Personally, I do not feel capable of being like this on an hour-by-hour basis throughout my life and do not always pay attention to what friends or colleagues say, let

alone try and empathically understand them. However, as with the other qualities described above, it is possible to aim to do this more in one's life, and during the period one is actively facilitating a group it is possible to put a great deal of effort into achieving this during the couple of hours that the group runs for.

Evaluations of *Psychology in the Real World* groups have referred to these qualities in terms of facilitation many times, linking them with positive outcomes, with reference to, for example, the facilitators' *'honesty', 'clarity'* and *'sympathetic response to some of my obvious past problems'*. Modelling self-disclosure – the facilitators talking about their own breakdowns, difficult family experiences, and other personal experiences that seem relevant and illustrative – has been remarked on in evaluations in helping to create a therapeutic group environment.

Therapists skilled in one-to-one interventions who have done little or no groupwork will nonetheless have many transferable skills, such as those identified by Rogers, and people who are used to creating environments that enable people to talk intimately can often enable this to occur in group settings. Rogers' core conditions, however, in one-to-one therapy are centred on deepening relationships and enabling individuals to conduct their own self-analysis and be healed through the holding relationship that the therapist provides. In contrast, in groupwork it is the other group members who provide the bulk of these interventions. The facilitator needs to enable group members to be genuine and have unconditional positive regard and empathy towards each other. A facilitator's role is not to individually heal each group member in turn. The sense of the group as a whole can 'hold' the group members in similar ways to which counsellors feel that therapeutic relationships hold people in individual work.

As well as enabling individual group members to talk more intimately about things (a transferable skill from one-to-one work), groupworkers also have to be skilled in closing down conversations (for example, to prevent one person's personal story taking up too much time in a group session or to enable the group to move on to another task). At such points skills learned in counselling training can be counter-productive: maintaining eye contact, nodding and smiling at someone you want to stop talking will have the opposite effect. Trainees in groupwork often have to rein in their habit of closely attending to the person talking and learn to direct their gaze to others in the group, for example, to catch the eye of someone else who wants to speak in order to encourage them to express their view and thus enable a more interactive debate.

46

On co-facilitation

When two workers are exploring whether to work together, an exchange about personal values will probably be the most important of all.
  Allan Brown

The group content and facilitation styles of many *Psychology in the Real World* groups, especially those solely facilitated by myself, have clearly reflected some aspects of my personality and background as well as my values. A Jungian analyst or student of personality theory might see them as reflective of the 'rational' personality style that Keirsey's temperament sorter indicates is my core temperament; a Freudian might see my aversion to authoritarian styles of facilitation as part of an unresolved Oedipus complex; a transactional analyst might identify key life scripts mirrored in the work (from my grandfather – 'no one is better than you but you are no better than anyone else'; from my father – 'the most important thing to strive for in life is justice and fairness for all'); a political analyst might match the groups to my recent gravitation towards the socio-political ideas of libertarian socialism. Obviously I would find it difficult to co-facilitate a group with an extremely judgemental person with fascist views and treasured life scripts that emphasise the need for elites to be in charge of the majority of the population who need regulation not liberation. However, I have found it helpful to co-facilitate groups with people who have different views, come from different backgrounds from my own and who have different ways of seeing the world.

Co-facilitation works well provided the facilitators find such differences tolerable and the differences do not prevent sufficient coherence in terms of course content and facilitation styles. Difference can lead to creative ideas about how to run groups and structure individual sessions. When doing a group on one's own it is possible to design a group that is solely attractive to (and overly aimed at meeting the needs of) people who are very similar to ourselves; but, as Keirsey's book *Please Understand Me* reveals, this will always be a minority of the population in terms of personality temperament let alone aspects of character (which are always unique). In short, any group is likely to reflect the background, interests and personality style of the facilitator and having co-facilitators who are different but not so clashing that they are unable to work together enables groups to be run and individual sessions to be devised that can be of interest to and meet the needs of a wider range of people.

There are many benefits regarding co-facilitation of *Psychology in the Real World* (and other types of) groups. These include:

1. *Creativity in the planning stages* – Two heads are often better than one, and two (or more) people chewing over an idea often sparks creative thinking.

2. *Sharing of workload* – Co-facilitators can share the tasks of organising the group, e.g. booking and liaising with the venue; designing and distributing the flyers; setting

up and tidying the room after the group; taking responsibility for preparing the content and designing the structure (session plan) for each session.

3. *Sharing of roles* – Having two facilitators offers opportunities for each to take up different roles. Co-facilitators may take roles that suit their skills or take roles that they wish to develop skills in. One division is in terms of who might focus on individual group members needs and who might primarily focus on the whole-group needs; similarly, who might mostly focus on the content of the session and what individual people say and who might focus on group process. I have found that inexperienced groupworkers, such as trainee psychologists, have tended to be very skilled at responding to individual group members comments and needs but are less accustomed to 'thinking group' and in supervision have often reflected on how they get overly focused on group members who are talking rather than having space to think about the other members (e.g. *Are the rest of the group bored? Do others want a chance to respond to the speaker – perhaps empathically, perhaps in a challenging way? Do some group members want to speak about something else? Do people need a break as their concentration is waning?*) Similarly, their focus is less commonly on whole group process (e.g. *Is this the kind of norm or culture we want to see established? Are we on task? What is the emotional temperature in the room like at the moment? Have things become too conceptual and impersonal in a way that is preventing experiential learning?*) Co-facilitation enables people to have space to think in these ways and learn and practice these skills without having to concurrently attend to individual member's needs.

4. *Covering absences* – If a facilitator is off sick the group can still function without a need for cancellation or for the group to run without a facilitator (which tends to be a very different experience once a group norm encompassing facilitation has been established – most groups tend to struggle to keep on task if no one fills the gap and takes on this role). Having more than one facilitator also enables people to take annual leave during the time-scale of the group without too disruptive an impact on the group. Additionally, co-facilitators who have not taken on certain roles have opportunities to do so during absences. For example, co-facilitators who see themselves as 'not the main facilitator' or who are being assessed in some way (e.g. on a placement as part of their clinical training) have felt they benefited from having some opportunities to be the sole facilitator.

5. *Mutual support* – co-facilitators can provide each other with support. Facilitating groups is a frightening experience for virtually all people. It would be odd for even the most experienced of group facilitators not to be nervous before the first few sessions of any group. For most of us it remains an anxiety-provoking experience even when we enjoy groupwork, highly value it and feel we are 'good enough' groupworkers. Such anxiety might be a primitive reaction – in any group the facilitators tend to be outnumbered and there is perhaps a fear of the group turning on the leaders (even though our conscious brain tells us this is unlikely in *Psychology in the Real World* ventures where members are free to attend or leave at any time). Co-facilitators can also provide mutual support during the session if needed. In my experience this mostly takes the form of reassurance that calms anticipatory anxiety –

What if I can't cope? What if I can't think of anything to say? What if my mind goes blank? What if I say something stupid? Calming each other's anxieties also enables facilitators to run groups with less content and structure (allowing more free-floating discussion and the group to generate the bulk of the material to be discussed), as most facilitators respond to their fears about how a session will go by preparing more content, taking more control and erecting more structure than is often needed. Bion said that group workers need to be able to 'think under fire' and sometimes, if one's mind goes blank, a co-facilitator can come to the rescue of a colleague who feels under fire. After the session, when co-facilitators usually stay and discuss what went well, what not so well and generally calm down after the adrenalin rush that flows through most group facilitators during the sessions, co-facilitators can also counteract overblown reactions each has to perceived mistakes and help each other to put things in context and in perspective. Co-facilitators can also serve to inspire each other and maintain each other's morale and motivation.

6. *Multiple perspectives* – When both facilitators have been psychologists this has had benefits in challenging the idea that one psychologist's view is representative of all psychology. This fits with a core philosophy associated with *Psychology in the Real World*: that it is helpful to explore and critique all ideas purporting to explain human behaviour and we should be wary of passively absorbing what we are told by supposed experts. Having two psychologists espousing different views on the same subject encourages people to see that they have to make up their own mind, come to their own conclusions and treat psychology as a broad church that encompasses very different ideas, many of which are in conflict. Similarly, groups have benefited in many ways from having co-facilitators who have had experiences of receiving mental health services, for example, in terms of their planning, content and group dynamics. When speaking from direct experience of being in psychiatric hospitals, taking or coming off medication, attending ward rounds or receiving various therapies people are listened and responded to by group members in very different ways to hearing comments on these matters by people without direct experience. Marese Hudson, who co-facilitated the *Thinking about Medication* and *Out of the Box* groups, had a vast array of encounters with mental health staff from which to draw upon, and had a wonderful way of saying: 'This was my experience, yours might be different, but I found that …' Group members who have had involvement with psychiatric services often feel a service user consultant facilitator has quickly and naturally understood them and what they have been through – there is often a quicker build-up of trust than with people who are identified as professionals, a greater sense of affiliation, and less 'us and them' dynamics, especially in the early sessions. In terms of advertising the groups, service user consultant facilitators have also been instrumental in letting people from 'hard to reach' groups know about the sessions and have actively encouraged such people to attend.

7. *Personal benefits for facilitators* – The benefits for service users who have co-facilitated *Psychology in the Real World* groups are elucidated by Anna Hughes in the next chapter and by other chapter writers in this book. Co-facilitation with an experienced

groupworker is the best way to learn how to run groups and psychology trainees and service user consultant co-facilitators have developed skills in this area and gone on to organise and facilitate groups in other NHS and non-NHS services (for example, run writing groups and women's groups). Experienced groupworkers also, of course, learn much from novice groupworkers: from being exposed to new ways of doing and thinking about things, as well as from being asked questions about why something is best done in a certain way – so-called naive questions can provoke much reflection.

The potential downsides of co-facilitation include:

1. *Lessening of commitment* – Sometimes having more than one facilitator can lessen each facilitator's commitment to the group (e.g. people are more likely to take annual leave during the group, not come in when a little unwell knowing that the co-facilitator will be there, lose some interest in the group and 'drift off' in sessions) which can have a knock-on effect on group members' commitment to the group.

2. *Inconsistency between facilitators* – This can be confusing for group members, especially when it impacts on the perceived structure of group sessions, leading people to feel less safe in terms of what might happen next. A loss of a sense of safety can lead group members to be less likely to take risks or speak about very personal experiences.

3. *Splits* – Sometimes group members may wish to provoke splits between facilitators, perhaps acting out family dynamics or old patterns of behaviour where inconsistencies between parents were evident. This can take the group off task and be difficult

experiences for group facilitators who need to avoid unhelpful splitting whilst modelling an acceptance of being different people with different views. This is often difficult to achieve in practice when emotional states induced in co-facilitators can be powerful and not easily understood or contained (see Chapter 31 on group dynamics).

4. *A feeling of pressure to perform* – Less experienced or less confident facilitators can feel under pressure to perform, that their interventions are not as apt as those of a more experienced partner, and can consequently become overly self-critical. Self-critical thoughts such as '*I'm not really needed … This group could function without me*' can come to the fore. The results of this can impact on co-facilitators who sometimes become quiet and do not feel confident enough to make what might have been helpful observations. At other times people have found themselves not quite quick enough to come in with a comment or too anxious to show what they know. Psychologists in training can be self-conscious and nervous as they are being assessed by their supervising co-facilitator in vivo (Ruth Howard has written a very honest and interesting paper on this and the chapter by Lucy Gahan in this book also remarks on it). Such difficulties are best spoken about honestly in meetings outside the group, but even when this occurs they can be hard to manage and can have a knock-on effect on the group as members pick up on such power dynamics and can become distracted from achieving the group task.

5. *Time and resources* – Two people facilitating not only takes up more resources it needs more co-ordination – people need to know what each will be doing, discuss how to separate roles, let each other know what the

other is planning, and so on. Of course there may be benefits to these meetings but it all increases the time spent in planning sessions outside the group, which impinges on other work and adds to workload stress that each facilitator may be experiencing.

6. *Difficulties with feelings for each other* – Co-facilitation can be an intimate experience with people working closely together on a project often in a different kind of relationship than they previously had. There can be a blurring of boundaries that might have been very different and clearer in other kinds of relationship (e.g. between a senior and junior colleague, or between a group facilitator and someone who has previously been a group member). Groups that feel very intimate in the session can infuse facilitators with feelings of intimacy and this can be confusing, especially for people who have not received any training in making sense of and containing emotional states induced in them by their work. Facilitators can also feel great anger and irritation with each other, for example, when having different ways of doing things, or relating to perceived differences in commitment or regarding the sharing of tasks. Some feelings may relate to the current situation; others may be manifestations of a facilitator's past experiences that might have been triggered by the current situation; others may be counter-transference reactions to transferences onto them by group members or each other. All of this needs to be recognised as far as possible and managed by both parties, with care to ensure that 'acting out' behaviours both in and out of group sessions do not take place.

On co-facilitation and supervision

On the whole I have found *Psychology in the Real World* groups (and other groups) have run well with sole facilitation and co-facilitation. I have only co-facilitated *Psychology in the Real World* groups with people I have got to know quite well and with whom I have a mutually respectful relationship. Experience has shown it has been important to: meet regularly before the start of the group, with planning sessions starting at least a few months before the first session; discuss each session for at least half an hour before and after the end of each meeting; meet on days other than when the group takes place in order to more generally reflect on the overall progress of the group, with some of these meetings taking place with a separate person acting as a supervisor.

An outside supervisor can help co-facilitators:

- unburden any stresses or worries about the group, and detoxify impacts of the group on them

- reflect on the group, e.g. on power dynamics between group members, group members and facilitators and between the facilitators themselves; on whether the group dynamics as a whole are helping or hindering the group

- reflect on how they are dovetailing in terms of co-facilitation, e.g. by enabling differences of opinion to be aired

- clarify and modify respective roles and ensure that co-facilitators are happy with the roles they are taking up, e.g. not holding each other back or feeling over burdened as one co-worker is perceived as not 'pulling their weight'

- bear in mind the bigger picture not just the previous and forthcoming session (e.g. discuss ending issues)

There is a lack of people offering supervision for groupworkers so finding such supervision can be difficult. We have found that outside supervision with someone who is not especially experienced in groupwork, even if they only ask very general questions (giving each facilitator in turn an opportunity to answer), is often better than no outside supervision.

SECTION 10

Walk and Talk

47

Walk and Talk, co-facilitation and service user involvement

ANNA HUGHES

Guy Holmes first introduced the idea of a 'walk and talk' during the autumn of 2006 towards the end of our coming off medication support group *Out of the Box*. Having suffered depression I was very interested in this idea, as I had always found the combination of exercise and fresh air a tonic during my darker days. In the spring of 2007 I met up with Guy to discuss publicity, timings, the practicalities of the walk itself and how we would run it. We decided that it would be helpful to choose the same time and day of each week. We felt that this would help give routine and consistency to those who wanted to participate. May until September gave people four months of weekly walks, hopefully to enjoy some fine weather and observe the natural wildlife along the banks of the River Severn.

The tranquil and beautiful location of the River Severn path proved to be an excellent choice of walk. Frankwell car park, with the easy meeting point at the bottom of the footbridge, close to the bus and train station as well as the car park, and being a town centre location is a good place to meet up. The walk itself is very gentle and relaxed. There is no expectation that you need to walk the whole distance. You can go entirely at your own pace, perhaps chatting to fellow walkers or keeping your thoughts to yourself. At the end of the walk, for those who wish to, there is the welcome opportunity of a drink or lunch and a well-earned rest at a local pub.

Having a project to focus on was a great help to me. It gave me a focal point outside my own problems. Helping to facilitate the group greatly improved my confidence and self-esteem. Without there being any pressure, I enjoyed the company of like-minded people. I would like to think, in my own small way, I encouraged other service users to join the group and to continue 'walking and talking' over the summer months. I tried to lead by example, in that I believe actions speak louder than words. By being open about the fact that I am a service user I hoped that it made others feel welcome and comfortable in the group. I also hoped that other service users were encouraged by seeing that it is possible to facilitate a group activity. I was delighted to hear that several group members continued to walk and talk over the winter months (without Guy's or my presence) and were very proactive in verbally advertising this to new people, handing out posters, and keeping the walk and talk concept going. Each year the group takes place the number of people from a service user background involved in running the group increases. I no longer take a facilitating role in *Walk and Talk* but have initiated a similar project connected to a local crisis house. I meet people who are staying there and we have an amble along the local paths with a stop midway at a community café. As there is a maximum of four people staying at any one time in the crisis house, and people often feel unwell, only one person per week tends to come, but the feedback from people (and staff) has been very positive, and we have opened it up to anyone who has previously stayed at the house being able to come along.

I remain positive that exercise and fresh air really help reduce mental health problems, and that even when you don't initially feel like it, the company of other like-minded people is of benefit. I know how much routine and comfortable company helps me on a day-to-day basis. With the opportunities of a good stroll and the picturesque Shropshire countryside, I hope that many others too have felt the benefit. Whilst on the walks several service users have mentioned how helpful it is to them to have a weekly routine to stick to. People have said that it is good to keep busy. One person whom I got chatting to told me that out of all the therapy he had received, and all the various professionals he had seen, *Walk and Talk* was the thing that had helped him most of all. He went on to explain that he thought that this was because there was no pressure, and that you were outside in a large open space doing a gentle activity with like-minded people. You could choose who you wanted to speak to, or not speak to anyone at all. I couldn't put it better myself.

48

Walk and Talk

You forced me to walk and talk
Like I'd never done before
We'd took on such a load
Treading down that lonesome road.
    Paul Robeson

Origins

Walk and Talk was born out of a confluence of several aspects of my working life. In 2006, during *Toxic Mental Environments,* the session *Making and Breaking Children's Lives* encouraged participants to think of a time during their childhood when they were happy. A surprising number of people talked of being in the countryside, often some distance from home, usually without their parents being present. This led us to consider how few opportunities there are for children nowadays to enjoy this kind of experience, with fears of the ever-prowling paedophile and lack of wild areas to play contributing to the justifications of having our children at home. In the session *Creating and Maintaining Healthy Environments* Penny Priest had presented her own research about the psychosocial impacts of walking in the countryside. At the end of this session (and end of the *Toxic Mental Environments* course) I made a commitment to do something to help people access and gain benefit from the beautiful countryside around Shrewsbury.

The *Toxic Mental Environments* sessions reminded me of a series of half-day events entitled 'Using Common Sense and Personal Experience to Help People' that Craig Newnes and I conducted in the mid 1990s. These followed a regular format where participants – mostly a mix of people involved with mental health services (both as recipients and as staff) – were initially invited to identify and discuss one thing that they felt had 'helped them when they had been in a mental health crisis' and one thing that they felt 'helped them maintain their mental health'. We would list what people identified and then compare our list with what was generally understood to be the evidence base. We also encouraged participants to assess whether local mental health services provided any of the things we had listed and, if not, whether anything could be done to bring about changes that might enable things on the list to be provided locally, either through statutory services or outside these structures. People tended to generate wonderfully eclectic lists of things that helped them. However, two repetitive themes kept cropping up in these sessions:

1. People felt they benefited from being with like-minded people who had had similar experiences.

2. People felt they benefited from being in the countryside and/or with animals.

The National Institute of Health and Clinical Evidence (NICE) guidelines, with their emphasis on evidence gleaned from randomised controlled trials (RCTs), inevitably provide a skewed view of the evidence as they give most weight to published research which only very well-funded organisations (e.g. pharmaceutical companies) tend to be able to afford to conduct or sponsor. Our sessions were providing a type of evidence that rarely makes it onto lists of research projects considered by NICE (and if it was ever published would only warrant the lowest type of weighting – that accorded to service user testimony about what is helpful). Personal testimonies are highly subjective and psychologists are aware of the flaws in drawing too strong a conclusion from such data. Nevertheless, I found this type of evidence, accumulated from sessions with over 100 local people, compelling and, applying a scientist-practitioner model to it, endeavoured to try and apply it.

During 2006 *Thinking about Medication* and *Out of the Box* had also run. At the end of *Out of the Box* some participants had said that they found the informal support invaluable but they now wanted to engage in something outside the confines of a support group primarily focused on coming off medication. I invited members of the group to think of what they might like to be involved in, and what they might like to help set up, and Anna Hughes and I started to meet to develop the *Walk and Talk* concept (see Chapter 47). Anna's enthusiasm for walking outdoors and reflections on the importance of it regarding her own wellbeing helped me realise how much I benefited from regularly walking my dog on the Severn Way. How the frustrations of the day can ebb away, almost carried along by the waters of the river flowing by. How watching the swallows and martins brings me out of my inner world and helps me connect with something much greater than the irritations and stresses that can envelop me. How seeing the sun rise and set, the seasons come and go, the leaves appear and fall can help me connect with a concept of continuing change which is

inherent in nature, and can connect me to ideas at the centre of psychological models that are important to me. This includes the *Tidal Model*, which emphasises that nothing lasts and change is inevitable. As Phil Barker remarks: the pain of emotional distress only *feels* as if it is unceasing, and if we could hang on to this enduring wisdom we might begin to live in, and for, the moment.

On mindfulness and *Walk and Talk*

Toxic Mental Environments had led me to reflect on the need for all of us to spend increased time in environments that are good for us and that might repair some of the damage done to us by toxic environments. However, whilst walking beside the River Severn, I realised that on many occasions I remained stuck in my head – re-experiencing the problems of the day, the troubles of the past or the worries of the future, and oblivious to the present. The concept and techniques of mindfulness are helpful at times when we are sucked out of the moment, especially when it can be helpful to notice our surroundings and bring our attention to the present – what we can see, hear, feel, experience. To learn how to catch ourselves being dragged down repetitive chains of thoughts and into memories and fears that regularly trouble us and to gently bring our attention back to the present, and what our senses are connecting us to, can be of great help. I had begun to explore these ideas with people during one-to-one sessions at the CMHT base. *Walk and Talk* would enable me to discuss this concept and encourage people to train themselves to do this in the here and now of the countryside – a very different thing from discussing it in the cold confines of the clinic.

WALK AND TALK

Might you enjoy...

A regular walk along the stunning river Severn.

Opportunities to talk with like minded people.

A chance to pick the brains of a local psychologist?

2009

Thursday, from 4th June to 3rd September

We meet at:
Frankwell car park by steps to footbridge.
Leaving at **11:00am**

Someone will be at the meeting point from **10:45 am**

11:00-12:30 we walk along a beautiful stretch of the river Severn.

12:30 onwards option of drink and something to eat at local pub with a beautiful garden.

Who are we?
Mike Atkinson, Gio Azzolina, Nicki Evans, Guy Holmes & Gary Stevens.
All of us are passionate about the countryside and Walking.
Guy is a local clinical psychologist.

Walk and talk is open to anyone.

Bring along:
Boots or shoes you don't mind getting muddy if it's been wet.

An open mind, a friend or a (friendly) dog!

People who come along are responsible for their own welfare and can choose to join in as much of the walk that suits them.

SEE: WWW.SHROPSYCH.ORG FOR REPORT ON WALK & TALK OR JUST TURN UP.

The flyer

Shared joy is doubled joy, shared sorrow is sorrow halved.

    Swedish proverb

The flyers we have designed to advertise *Walk and Talk*, as the black and white copy of the 2009 version designed by Nicki Evans reveals, have emphasised both the beauty of the walk and the informality of the venture. They have also often included the above quote. This fits with an ideology that sharing experiences (in both senses of the word – doing things with others and talking about the ups and downs of our life) can in very ordinary ways be of help to us. This also fits with the research literature. Emory Cowen conducted a series of research projects that revealed people often talk about the same kinds of things with hairdressers, lawyers, bartenders and work supervisors as with professional therapists, and can derive similar psychological benefits from such encounters. Paul Gilbert's book *The Compassionate Mind* cites numerous research projects that reveal that kindness, support, affection and compassion release endorphins, opiates and hormones such as oxytocin in the body and this alleviates the damaging effects of high levels of cortisone caused by prolonged experiences of stress. Both providing and receiving such support can be psychologically and physically beneficial. The research into psychological therapies (e.g. Bergin & Garfield, 1994) has consistently revealed that it is the quality of the relationship rather than the qualifications, experience, training or techniques of the therapist that has the biggest impact on outcomes – in short it does not matter whom we have healing relationships with, it is relationships that seem to heal.

The flyers advertising *Walk and Talk* are put up in various mental health service venues as well as pinned up on notice boards in voluntary sector organisations, community centres, local cafés, shops, pubs and libraries in order to attract as wide a mix of people as possible. Staff in the local CMHTs are given copies to pass on to people they work with who might be interested. The meeting place from which we set off is opposite the Guildhall – flyers are also put up in this building in order to bring it to the notice of local civil servants and councillors, with the hope that they might come along both for their own benefit and in order to provide access to them for a group of people who do not normally have much contact with their elected representatives. Sending *Walk and Talk* flyers and information about it to local councillors has also led to good support from the local authority and links with other local initiatives that are trying to increase access to the countryside.

Walk and Talk participants

A salient principle of community psychology is working with communities as well as individuals. That is, groups that share common interests. Building alliances with marginalised groups. A recognition that peer support can be mutually benefiting and an effective means to change.

    Bob Diamond

As with other *Psychology in the Real World* ventures, *Walk and Talk* is open to anyone. People come from all walks of life. What brings them together are shared interests – in the countryside, wildlife, walking, being outdoors, engaging in conversations in an informal setting. We have professional people coming on their day off or during their summer holidays, local unemployed people, people who have current or past involvement with community mental health services, local authority staff, youngsters with ASBOs preventing them from entering the town centre, patients from the local psychiatric hospital, people who live in residential rehabilitation services, retired people who have caught a free bus into town from outlying villages, people with learning disabilities, teenagers who have been excluded from school, and people who saw the flyer in town that morning and just decided to turn up. Some people bring a friend or family member, some their children, others their dog. Some come with a member of staff or someone they identify (or who identifies themselves) as a carer.

Mental health service staff who attend quickly come to realise that the group is set up for them to participate in as individuals alongside other people on the walk (including the person they might be accompanying) in a way that feels very different from most services which tend to emphasise and reinforce hierarchies and lines of difference between staff and patients. Some residential staff have appeared to find this difficult at first but have quickly come to enjoy it. I try to create a feeling of informality between myself and staff that mirrors the informality between me and the 'patients' they come with. This enables an openness of communication which often seems more useful than the rather stilted and awkward exchanges I have had when asked to provide consultation or training in residential services. For example, I have been able to engage in conversations about the recovery model and ways that this is applied in residential settings whilst walking alongside residential staff during *Walk and Talk* and been able to bring the residents they accompany into the debate. There is no expectation of my 'intervention' having to be associated with change – the conversations are conducted in the spirit of exchanging ideas. Whether this has more or less impact than the more formal consultation or training that psychologists usually provide is not known. What I do know is that the exchanges are much

more open, rich and less characterised by defensive positioning compared to training and consultation work I have conducted in residential settings. The beautiful (and neutral) countryside seems a more conducive setting for such discussions than the non-neutral and often sterile environments I have experienced whilst 'delivering' training.

Some people who initially participated in *Walk and Talk* during the first summer it ran kept the walks going through the autumn and winter (without my involvement) and have become part of an organising collective that ensures *Walk and Talk* goes on through the year. As such, some of these people have developed greater skills in running groups (e.g. designing and distributing flyers; taking responsibility for ensuring someone is there to welcome people as they arrive and for the smooth running of the venture; encouraging people to come again; ensuring time boundaries are kept; keeping an eye out for people who might not be getting what they want from the experience). Several have remarked on the benefits they feel they get from taking a role in organising something rather than being a passive recipient of help delivered by others. Together we have met up to lobby the local authority to improve the condition of the path; formed working parties to fill pot-holes with bark to make the path less muddy and more safe for *Walk and Talk* participants and the wider community; sat on committees in order to protect the route from developers and help part of the path be recognised as an 'official local authority trail'; and in doing so enjoyed feeling part of something that has benefits that go further than the therapeutics of being with others in the countryside.

Walk and Talk Group

I'm early today so I sit writing
Will anyone show?
I know they will
But I get anxious anyhow
Walking has proved good for me
Talking has helped me grow
It's so difficult to get out
I've been shut away for a long time
That's what I do
I have been shown there actually is a world out there
Maybe there's no need to be scared
It leads to opportunities I did not expect
I just need to take that step
I always freak out at a good opportunity
Whist walking along the Severn I find
Something to look forward to
The next thing is just round the corner
When this group ends
There'll always be something waiting
Something else to look to
Something to be involved in
That something that gives meaning

Nicki Evans, *Walk and Talk* participant, summer 2007

Box 19   On living where you work

Sometimes community psychologists do not live in the communities they want to help. Whilst the advantages for psychotherapists and their clients of having no contact outside their sessions are well-documented, I feel community psychologists risk missing out on too much information about a community if they only work in it. I am thinking of knowledge about public transport, which are the friendly and unfriendly pubs, what is going on in terms of entertainment and community activism, who to contact and who to avoid – the ordinary stuff of life. Nick Davies' book *Dark Heart: The Shocking Truth about Hidden Britain* graphically illustrates the lived experience of the poorest people in society, and how some of the most heart-rending and gruesome experiences poor people endure often go on around, but under the radar, of people who live very different lives. By living where I work I have been able to, for example, notice that one of the new 'stylish 1 and 2 bedroom apartments' (as they are advertised on the giant billboard that implores us to buy one of the 'last few that remain') is already being used as a crack house. Similarly, I would not have known about the route we go on during *Walk and Talk* if I had not explored the local area whilst walking my dog in the evening. The route is a gateway into the countryside coming straight out of the town centre but, when we started using it, was a relatively unknown and in places unkempt path. Whilst other towns might not have quite such a beautiful river and 'green corridor' running into them, I am aware that even when living in very deprived city centre areas of Birmingham and Nottingham I have been able to find hidden places – bits of woodland, parkland, canals and paths through wild areas where wildlife flourishes – often within a few hundred yards of my home.

Wild people feel comfortable in wild areas. Some parks can be too sterile whereas wild areas help people feel alive. Richard Mitchell and Frank Popham have published research indicating that green spaces ameliorate the body's response to stress and access to these can reduce the marked health inequalities that exist between poor and well-off people. In an editorial encompassing a review of the literature, Terry Hartig in *The Lancet* has argued for changes in social policy to enable people from poor backgrounds to have easier and greater access to green spaces in order to improve their physical and psychological health: the literature indicates that physical activity in natural environments yields more emotional, cognitive, and physiological benefits than activity in urban outdoor spaces, and significantly more benefits than inactivity indoors. If psychologists really want to be applied scientists we have to consider how to incorporate such evidence into our practice, and if we want to be directly involved then living where we work provides great advantages.

Whereas bumping into people only otherwise encountered in a one-to-one therapy relationship can be a discombobulating experience for both parties, bumping into people met through community psychology endeavours like *Walk and Talk* always feels great. And the best ways of bumping into people … to walk, cycle or take the bus. I have let many interested people know about forthcoming groups whilst cycling to work and seeing people in the street (for example, taking their children to school), and the sense of a loose nexus of people associated with *Psychology in the Real World* being connected by such chance encounters is perhaps not just in my head.

49

Access to psychology II

What is a highly paid clinical psychologist doing taking people out on a nature walk?
Senior NHS Trust manager

On *Walk and Talk* in early May 2008 we came across a swan's nest, just two feet off the river path. We all stared in awe at the swan on its giant nest of sticks, and at an egg that nestled beneath it, and reeled back as it hissed a warning for us to keep clear. One man turned around and quickly set off for home. As the weeks went by we got used to gently edging around the nest and caught glimpses of other eggs. Then one day in June six fluffy cygnets swam past us. We watched the cygnets grow in size and confidence and noticed one had a damaged leg and sometimes struggled to keep up. Some seemed bolder than others, swimming further from their watchful parents, and as autumn came we watched their plumes whiten as they all matured and steadily moved along their journey towards independence.

The manager quoted at the beginning of this chapter is right – it does not need a psychologist to set up a walking group and help people have wonderful experiences similar to the one described above. Indeed, for over a decade in Shropshire we have had a local walking group run by what was initially called Day Services and is now the Social Inclusion and Recovery Service and this has been shown to be highly effective (see Priest, 2007). For people who rarely venture out of their homes, who keep to well-rehearsed routes to and from their houses, who rarely raise

their heads to witness the world outside, a magical experience like we had with the swans is transforming enough. It perhaps does not need a psychologist to help people access or 'psychologise' such experiences. However, having me on the walks and being paid as a psychologist means that I inevitably bring psychology into many encounters on *Walk and Talk*. For example, just taking the swan example, this included explorations of the following:

1. Behavioural theory and exposure therapy: I helped others to calm the man who reacted to the hissing swan by running away. He initially angrily refused to rejoin the group. We discussed his fears, explored what fear reactions entail (e.g. physiological reactions such as the release of adrenalin that speed up breathing and heart rate) and used some basic anxiety management techniques to help him manage his fight/flight response. Other people on the walk witnessed and helped with this. We encouraged him to face his fear and walk past the swan's nest and, once he had done this, several of us engaged in a wider discussion of behavioural theories and therapies. The psychologist Bandura helped great numbers of people to reduce their fears through modelling and social learning techniques – *Walk and Talk* gave us an opportunity to do this and to model the benefits of facing fears. The following week a discussion ensued exploring why this person was very fearful of the swan again (despite

facing his fear the previous week) enabling me to explain the theory of spontaneous recovery – that his reactions (like all learned behaviours), until they have gone through a repetitive extinction process, spontaneously recover, especially overnight, and how the fear reduction process occurs quicker each time the fear is faced and a behaviour not reinforced. We tested the theory against his experience, and noted that he was able to face and calm his fear more easily each week.

2. Attachment theory, existential issues and developmental psychology: We all seemed to be profoundly moved whilst watching the swans and seeing their development each week. As the walk continued conversations turned to reflections on how the swans mirrored our own journey through life. At times we spoke of our own birth and early childhood experiences; discussed different experiences of being protected (or not) by parents; of sibling rivalry; of being handicapped or having a handicapped sibling; of separating from parents and the transition to adulthood; and of becoming parents ourselves, with the joys and difficulties that brings.

3. Comparative psychology, Freud and theories of personality development: We explored ideas about the fact that we are animals and debated how applicable studies of animal behaviour are to human behaviour. We discussed and critiqued Freud's theories of drives (the animal bits of us associated with sexual and aggressive urges) and whether psychological defences primarily relate to these drives or arise in different ways. We compared Freud's theory of ego development to other personality theories (e.g. object relations – the idea that aspects of our personality that we might be unconscious of might have developed as a result of our

relationships with significant people, largely our parents, in childhood).

All this (and more) from watching swans! Whilst I have questioned whether psychologists make the best healers, and certainly it cannot be claimed that we have better 'mental health' or are more successful in our relationships than any other group in society, we do have access to a wide range of theories and research evidence in an easily located library – our heads – and it is possible to enable many other people to access this library. The debates engaged in during *Walk and Talk* (and other *Psychology in the Real World* ventures) tend to be lively, broad, reflective and challenging in ways that only rarely occur in the media (which, for dramatic purposes, tend to favour two expert 'talking heads' vehemently disagreeing with each other). Whereas many *Psychology in the Real World* courses involve the facilitators initially introducing material to kick-start debates, as this chapter exemplifies *Walk and Talk* provides rich experiences that can serve this purpose; psychologists can contribute to ensuing debates by sharing their knowledge as well as be involved, alongside other group members, in *in vivo* therapeutic experiences.

On context

During *Walk and Talk*, especially when I am aware that other co-facilitators are keeping an eye on the group as a whole, I often get into fascinating conversations with people on the walk. Many of these differ from the conversations I have with people at the CMHT base. We might go from talking about the countryside to exchanging general social enquiries about our families. I might respond at length to (rather than 'bat back') direct questions about myself (ranging from what the community where I live is like to what helps me cope with life's pressures). Other conversations closely overlap with and seem more or less indistinguishable from those in the therapy room, as people sometimes talk at length about their painful life experiences, how these have shaped and affected them, their experiences of services, their dilemmas and future plans. What is different is the context.

Years of providing one-to-one therapy has revealed to me what a leap of faith it is to think that as people feel able to trust me more in the consulting room, as they disclose things they might not have spoken of before, as they learn to manage a (psychologically) intimate relationship, they transfer this learning to other contexts and relationships. Some do, but many have revealed that outside the consulting room they reveal very little to anyone else, only trusting me with their secrets, always fearful of being let down or hurt by others, shunning close relationships. *Walk and Talk* and other community-based groups offer a bridge between trust in the lone therapist and trust in others. People on the walk may choose moments when no one else can overhear them to speak about a deeply personal issue, but it is still in a public place, may be overheard, and may lead to a conversation that others might join. There is sometimes a fine line to tread, where counselling skills that readily lead people to speak more deeply in the therapy room might rapidly lead to

people opening up on *Walk and Talk* and disclosing more than they perhaps intended, but by and large this does not seem to have been a problem, and the friendly and trusting atmosphere in the groups seems to quieten people's fears about what they have revealed. Whenever people do imply they regret having spoken of intimate things with people they barely know, I tend to encourage a wider discussion within the group around us about how things like *Walk and Talk* are not confidential in the doctor–patient sense, but that we all know the importance of treating personal information that someone may have revealed with respect, not gossiping about it outside the group, and perhaps not revealing people's names if conversations about important but at times personal themes continue outside the group setting. Usually this seems to suffice.

Some people who come on *Walk and Talk* have had very fractious relationships with mental health services but this has softened when given an opportunity to meet people in a different context – not one where people are positioned as a patient expecting a cure but one where relationships grow in less entrenched ways. As Box 20 (p. 226) shows, this can bring unexpected benefits.

Box 20   Two participants' feedback on *Walk and Talk*

'Having read the title *Walk and Talk* I am still surprised that curiosity led me to find out more. As a child my parents recall that I had a reluctance to do either and as an adult I never acquired the love of walking for pleasure, it was just a means of getting from A to B. I checked out the website, slide show and poster. The appeal – the informality and accessibility. The suggestion simply to turn up with an open mind and sensible shoes. Happily what was not required – referrals, assessments, waiting lists and notes – appealed to me more. Armed with a promise to myself to do something different I turned up at the bottom of Frankwell Bridge steps. The experience – a time to be alone, to stop, briefly reconnect and to feel. To escape. A chance to take a risk and find courage. To listen. To be heard. I have been told that I need to help myself and take responsibility; this was one of the few times I was shown how. That the process of change is as important as the outcome. Ultimately an experience of not so much walk in my shoes as walk by my side. In the era of targets, specialist services, tight budgets and health and safety it makes a refreshing change for someone to take a simple idea ... and walk with it.'

'I am so used to writing letters lately complaining about a system that I think has been unfair to me, I barely know how to write a compliment. *Walk and Talk* was something that kept me sane over a long six-week summer holiday that can get very lonely. Even walking in torrential rain was fantastic! I would have sat at home depressed if not for the walk. The similar route each week was very different because of the things I saw and the different people I met. My psychotic mind connected everything personal to me and helped me bury old past memories ... freaky eh?'

50

Beginnings IV: *Walk and Talk*

All human experience involves flux. The idea that people might exist in constant states – like schizophrenia or depression – is an illusion. Instead people are in constant movement. This assumption suggests the value of helping people become more aware of how change is happening within and around them and how they might assist, influence or participate in its direction.

Phil Barker and Poppy Buchanan-Barker

When meeting people attending *Walk and Talk* for the first time I or one of the other co-facilitators introduce ourselves, welcome them to the group and explain something about the plan: what time we set off; where we go; what to expect; how it is very relaxed and people go at their own pace and do their own thing; how we don't walk on mass; how it's not a guided walk – rather an opportunity to enjoy the countryside in whatever way suits. As I shake people's hands and say my name most people reciprocate. Some start a conversation; many are very nervous and just listen and nod. One group of people occasionally behave quite oddly: people who identify themselves as 'carers' or 'staff'. Whilst many of these people quickly realise that the group is not an institutional endeavour and join in as individuals, chat to other people on the walk, give the person they have come with space to get to know others, and do not behave purely as an escort, others seem to struggle with this concept …

'Hi. Welcome. I'm Guy. It's your first time here isn't it?'

'I'm with him.'

'Oh that's nice; you've come with a friend.' Incredulous stare.

'Do you have a name?'

'Eric.'

'Well, enjoy the walk, Eric. Some people here have come before, but for others it's their first time too.'

'When does it end because I've got to get him back for his lunch?'

'It doesn't work like that. People walk as far or as little as they want. Some people come to the pub for something to eat or drink, others don't; some stay a couple of hours, others walk just part of the way then do their own thing.'

Incredulous stare.

'It's a beautiful walk,' I continue. 'It's hard not to be moved by the countryside we are walking through – I hope you enjoy it and get something out of it. I'll perhaps catch up with you later.'

I turn to the person with them. 'Hi, I'm Guy …'

A more normal conversation inevitably ensues.

I am not sure why people behave like this. However, I do believe that institutions institutionalise the staff just as much (if not more) than the patients. Residential staff often seem to feel worried that people will think that they are the 'mad one' rather than the 'sane carer' – and of course this frequently happens as the only thing to distinguish the 'mad' from the 'sane' on first meeting is usually the impact of medication, such as people with a tremor who blankly stare with a stone face (suffering parkinsonian adverse effects of antipsychotic medication) or people who pace up and down (suffering drug-induced akathisia). But of course all people who come to *Walk and Talk* for the first time are nervous, unsure what to expect, worried about what people might think of them, and feel awkward as they wait to set off. That is why members of what we now call the *Walk and Talk facilitators' collective* shake people's hands (hoping to calm people through touch); explain what will happen (aiming to settle people by giving them a mental map of what will unfold – like nature, people abhor a vacuum: we tend to fill it with fantasies, often malign, catastrophising fantasies); don't put people on the spot or expect them to speak much; smile and try and convey a sense of calm friendliness; and above all else normalise things.

Compared to other group situations, it is not possible on *Walk and Talk* to have the same kind of influence in creating a group matrix (see Chapter 12). Inevitably exchanges between people on the walk involve a more random and chaotic process, and the group often takes place as a fluid set of subgroups as people talk with whoever is walking alongside them. It is possible though to introduce people, and when someone says something it is possible to link their comment (and them) with other people on the walk who might think similarly (or differently). Some people come to connect with nature rather than other people – in a sense the countryside can be thought of as part of the matrix. The organisers use the facilitating style we call 'unobtrusive shepherding' (see Chapter 43) which involves a very loose boundary. Every walk has a new beginning (and end) as the people making up the group differ each week. Unlike other *Psychology in the Real World* groups, which are closed groups, *Walk and Talk* in many ways is always involved in the beginnings stages of development – in Tuckman's model (see Chapter 29) is always 'forming' (although for some regulars the group may be passing through other stages of development as well). As such, the skills described in other *Beginnings* chapters need to be utilised every week.

51

On horses, the healing power of animals, and concurrently attending community-based groups and one-to-one therapy

I had been seeing Jim for nine months on a one-to-one basis when, during a review, he stated a wish to continue the one-to-one sessions *and* come on *Walk and Talk*. I had suggested he might consider one of these options but he chose both. My psychoanalytic group training warned against seeing people for individual and group therapy at the same time, but I had not thought this through regarding *Walk and Talk*. Jim had identified a need for individual therapy to help him live with the long-term impacts of abusive experiences but he also wanted to do something about his 'social isolation' – to spend some time outside the sanctuary of his flat; to try and cope with being with people; to try and spend less time 'in his own head being bombarded by voices'. In this sense requesting both seemed logical. I felt uneasy but decided to go with the request and said I would see him by the River Severn the following week …

As soon as Jim arrives at the meeting point I realise it might not be such a good idea. Social anxiety seems a poor term to describe what he seems to be going through – this looks more like sheer terror, probably of being with other people and leaving the refuge that his home has become. I wonder what effect seeing me talking with others might be having but Jim does not catch my eye, just paces up and down on the edge of the group. As soon as I say 'Let's set off' he tears away, striding as fast as possible, apparently determined to get as big a gap as possible between the rest of the group and

himself. Half way through the walk I get a bit worried – he has left the path and appears to be talking to himself. He looks distressed. I leave the group – there are others who have been on *Walk and Talk* before and know the route. I feel awkward … is it because boundaries are being breached? My group analysis training would predict that, perhaps unconsciously, Jim might be 'wanting me for himself' (as he is used to in therapy) rather than joining the group and getting help from other people. I trust the group to look after itself, and feel relieved to have a co-facilitator – Anna is merrily chatting to various people, helping everyone feel at ease, modelling social skills I know I don't possess.

I find Jim in the middle of a field. He won't look at me.

'What's up?'

'There's no escape. They're everywhere.'

'Who?'

'There's no point. Even here they follow me, ruining things.'

I try everything I know to calm Jim, but my training seems ineffectual. I think he is talking about his voices but he seems to be trying to explain something about seeing someone come towards us on the path who once bullied him. In the one-to-one psychotherapeutic environment we would have time to talk this through, but here my comments seem to get lost in the wide-open spaces. He looks petrified – perhaps fearing that someone else might come over? I feel that he needs to get home (or do I need him to go home so I can focus on the group?) I am not sure he even knows where he is, such is his level of his distress.

'The voices are going mad,' Jim says to his shoes.

The group is ready to turn back down the path and head off to the pub. A quick glance across the group reassures me – people seem happy enough, content to let me concentrate on Jim. The two of us walk though a gate to the next field. I'm keen to get us back to the road as quickly as possible – for once being in the fields doesn't seem such a comforting place. Suddenly a horse trots up and bars our way. I have always been scared of horses but steel myself to shoo it away. And then the horse nuzzles Jim, rubbing its head against his. I panic and think it's trying to bite Jim's ear off! I expect him to scream but he doesn't. He nuzzles the horse back, stroking its neck. They lovingly caress and Jim calms. He smiles and giggles – I've never seen him do this before. As he strokes the horse, giving and receiving affection, his tortured features appear to ease. A look of serenity replaces his usual pained grimace. I patiently wait for a few minutes watching them. They seem conjoined.

On the way back Jim talks freely, more freely than I have ever witnessed before. He tells me that he helped to muck out stables and look after horses as a teenager and has always had an affinity with them. The mocking voices have let him be for now. Evidently there is a field with horses near where he lives but he has never gone down there; perhaps he will from now on, especially when he feels things are getting too much. Maybe one day he will work with horses again. Someone else from the group joins us and talks about how they have only ever truly felt happy when with animals. How it's easier to love animals than people – how you can trust them because you know if you treat them right they won't hurt you. I cite some research done by Deborah Wells on the benefits of having a dog in terms of loneliness, depression and various

measures of psychological and physical health. A silence ensues and I wish I'd just talked about how much I enjoy being with my dog, Marley. Jim has become quiet but the need to escape seems to have ebbed away, and the three of us stroll through the fields and back to the road.

Jim doesn't join us in the pub, but he does say that he feels well enough to make his own way home. The perpetual heaviness that he carries through life seems to have left him for now, and he sets off, head held high, not rammed into his chest as usual, facing the world rather than averting his gaze.

Through therapy we hope that people introject (absorb) something of the calm therapist. As I watch Jim walk down the road I get a feeling that something similar has happened here: the nuzzling horse is still with him, and I hope it always will be.

Postscript

Professional people like maps. Maps help us to not get lost. Without maps we can readily sink into doubts and paralysing fears: *I don't know what I'm doing; I feel so inadequate – I don't have anything to offer; How on earth do you help people who have such overwhelming problems?* For some of us our training provides an overall, general map. Others relate what each person says to one specific model or theory. For others a bag of techniques might suffice. Although I feel comfortable going 'off map' and have found over the years the people I have seen have introduced me to many new maps of what can help people, in the future I think I am unlikely to concurrently see people on a one-to-one basis whilst at the same time they attend a group I am facilitating. My experience is that the groups work well for people I have never met before and for people whom I have stopped seeing on a one-to-one basis. But I am concerned that it clouds my thinking, and that of the other person, when we try and do both at the same time. I get into muddles about what has been told me in the confidential setting of the clinic and what I have learned in the more public arena of the group. Boundaries perhaps do not need to be as set in stone as many therapists insist, but when blurred there can be muddles about intimacy and about the type of relationship two people are engaged in.

More is not necessarily more.

SECTION 11

Countering the impacts of stigma and working with diverse groups

52

On stigma

The sheer lack of respect and understanding given to the disadvantaged in Britain is highly corrosive of wellbeing and all the more so because it is constant and overwhelming.

C Jones (cited in Lynne Friedli's WHO report *Mental Health, Resilience and Inequalities*)

The work of Wolf Wolfensberger and others on social role valorisation has had an effect in shaping some of the philosophies and practices of *Psychology in the Real World*. A day with Wolf is a day where you will be taken through an exquisite analysis of the myriad of factors that lead certain people to be devalued, stigmatised and treated badly in our society. He often tracks this carefully back through historical accounts over a few hundred (sometimes thousand) years and reveals how certain human characteristics have come to be seen as 'desirable' and people who differ in some way from these norms have come to be 'negatively valued' (and usually treated badly) in our society.

Powerful groups tend to treat people who do not fit what society at that time has defined as desired norms as 'other' and start to classify them as a member of a (socially devalued) group. Modern phrases such as the 'mentally ill' and 'learning disabled' might seem more acceptable than older terms such as 'fools' and 'idiots' which were used to characterise (and legally categorise) people in the past, but Wolfensberger's analyses reveal that attitudes and behaviours to people assigned to these groups have, in many ways, changed little over the years.

In the terminology of social role valorisation such people tend to be assigned *negative deviancy roles*. For example, they might be seen, described and treated as: *not human*, *clown-like*, *a threat*, or *a charitable burden*. Opportunities to take up certain roles in life available to members of socially valued groups may be subtly or brutally denied to such people – roles such as *breadwinner*, *teacher*, *parent* or *therapist*. Members assigned to socially devalued groups become embedded in roles such as *patient* where they receive help designated as best for them by socially valued providers of care and have limited access to opportunities to learn skills needed to take on more socially valued roles. People cast into such negative roles tend to be denied 'the good things in life' such as being an integral member of a family; having an intimate group of friends with whom one freely socialises in settings enjoyed by most people in society; working in enjoyable and decently paid jobs seen by others as valuable; and being treated as an individual.

Socially devalued people have historically been grouped together and have suffered what Wolfensberger calls 'wounds', such as:

- relegation to low status and low power positions (e.g. service user)

- branding with stigmatising labels (e.g. schizophrenic)

- impoverishment of relationships, which might be largely limited to relationships with paid workers who are in roles that are more highly socially valued (e.g. psychologist)

- congregation with other branded people and separation from non-labelled people (e.g. through living in hospitals or group homes)

- impoverishment in terms of material resources (e.g. suffer the impacts of poverty and insults of receiving benefits where qualification for that benefit involves acceptance of devaluing labels)

- loss of control of major and minor decisions over what happens (e.g. institutions are inevitably run in ways that meet institutional and staff needs rather than individual needs which are so varied they cannot be met in such settings)

- impoverishment in terms of experiences (e.g. through suffering social exclusion)

The devaluing process leads people to devalue themselves (despite exhortations from cognitive therapists not to). Some come to feel that their life has been wasted – one man who had been involved with psychiatric services for over 25 years said to me that the only point of his life seemed to be to provide work and therefore pleasure and meaning to staff that were paid to help him. When alienated and treated as alien, people start to feel alien (which can become part of a person's core identity and can manifest itself in behaviours that get labelled psychotic, leading to greater labelling and stigmatisation). Some people may withdraw from life, others might become more demanding. Some may develop fantasy relationships, whilst others might display the resentment and rage felt about such processes. All of these and a myriad of other reactions can be labelled as psychiatric symptoms and can serve to fuel a stigma cycle (see Fig. 17, p. 236).

Social role valorisation argues that state-provided helping professions and institutions are often part of the problem rather than the solution. The helping professions have long histories of harming 'different' people. Treatments in the past can be seen as horrific and ridiculous now: from the electrocution of black men's testicles who were suffering drapetomania – a mental illness that only affected black slaves and caused them to run away from their white masters; to the hysterectomies given to women whose hysteria was 'scientifically proven to be caused by wandering wombs'; to the mushing of vital parts of people's brains done by the Nobel prize-winning pioneer of lobotomy Egon Moniz; to the electrocution of homosexual men when their penises reacted to homoerotic images presented to them by psychologists trained in behaviour therapy. But treatments today are often characterised by similarly 'heroic' attempts to change people designated as deviant: the electrocution of elderly women in order to induce epileptic fits to treat their depression; the widespread proliferation of what psychiatrist Peter Breggin has termed 'brain disabling' medication given to people aged from 4 to 104; personality disorder clinics providing specialist treatments even though there is no agreement of what constitutes an 'ordered personality' or even agreement on what the term personality means; the taking away of basic human rights (such as the right to refuse damaging medical interventions) from people deemed to be a risk to themselves or others even though individual behaviour is unpredictable (beyond the aphorism 'nothing predicts behaviour like behaviour' which is not particularly helpful regarding risk assessment and management); and the compulsory detention of people in environments that even the clinicians involved in the detaining feel are not conducive to good mental health (such as poorly staffed acute psychiatric services where the bureaucratic demands on nurses result in patients being

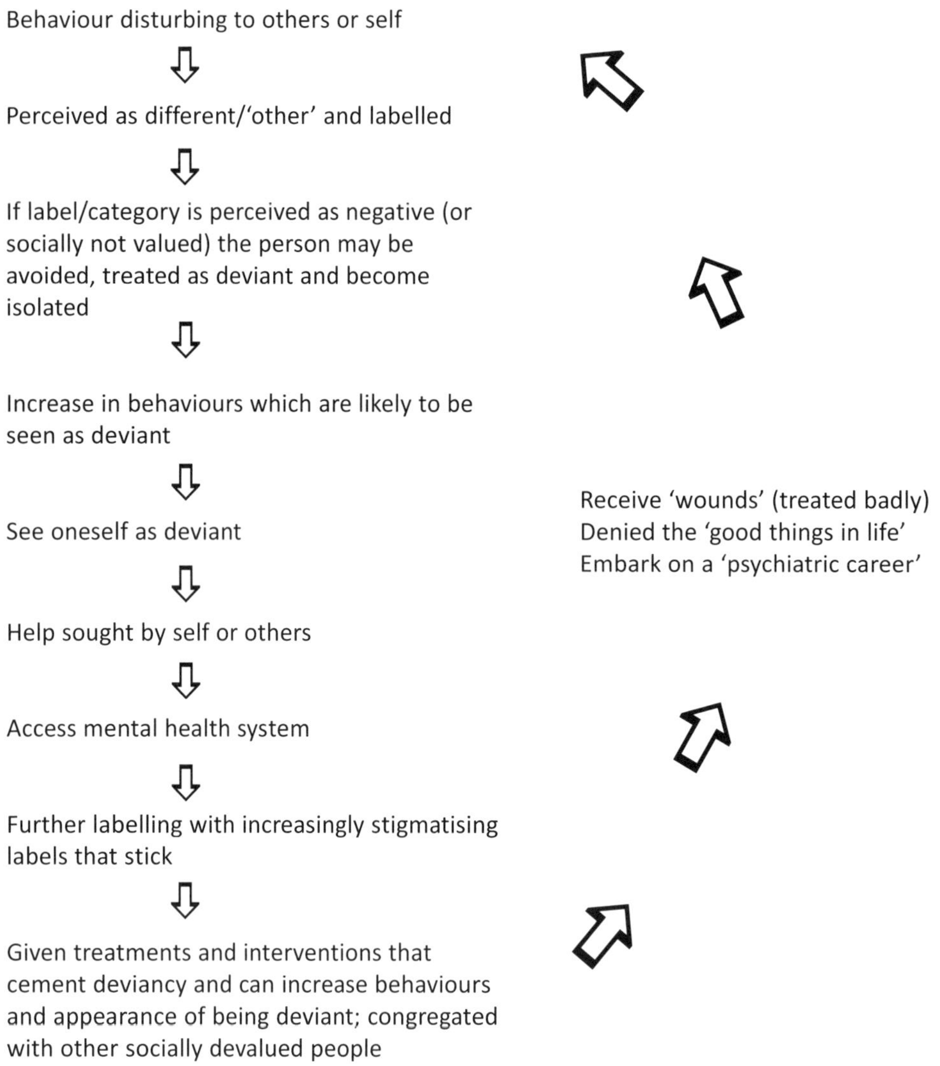

Behaviour disturbing to others or self

Perceived as different/'other' and labelled

If label/category is perceived as negative (or socially not valued) the person may be avoided, treated as deviant and become isolated

Increase in behaviours which are likely to be seen as deviant

See oneself as deviant

Help sought by self or others

Access mental health system

Further labelling with increasingly stigmatising labels that stick

Given treatments and interventions that cement deviancy and can increase behaviours and appearance of being deviant; congregated with other socially devalued people

Receive 'wounds' (treated badly)
Denied the 'good things in life'
Embark on a 'psychiatric career'

Fig. 17   A stigma cycle (developed from the ideas of Goffman and Wolfensberger)

continually assessed but rarely attended to, and which result in mountains of records but patients saying nothing helpful happens in the unit).

Wolfensberger has written on what dangerous places health services can be for people and of the process of 'death making'. In short, services are often places people at risk of being devalued may need to avoid.

Social role valorisation advocates helping people access and engage in positive, socially valued roles. People should be helped to attain competency in those roles (e.g. learn new skills) if they do not possess sufficient competency to presently carry them out. Its proponents advocate action at different levels, not just the personal, but also in the immediate environment of the person (where they spend their time) and in society as a whole – it is incumbent on those who really want to help to bring about political, legal and attitudinal change throughout society. Wolfensberger advocates alliances between socially valued and socially devalued people in society – such alliances can serve to unify people, broaden acceptance of differences, and encourage the coexistence of people.

There might be much in social role valorisation that is open to critique. Mad Pride and similar organizations have brilliantly countered prejudice not by having alliances with socially valued groups (people judged as 'sane') but by extolling the virtues of being mad and being different. As Peter Campbell has argued, alliances between different socially devalued groups (women, gay men and lesbians, black and minority ethnic groups, people with physical and learning disabilities, etc) can be helpful when trying to bring about political change and fighting for universal civil liberties. But the analyses of social role valorisation do pose a significant challenge to all people in the helping professions to reflect on what we do. I have spent most of my career doing research, training and consultation work with members of the helping professions that has largely focused on the harm that is done in the name of help. *Psychology in the Real World* ventures have provided opportunities to minimise and counteract some of that harm.

Countering the risks and effects of social devaluation and stigma

It was so good to realise that in spite of or because of all our faults and failings we are all mortal and members of the human race and it's OK not to be scared of those who live and express themselves differently.

Participant on *Understanding Ourselves and Others* course

Some of the people who get involved in *Psychology in the Real World* ventures have for years been involved in CMHT services that are aimed at helping 'people with severe and enduring mental health problems'; some have had periods in psychiatric hospital; some have diagnoses such as schizophrenia, manic depression and personality disorder; some until recently lived on long-stay hospital wards receiving years of rehab characterised by token economies (a recent conversation on *Walk and Talk* led to us renaming this as 'earning the right to get your fags back'). Such people are at high risk of social devaluation, and suffering discrimination resulting from stigma and prejudice. Over several decades John O'Brien has published work not just on the harm that services can do, but also on *what is worth working for?* He identifies five closely linked service accomplishments that do not prescribe how staff working with people assigned to socially devalued groups should behave but identify outcomes worth struggling for. These are:

1. *Community presence* – Countering the risks or effects of social devaluation involves people sharing the ordinary places and engaging in the ordinary activities that define community life, increasing the number and variety of places a person knows and can use, and avoiding segregated services that increase the process of social devaluation and the risks of being treated badly because of that process.

2. *Community participation* – This emphasises the importance of people being part of a network of personal relationships that include a variety of people not just those people one is congregated with as a requirement of receiving help.

3. *Having valued social roles* – This points to the importance of dignity, respect and a place among a network of valued people coupled to the avoidance of low status activities.

4. *Making choices* – People should have as much autonomy as possible (and much much than they are often permitted) in small everyday

matters (e.g. what to do) and large life-defining matters (e.g. who to live with).

5. *Contributing and increasing competence* – This involves people contributing as fully as possible and skilfully performing meaningful activities (with training and assistance when required).

Some of the ways that *Psychology in the Real World* ventures have tried to accomplish some of these aims are covered in other parts of the book (e.g. Sections 1 and 4). For example, people attend the groups as participants, students, writers or walkers not as patients or clients. They come along not because they are referred or because they are ill or needing treatment or therapy but because they are interested in something. Participants chose to come having seen the flyers rather than being referred in letters detailing their problems and deficits or forced to attend as part of a community treatment order. The venues are free of the stigmatising signs and messages that characterise many mental health settings and tend to be full of people attending courses rather than being assessed or receiving treatments. The groups occur in the ordinary places of life not places where socially devalued people are congregated in order to receive help and be efficiently processed through systems by (socially valued) professionals. Participants are treated as autonomous individuals, as equal members of the group whatever their background. People with long histories of involvement with mental health services mix with people with no involvement with these services – this not only enables community presence and participation, it lessens stigmatising attitudes in the wider population. For example, many who have attended mental health services disclose this fact at some point. Participants who have not had this experience are often surprised to discover

that group members they have got to know as people have been in the local psychiatric hospital, hear voices, have self-harmed and so on. As a consequence they can come to having some of their stereotypes and prejudices challenged.

Many *Psychology in the Real World* courses can be conceptualised as adult education. As Sue Arnold has written, by insisting that adult education became focused on academic achievement the government spoiled the enjoyment people got from learning in an environment that was freed from the continual need to achieve and get qualifications and missed the fact that informal education provides social glue for communities, as many people go on courses in order to make friends. This is often openly acknowledged by *Psychology in the Real World* participants who reveal that one reason they signed up for the course was that they were lonely. The groups offer people from all walks of life opportunities to become friends and feedback shows that this often occurs, assisted by the fact that we have breaks which enable more informal contact between people, and participants often lunch together after the main activity has taken place in the venues' cafés or in local pubs after *Walk and Talk*.

As well as making friends, people on the courses have gone on to set up formal and informal groups aimed at supporting each other and other people. One *Black Dog* participant set up a *Changes* group, initially with a membership made up of several people who had come on the course, but later with a much wider membership, which ran under the auspices of this voluntary sector organisation for several years with people meeting on a weekly basis. Other *Psychology in the Real World* group members have set up very informal groups that meet regularly and engage in a variety of activities that reflect the myriad of things people find helpful. Some members of *Psychology in the*

Real World groups have later taken on a variety of socially valued roles regarding projects connected with *Psychology in the Real World*. These include:

- consultant and contributor to the planning of other groups and projects
- group leader/facilitator
- researcher
- sole or co-author of articles in peer-reviewed journals
- chapter writer
- lecturer
- trainer of staff
- conference presenter
- campaigner
- committee member on local authority committee
- consultant to other people wanting to set up similar groups

The majority of people who have taken up these roles have had long histories of involvement with psychiatric services and have suffered many of the wounds described by Wolfensberger. Several have written chapters about their experiences in this book. Some have needed help to attain some specific competencies in these roles – assistance preparing talks given to staff teams and at conferences (including role-play preparation and psychological support on the day); training in facilitation skills; training in research skills; editorial help regarding writing in an academic style. I have tried to offer encouragement coupled to the minimal necessary support and followed Erich Fromm's maxim: *There can be no real freedom without the freedom to fail.* Having said that, no one has failed in these roles. People's inner critics have often lambasted them after they have, for example, given a talk about one of the groups, but the actual feedback from listeners has tended to

highlight their contribution rather than mine when it has been a joint endeavour. Many people who have gone on from being a participant in a group to taking up other roles have been naturally gifted in these areas, or re-acquainted themselves with skills not utilised since perhaps having a breakdown. Others have been keen but at the outset did not appear so well suited to such roles. Yet perhaps through being relied upon, they have become reliable, and through being depended on, they have become dependable. Similarly, through being trusted and respected they have perhaps grown to trust and respect themselves. All have contributed in unique ways and I have learned much about, for example, facilitating groups from co-facilitating with people with no prior experience of this kind of work.

Whilst some people have preferred to take on these roles as a volunteer (retaining independence from the NHS Trust and a greater sense of freedom to say and do what they want, e.g. be openly critical of services) many have been paid for their time and contribution. Policies in our NHS Trust have developed as a result of these contributions and a wish on behalf of Trust management to involve service users more in the running of the organisation and to pay people for their time. In early *Psychology in the Real World* ventures service user consultants were able to be paid £20 for attending meetings (e.g. to help with the preparation and planning of a new project), but not for co-facilitating groups. Partly through the example of *Psychology in the Real World* ventures and lobbying by members and their allies, Trust policies have since been modified to include payment for running groups.

Through *Psychology in the Real World* we have been trying to do something locally but at the same time there have been nationwide attempts to address stigma and social inclusion. These include:

1. *The National Service Framework for Mental Health (Standard 1)* which states that services should 'combat discrimination against individuals and groups with mental health problems and promote their social inclusion'. The government's proposed strategy for 2010–20, *New Horizons,* also emphasises the importance of reducing stigma and aims to put equality and human rights protection at the heart of its plans regarding mental health.

2. *The National Social Inclusion Programme,* which is updated annually by the government cabinet office and is given a high profile alongside the Social Exclusion Task Force. In 2004 the Deputy Prime Minister, regarding the report *Mental Health and Social Exclusion* from the Social Exclusion Unit, said: 'This report shows people with mental health problems are one of the most socially excluded groups. Too often they do not have the support they need to participate fully in society, yet we know that employment and community activities are important in promoting both mental and physical wellbeing.' The report advocated a redesign of Health and Social Services to challenge stigma and discrimination and assist access to employment, community activities, education and training.

3. *The National Institute of Adult Continuing Education (NIACE),* which identified the benefits of learning regarding young people with mental health difficulties as: the provision of structure and stability; opportunities to gain confidence and self-esteem; the building of support networks; empowerment; and the provision of opportunities for people to progress, fulfil potential and gain personal satisfaction. Benefits to society included: greater inclusion of a marginalised group; enhanced understanding, acceptance and tolerance of people; reduced expenditure on health and social services; and improved mental health.

4. *The British Psychological Society*, which has published a discussion paper on socially inclusive practice that highlights the work of Janet Bostock in combating discrimination in the workplace and reducing workplace stress, Catherine Sholl's work in schools combating prejudice and Rufus May's work with *Evolving Minds* (a similar project to some *Psychology in the Real World* ventures).

5. *The Combating Stigma: Time to Change* campaign, which is a national campaign that has been given a high priority in our NHS Trust.

Mental health services (Wolfensberger would say by their very nature) have a poor record in this area but there is scope to move from labelling, congregating and treating the mentally ill (and thus inevitably contributing to the devaluing process) to primarily focusing on reducing the amount we, as service providers, stigmatise people and enabling access to activities in 'the ordinary places of life' that help people and repair rather than inflict such wounds. It is important that this should be driven by ideology and evidence of what works best for local people, though, and not be used as justifications by people whose main aim is to reduce costs and cut services.

One evaluation of *Psychology in the Real World* groups specifically looked at stigma and social inclusion (see Holmes & Gahan, 2007). Based on questionnaires sent to people who had attended three *Understanding Ourselves and Others* groups in the preceding two-year period, the evidence indicated that members of the groups appeared to have more understanding and acceptance of people who have been diagnosed as mentally ill, e.g. one person commented: *I feel a lot less fearful of people with mental health problems. I see mental health now as a scale that we are all on somewhere rather than 'them and us'.* This reduction in 'us and them' thinking seemed to apply to people who had never been involved with mental health services *and* people who had, with an ethos 'that we are all people who can and will struggle when life overwhelms us' replacing means of categorising and differentiating the well and the ill, the sane and the mad, the depressed and the clinically depressed, which can be seen as a core part of the stigmatising process. This fits with an ideological belief that commonly permeates many *Psychology in the Real World* ventures: if we all see each other as part of the human race then categorisations such as these will lose their power and prejudice against people who have been assigned to socially devalued groups such as the 'mentally ill' may lessen. The groups are aimed at helping us notice similarities between people whilst accepting individual differences, and seeing those differences as characteristic of the individuals not general characteristics that are emblematic and symptomatic of a socially devalued group they might have been assigned to.

If one takes Wolfensberger's critique seriously one would accept that services are part of the problem regarding stigma and would want to be wary about bringing new people into such services. This evaluation indicated that, unlike many mental health promotion schemes which inadvertently advertise the wares of mental health services and attract more people to them, *Psychology in the Real World* courses do not bring people into the services and assist some people

to have less contact with them: 13% of respondents reported having had less contact with NHS and Social Services since doing the course, with 0% having more contact.

It is important, however, not to over-emphasise the impacts of *Psychology in the Real World* groups. In the evaluation cited above people were asked if, as a result of coming on the course, they 'felt a greater part of a community or group': 39% responded 'Yes' but 43% said 'No' (18% either did not answer or answered 'Not relevant'). Comments included: '*It certainly helped to be part of a group of people who were understanding and accepting, and that helped me to go on to a group where there was a greater mix of people and experiences'; 'I feel I can join in groups more – before I felt rather hesitant and felt I shouldn't – that perhaps I wasn't wanted (pathetic but true).'* However, other participants pointed out the transitory nature of this sense of belonging: '*Not as a permanent state. Whilst the course ran there was a group member feeling.*' Similarly, only a minority reported feeling less lonely (26%). A number of positive comments were made, e.g. '*It was nice to feel accepted and talk openly with such a nice group of people who I look forward to seeing sometime in the future.*' But it is hard to have a significant impact on social isolation. Although some people said they never feel lonely, others said they always feel lonely or alone whatever the circumstances, e.g. '*I always feel lonely. No amount of interaction will change this. It is the way I am and always have been.*' Such modest changes in a minority of group members indicates the size of the task when trying to reduce loneliness, isolation and stigma and increase social inclusion.

53

Psychology in the Real World for people from diverse cultural backgrounds

ZOUNISH RAFIQUE

Employers always seem really pleased to have an Urdu and Punjabi-speaking psychologist working in the service. However, in the seven years that I have worked in NHS psychology services I have only been asked to see an Urdu or Punjabi speaker for individual therapy on four occasions. There are many reasons why people from diverse cultural backgrounds do not engage with mental health services: research shows these include lack of knowledge about what mental health is and what services have to offer; fear around the consequences of asking for help, e.g. getting labelled as 'mad'; being sectioned or prescribed medication with unpleasant side effects; a sense of hopelessness that anything can help; shame around not being able to cope; and practical factors such as lack of transport, childcare and availability of interpreters or multilingual workers. Services are working hard to help people overcome some of these barriers, to educate people, to combat stigma and make it possible for people to talk with someone in their first language (as evidenced by the NIMHE report *Celebrating our Cultures*). Underlying these efforts seems to be the assumption that people working in services have the knowledge, skills and evidence-based interventions that would help.

But what about those people who *do* know what services have to offer but cannot reconcile this with their understandings of what causes their distress? It would make little sense to a woman who feels trapped in a culture where she would be blamed for the breakdown of her abusive marriage and for the shame this would bring on her family to be offered cognitive therapy to challenge the way she thinks about things or psychopharmacology to alter the levels of serotonin in her brain. She may see more relevance in interventions that might lead to changes in the attitudes in her community, or might provide her with more power such as an education so she could get a well-paid job and be independent, or interventions that led to her family not being so stressed or poor. For such people mental health services can feel so far removed from their worlds that they have little to offer. So rather than spend lots of resources trying to get people into existing services it seems to me that it would make sense to go to people who are not attracted to these services, i.e. to take psychology out into their real world.

My desire to work with people from different cultural backgrounds in a way that seems meaningful, relevant and respectful to them drew me to finding out more about the work that Guy did and the philosophies underlying this. I learned about the groups that he had run, what went well and what didn't go well, and thought about how I might use the ideas. I felt really excited thinking about applying community-based groupwork in ways that would appeal to a culturally diverse group of people. Guy and I agreed to continue to meet to think through and plan how this might be achieved. For me what made these consultations really exciting was that I felt like I had permission. I hoped to be able to facilitate a group where I could share that feeling – permission to ask questions, to not accept assumptions, to try new things, to get it wrong, to think! To facilitate a group where understandings could be shared openly, where everyone's views and contributions might be viewed as of equal value, in a place where no one person (or subgroup) was able to dominate how people should think and what should be done.

One major consideration was whether the group should be open to everyone or solely for people from a specific cultural group. I have worked with South Asian women in the past and know that many of them would be less likely to attend a group which included men (of any cultural group) and non-Asian women. This can be due to cultural disapproval of mixing with male strangers, embarrassment about not being able to speak English well, and a feeling of being different. For South Asian people what John Berry has termed a 'separation strategy of acculturation' – maintaining one's own culture while avoiding participation in the host culture – is often highly valued. This can be motivated by fear of being pressurised to conform to dominant cultural practices and consequent loss of cultural identity for current and future generations. Consequently such people are more likely to live a segregated existence.

Some South Asian women fear suffering prejudice in group situations where they might be with people from different backgrounds. Some hold prejudiced views towards members of other cultural groups. For example, the British norm of socialising with the opposite sex is often viewed as sinful for women. Many harbour racist views and some demonstrate these very openly; for example, I was told of a Pakistani woman who refused to attend a group 'because it's full of Indians'. The opportunity to be part of a diverse group, in which people are not expected to conform or agree with each other, but instead provided with a safe place from

which to explore differences and recognise similarities, has the potential to challenge such fears and prejudices. A more homogenous group can be more comfortable for people, and often offers opportunities for solidarity, support and empathy, but there is less scope for wider understandings to be gained and less potential for life scripts, attitudes and behaviours to others to change.

Conversations with Guy around practical considerations have been really important in helping me to focus on these issues. There is so much to think about, including where the group might meet, at what time, for how long, how structured the group might be, etc. I also needed to think about what to call the group and the impact the name can have on the appeal of the group. How to advertise the group so that it might reach the desired audience has also needed careful consideration. I have come to realise that there will always be pros and cons to any decision and that one group cannot appeal to everyone. It has helped to think about my hopes and aims for the group and how these might overlap with the hopes, aims and needs of people who might attend, and the needs of the cultural groups they come from.

I have also found it helpful to reflect on my practice and the kind of clinical psychologist I want to be. Through discussing *Psychology in the Real World* projects I have realised that, rather than just feeling helpless and frustrated with the limitations of the impact of individual therapy on people's lives which are severely affected by stigma, prejudice and isolation, there is something I can do. Such a project would also provide increased access to psychology for a wider group of people than solely those who meet the stringent criteria for the Community Mental Health Team I work in. I have also reflected on how my style as a one-to-one therapist may contrast with my style as a group facilitator. For example, Guy has talked a lot about the benefits of talking about his own experiences in addressing the imbalance of power between group leaders and group members and in terms of establishing group norms, which has encouraged me to reconsider my stance on self-disclosure.

In the future I am planning to set up a group to explore different experiences and understandings of depression and how these influence people's views on what is helpful in coping with depression. I chose to focus on depression as it is a concept that is increasingly recognised by people from different cultural backgrounds (of all ages, and by men and women). This offers an opportunity for the group to be of interest to and be open to everyone. I hope to attract people from different backgrounds by advertising widely and through contacting people I know who have links with different community groups. I also intend to publicise my ability to speak Urdu and Punjabi in order to attract people from Asian communities. I have begun to think about questions that would facilitate discussions, including exploring ideas proposed by Paul Gilbert around the role of entrapment and shame in depression which have been found to be particularly relevant for South Asian women. Questions might include: What role does powerlessness play in causing people to be depressed? Why don't people get away from situations that they are unhappy in? Is depression a natural reaction to suffering prejudice? Below is an example of the kind of handout that might be used. There is still a lot to think about and I am sure I will discover more things along the way. For now, I am pleased to have made a start.

Some Thoughts on Prejudice

Is prejudice a consequence of categorisation?
It has been argued that prejudices are formed through our tendency to categorise information and to form heuristics (mental short cuts), which are used to make sense of new information. Thus, the first stage in forming prejudices is the creation of a category into which people are included based on identified characteristics. This then allows us to react to new people based on our existing beliefs. Whilst there are advantages for us in being able to do this, one of the downsides is that it leads to the formation of 'in-groups' and 'out-groups' which can come to be seen as more homogenous than they actually are (e.g. the belief that 'they're all like that'). Members of out-groups are prone to being seen as having less favourable attributes and so prejudices about them are more likely to develop.

Does prejudice maintain self-esteem?
This idea suggests that prejudices maintain and enhance self-esteem by allowing people to view the groups of which they are members, and consequently themselves, as superior to out-groups, whose members are seen as inferior; thus people elevate themselves in terms of perceived status and consequently self-esteem. Tajfel (1982) designed an experiment to test this in which strangers were assigned to groups based on arbitrary criteria. He found that people very quickly rated the members of their group more positively and allocated more rewards to them. So, even when the reasons for in-group membership are fairly innocuous, people appear to be motivated to 'win' against the out-group, and this serves to enhance self-esteem for individuals and pride and unity in their group. One result of this, however, is that it can result in the unfair treatment of members of the out-group (discrimination).

Are we conditioned to be prejudiced?
Many of our behaviours can be thought of as becoming acquired through conditioning and our views and attitudes might similarly be learned. The repeated pairing of a negative attribute with a specific group might lead to prejudice, e.g. 'all schizophrenics are dangerous'. Views acquired in this way by classical conditioning (the repeated pairing of two stimuli, e.g. in newspaper articles 'schizophrenia' and 'violence') might be reinforced by operant conditioning processes, such as approval from peers for stating such views or for behaving in a discriminatory way towards someone from that group (e.g. applause from people in a public meeting for stating that 'a residential facility for the mentally ill should not be allowed in our neighbourhood'). In this way, explicit and implicit messages can be transmitted from generation to generation and become part of a general culture of prejudice. Research studies have shown that children can learn prejudiced attitudes from their parents, but these correlations are typically low (e.g. Connell, 1972), suggesting that learning theory may not provide a comprehensive explanation of prejudice.

Is prejudice caused by competition for limited resources?
The *realistic conflict theory* (Sherif, 1966) proposed that conflict and prejudice arise when people are competing for limited resources. It has been documented that prejudice, discrimination, and violence against out-group members is positively correlated with times of economic difficulty. This phenomenon may interact with other processes that lead to prejudice and discrimination (e.g. scapegoating – where a group seeks a simple cause of a social problem in order to easily solve it by getting rid of the cause and therefore the problem). When jobs are scarce, immigrants are more likely to be blamed: 'They come over here and take all our jobs – send them back.'

Is prejudice a defence?
In psychoanalytic theory, defence mechanisms are used to cope with uncomfortable feelings and to maintain self-image. The use of some defences (such as projection) may be highly likely to lead to prejudice. Projection occurs when we deny particular characteristics in ourselves that we feel disturbed by or uncomfortable with and project them onto others, e.g. sexual attraction that we feel towards members of the same sex might disturb us, we see it as dirty, and we project this onto others, seeing homosexual men or lesbians as dirty and disturbing. The more we fight against our feelings (e.g. the complexities of who and what we find attractive) the more we might need to project out. This can tie in with the process of scapegoating, where if the scapegoat is got rid of (the extermination of gay men and lesbians, as tried in Nazi Germany) then there is hope that the disturbing feelings will also go.

Are certain types of people more likely to categorise in this way?
Within the four types of temperament that Keirsey has proposed, *guardians* score highly in terms of 'judging' – they seem to be more wired up to constantly make judgements about what is right and wrong/good and bad than people with other temperaments. This might lead people to readily see groups of people as good or bad, e.g. 'black people are lazy' or 'black people are tremendously hard working'. In terms of character (the part of our personality that is shaped by experience), Adorno's work centred on the idea that people with harsh, disciplinarian parents are more likely to develop authoritarian personalities themselves, which includes traits centred on conformity, intolerance, and insecurity. People with this kind of character appear to be prone to holding prejudiced views.

Do mental health services, through the process of categorisation, add to prejudice?

Diagnoses regarding physical health problems provide doctors with short cuts for describing people who are exhibiting particular symptoms, but this way of categorising people appears to lack validity in the area of mental health (see Boyle, 1999). In other areas of medicine the use of diagnosis has enabled access to specialist help that is more effective than home treatment and assisted research that has provided accumulative insights into the underlying causes of health problems. These benefits are not so apparent in the area of mental health, where the disadvantages of diagnosis are significant, for example, the prejudice and harm suffered by people thus labelled (which in Nazi Germany involved the easily located 'mentally ill' being given a 'mercy death'). The differences between 'them' (the mad) and 'us' (the sane) can be exaggerated, resulting in a homogenised view of 'the mentally ill', whereas the evidence points to great variation in people's behaviour, even between two people with the same tightly defined psychiatric diagnosis. A 'mental disorder' can come to be viewed as representing a stable characteristic of a person, rather than each individual being seen as unique and whose behaviour largely consists of moment-to-moment reactions to environments. A psychiatric diagnosis can become an explanation for behaviour (rather than solely a description) – ordinary and predictable reactions to extreme situations (e.g. anger and depression about losing one's liberty) may then be attributed to a psychiatric disorder that a person is suffering with rather than a fairly predictable outcome attributed to a particular environmental situation. Having formal ways of categorising people as 'mentally ill' or 'sane' perhaps enables the 'sane' to bolster their sense of sanity at the expense of the 'mad', onto whom they can project their fears (e.g. of their own instability, eccentricity or lack of self-control). As social historians such as Michel Foucault have revealed, there is a long history of categorisation, confinement and experimentation on people who behave in ways that disturb, frighten, or create inconvenience for the people with power to categorise and confine, and prejudices with such long histories are not easy for societies to let go of.

How can prejudice be reduced?

Allport (1954) proposed that, under the right conditions, interpersonal contact is one of the most effective ways of reducing prejudice. The basic premise is that, as we get to know more about individual people, we will find our ways of categorising them, and our views about the group into which we categorise them, challenged. We will thus come to have views that are more fully rounded than those based on stereotypes and prejudice. According to the *contact hypothesis,* in order for this to occur the following must be present:

1. Mutual interdependence
2. A common goal
3. Equal status of group members
4. Social norms in place that promote equality

54

Connecting people

Only connect.
    E.M. Forster

*Here lies constructive, connective power that can
be so healing and valuable.*
    Don Harris, *The Writing Group,* 2008

Forster's oft-quoted epigraph to *Howard's End*
has served as a guiding principle regarding
Psychology in the Real World ventures. Some
interpretations take *only connect* as
encouragement to accept Donne's philosophy
that 'no man is an island'. Psychoanalyst Adam
Phillips and historian Barbara Taylor have
written on the importance of what the
Victorians called *open-heartedness* and the
Christians *caritas* in terms of bringing
connectedness with and kindness to others into
our lives, not just to help others but also for our
own mental health. This is similar to the
Buddhist emphasis on loving kindness,
compassion to others and connectedness to all
living things. Others see *only connect* in terms of
the importance of individually feeling fully
connected regarding the various aspects of
ourselves, for example, feeling connected to our
emotions. Some see the aphorism as
encouragement to *seize the day* and unite the
spiritual and material aspects of life. *Psychology
in the Real World* groups try and provide
environments for people to do these things. For
example, there are opportunities to be kind to
and receive kindness from others; to have less
narrow conceptualisations of who we are and to

try and accept and connect with all aspects of
our selves; and intellectually to blend the social
materialist standpoint with others, including
what might be termed spiritual ideas. Different
ideologies are introduced and sit alongside each
other, as do the people on the courses – people
with different personality types, people from
different cultural and socio-economic
backgrounds, 'the mentally ill' and those who
have escaped diagnosis – all with the aim of
helping people to connect with others. Perhaps
the more we can connect with and understand
each other, with space for open and honest
exchange of ideas but without the drive to
impose our beliefs on others, the more we feel
connected, whole, held, part of something.
Much of the feedback we get at the end of these
courses finds eloquent ways of expressing this, as
Don Harris' quote at the beginning of this
chapter illustrates.

    Don's experience of *The Writing Group*
matches Daniel Goleman's analysis in his book
Social Intelligence regarding what goes on when
people engage with each other. He cites evidence
that indicates connections between people are
not simply metaphorical, they can be mapped in
terms of brain activity: when people link up and
feel connected to others there appears to be a
corresponding neural link-up where people's
brains 'engage in an emotional tango, a dance of
feelings'. Brain scanning experiments indicate
that social interactions operate as modulators
(Goleman likens them to interpersonal
thermostats) that continually reset key aspects of

our brain function as they orchestrate our emotions. This impacts on hormonal and other biological systems including specific genes that regulate the immune system. In short, our relationships appear to mold not just our experience but our biology. As Goleman puts it: 'nourishing relationships have a beneficial impact on our health, while toxic ones can act like slow poison in our bodies.' This fits with a great body of research into counselling and psychotherapy that repeatedly reveals that it is the quality of the therapeutic relationship (rather than techniques, models or therapeutic background of the therapist) that is the main medium of help (see Hubble et al, 1999).

Partly as a result of a successful marketing campaign by the pharmaceutical and therapy industries to get individual people to diagnose themselves and be diagnosed as individually flawed and in need of drugs for their brain biochemical imbalances and individual therapy for their psyche, the NHS and social services are overrun with referrals. One response has been to widen the number of people who can prescribe and monitor medication. Another has been to increase the number of people providing short-term psychological support and therapy (for example, through IAPT – Improving Access to Psychological Therapies – services). These approaches are likely to fail significant numbers of people. We have long known that people with very early experiences of deprivation and abuse often have long-lasting difficulties, especially in terms of social interaction, that are not easily overcome by long-term support and therapy let alone short-term quick fixes. Harry Harlow's monkeys that were severely deprived of contact with their parents or substitutes became 'psychotic' and never acquired skills or behaviors needed to interact with other monkeys. Psychotherapist Michael Balint identified that some of us with very early experiences of neglect and abuse appear to have a 'basic fault' (like a

fault line in geology) running through us that is always susceptible at any point in life to opening up under certain conditions. Brain imaging research cited in Paul Gilbert's book *The Compassionate Mind* reveals that 'neurons that fire together wire together': early maladaptive experiences and connections (e.g. associating physical contact and intimacy with abuse) are therefore not easily undone. But the latest research is also revealing that the plasticity of the brain carries on into adulthood and even old age (see Sharon Begley's *The Plastic Mind*) – there is thus hope that decent, respectful, kind, loving relationships can heal people and rewire their brains (e.g. physical contact and intimacy can be associated with mutual love and tenderness – neurons firing together in such association will also wire together). Such associations however are likely to take time – once trust is wrecked it is hard to be rebuilt. Community-based groupwork may offer opportunities for people to connect with others in ways that go some way towards healing previous hurts that short-term one-to-one interventions are unable to do.

The groups are aimed at providing a place for lonely people to connect with others. Richard Wilkinson's research into income inequality and health problems led him to conclude that countries with high levels of inequality (such as Britain) have low levels of social capital – helpful interconnectedness between members of communities (and society in general), where people feel part of a social network that provides them with increased power and eases physical, psychological and social distress. The level of social isolation of many people who attend CMHTs is truly astonishing. I have met many people who have no supportive relationships with anyone outside mental health service staff. Similarly, people have told me they can think of not one kind, positive or supportive comment from anyone in their life, ever. The groups are no panacea and many lonely people even when they have appeared connected with others whilst the group has been running have returned to very isolated existences after the end of the group. But, as several chapters in this book reveal, some have joined other groups, signed up on other courses, set up their own small informal groups, and several have entered into lasting friendships.

The groups are also aimed at connecting people who want to engage in social action. In order to bring about social change one normally needs allies. People frequently feel impassioned about perceived social injustices but relatively powerless to bring about change. Allies help us maintain morale and share the tasks of campaigning as well as leading us to be perceived as a campaign group rather than lone mavericks. And whilst coming together to discuss theories is important, we are also guided by one of the most influential theoreticians of all time, Friedrich Engels, who said: 'An ounce of action is worth a ton of theory.'

55

On progress and seeking truth

Those who seek to avoid truth end up in delusion. And while all science aims at truth, psychoanalysis is unique in recognising that the search for truth is, in itself, therapeutic.

Hanna Segal

In many of the groups we individually and collectively do something that can seem rather old-fashioned in a postmodern era – we seek truth. The psychoanalyst Hanna Segal in an interview in *The Guardian* emphasised the importance of 'not seeking The Truth with a capital T, an omniscience, but truth that is the same as reality'. Evaluations of *Psychology in the Real World* groups have indicated that seeking truths has been experienced as therapeutic and people have described the importance of 'raising veils that mask certain ways of seeing ourselves and the world'. Whilst we seek truth we also heed Einstein's aphorism: 'Whoever undertakes to set himself up as a judge of Truth and Knowledge is shipwrecked by the laughter of the Gods.' In the groups there tends to be an acknowledgement that postmodern critiques help us question the validity of any knowledge base. Such critiques have also helped us to be aware that any statement about human beings perhaps says as much about the person making the statement (and the cultural influences on him or her) as the people the statement purports to apply to. Having as diverse a group as possible in terms of cultural backgrounds helps us to recognise this. In the groups we also appreciate that 'reality' and 'knowledge' can

never be said to be fixed and completely known and understood – they can only be seen as needing constant exploration in an area as complex as human behaviour. Unlike other areas of science, there are no precise, unbending laws of behaviour that apply in all situations. *Psychology in the Real World* ventures do not have an ideology that one thought system should govern all people's beliefs or be the only way of investigating what might be called *truth*. We try and give great weight to people's experiences, and reflections on these, in comparison to what can sometimes seem to be rather fixed principles as set out in textbooks on psychology, principles that are often based on studies of one particular ethnic or social group.

On the courses we engage with Peter Hulme's 'Uncertainty Principle' which states that importance and certainty are inversely related. This is similar to Niels Bohr's statements about the search for 'deep truth': if we want more clarity we have to settle for less truth, but if we want more truth we will have to suffer less clarity. But this is not the same as believing that 'nothing can really be known for sure therefore all that can be said is that people have their own narratives or competing theories'. Not many *Psychology in the Real World* participants, or facilitators, have held a belief that each person's narrative or theory is equally valid (or equally lacking in validity). We therefore try and heed David Smail's warnings about the risks of 'drowning in relativism'. Readers interested in different ways of categorising philosophical enquiry may agree with community psychologist *Paul Moloney*, who distinguished the philosophies underlying *Psychology in the Real World* from the post-structuralism that has dominated much academic thinking in the last 20 years by describing them as 'critical realist – epistemological relativism combined with ontological realism'.

Some of our brightest people have spent the bulk of their time and energy over the past couple of decades engaged in lengthy analyses of language and deconstructing the notion of reality. This type of critique has led to helpful ways of looking at the world. However, over the same period our society has become more unequal in terms of wealth and income, the psychologically damaging effects of this inequality appear to have become even more pronounced, and fewer and fewer people seem to be putting their energy and time into bringing about more democratic and less psychologically toxic systems. We do not want to mirror this in *Psychology in the Real World* ventures. As the chapter on collaborative conversation emphasises, we hope to introduce people to a range of different ways of understanding themselves, other people and the world we live in. Not everyone who comes has a wish or interest to go beyond this, but many see the personal as political (as Ghandi said: 'Be the change you want to see in the world'). Other members and facilitators want to try and have a more direct impact on things, heeding Karl Marx who said: 'Philosophers have only interpreted the world in various ways; the point is to change it.'

On Schopenhauer's idea of truth passing through stages

All truth passes through three stages. First it is ridiculed. Second it is violently opposed. Third it is accepted as being self-evident.

The ideas and practices that underpin *Psychology in the Real World* ventures have often passed though the stages Schopenhauer outlines. Many have initially been ridiculed, trivialised and seen as unimportant within the context of 'treating serious *mental illnesses*'. At other times they have been challenged or opposed. I would add to Schopenhauer's second stage the idea that, if not violently opposed, then inconvenient truths are often deliberately ignored (Segal believes this process is more unconscious than conscious). The third stage, when truth is accepted as self-evident, can lead to changes in practice but is sometimes used in a Machiavellian way to retain a status quo rather than lead to revolutionary or progressive changes that one would expect from such acceptance.

Changes do occur, however. Early in my career I was ignored and at times aggressively dismissed for trying to shape services in accordance with what the people using that service said they wanted to happen rather than carry out what managers deemed 'needed to be done' or clinicians stated 'their training and knowledge base revealed worked best'; now every part of our NHS Trust has in-built official mechanisms to *Listen and Respond* to the people who use the service. Walk and Talk was ridiculed (seen as a joke compared to 'proper' mental health interventions such as medication and therapy); now 'ecotherapy' is widespread and Local Authorities and NHS Trusts are setting up similar schemes across the country. Groups where people could access the work of critical psychiatrists and which might support people who decided to come off psychiatric drugs were seen as dangerous by some people and not the kind of thing psychologists and service users should be involved in; now *New Ways of Working* documents are entitled *Medicines Management: Everybody's Business*. People who access mental health services have gone from being members of *Psychology in the Real World* groups to setting up and facilitating similar groups. This was seen as radical many years ago, but our NHS Trust has similarly progressed from seeing people as passive recipients of psychiatric treatments to paying people to plan and run these groups. When trying to bring about changes that are not initially welcomed by people with power it helps to have allies, it helps to have the kind of temperament where one is not that fearful of being told off, but it also helps to hold in mind Schopenhauer's concept of truth passing through stages.

Box 21   On the need for humility about our ways of understanding the world

Philosophers dating back to Plato have argued that we do not see reality – we have experiences that are approximations of the real world, if indeed we could ever be sure there is a real world 'out there' to be discovered. Students of psychology are often poorly schooled in philosophy and given an impression that it is only since the onset of the twentieth century when psychology became established as an academic subject that people have become aware of how flawed and biased our ways of interpreting the world can be. Francis Bacon in the sixteenth century described four ways people erroneously make sense of things – four 'idols', perhaps better translated nowadays as illusions or bad habits of mind. These seem as relevant today as they were then:

Idols of the tribe – systematic errors common to all human beings, probably relating to the ways that the brain or conscious thought operates, such as the tendency to see more order or pattern in things than may be the case.

Idols of the cave – personal prejudices that are individual, e.g. transference reactions (such as expecting people to behave to us like our parents did), or the notion of 'to the man with a hammer everything looks like a nail'.

Idols of the market place – misunderstandings relating to the difficulties we have in putting complex things into words, or through mystification relating to the misuse of language.

Idols of the theatre – errors relating to received systems of thought. We find it hard to accept information that does not fit in with our preconceptions of the world, and our preconceptions can be misconceptions that have been drilled into us by authority figures that have come to be unquestioned by the vast majority of us.

Psychology has not discovered such biases. However, it has experimentally tested some of them. Eliot Aronson's *The Social Animal* provides illuminating data to support the notion that as human beings we are often convinced we are right, or in a post hoc way explain to ourselves and others that we have done things for rational reasons, when experimental evidence does not support such notions. This has been a popular text on many *Psychology in the Real World* courses.

On progress

The reasonable man adapts himself to the world. The unreasonable man persists in trying to make the world adapt to him. Therefore all progress depends on the unreasonable man.

George Bernard Shaw

Shaw's quote should act as a jolt to all those who have gone along with the idea that what is needed in Britain is a massive increase in the number of people accessing cognitive and other therapies that are solely aimed at enabling people to cope better with the demands of their lives. Whilst the concept of progress has been critiqued by many post-structuralist intellectuals, it has its place in *Psychology in the Real World* ventures that encompass people's wishes to bring about social change. A look at the history of psychiatry indicates that ideas and practices go in and out of fashion rather than progress in the way the era of modernity led us to believe, but without a vision of how things could be different and a drive to make the world a better place I fail to see how there can be sufficient motivation to try and bring about changes that are thought to be of potential benefit to people. Of course we have to be constantly aware of issues of power in terms of who defines what progress is. As one African proverb states: *Until the lion has a historian of his own, the tale of the hunt will always glorify the hunter.* We also need to accept how flawed our concepts of 'better' can be and ultimately misguided our attempts at change might turn out. I am also very aware of the law of unintended consequences: in the 1990s I researched and wrote about the need for greater awareness of the number of boys who are sexually abused every year, never for one moment thinking that greater awareness and public debate about childhood sexual abuse would lead to the levels of paranoia and over-the-top State policies that have characterised the last decade.

Even progress that most people see as beneficial can take a lot longer than was originally envisaged. I have found it helpful to think of working alongside people with similar views to achieve things over a period of years (and even decades) rather than weeks. And as well as progressing things, we often have to defend things, perhaps following Hanna Segal's allusion to Cormac McCarthy's *The Road*: 'Sometimes one has to keep a little fire burning, no matter how small, and sometimes no matter how hidden.' But by giving up, just keeping our head down or accepting that all we have are competing narratives, we run the risk of spending our lives disengaged from the struggle to make the world a better place for ourselves and others, whilst allowing other people to take positions of real power and do real harm.

Goebbels said: 'If you tell a big enough lie and keep repeating it, people will eventually come to believe it. The lie can be maintained only for such time as the State can shield the people from the political, economic and military consequences of the lie. It thus becomes vitally important for the State to use all of its powers to repress dissent, for the truth is the mortal enemy of the lie, and thus by extension, the truth is the greatest enemy of the State.'

People who seek truth may never find *The Truth* but they may reveal *The Lies*.

SECTION 12

The Writing Group

56

Becoming a community psychologist through groupwork: A trainee's experience

LUCY GAHAN

Before doing my clinical psychology training I carried out an evaluation of several *Understanding Yourself and Others* groups with Guy. I was struck by some of the group members' comments, which movingly described how the course had impacted on many areas of their lives, and this fuelled my interest in the power of groups and community-based work. By the time I was a third-year trainee I felt I had a greater understanding of what community psychology entailed – the Staffordshire and Keele training course takes a critical stance towards mental health and illness, considers a broad view of the influences on human behaviour and pays attention to the contexts in which people live their lives. However, specialist groupwork and community psychology placements seem few and far between. It may be that trainees and qualified clinicians prioritise skills in individual therapy, particularly with the current emphasis on short-term one-to-one interventions, and difficulties clinicians have in finding the time, resources and energy to go beyond this in their work. Or perhaps many share my own anxieties about groupwork and working outside the comfort of the therapy room. I wanted to spend time with people who appeared to 'live' some of the ideas I had encountered on the course and I elected to do a specialist placement in community-based groupwork with Guy.

During the first half of the placement I planned and co-facilitated an *Understanding Ourselves and Others* group. This experience challenged me on many levels. I regressed to my default position of preparing a lot of material for each session, which helped me feel more in control of my anxieties about group facilitation. However, through supervision, I quickly identified that this served as a distraction from facing the unpredictable nature of groupwork and from developing my skills in facilitation. By hiding behind my material I was avoiding fully connecting with the group. The year-long nature of the placement allowed me to try different styles of facilitation in two subsequent groups – *Walk and Talk* and *The Writing Group*.

Whilst co-facilitating *Walk and Talk* I discovered that my skills in working with individuals were useful but did not necessarily transfer to groupwork as directly as I had hoped. I needed to develop a balance between offering group members access to particular psychological perspectives through talking with me on the walk and avoiding being drawn into a therapy-type relationship with one group member at the expense of encouraging and facilitating a cohesive group. Reflections on observations by Guy and supervision on the group provided by another psychologist helped me to focus more on group needs and processes and realise that group dynamics are not helped if members see a facilitator predominantly attending to the needs of one person on the walk (e.g. this can spark old wounds regarding sibling rivalry). I came to realise that I had assumed groupwork skills are innate, something groupworkers are born with, rather than something that can be learned through practice and reflection on our ways of facilitating groups, and endeavoured to try and focus more on group processes in the final group I was to be involved in – *The Writing Group*.

Whilst *Walk and Talk* had been co-facilitated with people from a service-user background, I had not been involved in the original setting up of the group. Service user consultancy and service user involvement are emphasised in clinical psychology training and in NHS policies. Planning and running *The Writing Group* with Nicki Evans enabled me to be involved in something that encompassed these practices. It was decided that Nicki and I would take the lead facilitator's role and the two of us met many times to plan the group. I was surprised by the detail of the decisions we had to make: What sort of message did we want to give about the group in the flyers? Who was it aimed at? How should we advertise it? Should it be an open or closed group? How many people should it involve? For how long, and how often, should we run sessions? All these questions caused us to reflect on the philosophies and aims of the group and make decisions in keeping with these aims.

Working with Nicki also led me to reflect on power issues in groupwork and my personal style of co-working. My ideal of planning and facilitating the group as equals proved trickier than I envisaged. For example, both Guy and I received a salary that paid for all the time we spent preparing and facilitating the group and had access to power that was unavailable to Nicki, for example, to book and arrange payment for the room we hired. In addition, my personal style, when anxious, is to take the lead, and I found myself needing to rein in this inclination. This was a dilemma for me every meeting, particularly as I knew of some of Nicki's anxieties about facilitating the group (see Chapter 58). I wanted to support her but not

'take over', whilst at the same time staying faithful to her original vision of the group. Power dynamics were also made complicated by Guy's role, which was like a cross between a group member and support facilitator: whilst he read his own poems, commented on other people's writing and joined in the debates about what the material brought up for people, he also occasionally made facilitating comments when he thought we were floundering. In addition, he offered Nicki and me support and feedback after the end of each session and in supervision between sessions. Power issues were made even trickier by the fact that Guy was observing me and would assess me on a pass/fail basis at the end of my placement. Although we made it clear that Nicki and I were the main facilitators, Guy's role as my supervisor was made explicit to the group, which meant that at times group members would look to Guy as being 'in charge' – something we explored in supervision. This highlights some of the challenges of co-facilitating groups where differences in power and status exist between facilitators.

Groups can feel like an unpredictable monster, where anything can happen at any moment, and the perceived safety of individual work can seem like a welcome sanctuary to the novice groupworker. Hearing about Guy's own anxieties about groupwork helped me manage this anxiety as I realised that being in a group is challenging for most people. I also found that, despite my anxiety, which would reach a peak on the day of each session, or sometimes the day before, I experienced a sense of awe at the potential power of groups. In the planning stages of *The Writing Group* we feared long silences where group members might find it difficult to share their work. However, in the first session one member read out an exceptionally powerful piece of writing, which revealed very personal aspects of her own story, including something that she had struggled with for many years. This bravery and openness set the tone for the group, which became a very intense experience for group members and facilitators alike.

Particularly striking was the feeling of solidarity that grew within the group as the weeks went on. Hearing not only the beautiful words that people had written, but learning about the author, the situation in which the work was written, the tragedies and triumphs of their lives, and the depth of emotion in their voices as they entrusted their work to the group was exceptionally powerful. When groups generate this degree of intimacy it can be tempting to overestimate the power of the group to bring about change. However, when reflecting on the group in the last couple of sessions, group members described the experience as 'moving', 'validating', 'healing' and 'liberating'. Several people described how it had given them confidence or helped them feel accepted in groups in general. As someone starting to create a professional identity and looking for creative ways of working that bring benefits to people, it greatly encouraged me to be open to the power of group and community-based ways of working in terms of providing many things that individual therapies cannot.

57

The Writing Group

LUCY GAHAN and GUY HOLMES

A moment of madness
A second of sense
To sit here with strangers
Life without pretence
Like ripples on a pond
We drift far away
Our temples
Are different
Or the same would you say?

    A participant in *The Writing Group, 2008*
    (writing about the group experience)

The therapeutic benefits of writing, whilst recognised for centuries, are increasingly being utilised and researched in the field of psychotherapy (see Bolton et al, 2004). The benefits of writing have also been extolled in the mental health service survivor movement, not just in relation to personal gains, but also in terms of people getting across their experiences of services and other life events (see www.survivorspoetry.com). Matthew Lieberman has conducted brain imaging (MRI) research that indicates writing about personal experiences impacts on parts of the brain, such as the amygdala, that are connected with high emotion and fear, reducing activity in these areas, whilst at the same time increasing activity in areas associated with emotional regulation, such as the prefrontal cortex. Lieberman describes this as a seesaw effect, where the more frontal activity there is, the less amygdala response, and it seems to be apparent even in people who do not feel that writing and putting feelings and experiences

into words helps to manage emotions.

The Writing Group was initially inspired by Nicki Evans, one of the group facilitators, who, whilst attending an *Understanding Ourselves and Others* course, had discussed her poems during the breaks in the sessions. Nicki was interested in meeting other people who found writing to be cathartic and helpful (see Chapter 58). These discussions led to the idea of setting up a writing group that would have similar philosophies to other *Psychology in the Real World* courses (see Section 1) and bring benefits beyond those associated with people sharing their written work. For example, Peter Campbell, who describes himself as a mental health system survivor and poet, has written about how such groups can enable a sense of connection and solidarity with others, challenge discrimination and help people to experience a greater sense of meaning through participation in a shared activity.

Whilst Guy was involved in a couple of initial planning meetings about the group, it was Nicki and Lucy who met many times, and liaised by email, to design the flyer, discuss core philosophies, and devise the structure and facilitation process to be used in group meetings. Putting some of these ideas into a few words on a flyer was quite a challenge and this led to creative discussions about what the group might be like. It was decided that, unlike many other writing groups, people would not write in the sessions. Nor would the group be a creative writing group where people learn and practice technique, critique each other's work in terms of style and discuss how to get published. The intention was to create a safe, encouraging environment where people could share work they had already written in an accepting atmosphere without feeling judged or criticised. We aimed to communicate clearly that people could participate in any way they felt comfortable, such as asking another group member to read their work aloud, with the hope that people's confidence in sharing their work might increase and people might benefit from discussing their own and other people's writings. With this in mind we settled on a small group of seven (plus Nicki, Lucy and Guy). Flyers were circulated in mental health services as well as being pinned to notice boards at many non-mental health settings. The group was quickly booked up, with one person keen to be on a waiting list should anyone not turn up or drop out.

When planning the group we had aimed for a loose structure. During the first session, where members of the group introduced themselves and described their hopes for being part of the group, people quickly offered to read their poems and other types of writing such as articles, stories, obituaries and diary entries. Some of these had been written many years ago, others were more recent. The facilitators felt this went well, but feedback formally obtained at the end of the group matched some comments made during the third session that initially people seemed unsure of how to use the group, perhaps due to the loose structure, perhaps due to some chaos regarding two facilitators not being present in session two. A couple of people dropped out (allowing the person on the waiting list to join us). By the fourth session, however, the group appeared to have become the safe, cohesive group that we had hoped for and had settled into a (perhaps better understood) pattern each fortnight. One group member

would start off by introducing a piece of writing that they had done and give some background information regarding the work. After reading the work the whole group would discuss the things it brought up – not its merit in terms of grammar or style, but rather the themes expressed in the writing. Each person in the group was given sufficient time to describe and read at least one piece of work each session.

The themes referred to in the writing were very varied. They included: death and mourning; psychiatric treatments; impasses in family life; fears of going mad; war; motherhood; how to survive the rigours of life; painful and frightening childhood experiences and their impacts; loneliness and depression; and smiling. The discussions also touched on the benefits of writing – the cathartic effect of getting something buried inside out into the open; the possibility of expressing something that we feel unable to say in conversation; the conjuring of something that has troubled us but seemed inexpressible. At times the group felt reminiscent of psychotherapy groups when they are working well – the writings provided the material that the group then analysed, with members' empathic comments providing each other with considerable support, and there being plenty of opportunities to personally reflect on how the various things discussed related to our own experiences. As one member put it:

'The Writing Group has helped me to realise that I use writing to gain insight; so far primarily for myself, but some of it is also relevant to others and worth sharing. One of the greatest achievements ever is that I have learned to listen to poetry. I have heard the often very intense feelings of the writer and the way they have expressed these feelings with image and metaphors; this has given me a much more 'real' sense of the emotion they experience than mere feeling words can do on their own.'

The Writing Group

Have you written poetry or done some writing but not had the confidence to share it with other people?

Has writing helped you feel better or helped you express things that are difficult to say?

Would you like the chance to share and talk about your writing in an informal and relaxed atmosphere?

- Come along to this group, bring things you have written and discuss your own and other people's writings without the pressure of it being criticised
- People might be nervous but we hope to find ways of helping everyone feel safe and confident enough to join in; for example, people might ask someone else to read what they have written

Venue: Gateway Education and Arts Centre, Chester Street, Shrewsbury

When: Mondays, fortnightly from 19th May to 11th August 1.00 – 2.30 pm

Who are we? Lucy Gahan, Nicki Evans and Guy Holmes. All three of us are interested in the benefits of writing and how it can help us get through difficult experiences. Lucy and Guy are local psychologists.

How to join in: In order to keep things friendly and informal, places are limited to a maximum of 7. Phone to book a place. It is free to join.

As well as taking on some of the facilitation roles, Nicki and Guy read poems that they had written. As the poems often revealed very personal things about them this perhaps helped other members to take risks and an atmosphere of trust and intimacy to develop. Lucy took the lead role in terms of conducting the group, utilising the *model railway operator* style of facilitation described in Chapter 43.

Reading poetry, especially reading it aloud or hearing it read, can at times be an intensely emotional experience. But on other occasions one can feel confused about what a poem is about or left wanting to know more about what the poet was trying to convey. In *The Writing Group* we were in the privileged position of not only hearing people read their own work but hearing something about the context in which it was written and the author's own thoughts about the writing. People talked about what was going on in their lives (and in their heads) when they wrote the piece and this often brought the writing to life.

Evaluating the group

'For me it was a privilege to meet other writers, be alongside the ways they saw things, and to feel welcome … in the group I felt I had understood more clearly, and had BEEN understood – that makes such a difference.'

The main aims of evaluating the group were to assess benefits that members had experienced through being part of the group and obtain feedback on how any future venture of this type might be changed in order to maximise benefits for participants. This was important as this was the first time a group of this nature had been run. Whilst the facilitators had discussed and reflected on each meeting of the group after each session ended, and in supervision sessions between groups, we were keen to hear individual group member's thoughts and reflections on *The Writing*

Group experience. At the penultimate meeting all group members (including the facilitators) were invited to write about their experiences of the group between that meeting and the last with the aim of reading these out in the last session. Although there are difficulties in utilising such 'data' for research and audit (for example, this type of evaluation provides no quantifiable data on the impacts of such a group on psychiatric symptoms experienced by group members who have a long history of involvement with mental health services), people who regularly run therapeutic writing groups (such as Gillie Bolton) often utilise such means of obtaining feedback. All group members contributed by writing poems and narrative pieces describing their experiences of being part of the group and of their feelings about it coming to an end.

The original evaluation report of the group included each member's writing about the group in full as we decided not to analyse and categorise the comments – such research can be critiqued as revealing as much about the researchers as the participants and much can be lost in the analysis. The report is available on www.shropsych.org/psychologyintherealworld. htm; some quotes from it have been incorporated in this chapter. At the instigation of group members, a booklet containing examples of people's work read during the course of the group was compiled. This was presented to members of the group in the last session as well as being made available on several local websites thus publicising people's work. A copy can be downloaded from www.shropsych.org/ psychologyintherealworld.htm.

'Writing is an extremely lovely hobby and the group was great to give me some confidence to start writing again … I'm trying hard to fight the urge of writing. Why fight? Why not just indulge?'

58

Experiencing the journey from service user to group facilitator

NICKI EVANS

I feel I never progress in achieving 'mental health': just years of medications and care workers and diagnoses that really mean nothing, and endless hospital admissions that wear me out. I have always managed, however, to attend *Psychology in the Real World* groups. I originally found it difficult to even talk to people and was racked with anxiety and sheer terror wondering why I was subjecting myself to these groups. At the end of the first group I attended (an *Understanding Ourselves and Others* course) I told Guy that I had previously been unsure whether I or any other people really existed. I did not feel real, but through being on the course I had started to believe and feel that the other people on the course were real and did actually exist. I found that gradually the knowledge I was gaining was of interest to me. I was introduced to ways of thinking I knew nothing of; alternative points of view that made me challenge things within myself and question things in the world around me.

For years I lived in a shallow, blinkered world and knew nothing else but psychiatric hospitals and severe attempts on my life, an endless cycle. Not by any means are things now perfect: I still have my daily struggles and the odd relapse, but through my various involvements with the *Psychology in the Real World* groups I feel empowered with an internal sense of expansion through actively learning, talking, taking part and pushing myself out of my comfort zone. I feel no shame in being open about what I have been through. I believe many issues should be brought out into the open and these groups greatly encouraged this in me. In the groups I mentioned aspects of my life (such as self-harm) that people often find themselves condemned or ostracised for. But in *Psychology in the Real World* groups I have always found an acceptance and acknowledgement of who I am regardless. The *Walk and Talk* group in particular was a life-saver. I attended during a year-long psychiatric hospital admission and it got me out, got me talking, got me back with nature. This was of far more benefit than being told to go to Occupational Therapy which I actively defied. I don't think people quite understood why I did this, but it is a bit like feeling people are running your life so you fight against them and try in small ways to do something that they have not suggested (maybe my defiance at times is what keeps me going). To attend *Psychology in the Real World* groups was my own decision as opposed to a referral which I would have defied.

I had gone on *Walk and Talk* regularly and taken some photos. Guy asked me if I would co-present a talk with him about this group to some psychologists as part of their staff training. I planned and prepared the session with Guy. We used a lot of photos I had taken on the walk to give a flavour of what it entails. In the session I read a couple of poems that I had written about the experience, described the group, and answered questions people had about it. I was amazed I managed it. This meant a lot to me, that I was even asked to do this. It went really well and I had not thought I was capable of such things.

I write a lot of poetry. I find it helps express what I cannot say in speaking. It is my way of trying to get people to understand what is going on for me. I have always craved simple acknowledegment. I have always wanted to make a difference, however small. Initially I wrote so that I would leave something behind as I saw my life as hopeless and lonesome. However, I plucked up the courage to talk to Guy about my poems during the first *Psychology in the Real World* course I attended and to let him read some of them. To my delight his response was to suggest that he and I set up a writing group sometime in the future. I thought 'someone believes I am capable'. I was keen to do this, although the thought of it also freaked me out … running a group – I could barely speak to people or look them in the eye! I considered myself incapable of anything. I considered myself not even part of the human race.

From that moment on there was no pressure to do this group – it was a case of when I felt ready to organise things with Guy. A couple of years passed by during which at times I was severely unwell in terms of my mental health, often hospitalised and medicated to the point where I could not write or even think of future possibilities. After various flat moves and encouragement and support (from people within and outside mental health services) I became more active and communicative, although still anxious and depressed. Throughout this period I kept some contact with Guy. He was not part of the CMHT that I was involved with. Rather, this contact was through me occasionally coming to one of the *Psychology in the Real World* groups or through emails we periodically exchanged about *The Writing Group* idea. We never let the idea of *The Writing Group* die, although we did not progress it beyond the stage of it being an idea.

When Guy approached me in 2007 and said

he had a trainee clinical psychologist, Lucy Gahan, working with him who was particularly interested in groupwork I felt there would never be a right time to sort this writing group out. The thought of it terrified me. I was not sure how I envisaged it, thought I would be a bit useless and did not feel I had any good ideas for it. However, when I met Lucy and Guy and we threw our ideas around all my apprehension dissipated and I was able to come up with ideas and suggestions. I left the meeting with a sense of achievement.

It was agreed that Guy would take a lesser role in the group and be more of a participant than facilitator which I guess is unique for him as he usually runs the various groups. This allowed Lucy and I to take the leading roles in running the group. Lucy and I regularly met, initially doing the flyer for the group. I had no idea that it would be so hard getting the wording right and it took us some time to get it clear what the group was about – that it was about people sharing their own work, that it was not a creative writing group (we wouldn't spend time in the group writing) and that the emphasis would be on the benefits of writing as a way of expressing things and certainly not for people to feel that their work would be criticised. We wanted people to feel it would be in a relaxed atmosphere; that is why we designed it for a small number of people. Finally the flyer was finished with location and dates decided. I had been keen for it to be at a non-mental health venue, particularly The Gateway which is an Arts and Education centre, and Guy was able to get the NHS Trust to fund this. Flyers were put up in various places, including mental health service waiting rooms and The Gateway itself, and soon the seven places available were filled. One fear (perhaps for all of us) was: *What if no one wants to attend?* This proved to be unfounded, but was replaced with: *What if they all drop out?* As the date for the first meeting of the group loomed I freaked out and considered dropping out myself.

I wrote a few panicky emails to Lucy about this, often late at night being unable to sleep. I was worried about my own writing, about reading it out, about ending up in floods of tears or generally making an embarrassment of myself. The 'what ifs' flooded around in my mind. Lucy and Guy were very reassuring to me. Guy said that he always felt like that before the start of a new group, to the point where he often felt sick. He also said that everyone in the group would also be nervous so it gave us a good insight into what it would be like for them and would assist us relate to and help other members of the group manage this in the first session.

Before the first group meeting we met up to discuss who would say what and Lucy and Guy asked me how much I wanted to say. I was thinking 'Nothing! I don't want to be here!' But I did not say this out loud. I felt like I was going to run off or be physically ill. But when people started to arrive for the group I started to calm down. I felt genuinely friendly to everyone and more settled. Once there and immersed in it there was no way I was going to run out – I wanted to be there.

We all introduced ourselves and as part of the general introductions a couple of people read out their poetry. Some did not feel able to do so straight away and simply listened, which is understandable as none of us knew quite what to expect or what would be read out. The poem I took to read out I asked someone else to read as I felt quite anxious and thought I might cry. Guy said later that this was good as it enabled other group members to ask others to read out their work should they wish to do so (which some did in subsequent sessions). On the whole the first meeting went well, everyone seemed very open and the reading of the poems and other pieces of writing seemed to help people feel comfortable and engaged. People were very brave with what they were willing to share which was quite touching.

The following group meeting was very dramatic. I knew in advance that Guy would not be there but Lucy and I had prepared for this. Unfortunately on the day of the group Lucy became very ill and could not come. Panicked messages were sent out cancelling the group but only one group member got the message. I went to The Gateway and, as people arrived, I received the message that it was cancelled. I told the group members that it was cancelled, however they persuaded me that I could run the group on my own. I was thrown in at the deep end. Much to my amazement, although perhaps it was a bit disorganised, I managed it. I started by asking for some feedback about the first session. I thought it would be useful to share this with Guy and Lucy later. People talked about the lack of structure and that they were not quite sure about things, about what they were meant to do or say. I suppose the same applied for that day that I ran the group by myself! But I felt I did the best I could and couldn't believe that I had managed it. I left The Gateway with a grin on my face and wrote excited emails to Guy and Lucy as soon as I got home. I realised that I can actually do things and it helped my confidence greatly.

My doctor and various mental health workers were greatly impressed and surprised when they learned that I had managed this. The impacts on me of attending some *Psychology in the Real World* groups have not always been met with such a positive response. When I have openly questioned psychiatry and certain ideas regarding mental health (having learned little bits of psychology) there has sometimes been a harsh response and dismissive attitude: 'Who have you been talking to?' 'What group are you on now?' I generally find this amusing but there is a deeper, more serious side to such matters. I believe there should not be such a huge separation in various areas of mental health and things should be looked at and viewed from all angles and aspects.

I was very touched to receive a thank-you card from everyone in *The Writing Group* a fortnight later when we next met. As the weeks went by the group seemed to settle down, everyone bonded well and some fantastic things were read out. I started reading my own work, and this became easier and easier (for all of us). There were many poems that brought me close to tears as they were so moving and well read. The initial sense of disorganisation dissipated quickly as we developed routines in the group that we all understood. People in the group, and I, felt it was a great success.

To go from being a group member to a group facilitator was huge. It meant everything. For years it had been drilled (probably non-intentionally) into my head that I was flawed, incapable and ill. In the years between discussing the idea of a writing group and it actually starting I often thought that I would not be alive to run it. This experience broke the chains of this thinking and sparked a huge enthusiasm for writing and thinking of the future. It is as though this has been a journey for me from despair and being self-destructive to growing slowly into a more mature, level-headed, confident individual that does have a place and indeed a purpose. When *The Writing Group* ended I felt so sad I held back the tears. I feel all aspects of the experience – the setting up of things, the running of the group and the warmth and kindness of everyone involved – helped in ways no pill or therapy could ever come close to achieving. Being active and out in the world is far more healing than hiding away in a flat or hospital. I can now talk to people and this is truly liberating. I know that I matter and I have made a difference. I hope that maybe next year another writing group can be run and that many ideas will follow on from all of this. Through connecting and engaging with people, in a variety of roles, I think I may have just rejoined the human race that for years I denied I was part of.

SECTION 13

On groupwork IV: *Endings*

59

On retaining a sense of humility about the impacts of community-based groupwork

One can't complain. I have my friends. Someone spoke to me only yesterday.
    Eeyore in *The House at Pooh Corner*

Many people seem to have experienced a wide variety of benefits from being involved in *Psychology in the Real World* groups, but it is important to not make the kinds of ludicrous claims that characterise many books on mental health interventions. Hopefully the chapters have revealed these groups to be very much in the real world rather than the made-up world that appears to be described in some books about mental health: community-based groupwork is no panacea for all individual and social ills, and there are considerable limitations in terms of its potential impacts. Gary Hosty's quote about medication being 'of some help to some people with some of their problems some of the time, but usually at some cost' equally applies to individual therapy, groupwork and community-based interventions of the types described in the previous chapters.

Both formal and informal evaluations of the groups have indicated that many people relate positive changes in their personal wellbeing/ mental health and in their life situation to being involved in *Psychology in the Real World*. For example, one person with a long-term addiction to heroin came off the drug whilst attending a group after discovering that people uninvolved in the drug scene were not as narrow minded as he thought (they did not condemn him when he revealed his addiction) and were not as dull and uncaring as he had feared. He made friends with people whom he felt were interested in him (rather than interested in taking drugs with him). However, not everyone experiences such transformative benefits. A couple of people who regularly took crack cocaine contributed little and did not seem to benefit from one group that they (irregularly) attended, and one person who mentioned their past heroin addiction during an initial round robin did not come back (I feel that as facilitators we failed to sufficiently connect this person with others during the formation stage of the group).

Many chapters have revealed some advantages of community-based groupwork in bringing about change in people's lives when compared to one-to-one work, however there are some disadvantages. Compared to individual therapy there are fewer opportunities for individuals to describe in detail their difficulties, history and life situation and less time in the session to talk through what needs to happen to bring about some change in these difficulties. Group members have fed back that they found some things too personal to disclose in *Psychology in the Real World* groups. Such people may have needs that these groups are never going to be able to fully meet and feedback has indicated that some group members felt they needed one-to-one interventions prior to, alongside or subsequent to coming to the groups.

Whilst many people have found sessions such as *What is the point of being alive?* positive experiences, and even transformative, a minority have described being disturbed (one said 'haunted') by such sessions. It is important to remember that psychological defences are necessary for all of us to survive the rigours of life. Mental health professionals can at times recklessly strip people of their defences and, although we hope we have not thoughtlessly done this in the groups, undoubtedly there is a risk of disturbing people who may gain insights about their defences but insufficient help to utilise alternatives. No group experience can provide the individual attention some people sometimes need to clarify how to replace potentially maladaptive coping strategies with more helpful ones. Facilitators are often unaware of how disturbing a session might have been (for example, I did not realise that person was haunted by *What is the point of being alive?* only learning about it a year later when the group was formally evaluated). I am aware, however, that even for people who have described significant benefits from attending the groups, general progress in terms of psychological wellbeing has often been 'two steps forward, one step backwards' as impacts of traumas and stress have at times overwhelmed them. Similarly, whilst many people who have attended the groups have subsequently reduced and come off their medication, it would be wrong to think that this has been plain sailing – many of these people have had periods in their lives of intense pain and considerable disturbance requiring significant support from friends, family and professionals.

Although *Psychology in the Real World* groups enable access to professional psychologists and the provision of psychological analysis and support to a greater number and range of people than can be achieved by solely providing individual therapy in a narrowly defined service, they still only involve relatively small numbers of people compared to the proportion suffering in

any community. In addition, the groups have not always attracted people from all aspects of society. Although effort is made to get as mixed a group as possible, working-class young men and people from black and ethnic minority groups have been underrepresented in many of the groups. The marketing strategies might not have appealed to such people (for example, they may not know of Churchill's conceptualisation of depression as 'the black dog'). Perhaps the content and focus of the groups has not provoked interest or has been off-putting (e.g. young men with substance misuse problems might be more interested in, and receive more benefit from, joining a football team that encompassed ideas from *Psychology in the Real World* than what might be perceived as a 'talking shop'). The philosophies underlying the groups might be conceptualised as white, Western and liberal, and clash with some philosophies that are important to people from some black and minority ethnic groups. People from under-represented groups may want to join different types of community-based groups or might respond to a different type of approach to ones we have tended to employ (see Chapter 53).

As Chapter 62 describes, the evaluations on which much of this book is based are open to critique in terms of methodology despite our intentions to obtain as honest feedback as possible on the groups. Both formal and informal feedback from group members has taught us a lot – the book undoubtedly gives a false impression of the groups being much better planned with well-thought-out philosophies prior to their commencement than has actually been the case. In reality they have been much more experimental, becoming more refined (and understood) each time they have been repeated. As such we have undoubtedly made many mistakes along the way, missing opportunities to help and perhaps inadvertently harming more people than we are aware of.

Co-facilitators have described many benefits of taking up a socially valued role, but I have also been aware of the strain on them, especially when aspects of their own lives have been disturbing and painful and they have had to suppress their needs and their pain 'for the sake of the group' (see Box 22). Understandably, at certain times all of us facilitating these groups have found our private lives and personal distress spilling over into the time we have set aside for preparing, discussing and facilitating the groups. For people with no professional training and little outside psychosocial support, co-facilitating has sometimes been simultaneously experienced as a great strain, as well as something worthwhile and personally rewarding. Containing the pain expressed by many members in these groups can be quite a challenge and when feelings about our own lives are particularly raw this can push us to the limits of what we can bear. At times I feel I have naively expected too much from people who might have natural skills in facilitation and great motivation and commitment to running groups but no training (or prior experience) of groupwork. Many of these people have also been paid only a fraction of what I am paid for facilitating the groups, with others working purely on a voluntary basis. As Chapter 46 describes, co-facilitators can provide each other with support both in and out of sessions, but as in any peer relationship there are limits to this regarding the wide range of needs and intense personal pain that some people experience. This book has been written to encourage and help people, whatever their background, to get involved in groupwork, but there is potential for personal strain and pain as well as gain when facilitating groups. With this in mind we are planning to run local training courses for people who want to set up groups and are establishing more comprehensive systems of support and supervision for people doing groupwork.

Box 22   How upset one can get whilst facilitating a group: Extracts from a reflective piece written by a co-facilitator shortly after one group session

After everyone left I kind of fell apart. I cannot remember when I last cried like that. Guess I couldn't suppress it. Maybe I needed to cry after so long trying not to, but I'm not good on the where and when I decide to burst into tears. I just couldn't help it. At least I didn't run off or do something rash, and at least I didn't cry in the group – I think that would have been a huge embarrassment.

Why did I say the group is killing me? Why? I'm just having a bad time (very bad if I am honest). I cannot completely act with pretence in the group. I am not a professional person. I cannot just turn my feelings off and suppress things when I hear things I relate to. I am ruled by a battered heart that at times does not always engage the brain. I have nothing else to immerse myself in and give myself a break. I cannot escape things. I lack structure in my general life. If I were on an even keel I would be working full time, but I'm not. I've lost everything. I'm still upset about everything. I may not be the most stable person. I hope Guy realises this (well he does now).

I'm not going anywhere. Sure, 'I don't have to do this group', but I need to. If I threw in the towel I'd unravel to a point of no return and it would be a huge regret. It would set me back to a place I don't wish to go. The group triggers many things in me that are painful. I do not choose that pain but I cannot avoid it. It's better for me to face this and continue. When I look back on this group it'll be without regret and represent achievement to me.

The fact that most *Psychology in the Real World* groups have been time limited has provided many advantages for group facilitators and group members (e.g. has enabled new groups to be set up and group members to take the lead in later projects), but this has also impacted in terms of the loss of support that many people experience whilst attending the groups. There has also been a loss in terms of bringing about systemic and social change as time-limited groups offer fewer opportunities for people to work together on projects that take a great deal of planning. The 'Living with Medication' group in Leicester have achieved more than our *Thinking about Medication* group in terms of having an impact on their local health services perhaps because their group is not time limited and people have gone on from analysing problems to collectively campaigning for change. Future *Psychology in the Real World* groups are planned to incorporate opportunities for people to move from analysis to bringing about social change by having this process built into the course programme (e.g. *This is Madness,* which intends to bring people together who want to address problems of stigma) and by having more formal ways of providing support for people to campaign or set up projects after the last session of the group.

By coming on the courses some people have made friends and become less lonely but many in their own and any objective person's analysis have remained as socially isolated as Eeyore. Groups that provide ongoing support have been set up by ex-*Psychology in the Real World* members and more are planned (e.g. Anna Hughes is developing a *Walk and Talk* for people in the local mental health crisis house; Nicki Evans and a past member of one of *The Writing Groups* are setting up an informal group for people interested in sharing their writing). However, such groups have often proven difficult to get off the ground and, like many

support groups, have been quite fragile entities in terms of their ability to provide long-term, ongoing support.

As regards bringing about changes in the mental health system and wider social change, the last decade, as many before it, seems to have had tides of opinion and policy going in opposite directions. For example, many *Psychology in the Real World* groups have given weight to the oft-neglected social causes of distress, and recently the work of people such as Richard Layard and Richard Wilkinson have come to national prominence (for example, revealing that in Western countries increased personal wealth does not lead to increased happiness once basic needs are met, and countries with the greatest inequality of income have the greatest social, physical health and mental health problems). At the same time little has been done to reduce poverty and inequality, and recent investment in mental health appears to have been driven by a government agenda to target individuals and process them through systems designed to patch them up via short-term therapy in order to get them off benefits and back into the kinds of work systems that may well have been instrumental in causing their breakdown. At a more general level, it is not clear if individualism has reached its zenith despite many people (in *Psychology in the Real World* groups and the general population) recognising the problems caused by structuring our society in ways that encourage individual people to seek individual solutions to their individual problems. Whilst professing 'the right to be whoever we want to be', there seems to me to be astonishing levels of conformity to authority figures, resigned acceptance of the loss of civil liberties, and exhausted apathy when it comes to struggling against injustice and what is perceived as wrong or lacking in 21st century Britain. *Psychology in the Real World* projects have led to a few people trying to bring about changes in local mental health services and in wider social systems, but they have hardly led to the kind of revolutionary campaigning that characterised previous eras (e.g. during the protests in Europe in the late 1960s the 'lunatics' literally did take over some of the asylums), even though one might have expected this from listening to some of the impassioned discussions in the groups. This fits with research cited by Wilkinson and Pickett that indicates that when people come together to discuss social issues they are often surprised by how many others recognise the downsides of individualism and materialism, but when they return to their atomised lives they feel isolated and cut off from such people and unable to bring about any change.

Although *Psychology in the Real World* groups have looked at the medical model as one way of explaining human distress, they also provide access to many alternative ways of thinking about mental health, and many participants have experienced them as a challenge to what is sometimes called 'the medicalisation of misery'. Critiques of the illness model appear to be gaining ground in Britain, with increasing numbers of conferences, books, and academic and newspaper articles focusing on the limits and harmful aspects of this model. There is even a campaign for the abolition of the label schizophrenia (see www.caslcampaign.com) and *DSM* (the Diagnostic and Statistical Manual that psychiatrists use to formally diagnose people with a psychiatric disorder) has come under much criticism. Robert Spitzer, who was head of the *DSM-III* and *DSM-IV* task forces (and as a result instrumental in formally defining more than a hundred mental disorders) has publicly admitted the folly of this process. In the 2007 BBC2 documentary *The Trap* he said: 'What happened is that we made estimates of the prevalence of mental disorders totally descriptively, without considering that many of

these conditions might be normal reactions which are not really disorders. That's the problem, because we were not looking at the context in which those conditions developed.' Even the introduction to *DSM* notes how it would be more sensible to think of mental health problems on a continuum (that we are all on) rather than the discrete categories that *DSM* delineates (you are either mentally ill or sane depending on how many of a specified list of behaviours you are deemed to exhibit). Spitzer wrote the forward to Horwitz and Wakefield's seminal book *The Loss of Sadness: How Psychiatry Transformed Normal Sorrow into Depressive Disorder*, which, as well as critiquing the whole notion of categorising mental illnesses, argues that psychological distress is a necessary part of human development and without painful experiences human consciousness could not have evolved. Despite this, large numbers of mental health professionals remain unaware of such critiques; NICE dictates what are deemed to be effective treatments for mental illnesses, only occasionally mentioning (then completely ignoring) the fact that psychiatric diagnoses lack validity (see Boyle, 1999); increasing amounts of training of NHS staff is conducted by people in the pay of pharmaceutical companies; new services (let alone existing ones) continue to be geared around diagnoses and their treatment; and 29 million prescriptions were written by doctors for antidepressants in 2005.

In our local NHS Trust the machinations of the corporation and the increasingly privatised system in which it operates seem to frequently override the practices and potential impacts of *Psychology in the Real World*. The need to record (and ever-increase) the number of individual 'episodes of care' that are 'delivered' to 'identified patients' inevitably grates with models based on community psychology. The complexities of what gets called 'depression' (as explored in *The Black Dog*), let alone 'mental health', and the diversity of what helps people cannot easily be operationalised into contracts where money is exchanged based on numbers of identifiable patient contacts. Elisabeth X (in Chapters 6 and 20) directly relates the benefits of *Psychology in the Real World* groups to the absence of referrals, assessments, questions about risk, record keeping and statistical recording. Nicki Evans (in Chapter 58) reveals the power of co-facilitating a group in terms of impacts on her own mental health. All of this points the way to services being freed up from top-down governance and bureaucratic requirements so people can benefit from very diverse ways of being involved in mental health services. Yet bush-fire panics relating to clinical governance (such as those about risk assessments) sweep though NHS and Local Authority bodies, with top-down solutions being implemented by decree and enforced in all situations, no matter how ludicrous. Managers, under so much strain from continual fire-fighting and demands to immediately implement wave after wave of reform designed by people who have never worked in services, seem to have few opportunities for true reflection or to escape what Bion called fight/flight states and operate in work group mode. At times their only relief from the heat and strain of one pressing situation seems to be the distraction of having to respond to the next bush fire.

The fear that some staff groups have historically felt about openly questioning practices in mental health services appears to be infecting all professions. In a system where Foundation Trusts have to compete against each other (and against private sector organisations) for business, reputation is everything. In such cultures it is hard to envisage any Trust welcoming its practices being publicly shown to be ineffective or inefficient, let alone misguided, harmful and foolish. In such climates radical community-based groupwork might initially have to be conducted under the radar, at least until such groups can establish their own evidence base and support from local people and clinicians (although there are many arguments to justify such groups to service managers and commissioners – see Chapter 63). Thus, whilst some progressive people feel the battle for ideas seems to be being won, power and control of the structures in which health and social care are delivered, as well as the purse strings, seem to be increasingly in the hands of people whose interests are not those of revolutionary change towards systems where local people really would have greater power over the ways that they might be helped, and where a great diversity of approaches in the arena of mental health could be assisted to flourish.

60

Attachments, separations and groupwork

There is nothing so practical as a good theory.
    Kurt Lewin

Some theories about groups and groupwork are impenetrable for all but the most intellectual expert in the field yet the majority of people running groups in the statutory and voluntary sectors have received little academic (or indeed groupwork) training. Attachment theory, as described in the work of John Bowlby, may offer something more useful. Jeremy Holmes wrote a brilliant paper in 1994 entitled *Attachment theory – a secure theoretical base for counselling?* where he related basic principles of attachment theory to the practice of counselling. Yet most childhood experiences do not occur in one-to-one dyads but in groups – in the family home, nursery, classroom and playground, where children and adults are together and operate as a family, sibling, school class or hobby group. Similarly, many of our adult experiences occur in groups – in a shared home with friends, or in a family home where we are now the parents, in work groups or teams, with friends on holiday, in pubs and clubs. Many services set up to help people offer opportunities for people to come together in groups, some more formal or therapeutic, others more informal and social. In this chapter I therefore plan to mirror the structure and style of Jeremy's paper but apply attachment theory to groups rather than individuals before going on to indicate how, with its emphasis on attachments and separations, attachment theory can provide 'a secure theoretical base' for groupwork.

Some basic principles of attachment theory and how these can be expanded to thinking about groups

Bowlby (and many researchers who have experimentally tested his theories) observed that children, like most animals, will seek proximity to an 'attachment figure' (e.g. their mother), especially at times of distress or illness, apparently seeking protection, comfort and reassurance. As well as responding to these needs, the attachment figure can provide a 'secure base' where the child comes to feel safe enough to explore the environment beyond. This not only includes the physical environment: it can be conceptualised as encompassing the emotional terrain whereby the child might try out different ways of reacting to external events or internal states. However, when it feels parted from the attachment figure, a child's natural response will be one of protest – usually displayed as distress or aggression ('separation protest'). The way these patterns of proximity and separation evolve between the child and the attachment figure – the attachment relationship – becomes stored as 'an internal working model' from which the child makes assumptions about how people will behave to him or her, especially at times of distress. 'Insecure attachments' in childhood (which might arise in response to repeated patterns of the child not being helped to leave the safety of the secure base, or being met with rejection or very confusing behaviours when seeking the attachment figure at times of distress) can have lasting impacts on the way a child manages difficult emotional states, and lead to expectations regarding the responses of others should they seek help or display distress that can make intimate relationships difficult in later childhood and adulthood. However, experiencing 'secure attachments' later in life can mitigate some of these impacts (people can develop new 'internal working models' – for example, ones where there is less fear of rejection when seeking comfort from someone at a time of distress).

Attachments have thus been traditionally conceptualised as centring on one-to-one relationships. However, the role of the mother may have been overemphasised in the theory: there are often several attachment figures during a child's development – parents, grandparents, siblings, close friends of the family, teachers, hobby group leaders – who operate as attachment figures individually and at times as a group. It may be that groups, including the 'sense' of the family home, the nursery or school class, can also provide a secure base. When we feel safe and secure in our group we may feel more able to manage difficult feelings and to try out being different – both within the group as well as being more open to experiences (and encounters with people) outside the group. Whilst separation protest undoubtedly occurs in one-to-one situations it can also be conceptualised as occurring during separation from the groups to which we have a sense of belonging – just look at the anxieties children have when being separated from their class at school. The concept of internal working models of attachments can also be applied to groups: our experiences in groups will lead to expectations of what will happen in future groups. Hurtful encounters will affect the ways we behave in groups – we may, for example, fearing rejection, desperately cling on to being a member of a group we would be better off leaving, or be avoidant of all groups in case we

experience another rejection. Later healthy group experiences may help us to discover and practise different ways of being in group situations, and thus develop new internal working models of group interaction.

Applications of attachment theory to groupwork

Jeremy Holmes looked in detail at six aspects of attachment theory and applied them to one-to-one counselling. Below I apply them to groupwork:

1. *A secure base* – Once the initial anxiety of joining and being in a new group eases, the group experience as a whole can provide a secure base from which people can feel safe enough to discuss challenging things, 'be themselves' or try out being different. Meeting in the same place each time (people often like to sit in the same place); the reliability of the same facilitators always being there when people arrive; the predictability of the experience (each session tends to be different but have a similar routine); a calm atmosphere and overall sense of safety; some degree of confidentiality or sense that what is spoken of will be treated as private; the keeping of time boundaries; a sense of being held and comforted by people in the group and by the overall group experience – all these can lead to the group being experienced as a secure base which can serve to calm anxieties and distress and provide the necessary security from which one can explore the (psychological and physical) world. The facilitators are important in this. For example, one participant on an evaluation form commented: *'An excellent tutor who at all times encouraged group participation and enabled us all to allow our vulnerability to be revealed.'* But each group is also dependent on its members working together to create this sense of a secure base.

2. *Attunement and empathy* – A mother might be attuned to and able to empathise with her child when sought out at a time of distress, thus enabling the child to calm and regain a sense of equilibrium before venturing out into the world again. Adults need this too. But a group in which we feel safe can also provide such encounters. Empathy is a difficult thing – we never really know what another is experiencing and even our best efforts can be misguided. In a group there tend to be more (and more varied) comments and reactions when a group member reveals their distress, and as such, there is a greater chance of someone being empathetic. The group as a whole can provide a containing experience within which this can occur. For example, an *Understanding Ourselves and Others* participant stated: *'There was lots of mutual support and encouragement for those who may have been feeling rather vulnerable during some sessions.'*

3. *The chance to develop a coherent narrative* – In secure attachments the distressed child learns to put their distress and reasons for the distress into words and for it to become a coherent story. Group experiences offer similar opportunities. People who had never been in groups where they could express their feelings and describe their experiences in ways that made sense to others and themselves can have opportunities to do this, and as a consequence can learn to become comfortable doing it in other group (and one-to-one) situations in the future. The narrative of their story – how they have come to be who they are – can start to make sense and can open up new ways of being in the world. *'When I went from talking generally about the topic to talking about my life I felt OK, I felt understood – something that doesn't often happen,'* commented one *Psychology in the Real World* participant.

4. *The metabolism of powerful feelings* – In attachment theory the child is seen to benefit from encounters where powerful feelings (especially anger) are expressed to the parent and contained and metabolised – the feelings do not overwhelm the parent, who does not silence them, but by containing them enables the child to achieve a state of calm and, through repetitions of this experience, the child comes to learn to do this him- or herself. In groups people temporarily overwhelmed by emotion can benefit from experiences where such emotions are expressed; where this expression is seen not to overwhelm (or destroy) the group as a whole or any individual in it; where such feelings are absorbed and contained by the group; where the person is calmed by the experience; and, in time, the person may come to internalise the group as a calming presence at times of future overwhelm. *Psychology in the Real World* ventures often bring up powerful feelings in participants, which are usually contained in the group (e.g. distressed people have only rarely left the room), and which are not often met with awkward silence but rather recognised and accepted for what they are (by group members or, failing this, the facilitators). This has included, for example, anger about hurtful psychiatric treatments and being sectioned (in *Thinking about Medication*), deep pain relating to past abusive experiences (*Understanding Ourselves and Others*), profound sadness relating to experiences of separation and loneliness (*The Black Dog*) and yearning for deceased family members (*The Writing Group*). One group member commented: *'The group has felt safe and comfortable. Over the weeks I have grown to feel increasingly safe in myself (rather than out of control) and increasingly comfortable (rather than anxiously thinking I'm disturbed).'*

5. *Opportunities to manage experiences of loss and mourning* – Bowlby felt that attachment theory is as much about loss and separation as it is about bonding. Experiences of separation and loss occur in groups as people leave and eventually the group comes to an end. Good group experiences engender powerful emotional states, particularly the wish for the group to continue (see Chapter 61). Groupworkers can enable feelings about the loss of contact with other members and loss of the group as a whole to be expressed, contained and learned from. *Psychology in the Real World* groups always offer opportunities in the last session for members to reflect on their own feelings about the group coming to an end and to link this to the literature on endings and separations, including Bowlby's theories.

6. *The modification of maladaptive internal working models* – Just as in counselling, groupwork offers people opportunities to develop insights about the roots of their relationship difficulties and to have new 'corrective' experiences. Children that have been scapegoated, ignored, bullied, oppressed, judged, humiliated, silenced or rejected in family, school or friendship groups have very different expectations of future groups compared to children who have been respected, comforted, praised, given valued roles and encouraged to take responsibility in such groups. Later in life, during opportunities to be members of healthy groups, people who have had damaging experiences in groups are likely to behave in ways that might impede their ability to have

some of that damage repaired (e.g. they might have learned to protect themselves by shunning groups, or by not revealing vulnerability in group situations, keeping silent or unnoticed, or using bravura to keep other group members at a distance). Everyone has internal models of how people behave in groups, what goes on in groups, and what happens to us in groups, which affect our commitment to groups and our responses to group dynamics and experiences. Sometimes this leads to patterns in previous groups repeating themselves, however there remain opportunities for all of us to develop more secure attachments in group situations and thus incorporate new working models which allow us to respond and behave differently in future group situations.

By running different groups in the same locality over a long period of time I have been able to witness this process many times: the woman whose rage erupted about the way she had been treated in the mental health service, calming when this was met with empathy (rather than finding her rage transforming into madness or destruction as had previously occurred), and as a result learning how to put anger into words that could constructively get her views across to workers in the mental health system; the man who was very emotionally restrained in one group, being terrified of expressing his views or feelings, being able to openly talk about painful events and cry in a subsequent group, and learn that catastrophic things do not happen after emotional outpourings.

61

Endings

The end is built into the beginning.
　　Hazel (*Synecdoche, New York*)

The endings of *Psychology in the Real World* groups, like endings of therapy groups and of individual therapy, offer opportunities for participants to explore the impacts on them of such experiences. The title of the last session of *Understanding Ourselves and Others* courses is usually *What happens when things come to an end?* This provides opportunities for participants to reflect on their thoughts and feelings about the group ending and how these might mirror similar feelings when other things in life end – jobs or careers, certain roles (e.g. of being a parent when children leave home), relationships, the death of loved ones and the prospect of one's own death. The literature on loss and separations (e.g. the work of Elisabeth Kübler-Ross and John Bowlby) is introduced and discussed in the whole group before group members are encouraged to reflect on endings that they have experienced and what it feels like for the group to be coming to an end. Other *Psychology in the Real World* groups offer similar possibilities. For example, the literature relating loss and separation to depression is considerable, and insights pertinent to endings are a key part of the last couple of sessions of *The Black Dog*.

　As in other group situations there is a dilemma for facilitators regarding the ending of a community-based group. The more final the ending – for example, the facilitators not introducing any prospect of the group formally meeting again and not introducing scope to discuss how individual group members may stay in touch – the more powerful the ending experience will be and the more potential there will be to learn from reflections on the experience of the group ending. However, *Psychology in the Real World* groups have aims beyond those of personal insight and experiential learning. For example, they have specifically been aimed at having an impact on social inclusion and loneliness, and several groups have tried to gather people together who might collectively act to bring about social change. Having a final ending where the facilitators and group do not meet again does not prevent group members from subsequently meeting up after the group finishes, but it does not facilitate this either. For this reason some *Psychology in the Real World* groups have included time set aside in the last session for people to discuss how they might keep in touch with each other, whether they may want to meet in subgroups to take forward any action after the end of the group, and whether they want a follow-up session. Such discussions are not as easy to facilitate as one might think. They can be characterised by awkwardness, perhaps raising anxieties in people that no one from what might have been experienced as an intimate group will want to join them in a follow-up meeting or project, which might mirror previous disappointments or rejections that they have experienced. Alternatively, they can raise fears in group members of being obliged to meet up afterwards with people when they might rather not, and evaluations have occasionally revealed that some people have felt pressure to get involved in projects and make additional commitments beyond the end of the group.

Powerful feelings about endings can arise in the penultimate and final sessions of cohesive groups and this can lead to facilitators colluding with members and fudging the ending, for example hastily arranging a follow-up meeting without thinking through what that might achieve. This risks group members neither making their own plans to meet up outside the group nor learning something about their reactions to endings and developing their ways of expressing and managing feelings that accompany such experiences. I wonder whether this occurred when one *Black Dog* group decided to meet again at the same venue three months later. Only about half of the group turned up and no group members had in the meantime met up with each other. There did not seem to be the energy in the group that had been there during the last session when the follow-up had been suggested. The facilitators were left thinking that if the group had ended three months before as planned there might have been more likelihood of group members making their own arrangements to stay in contact – arranging a follow-up had perhaps led to inactivity rather than the kinds of activity we had hoped might occur. Undoubtedly a psychoanalyst would have interpreted events as the whole group (including the facilitators) avoiding the feelings associated with the original ending of the group by setting up 'another ending'.

Rather than, in the last session, handing decision making over to the group regarding whether the group might continue in some capacity and whether there might be follow-up meetings, which brings up difficulties of democracy (how can 14 people make collective decisions about such things in such a short-

time?) and risks decision making being skewed by powerful feelings about the group ending, it can be better to help the group end as planned but assist group members that are interested to later come together to plan a similar but different project. The end of *Thinking about Medication* led to the creation of *Out of the Box*. Although there were undoubtedly strong feelings at the end of *Thinking about Medication* and strong wishes within the group for it continue beyond the end date, we kept to the predetermined date for the last session then encouraged people who wanted something more to set up something different. This involved group members who were interested in being part of another group subsequently meeting to discuss their individual and collective needs, plan what kind of group might meet these, make decisions about how such a group might be facilitated and whether Marese and I were the best people to do that, and make practical arrangements such as where and when the group might meet. Thus, rather than *Thinking about Medication* being extended and becoming a long-term group (which would probably have led to dropouts), a new project was thus enabled that could meet the expressed needs of a subset of the original group, and group members were able to take responsibility for planning and organising that group.

Out of the Box operated more informally and more like a support group than other *Psychology in the Real World* groups and, unlike these groups, was not set up for a fixed period of time. This can lead to dilemmas in group members and facilitators about the length of time one might make a commitment for, and inevitably as months go by people decide to leave such groups. This then raises an issue about whether such groups should be open to new members, with the advantages and disadvantages this brings for existing members and new people, or whether a group with dwindling numbers should be brought to an end. Such issues need careful consideration but, in a support group that is supposed to concentrate on a specific task (e.g. help people reduce medication), whether to continue or end the group can be an issue that comes to repetitively dominate the dynamics and discussions. A psychotherapy group would use this as pertinent material to continually analyse and learn from, but a support group can become bogged down in such issues. In the end *Out of the Box* group members and facilitators decided to bring the group to an end as some people left and some wanted to commit to alternative projects and become members of different types of groups. However, as chapter writers in this book testify, others missed this type of ongoing support and wanted the group to continue. All of these conflicting feelings and needs need to be carefully considered by groupworkers and discussed both in the group and outside, where supervision on such matters can be crucial. This can help facilitators to clarify their personal feelings about the group ending; the impacts on them of the feelings group members have about the ending; the pros and cons of having further discussion in the group about whether it should continue; and the pros and cons of making various decisions (e.g. the facilitators saying they will no longer commit to an ongoing group with such small numbers and making an authoritative decision that the group should end and setting an end date).

One factor for facilitators to consider regarding endings is that ongoing groups with no end date prevent new groups from being set up as there is only a small amount of time any worker can spend each week on running groups (we have not had more than two *Psychology in the Real World* groups running per week at any time and only one group that requires significant preparation for each session). Psychologically and practically I have found it helpful to have one group in the preparation stage, one running, and one recently ended where I might be involved in writing a report for the group or preparing something for publication on that group.

Over the years, whilst many *Psychology in the Real World* groups have started and ended with many group members undoubtedly losing touch with each other, by having a succession of groups there have been opportunities for people to bump into people they met on one group if they sign up for a subsequent group. In addition, *Walk and Talk* helps to keep a loose nexus of people who have come to *Psychology in the Real World* groups linked together. Although I am normally involved solely in the summer, *Walk and Talk* now runs throughout the year having increasingly become a members-run venture. It offers opportunities for people to stay in touch and not retreat into a lonely, isolated existence, and has meant that goodbyes that have occurred in other groups need not be absolute endings in terms of contact, as there is always a weekly *Psychology in the Real World* venture to which people can turn up when it pleases them.

62

Evaluating groups

Research that produces nothing but books will not suffice.

    Kurt Lewin

When considering evaluating groups one has to first ask: what, and who, is the evaluation for? The answers will guide the methodology to be employed as well as the specific questions one might ask or hypotheses one might want to test. Each *Psychology in the Real World* venture has been evaluated in some way. Mostly this has been with the aim of obtaining relevant feedback for facilitators that might guide their general practice and improve the effectiveness of the group should it run again. A secondary aim has been to produce reports that provide a summary for participants of the group in order to help people remember and apply some of the things they might have learned whilst participating. Such reports also serve to advertise the group when it is next run – I put them on our department website and often refer to them on flyers advertising subsequent ventures. This allows people to be better informed as to what they are joining. One hears the notion of informed consent emphasised increasingly in terms of mental health service provision but most people are still given very little idea of what it might be like to see a psychologist or other health professional, go into a psychiatric hospital or attend a CMHT. Most information leaflets about services do not even attempt to convey this and just contain a few bland statements about the service, but the reports – full of quotes

of what people have said, with descriptions of the sessions and sometimes photographs (for example, of *Walk and Talk*) – do give a flavour of what coming to a *Psychology in the Real World* venture might be like.

The evaluations and reports on www.shropsych.org (like this book) are also written to guide other people who might be interested in setting up similar groups. Each evaluation adds to the evidence base: some have been published in peer-reviewed journals, others are solely available on the website. They can be used to reply to the query *Where's the evidence?* Sometimes it can seem like you are the character in Edvard Munch's *The Scream* when being challenged with this question in the modern NHS, as it has been used to intimidate people or justify cuts in services rather than be a proper question to ask regarding all health and social interventions.

Some evaluations have included questions aimed at evaluating whether the groups meet specific NHS Trust and social service priorities (e.g. Holmes and Gahan's 2006 study included five questions on the local authority's *Quality of Life Indicators for Learning and Culture,* i.e. on the impacts of *Psychology in the Real World* on group member's knowledge, skills, confidence, self-esteem, physical and psychological wellbeing, and employment prospects). The reports and evaluations thus provide data on how effective the groups have been in meeting these service aims as well as whether group members' individual aims have been met. They serve the purpose of justifying my involvement in these projects, provide service user feedback about the psychology service, provide information about what I do to my line manager and enable this manager and others in the Trust to respond to pressures to provide evidence about psychology interventions and the usefulness of the service. They also help people tick many boxes in terms of performance management, e.g. service user feedback about services, service user consultancy, service user involvement, mental health promotion and prevention, and combating stigma.

The process of continually evaluating *Psychology in the Real World* ventures can be thought of as audit. But this seems very different from what Mental Health Trusts often call audit and governance – processes that seem to increasingly echo the manoeuvrings of corporate bodies in the business world. Audit in these contexts often seems to relate more to meeting targets, lowering costs, avoiding complaints and being sued, displacing blame and responsibility, and controlling staff through creating fears of redundancy. In my view it is more important to be accountable to the people one is paid to help than be accountable to multiple layers of hierarchical management that many clinicians feel have been undemocratically imposed on them in order to control professional independence and bring about privatisation by stealth.

The specific methodologies employed in evaluating each group have not been described in great detail in this book but are published on www.shropsych.org/psychologyintherealworld.htm and further details can be obtained directly from the author. Chapter 38 on the 2006 *Thinking about Medication* group provides greatest detail on research methodology regarding an evaluation, but even here more detail can be found on the website, such as copies of letters and questionnaires sent and information on the

statistics used. The methodologies we have utilised are better conceptualised as audit and action research (see below) rather than pure research, and are certainly not above critique, for example, in terms of the rigour of methodologies and statistical analyses employed. For example, none have utilised control group methodologies. Such research, especially if conducted by an impartial researcher, could provide a good comparison between group participants and people perhaps on a waiting list. In the current climate, where NHS Trusts want staff to focus on meeting targets, clinicians such as myself do not have the time to be involved in large-scale research projects that need a year to get approval from Trust research governance boards and ethical committees before being initiated, and as a consequence (operating in the 'real world') we have to make do with conducting more low-key audits as a means of evaluating our work.

The evaluations involve small numbers, which raises questions about the generalisability of the findings. However, they are on local populations and therefore the data is generalisable in terms of applicability to future groups with similar people in the same locality. This contrasts with the generalisability of a lot of the published outcome literature on psychological interventions as the bulk of this has been conducted on populations that differ from those that access our local CMHT (e.g. American degree students and people who are relatively well off). Applicability of outcome evidence is a much more complex issue than is often portrayed, as outlined by Moloney and Kelly's article *Beck Never Lived in Birmingham: Why CBT may be a less useful treatment for psychological distress than is often supposed* and Clarke and Barkham's recent paper *Evidence de Rigour*.

Some *Psychology in the Real World* groups have run with only a few men, which raise even greater questions about making generalisations from some of the data in terms of what helps men. On the other hand, many of the groups had few dropouts, which is one of the main methodological problems with the outcome literature. Even heavily financed research tends to have high drop-out rates, which the authors frequently ignore, brush over, or use statistical gerrymandering to overcome. People drop out for a reason (normally they find the intervention unhelpful or harmful) and, as NICE has acknowledged, the lack of data from such people could mean that many so-called gold standard trials misleadingly indicate a drug or therapy is much more helpful and much less harmful than is actually the case.

Many *Psychology in the Real World* evaluations are done in rather a rushed fashion – working in the NHS gives people little time to think about and prepare for groups let alone design, plan and execute rigorous research projects. All standard groupwork textbooks recommend the careful planning of how to evaluate a group as part of the initial preparations for the group and emphasise the importance of having all the materials to do an evaluation ready before the first session. This is very laudable and sensible, but in the real world this is not always possible – the rush to get things prepared for the start of a group usually involves facilitators working well into the night on the evening before the opening session and evaluating the group ends up descending down the list of priorities. However, failing to prepare is preparing to fail, and utilising control groups, pre and post measures (both quantitative and qualitative) and having evaluations solely conducted by researchers who are not involved in the groups as facilitators would provide different types of data than that which we have been able to gather. Oded Manor's *Groupwork Research* is a good text on evaluating groups.

When evaluating the groups we have

endeavoured as much as possible to be scientist-practitioners and to limit biasing effects on the data. For example, although most participants (having taken on board the ethos of 'speaking one's mind') seem happy to provide honest and constructively critical feedback during the last session, we also give people opportunities to feed back anonymously in order to capture comments that people might not feel comfortable saying in front of us or the whole group. Our primary aim in obtaining feedback has not been to show that our interventions 'work', to obtain evidence to secure funding or to generate profits from selling evidence-based treatments; rather it has been to find out what went well and what did not go well so as facilitators we could change the way we work next time. As *groupworkers* we have invested a lot in facilitating a group that aims to help as many people as possible have outcomes that they hoped for and this may well have a biasing effect on the evaluations, but as *researchers* we have not started from a position of having an interest in obtaining positive results from the evaluation – we have genuinely had an interest in obtaining honest, constructively critical feedback.

The evaluations usually centre on people's general views of the groups, including what they have found helpful and what they have not found helpful (or found harmful) about being involved, and the extent to which their aims have been met. This is very different from research that is set up to solely evaluate whether a specific, uniformly delivered treatment has brought about changes on a specific measure of each research subject's supposedly uniform problem. *Psychology in the Real World* evaluations have enabled complexity and diversity to be recognised. For example, during a round robin evaluation of *Walk and Talk* people referred to very different impacts on them of being involved: improved physical health; reduced social isolation; improved psychological wellbeing through connection with nature; psychological benefit from sharing difficulties over a pint in the pub with sympathetic listeners; reductions in social anxiety; and introjection of aspects of the group (e.g. feeling increasingly safe and comfortable through spending time in a safe and comfortable group).

Methodologies used in the evaluations include:

1. *Participant observation and focus groups* – Normally the last meeting of a group is utilised as an opportunity to reflect on ending issues and includes discussion of what participants have got from coming on the course, how it has impacted on them, what they will take away, what plans they have for the future, and so on. Comments are usually recorded, written up in a way that ensures anonymity and incorporated into a report. This is then given to participants for them to amend inaccuracies, add additional comments and give consent to the report being sent to other people (e.g. managers), appear on the website and form the basis of a publishable article. The final report is then published and put on www.shropsych.org.

2. *Questionnaires* – In penultimate sessions questionnaires are often given out to be filled in anonymously and returned the following week (in sealed envelopes) or by post. These often include a list of individual and group aims agreed at the start of the group with requests to rate the degree to which each participant feels these aims have been met. Specific questions testing various hypotheses have accompanied more open and general questions; this has enabled the gathering of data that can be analysed by quantitative and qualitative methods. At the end of each questionnaire we give people ample space (one sheet of A4) to write general comments on what they made of the course. In several evaluations this has led to large amounts of information that can then be analysed with qualitative methodologies. Such open questions often provide the most interesting data – many of the quotes included in this book have come from such questions. Despite opportunities (and active encourage-ment) for group members (including those who have dropped out) to anonymously comment negatively about the groups if they feel anything has not been a good experience, the positive comments and ratings have always significantly outweighed the negatives in any evaluation we have done.

We do not usually use standardised research tools as they do not readily fit the philosophies of *Psychology in the Real World*. For example, the Beck Depression Inventory by definition defines what depression 'is' through the 21 questions it asks, whereas *The Black Dog* enables a more complex conceptualisation of depression, where each person's depression may be subtly or radically different from another. However, we have included specific questions that are used in some NHS Trust and Local Authority questionnaires to test whether interventions are helping these organisations' stated priorities to be met. We have also devised questionnaires to test our own hypotheses, e.g. whether the groups provide the 11 therapeutic factors identified by Irvin Yalom and whether the groups enable people to increase participants' proximal powers as identified by David Smail. Examples of these types of questionnaires and this type of research methodology can be found in two research reports conducted by Lucy Gahan and myself on *Understanding Yourself and Others* 2004–2005 and *Understanding Ourselves and Others* 2008: see www.shropsych.org/ psychologyintherealworld.htm

3. *Follow-up contact* – Participants have been asked for feedback up to 18 months after completion of a course in order to try and

measure longer-term outcomes (see, for example, Holmes & Gahan, 2007). Very little research is conducted on long-term outcomes. Drug company research usually only involves measuring people over several weeks. The long-term outcome literature for psychiatric interventions such as ECT and psychological interventions such as talking therapies indicates that they are rarely effective six months after the treatment has ceased (see Epstein, 2006). This is widely known but seldom referred to. Although my research methodology is open to critique and service satisfaction surveys are renowned for producing data with high satisfaction scores, I have tried to get some data on longer-term outcomes and the data has indicated some positive changes for people that participants related to impacts of the group occurring months and sometimes years after the group ended. This fits anecdotal evidence I have obtained. For example, several people have stopped me in the street years after completing a course to say that attending the group 'changed their life', and have provided rich descriptions of how this occurred. Of course, people who might have bumped into me years later and not had a good experience of the groups are less likely to be so effusive, but such encounters are one of the bonuses of providing community interventions where you live and work and are testimony to how powerful and lasting the impacts of *Psychology in the Real World* groups can be on occasion.

4. *Creative methodologies* – We have tried to utilise some novel and creative ways of evaluating the groups. For example, we have asked members of *The Writing Groups* to produce a piece of writing describing their thoughts and feelings about the group coming to an end and what they have got from participation. This has produced some wonderful poetry and moving pieces of writing which, along with the discussion that accompanies it, has provided rich feedback to the facilitators about the groups and has been made available for others to read on www.shropsych.org and on our local service user website www.well-scrambled.co.uk.

Action research

Psychology in the Real World ventures, individually and in terms of the progression from the ideas that led to the first venture right through to those that have underpinned the most recent ones, can be conceptualised as action research. Kurt Lewin coined this phrase in the 1940s to describe a way of operating that incorporates an interactive set of steps that involve planning, action and fact finding about the results. His framework involves people taking a research mentality to every aspect of a particular project: starting with the original idea, incorporating fact finding and research around the idea, planning the venture, the first step in implementation (the first action), evaluation of that step and the making of appropriate amendments, then planning and enacting the second step (action), and so on. Research, or audit, is not something that is therefore done in isolation or at the end of a project by outside researchers – it runs through every step of the process and involves collaboration between everyone involved. In a sense, since groupwork of this type was not something I was formally trained to do, every step of every *Psychology in the Real World* group has felt like an experiment and I have been keen to shape and adapt each venture at every step of the journey. This book may give some readers a misleading impression that each group was mapped out in advance and conducted according to a careful plan before being evaluated at the end. Nothing could be further from the truth. Doing the groups has been just as much a voyage of discovery for myself and other facilitators as for the participants who, every step of the way, have influenced the philosophies and practices that underpin *Psychology in the Real World* ventures, through their thoughtful and honest comments, and sometimes their non-verbal reactions, in each minute of each session of each group. Reflection on this – with group members in breaks, over lunch after the group session has ended, often with co-facilitators, and in supervision in between sessions – has enabled us as scientist-practitioners/reflective practitioners/action researchers to learn about, adapt and shape the groups. It has involved moment-to-moment theorising and us treating every minute of every group as 'data' that might inform our thinking and ways of doing things. It has led us to understand more fully what we have been doing. This process can be expected to go on forever – it would be so boring if it didn't!

SECTION 14

Final thoughts

63

'How can this be done in the modern NHS?'

Not everything that counts can be counted, and not everything that can be counted counts.
  Albert Einstein

When hearing *Psychology in the Real World* ventures described at conferences, training events and on clinical psychology training courses, people frequently say they feel inspired. However, this tends to be accompanied by another set of feelings, especially in NHS professionals, that seem to relate to feeling crushed, exhausted and worried, especially when considering doing anything outside NICE guidelines and outside the narrow confines of providing individual therapy. One of the most common questions I am asked is 'How can you manage to do this in today's NHS?' Several people who have seemed interested in setting up their own projects have later become a bit despondent, saying: 'It's alright for you, but I would never be allowed to pursue my own ideas in this way and do this kind of work.' For me it is quite frightening to witness the constriction (some might say crushing) of professional independence about how people deliver a service, not through what recipients say would meet their needs but through the domination of managerialism in the NHS.

I normally tell interested people that I have set up (and helped others set up) these ventures as part of fulfilling my job description and have not felt a need to request permission or obtain express approval from people who have acquired (or are perceived to have acquired) power to stop me providing psychology services in ways that best meet the expressed needs of the local people I am paid to help. My experience is that asking highly stressed people in managerial positions for permission often triggers in them fears about what might go wrong and discussions get skewed by the pressure they feel to meet the latest targets. Managers at all levels in the hierarchy are under enormous strain to react to unreasonable demand after unreasonable demand, and what they were bullied to do last month seems to get forgotten as they get bullied to fulfil this month's priority. Consequently, there is a high risk that they will come up with lots of reasons *not* to do something. On the other hand, support from managers helps people to feel more confident in what they are doing: Doel and Sawdon researched factors that enable and prevent groupwork being done in mental health settings and found that official sanction from people in managerial positions was perceived by staff as one of the most important factors.

When justifying or seeking permission for groupwork in community settings, it should not be too difficult to marshal arguments to persuade managers or commissioners that the types of groups described in this book should be conducted. When doing them for the first time we have found it helpful to talk of 'projects' rather than 'services'. Arguments that justify the need for such projects can refer to:

1. Government frameworks for the delivering of services, such as the National Service Framework and *New Horizons* (its proposed replacement). National Service Framework Standard 1 emphasised the need for mental health promotion. It was given equal weight alongside the other frameworks yet received comparatively little attention from managers and very little funding. *New Horizons* aims to put equality, combating stigma, mental health promotion, and service user-driven initiatives at the fulcrum of mental health services for the period 2010-2020. *Psychology in the Real World* ventures have enabled managers to tick boxes and assure commissioners and the Department of Health that there is 'activity' in the area of mental health promotion and the similarly ignored areas of prevention and stigma, and can be seen as a template for how services might be structured under *New Horizons*. The groups fit with many government initiatives that are given great emphasis within NHS Trusts. For example, my employing Trust in 2009 launched a prominent *Combating Stigma Strategy* and became a partner in the national high profile *Time to Change* campaign. The groups enable managers and commissioners to show that something is being done at ground level, not just in the arena of policy statements.

2. Mental Health Trusts' expressed aims and objectives. Many services struggle to live up to these aims, but *Psychology in the Real World* ventures sit easily within such frameworks. For example, my Trust's 'Headline Strategic Objectives for the Board of Directors' include: *Ensure delivery of fair, equitable and values-based services; Ensure delivery of personalised care offering choice; Ensure delivery of effective, outcome-based care; Ensure our position in the NHS marketplace is predicated on innovation and quality; Ensure we continue to modernise, innovate and refine services through the deployment of*

Research & Development. Similarly, the Trust's plans for the future as set out by the head of adult mental health services ('2020: The Vision') include amongst five key areas of focus: reduced stigma and increased social inclusion; using educational approaches to promote and extend knowledge and availability of skills for mental health and wellbeing; working with media and marketing to raise general awareness of protective factors and risk factors. Such official documents provide a general umbrella under which *Psychology in the Real World* ventures can be protected and valued.

3. The projects have involved NHS Trust service users in many ways, thus meeting one of the organisation's main aims regarding service user involvement. For example, they have been set up in response to service user requests (directly to me or as recorded in local surveys); have involved service users in terms of planning and co-facilitation; have involved service users in their evaluation, including people learning research skills and publishing academic articles in journals and books.

4. The groups are evidence based. The evidence base for the benefits of walking, exercise and being in the countryside is strong and supports the setting up of something like *Walk and Talk* (see Chapter 48). It is just less commonly cited than the evidence base for psychiatric drugs and cognitive-behaviour therapy, which are bound to dominate NICE guidelines as this organisation was explicitly set up to look at cost-effective *treatments* not the whole range of ways in which a mental health service can be provided. For example, NICE guidelines rarely mention recovery despite this concept dominating other areas of policy in mental health. Similarly, social inclusion is given a high profile in many government documents but you would not know this from reading NICE guidelines.

Psychology in the Real World groups are evaluated. Although the methodologies of these evaluations are open to critique (see Chapter 62), they are done in ways to obtain as much information as possible about participants' experiences of the groups, and thus provide a local evidence base of their own. This evidence is more likely to generalise to the local population CMHTs are paid to help compared to national and international databases that might be based on research on very different populations.

5. It can be argued that the groups are examples of innovative practice. To solely follow NICE guidelines and other protocols is not the true vocation of a scientist-practitioner. Science is about innovation, experimentation, testing hypotheses, generating new theories and providing new evidence for scrutiny by peers, without which progress cannot be made. Each Department of Health document is based on research that was done many years before publication and some of this is often out of date by the time pressure is exerted for its implementation.

When we published *This is Madness* (Newnes, Holmes & Dunn, 1999) much of it was seen as extreme by many people in mental health services; within a decade many of its premises had become accepted by the majority of staff and managers. *Thinking about Medication* ruffled feathers – *should psychologists be involved in medication? … how wise is it to provide disturbed people with a full account of the downsides of psychiatric drugs? … shouldn't medication be the sole realm of psychiatry and nursing?* Yet several years on, *New Ways of Working* documents sent to chief executives of each NHS Trust for immediate implementation had the slogan that 'medicines management was everybody's business' and recommended that projects like *Thinking about Medication* and *Out*

of the Box should be available in all NHS Mental Health Trusts. Similarly *Walk and Talk* was initially perceived as innovative. Years later the Health Secretary Andy Burnham said: 'I will make it a personal priority to embed in the NHS culture the promotion of physical activity.' Waiting for the government to catch up is not commensurate with the modus operandi of scientist-practitioners who should be changing their practice as they constantly analyse and evaluate what they do.

6. The groups have wide-reaching support. *Psychology in the Real World* groups, and evidence supporting them, have been presented to a large number of people locally and nationally and have therefore gained approval and support from a wide variety of sources. This includes both professional and service user organisations. Senior people in the Department of Health and in organisations involved in shaping current and future national mental health policy have remarked positively on the philosophies that underpin *Psychology in the Real World* (for example, in terms of making psychology and NHS psychologists more widely accessible to people). Publicising the groups through presenting the work at training events, national conferences and in journals such as *OpenMind* (as well as academic journals) helps increase awareness and leads to a wide range of contacts with people nationally, which bolsters confidence in their validity and importance.

7. The groups are encapsulated within a job description and annual job review (KSF) process and have support from line management and other clinicians. It is clearly helpful to have a line manager who has an understanding of the ideas behind the work. I was perhaps lucky during the period when some of the original projects were planned and set up in that I benefited from having Craig Newnes as my line manager. Craig

and I had worked closely for many years and had developed similar ideas about mental health services. Subsequent psychology managers have had significantly less knowledge of this aspect of my work but have also been supportive once the philosophies and practices have been explained. I have a job description which states I am responsible for providing a clinical psychology service to the people in the catchment area of the CMHT where I am based – this makes it hard for non-psychologists to directly intervene to prevent me providing this service in ways that I feel best utilises my skills as a psychologist in terms of meeting local people's needs. A key to the groups' success relates to providing people who attend local CMHTs with opportunities to mix with people who are not so embedded in psychiatric services and all of the groups have members who are CMHT clients (the core group I am employed to help). CMHT colleagues have heard people comment on the benefits they feel they have experienced from the groups and this has led to the groups being viewed positively by local clinicians. The managers of the CMHTs where I have been based have also witnessed the benefits of this work and have not tried to insist that other things are done instead (although the fact that the managers of these teams have not been my line manager might also have prevented this). Having good relationships with work colleagues of all professions and in all positions in the hierarchy is also important – this takes time and can only be achieved by staying in the same place of work for a considerable period.

In short, whenever I have made presentations about *Psychology in the Real World* groups to senior managers in the NHS Trust (e.g. at clinical governance meetings) the work has been met with considerable interest and universal approval, as indeed it has in a wide range of professional and service user forums locally and nationally. The groups also have a good reputation with service user activists in the local area and service user consultants who sit on various NHS Trust committees. It is not difficult to make a strong case for the need for this type of work and the fear of it being prevented perhaps infuses people more than it needs to.

On time pressures

Doel and Sawdon's research revealed that time pressure on clinicians was one of the main reasons people did not do more groupwork. Time spent in preparation and logistics when setting up community-based groups usually exceeds the time spent facilitating the sessions. On top of this is the time spent preparing each individual session (short in endeavours such as *Walk and Talk* or *The Writing Group*, many hours for each session in *Understanding Ourselves and Others* and *The Black Dog*), as well as the time spent debriefing with co-facilitators and in supervision afterwards. Then there is the time needed to evaluate the groups and publish reports. In an NHS that heaps ever-increasing bureaucratic requirements on clinicians in the name of performance management I have found it incumbent to ignore many requests to do certain tasks that have little or no relevance regarding helping local people in order to preserve the time needed to prepare and run these groups. Similarly, I quickly give up sitting on committees where decisions are never taken; where I am constantly outvoted and unable to influence decisions; where the committee has little real power so that decisions taken do not lead to significant changes in the way people do things; or meetings that are solely about box-ticking for performance management and audit purposes. There are more important things to do. Like fulfilling your job description, which may include sections on training, supervision, service user consultation and service user involvement, all of which are encompassed in community-based groupwork.

It is not easy to resist pressures to do things, even when those telling you to comply agree that the demanded-for actions are irrational, clinically unhelpful and a waste of time. The NHS at times feels like it has layers and layers of management, with each manager telling the person below them: 'I know it's not a good idea but there is nothing we can do – we just have to get on with it.' To help people be less conforming locally, partly inspired by a session on *Toxic Mental Environments*, a number of us have operated something called *Protest Against the Rising Tide of Conformity* over the past few years, where we send out emails and put up posters in local services citing prominent people's comments about the risks of conformity. In addition, a number of us have set up systems to support an ever-shrinking band of people who openly struggle against the alienating effects of bureaucratic requirements that suffocate impassioned clinicians' intrinsic motivation for their jobs and lead them to just process people through systems rather than really engage with people. Having allies and solidarity helps people resist many things, including well-meaning but often heavy-handed attempts to bring about conformity in the name of consistency, accountability and efficiency, that have the (often unwanted) effects of bringing about alienation, infantilisation, exhaustion, demoralisation and paranoid fears of being disciplined. An example of a poster for this campaign can be found at the end of this chapter.

On registering client contacts

People who come on *Psychology in the Real World* courses are not registered and counted as client/patient contacts on NHS databases. This is because the groups are not conceptualised as treatment or therapy. Those attending include

people who are already registered on NHS Mental Health Trust databases (through their contact with other professionals in the service) as well as people who are not registered, as they have had no assessments or mental health service interventions. An insistence on all people attending *Psychology in the Real World* groups being registered and having their attendance recorded as 'client contacts' would clash with core *Psychology in the Real World* philosophies (e.g. the challenge to the categorisation of people as either mentally ill or sane). It would also raise several intriguing possibilities – for example, members of the public with no other contact with the Mental Health Trust and members of staff who sign up for a course (conceptualising it as training) would get a mental health record and be officially registered as 'having a mental health problem' with concomitant knock-on effects.

Mostly demands to submit client contacts for everything we do should be countered by citing Albert Einstein's quote at the beginning of this chapter. The struggle against everything being recorded and put on databases that appear to be designed to enable the NHS to be privatised needs to be, in my opinion, struggled against. I have long argued against any recording of non-anonymised client contacts being used for non-clinical purposes (e.g. payment of contracts) due to the impossibility of letting people know who might have access to information that names them as receiving help from a mental health service. The Joseph Rowntree Trust has published a report stating that NHS databases are 'almost certainly illegal' under data protection and human rights legislation, the 'benefits claimed for data sharing are often illusory', and data sharing can harm the vulnerable through discriminisation and stigmatisation (Anderson et al, 2009). In arguing against the forced recording of people on such databases I have cited my professional duty to protect people's confidentiality as well as John Stuart Mill, who said it is unethical to force people to do something that they rationally object to on ethical grounds.

At present I have been able to avoid recording *Psychology in the Real World* participants on patient databases (and just feedback the total number of people attending each group to my line manager who keeps anonymous records of the various psychology interventions provided by CMHT psychologists). My face-to-face individual work in the CMHT is recorded on patient identifiable databases. It is essential that psychology and other staff are contracted to provide a low enough number of 'patient-identifiable face-to-face contacts' to enable work on top of individual therapy to be conducted, and historically Shropshire CMHT psychologists have been contracted to provide 400 per annum. Some clinical psychologists have contracts that demand twice this number of contacts with the result that they can only provide a therapy service, not the range of interventions that my (and probably their) job description expects (e.g. consultation work, training, research, supervision, community work, prevention, service user involvement work, groupwork). Managers in our NHS Trust and local commissioners in Shropshire have valued the range of work clinical psychologists do and have agreed contracts for face-to-face clinical work that ensure other types of work which require

considerable planning and preparation can take place. But like in *Catch-22* the number of 'missions' is always under threat of being increased in an NHS that seems to expect its staff to constantly provide more of everything. In 2009 our number of recordable face-to-face contacts was increased by 50% to 600 per annum without any guidance about what psychologists are expected to do less of. Some of the invisible glue that we try and provide in the system to enable other staff and service users to provide psychological interventions without suffering themselves or harming others is having to be spread much more thinly in a welfare state that seems to have lost all concept of welfare and increasingly only counts what it can count.

As well as meeting many organisational needs *Psychology in the Real World* groups can reduce waiting lists. For example, people are given the option of attending groups I run or seeing me individually but not offered both at the same time, and evaluations of the groups indicate that people have less rather than more involvement with services after attending the groups. However, to set up such groups just to reduce waiting lists or provide numbers of contacts to prove people are seen in order to meet performance management criteria would be depressing indeed. Surely we are in this line of work to do more than process people through systems and deliver rather meaningless data to fulfil contractual agreements?

protest against the rising tide of conformity

Good men must not obey the laws too well.

Ralph Waldo Emerson

Disobedience, in the eyes of anyone who has read history,
is man's original virtue.
It is through disobedience that progress has been made,
through disobedience and through rebellion.

Oscar Wilde

Liberty – individual liberty, the autonomy of the human – matters
because no one has the right to dictate to others how they should
live, what they should choose, whom they should love, or what goals
they should pursue, except if any of these things threaten harm to
others, where harm includes limiting others' freedoms to choose.

A.C. Grayling

Collective fear stimulates the herd instinct and tends
to produce ferocity toward those who are not regarded
as members of the herd.

Bertrand Russell

protest against the rising tide of conformity

64

The need for community-based groupwork in the 21st century

What is to be done when the forces of reason struggle so hard to withstand the machinations of interest?

David Smail

In my view the challenges of the 21st century are going to need much more than streams of individuals having their distress eased by streams of therapists providing one-to-one therapy. Psychoanalysts early in the 20th century had great confidence that psychotherapy would lead to a lessening of the ills in society. But that century saw more people killed in war and by avoidable famine than any other; gross inequalities of wealth and income, within countries and between countries, despite research indicating the deleterious impacts of this on the majority of people; mindless over-exploitation of the world's resources risking a desertification of some areas and the drowning under water of others; and the treatment of the planet as a dustbin into which people could chuck the waste from so many things that they do not need and at best bring only the most fleeting experiences of happiness. David Webster's historical analysis of the tipping points of civilisations indicates that when populations and empires seem at their most numerous and powerful this can be the point at which they are closest to environmental collapse. The environmental scientist James Lovelock has predicted periods of mass migration of people followed by a reduction in the world's population to one billion by the end of this

century (it is currently six billion). The consequences of this seem almost unimaginable, the only models for such events provided in science fiction novels.

Individual therapy has no doubt provided some relief for many people who have engaged in it (including myself), although, like psychiatric interventions such as ECT, the evidence for long-term benefits in the majority of recipients once the therapy ends is not strong (see Epstein, 2006). Individual therapy may help some people achieve what Maslow called self-actualisation of a person's full potential, but Maslow himself said that this is only realistically possible with a very small percentage of the population. Most people, especially those coming into services, struggle to have their basic needs met, such as the need for safety in their own home and neighbourhood; supportive relationships where they are respected and loved; freedom from abuse and exploitation; and engagement in meaningful activities that generate a sense of belonging and self-esteem. If the middle and latter parts of the 21st century include greater difficulties for people, whatever their country of origin, in terms of meeting these and even more basic needs (for shelter, food and water), psychotherapy could become an irrelevance. And by putting the vast majority of our resources into one-to-one therapies and medication we could be misguidedly providing the kind of comfort Nero got from playing his fiddle whilst Rome was burning – but this time it could be the whole planet that is set to burn.

Although Malthusian predictions have frequently proven unfounded and predicting the future of societies can be as hit and miss as predicting individual human behaviour, even if things continue pretty much as they are now I feel we need a different approach from the strategies and interventions that have dominated recent decades. The contents of this book provide no panacea. However, they perhaps do hint at certain things that might be important in terms of meeting some the challenges of the 21st century. For example, we might try to increase and deepen the interpersonal links we have with other people – those whom we see as potentially sharing some of our understandings of the world *and* those who do not, from whom there may also be much to learn. We can do this by perhaps engaging more in collaborative conversations, where we hold on to a sense of humility about our individual ways of understanding the world, explore ideas with others (rather than use power to get others to see the world in the way we do), and develop skills in resolving differences of opinion and conflict. There is perhaps more scope to utilise our capacities for building mutual aid systems – groups where we can receive *and* provide support, and act with solidarity to change things perceived as harmful. Rather than refine ever-increasing skills in one-to-one interventions, people might give greater focus to the neglected area of groupwork, developing their capacity to organise and facilitate groups, including how to manage group processes that interfere with

rational decision making (such as groupthink, scapegoating and splitting). We might learn to let go of our obsessions with categorising people, obtaining expert opinion and seeking the technological 'quick-fix'; instead, accepting the uniqueness of each individual, the great diversity of things that people find helpful, and the fact that change often takes a long time.

When people come together and pool their thoughts and ideas in group cultures akin to *Psychology in the Real World* it can become easier to analyse the roots of problems (both the causes and the causes of causes) and generate creative solutions to problems that might be taken forward by groups of people working together. This works well when we have learned to value the contributions of people who act and see things very differently from ourselves (providing their actions do not harm others) and committed ourselves to challenging forces in our communities that lead to the stigmatisation and marginalisation of people. In these ways communities can perhaps be built that utilise one skill that human beings have above all else – we are very proficient at changing our environment. In the West we have been misusing or wasting this talent (e.g. been seduced into spending our time and money on home improvements) rather than learning from histories of communities where the benefits of collectively working together to improve the psychosocial and material environment for *all* members of a community has led to great individual and communal benefits.

REFERENCES

Ackerman, D (1995) *A Natural History of the Senses.* New York: Vintage Books.

Adbusters: Journal of the Mental Environment. www.adbusters.org

Adorno, T, Frenkel-Brunswik, E, Levinson, D & Sanford, R (1950) *The Authoritarian Personality.* Oxford: Harpers.

Allport, G (1954) *The Nature of Prejudice.* Reading, MA: Addison-Wesley.

Anderson, R, Brown, I, Dowty, T, Inglesant, P, Heath, W & Sasse, A (2009) *Database State.* York: Joseph Rowntree Reform Trust.

APRIL (Adverse Psychiatric Reactions Information Link) www.april.org.uk

Arnold, S (2005) Lesson's Over. *The Guardian,* 14.06.05.

Aronson, E (1995) *The Social Animal.* New York: Freeman.

Asch, S (1951) Effects of group pressure upon the modification and distortion of judgment. In M Guetzkow (ed) *Groups, Leadership and Men.* Pittsburgh, PA: Carnegie.

Austin, T (1999) The role of education in the lives of people with mental health difficulties. In C Newnes, G Holmes & C Dunn (eds) *This is Madness: A critical look at psychiatry and the future of mental health services.* Ross-on-Wye: PCCS Books.

Bacon, F (1620) *Novum Organum* see www.constitution.org/bacon/nov_org.htm

Bakunin, M (1964) *The Political Philosophy of Bakunin.* New York: Free Press.

Balint, M (1968) *The Basic Fault.* London: Tavistock.

Bandura, A (1977) *Social Learning Theory.* Englewood Cliffs, NJ: Prentice Hall.

Barker, P & Buchanan-Barker, P (2005) *The Tidal Model: A guide for mental health professionals.* London: Routledge. See also www.tidal-model.com

Bateson, G (1973) *Steps to an Ecology of Mind.* London: Paladin.

Begley, S (2009) *The Plastic Mind.* London: Constable.

Bergin, A & Garfield, S (1994) *Handbook of Psychotherapy and Behaviour Change.* Oxford: Wiley.

Berne, E (1964) *Games People Play.* London: Penguin.

Berry, J (1997). Immigration, acculturation and adaptation. *Applied Psychology, 46,* 5–68.

Bion, W (1961) *Experiences in Groups.* London: Tavistock.

Blackmore, S (2000) The power of memes. *Scientific American, 283,* 52–61.

Boal, A (1995) *The Rainbow of Desire.* London: Routledge.

Bohm, D (1996) *On Dialogue.* London: Routledge.

Bolton, G, Howlett, S, Lago, C & Wright, J (2004) *Writing Cures: An introductory handbook of writing in counselling and psychotherapy.* London: Routledge.

Bowlby, J (1969) *Attachment and Loss (Vol 1) Attachment.* London: Hogarth.

Bowlby, J (1973) *Attachment and Loss (Vol 2) Separation: Anxiety and Anger.* London: Hogarth.

Bowlby, J (1980) *Attachment and Loss (Vol 3) Loss: Sadness and Depression.* London: Hogarth.

Boyle, M (1999) Diagnosis. In C Newnes, G Holmes & C Dunn (eds) *This is Madness: A critical look at psychiatry and the future of mental health services.* Ross-on-Wye: PCCS Books.

Breggin, P & Cohen, D (1999) *Your Drug May Be Your Problem: How and why to stop taking psychiatric medications.* New York: Perseus.

British Psychological Society (BPS) (nd) *More About Psychology.* www.bps.org.uk

British Psychological Society (2008) *Socially Inclusive Practice.* Leicester: BPS.

Brown, A (1994) *Groupwork.* Gateshead: Athenaeum.

Brown, G & Harris, T (1978) *Social Origins of Depression: A study of psychiatric disorders in women.* London: Tavistock.

Brown, J, Cochrane, R & Hancox, T (2000) Large-scale health promotion stress workshops for the general public: A controlled evaluation. *Behavioural and Cognitive Psychotherapy, 28,* 139–51.

Burke, D & Lotus, J (1998) *Get a Life!* London: Bloomsbury.

Burlingame, G, Fuhriman, A & Mosier, J (2003) The differential effectiveness of group psychotherapy: A meta-analytical perspective. *Group Dynamics: Theory, Research and Practice, 7,* 3–12.

Campbell, P (2001) Surviving social inclusion. In C Newnes, G Holmes & C Dunn (eds) *This is Madness: A critical look at psychiatry and the future of mental health services.* Ross-on-Wye: PCCS Books.

Campbell, P, Cobb, A & Darton, K (1998) *Psychiatric Drugs: Users experiences and current policy and practice.* London: MIND.

Camus, A (1955) *The Myth of Sisyphus.* London: Hamish Hamilton.

Camus, A (1956) *The Fall.* London: Penguin.

Casement, P (1985) *On Learning from the Patient.* London: Routledge.

Chadwick, P (2001) *Personality as Art: Artistic approaches in psychology.* Ross-on-Wye: PCCS Books.

Chomsky, N (1992) *Media Control: The spectacular achievement of propaganda.* Boston, MA: Open Media.

Clarke, J & Barkham, M (2009) Evidence de rigour: The shape of evidence in psychological therapies and the modern practitioner as teleoanalyst. *Clinical Psychology Forum, 202,* 7–11.

Cobb, S & Rose, R (1973) Hypertension, peptic ulcer and diabetes in air traffic controllers. *Journal of the Australian Medical Association, 224,* 489–92.

Coimbra, J & Menezes, I (2009) Society of individuals or community strength: Community psychology at risk in at-risk societies. *Journal of Critical Psychology, Counselling and Psychotherapy, 9,* 87–97.

Connell, R (1972) Political socialization in the American family: The evidence re-examined. *Public Opinion Quarterly, 36,* 323–33.

Cooper, C, Cooper, R & Eaker, L (1988) *Living With Stress.* London: Penguin Books.

Cowen, E (1982) Help is where you find it: Four informal groups. *American Psychologist, 37,* 385–95.

Cox, R, Holmes, G, Moloney, P, Priest, P & Ridley-Dash, M. (2010) Community psychology. In J Cromby, D Harper & P Reavey (eds) *Psychology and Mental Health: From disorder to experience.* Basingstoke: Palgrave Macmillan.

Crepaz-Keay, D (1999) Drugs. In C Newnes, G Holmes & C Dunn (eds) *This is Madness: A critical look at psychiatry and the future of mental health services.* Ross-on-Wye: PCCS Books.

Csikszentmihalyi, M (1998) *Finding Flow: The psychology of engagement with everyday life.* New York: Basic Books.

Curtis, A (2002) *Century of the Self.* BBC TV documentary.

Davies, N (1998) *Dark Heart: The shocking truth about hidden Britain.* London: Vintage.

DeGrandpre, R (2000) *Ritalin Nation.* New York: Norton.

Department of Health (2008) *Medicines Management: Everybody's business.* www.dh.gov.uk/en/ Publicationsandstatistics/Publications/PublicationsPolicyAndGuidance/DH_082200

Diamond, R (2008) Opening up space for dissension: A questioning psychology. In A Morgan (ed) *Being Human: Reflections on mental health in society.* Ross-on-Wye: PCCS Books.

Doel, M & Sawdon, C (2001) What makes for successful groupwork? A survey of agencies in the UK. *British Journal of Social Work, 31,* 437–63.

Easterbrook, G (2003) *The Progress Paradox: How life gets better while people feel worse.* New York: Random House.

Echo Research (2009) *Teenage Boys and the Media.* www.echoresearch.com/data/File/pdf/ echo%20teenage%20boys%20report%20of%20survey%20findings.pdf

Epstein, W (2006) *Psychotherapy as Religion.* Nevada: University of Nevada Press.

Evolving Minds www.evolving-minds.co.uk

Fanon, F (1986) *Black Skin, White Masks.* London: Pluto Press.

Fazel, S, Grann, M, Carlstrom, E, Lichtenstein, P & Langstrom N (2009) Risk factors for violent crime in schizophrenia: A national cohort study of 13,806 patients. *Journal of Clinical Psychiatry, 70,* 362–9.

Fazel, S, Langstrom, N, Hjern, A, Grann, M & Lichtenstein P (2009) Schizophrenia, substance abuse, and violent crime. *JAMA, 301,* 2016–23.

Feifel, H & Eells, J (1963) Patients and therapists assess the same psychotherapy. *The Journal of Consulting Psychology, 27,* 310–18.

Fernando, S (2009) Wellbeing for all. *OpenMind, 159,* 14.

Festinger, L (1957) *A Theory of Cognitive Dissonance.* Palo Alto, CA: Stanford University Press.

Festinger, L, Riecken, H & Schacter, S (1956) *When Prophecy Fails.* New York: Harper & Row.

Forgiveness Web, The www.forgivenessweb.com/RdgRm/research.htm

Foucault, M (1978/1997) What is critique? In S Lotringer (ed) *The Politics of Truth.* Cambridge: MIT.

Foucault, M (1991) *Discipline and Punish.* London: Penguin.

Foucault, M (2001) *Madness and Civilisation.* London: Routledge.

Foulkes, S & Anthony, E (1965) *Group Psychotherapy: The psychoanalytic approach.* London: Karnac.

Freire, P (1996) *Pedagogy of the Oppressed.* London: Penguin.

French, J & Caplan, R (1972) In A Marrow (ed) *The Failure of Success.* New York: Amacon.

Freud, S (1917) *Mourning and Melancholia.* In Penguin Freud Library (Vol 11). London: Penguin.

Friedli, L (2009) *Mental Health, Resilience and Inequalities.* Copenhagen: World Health Organisation.

Fromm, E (1960) *Science and Human Responsibility.* St Louis: Washington University Press. See also *Man's Needs: Interview with Huston Smith.*www.erich-fromm.de/data/pdf/1960g-e.pdf

Fromm, E (1996) *To Have or To Be?* London: Continuum.

Fryer, D (2009) International manifestations of community critical psychology. *Journal of Critical Psychology, Counselling and Psychotherapy, 9,* 59–65.

Gahan, L & Holmes, G (2008) *Psychology in the Real World: Understanding ourselves and others 2008 evaluation* (unpublished report available on www.shropsych.org/psychologyintherealworld.htm)

Gilbert, P (2000) *Overcoming Depression.* London: Constable.

Gilbert, P (2009) *The Compassionate Mind.* London: Constable.

Gitterman, A (2004) The mutual aid model. In C Garvin, L Gutierrez & M Galinsky (eds) *Handbook of Social Work with Groups.* New York: Guildford.

Goffman, E (1963) *Stigma: Notes on the management of a spoiled identity.* Englewood Cliffs, NJ: Prentice Hall.

Goleman, D (2006) *Social Intelligence.* London: Hutchinson.

Gordon, P (1999) *Face to Face: Therapy as ethics.* London: Constable.

Gourevitch, P (1998) *We Wish to Inform You that Tomorrow We Will Be Killed with Our Families: Stories from Rwanda.* London: Picador.

Grantham, P (2007) *Seminars in Effective Groupwork: The Essential Toolkit for Running Groups.* Birmingham. (See www.skillsdevelopment.co.uk for current courses.)

Grantham, P & Budnik, Y (2006) *Styles of therapeutic groups: Rethinking the model of White & Lippitt.* Abstracts from the All-Russia scientific conference on clinical psychology: The future of clinical psychology. Perm, Russia.

Grayling, AC (2004) *The Mystery of Things.* London: Orion.

Hagan, T & Smail, D (1977) Power-mapping I. Background and basic methodology. *Journal of Community and Applied Social Psychology, 7,* 257–67.

Hanson, S, McHoul, A & Rapley, M (2003) *Beyond Help: A consumer's guide to psychology.* Ross-on-Wye: PCCS Books.

Harlow, H (1986) *From Learning to Love: The selected papers of HF Harlow.* New York: Praeger.

Harper, D & Spellman, D (1996). Talking about failure. *Clinical Psychology Forum, 98,* 16–18.

Hartig, T (2008) Green space, psychological restoration and health inequality. *The Lancet, 372,* 1614–15.

Healy, D (2001) The SSRI Suicides. In C Newnes, G Holmes & C Dunn (eds) *This is Madness Too: Critical perspectives on mental health services.* Ross-on-Wye: PCCS Books.

Healy, D (2005*) Psychiatric Drugs Explained.* Guildford: Mosby.

Heron, J (2001) *Helping the Client: A creative, practical guide.* London: Sage.

Hillman, J & Ventura, M (1992) *We've Had a Hundred Years of Psychotherapy – And the World's Getting Worse.* London: HarperCollins.

Hodgkinson, B, Evans, D, O'Donnell, A, Nicholson J, & Walsh, K (2000) The effectiveness of individual therapy and group therapy in the treatment of schizophrenia. *Systematic Review by Joanna Briggs Institute for Evidence Based Nursing and Midwifery, 5,* 1–54.

Holland, S (1992) From social abuse to social action: A neighbourhood psychotherapy and social action project for women. *Changes, 10,* 146–53.

Holmes, G (2003) An audit: Do the people I see get better? *Clinical Psychology, 24,* 47–50.

Holmes, G (2006) Toxic Mental Environments. *Clinical Psychology Forum, 164,* 39–43.

Holmes, G & Gahan, L (2006) An evaluation of *Psychology in the Real World: Understanding yourself and others.* Unpublished report available on www.shropsych.org/rwgroupresearch.pdf

Holmes, G & Gahan, L (2007) Psychology in the Real World – Understanding Yourself and Others Course: An attempt to have an impact on stigma and social inclusion. *Groupwork, 16*(3), 9–25.

Holmes, G & Hudson, M (2003) Coming off medication. *OpenMind, 123,* 14–15.

Holmes, G & Hudson, M (2006) An evaluation of a *Thinking About Medication Group.* Unpublished report available on www.shropsych.org/evaluationmeds.pdf

Holmes, J (1994) Attachment theory – A secure theoretical base for counselling? *Psychodynamic Counselling, 1,* 65–79.

Horwitz, A & Wakefield, J (2007) *The Loss of Sadness: How psychiatry transformed normal sorrow into depressive disorder.* New York: Oxford University Press.

Howard, R & Holmes, G (2007) Reflections on a specialist groupwork placement. *Clinical Psychology Forum, 179,* 11–14.

Hubble, M, Duncan, B & Miller, S (eds) (1999) *The Heart and Soul of Change: What works in therapy.* Washington, DC: American Psychological Association.

Hughes, T (1998) *Birthday Letters.* London: Faber and Faber.

Hulme, P (1999) Collaborative conversation. In C Newnes, G Holmes & C Dunn (eds) *This is Madness: A critical look at psychiatry and the future of mental health services.* Ross-on-Wye: PCCS Books.

Icarus Project (2008) Harm reduction guide to coming off psychiatric drugs and withdrawal. Available on www.theicarusproject.net

Ivancevich, J & Matteson, M (1980) *Stress at Work.* Glenville, IL: Scott, Foresman & Co.

Jablensky, A, Sartorius, N, Ernberg, G, Anker, M, Korten, A, Cooper, J, Day, R, & Bertelsen, A (1992) Schizophrenia: Manifestations, incidence and course in different cultures: A World Health Organization ten-country study. *Psychological Medicine Monograph Supplement, 20,* 1–97.

Jackson, G (2005) Cybernetic children: How technologies change and constrain the developing mind. In C Newnes & N Radcliffe (eds) *Making and Breaking Children's Lives.* Ross-on-Wye: PCCS Books.

James, O (1998) *Britain on the Couch.* London: Arrow Books.

Janis, I (1972) *Victims of Groupthink.* Boston, MA: Houghton Mifflin.

Johnstone, L (2007) Understanding psychiatry's resistance to change. In D Double (ed) *Critical Psychiatry: The limits of madness.* London: Palgrave Macmillan.

Jones, C (2006) Studying social policy and resilience in families facing adversity in different welfare state contexts – the case of Britain and Sweden. *International Journal of Health Services, 36,* 425–42.

Kaner, S (2007) *Facilitator's Guide to Participatory Decision-Making.* London: Jossey-Bass.

Karasek, R, Baker, D, Marxer, F, Ahlbom, A & Theorell, T (1981) Job decision latitude, job demands and cardiovascular disease. *American Journal of Public Health, 71* (3), 694–705.

Keillor, G (1985) *Lake Wobegon Days: The original Radio 4 broadcasts.* BBC Radio Collection.

Keirsey, D (1998) *Please Understand Me: Temperament, character, intelligence.* Del Mar, CA: Prometheus.

Kelly, G (1955) *The Psychology of Personal Constructs.* New York: Norton.

Klein, M (1975) *The Writings of Melanie Klein, 4 vols.* London: Hogarth.

Klein, N (2001) *No Logo.* London: Flamingo.

Kornhauser, A (1965) *Mental Health of the Industrial Worker.* New York: John Wiley.

Kübler-Ross, E (1973) *On Death and Dying.* London: Routledge.

Layard, R (2005) *Happiness: Lessons from a new science.* London: Allan Lane.

Lehmann, P (2001) Coming off neuroleptics. In C Newnes, G Holmes & C Dunn (eds) *This is Madness Too: Critical perspectives on mental health services.* Ross-on-Wye: PCCS Books.

Lehmann, P (ed) (2005) *Coming off Psychiatric Drugs: Successful withdrawal from neuroleptics, antidepressants, lithium, carbamazepine and tranquillizers.* Berlin: Peter-Lehmann Publishing.

Lewin, K (1946) Action research and minority problems. *Journal of Social Issues 2,* 34–46.

Lewin, K (1951) *Field Theory in Social Science.* New York: Harper Row.

Lieberman, M, Eisenberger, N, Crockett, M, Tom, S, Pfeifer, J & Way, B (2007) Putting feelings into words: Affect labelling disrupts amygdala activity in response to affective stimuli. *Psychological Science, 18,* 421–8.

Living with Medication Group c/o Network for Change, 150–152 London Rd, Leicester, LE2 1ND. www.networkforchange.org.uk

Macgowan, M (2008) *A Guide to Evidence-Based Group Work.* Oxford: Oxford University Press.

Makkawi, I (2009) Towards an emerging paradigm of critical community psychology in Palestine. *Journal of Critical Psychology, Counselling and Psychotherapy, 9,* 75–86.

Malan, D (1995) *Individual Psychotherapy and the Science of Psychodynamics.* Oxford: Hodder-Arnold.

Manor, O (ed) (2009) *Groupwork Research.* London: Whiting & Birch.

Maslow, A (1970) *Motivation and Personality.* New York: Harper & Row.

McCrone, P, Weeramanthri T, Knapp M, Rushton, A, Trowell, J, Miles, G & Kolvin, I (2005) Cost-effectiveness of individual versus group psychotherapy for sexually abused girls. *Child and Adolescent Mental Health, 10,* 26–31.

McDermott, F (2002) *Inside Group Work: A guide to reflective practice.* Crows Nest, NSW: Allen & Unwin.

McRoberts, C, Burlingame, G & Hoag, M (1998) Comparative efficacy of individual and group psychotherapy: A meta-analytic perspective. *Group Dynamics: Theory, Research and Practice, 2*, 101–17.

Milgram, S (1963) Behavioral study of obedience. *Journal of Abnormal and Social Psychology, 67,* 371–8.

Mitchell, R & Popham, F (2008) Effect of exposure to natural environment on health inequalities: An observational population study. *The Lancet, 372,* 1655–60.

Moloney, P & Kelly, P (2004) Beck never lived in Birmingham: Why CBT may be a less useful treatment for psychological distress than is often supposed. *Clinical Psychology, 34,* 4–8.

Moncrieff, J (2008) *The Myth of the Chemical Cure.* Basingstoke: Palgrave Macmillan.

Moncrieff, J (2009) *A Straight Talking Introduction to Psychiatric Drugs.* Ross-on-Wye: PCCS Books.

Mosher, L & Burti, L (1994) *Community Mental Health.* London: Norton.

Newnes, C, Holmes, G & Dunn, C (1999) *This is Madness: A critical look at psychiatry and the future of mental health services.* Ross-on-Wye: PCCS Books.

Newnes, C & Radcliffe, N (eds) (2005) *Making and Breaking Children's Lives.* Ross-on-Wye: PCCS Books.

NIACE: The learning needs of young adults with mental health difficulties. archive./niace.org.uk/information/briefing_sheets/young_adults_MHD.htm

NICE (National Institute for Health and Clinical Excellence) (2004) *National Clinical Practice Guideline 23: Depression: Management of depression in primary and secondary care.* Rushden: The British Psychological Society and Gaskell.

NIMHE (National Institute for Mental Health in England) (2004) *Celebrating our Cultures: Guidelines for Mental Health Promotion with Black and Minority Ethnic Communities.* London: Department of Health.

O'Brien, J (1989) What's worth working for? In V Bradley & H Bersani (eds) *Improving the Quality of Services for People with Developmental Disabilities: It's everyone's business.* Baltimore, MD: Paul Brookes.

Office of the Deputy Prime Minister (2004) *Mental Health and Social Exclusion: Social Exclusion Unit Report.* London: HMSO.

Orford, J (1998) Have we a theory of community psychology? *Clinical Psychology Forum, 122*, 6–10.

Paykel, E, Myers, J, Dienelt, M, Klerman, G, Lindenthal, J & Pepper, M (1969) Life events and depression: A controlled study. *Archives of General Psychiatry, 21,* 753–60.

Phillips, A & Taylor, B (2009) *On Kindness.* London: Hamish Hamilton.

Pidgeon, N & Henwood, K (1996) Grounded theory: Practical implications. In J Richardson (ed) *Handbook of Qualitative Research Methods for Psychology and the Social Sciences.* Leicester: British Psychological Society.

Porter, R (2002) *Madness: A brief history.* Oxford: Oxford University Press.

Priest, P (2007) The healing balm effect: Using a walking group to feel better. *Journal of Health Psychology, 12,* 36–52.

Psychology Wiki. http://psychology.wikia.com/wiki/Main_Page

Read, J (2005) *Coping with Coming Off: Mind's research into the experiences of people trying to come off psychiatric drugs.* London: Mind Publications.

Read, J (2009) *Psychiatric Drugs: Key issues and service user perspectives.* Basingstoke: Palgrave Macmillan.

Read, J, Mosher, L & Bentall, R (2004) *Models of Madness.* Hove: Routledge.

Reich, S, Riemer, M, Prilleltensky, I & Montero, M (2007) *International Community Psychology: History and theories.* New York: Springer.

Rogers, C (1951) *Client-Centered Therapy.* London: Constable.

Roseth, C, Johnson, D & Johnson, R (2008) Promoting early adolescents' achievement and peer relationships: The effects of cooperative, competitive and individualistic goal structures. *Psychological Bulletin, 134,* 223–46.

Roth, A & Fonagy, P (2004) *What Works for Whom?* New York: Guilford Press.

Roth, G (1993) *When Food is Love.* London: Penguin.

Rowe, D (2005) *Depression: The way out of your prison.* Hove: Brunner-Routledge.

Sagan, C (1987) The Burden of Skepticism. *Skeptical Inquirer, 12.* Available at www.scribd.com

Sartre, J-P (2003) *Being and Nothingness: An essay on phenomenological ontology.* London: Routledge.

Seedhouse, D (2005) *Values Based Health Care: The fundamentals of ethical decision-making.* Oxford: Wiley.

Seligman, M (1975) *Helplessness: On depression, development and death.* San Francisco: Freeman.

Seroxat User Group www.seroxatusergroup.org.uk

Sharit, J & Salvendy, G (1982) Occupational stress: Review and reappraisal. *Human Factors, 24,* 129–62.

Sherif, M (1966) *In Common Predicament: Social psychology of intergroup conflict and cooperation.* Boston: Houghton Mifflin.

Slater, L (2004) *Opening Skinner's Box.* London: Bloomsbury.

Smail, D (1993) Putting our mouths where our money is. *Forum, 93,* 11–14.

Smail, D (2005) *Power, Interest and Psychology: Elements of a social materialist understanding of distress.* Ross-on-Wye: PCCS Books.

Smith, M (1997, 2004) Carl Rogers and informal education. *The encyclopaedia of informal education.* [www.infed.org/thinkers/et-rogers.htm. Last update: 5 February, 2009]

Solomon, A (2002) *The Noonday Demon: An atlas of depression.* New York: Scribner.

Spunk Library. www.spunk.org

Stock Whitaker, D (2001) *Using Groups to Help People.* London: Routledge.

Surowiecki, J (2004) *The Wisdom of Crowds: Why the many are smarter than the few.* London: Abacus.

Tajfel, H (1982) *Social Identity and Intergroup Relations.* Cambridge: Cambridge University Press.

Taylor, P & Gunn, J (1999) Homicides by people with mental illness: myth and reality. *British Journal of Psychiatry,* 174, 9–14.

Tillitski, C (1990) A meta-analysis of estimated effect sizes for group versus individual versus control treatments. *International Journal of Group Psychotherapy, 40,* 215–24.

Time to Change www.time-to-change.org.uk

Toseland, R & Rivas, R (2005) *An Introduction to Groupwork Practice.* London: Pearson.

Tuckman, B (1965) Developmental sequence in small groups. *Psychological Bulletin, 63,* 384–99.

Twenge, J (2006) *Generation Me.* New York: Simon & Schuster.

Tyrer, P & Kendall, T (2009) The spurious advance of antipsychotic drug therapy. *The Lancet, 373,* 4–5.

Waterson, J (2002) Redefining community care social work: Needs or risks led? *Health and Social Care in the Community, 7,* 276–9.

Watkins, M & Shulman, H (2008) *Towards Psychologies of Liberation.* Basingstoke: Palgrave Macmillan.

Webster, D (2002) *The Fall of the Ancient Maya.* London: Thames and Hudson.

Wells, D (2007) Domestic dogs and human health: An overview. *British Journal of Health Psychology, 12,* 145–56.

White, R & Lippitt, R (1960) Leader behavior and member reaction in three 'social climates'. In D Cartwright & A Zander (eds) *Group Dynamics: Research and theory.* Evanston, IL: Row, Peterson.

Wilkinson, R (1996) *Unhealthy Societies: The afflictions of inequality.* London: Routledge.

Wilkinson, R & Pickett, K (2009) *The Spirit Level: Why more equal societies almost always do better.* London: Penguin.

Wolfensberger, W (1992). *A brief introduction to Social Role Valorization as a high-order concept for structuring human services.* Syracuse, NY: Training Institute for Human Service Planning, Leadership and Change Agency (Syracuse University).

Workers Educational Association (WEA) www.wea.org.uk

Yalom, I (1980) *Existential Psychotherapy.* New York: Basic Books.

Yalom, I (2005) *The Theory and Practice of Group Psychotherapy.* New York: Basic Books.

Zimbardo, P (2007) The Lucifer Effect: How good people turn evil. London: Rider.

CONTRIBUTORS

MANDY BARRATT is married with two grown-up daughters. She has done foster care, volunteer work with orphans in China and co-leads a youth group. After 28 years of taking psychiatric medication she managed her own withdrawal and has happily been drug and symptom free since 2006. She currently works as a Support, Time and Recovery Worker in a CMHT.

JO CLARE is currently a CMHT service user who has attended three *Psychology in the Real World* courses. She is interested in psychology and likes fresh air and the sea.

KEN DAVIES is married with two grown-up sons, and lives in Telford. Most of his working life was spent in engineering and management roles in the communications industry. Ken's experience of mental health problems and treatment inspired him to work in mental health services, first in voluntary work and then as a Support, Time and Recovery Worker in his local Crisis Resolution and Home Treatment team.

NICKI EVANS – Having been given a diagnosis and medication, I feel that challenging ideas and practices in mental health has proved crucial for me. I am now aware there are many unimplemented routes, which do not include hospital environments or being heavily medicated, that lead to a better sense of wellbeing. I am currently a service user consultant with a fondness for animals, especially my dog, the outdoors, travelling, photography and writing poetry as a means of expressing myself, something that has developed since co-facilitating *The Writing Groups*.

LUCY GAHAN works as a clinical psychologist in Shropshire. Having trained on the Staffordshire and Keele clinical course, she developed a particular interest in community psychology. She is also drawn to narrative and systemic work, as well as psychodynamic models of therapy. She continues to explore ways of working psychologically beyond individual therapy.

GUY HOLMES lives in Shropshire with Biza, Ella and Marley. He was co-editor of the books *This is Madness* and *This is Madness Too* and has published over 35 articles on subjects such as the medicalisation of distress, impacts of abuse, medication and groupwork. He works as a clinical psychologist in the NHS.

MARESE HUDSON spent eleven years in the mental health system during which time she suffered many hospital admissions and was prescribed major tranquillisers, antidepressants and minor tranquillisers. When she decided to come off she came up against medical negativity and found no expertise or services within the mental health system regarding withdrawal. She was helped to come off by a substance misuse service providing a group for people on prescription drugs. She has not re-entered the mental health service since and has not taken psychiatric drugs for 17 years. She was a founding member of Shelton Hospital's Patients' Council and has worked for many years as a volunteer at MIND.

ANNA HUGHES – I have been a service user since 2000 and involved in service user involvement projects since 2004. My current involvement includes: facilitating satisfaction surveys on an inpatient ward; organising a weekly 'walk and talk' for guests at a crisis support house; and service user representation for a community-based printing workshop. Service user involvement has made a tremendous difference to my outlook on life, self-esteem and confidence, giving me a positive focus, a structure to the week and an important sense of belonging. I have met some fantastic people from all walks of life and hopefully have given something back.

CAROL JOHNSON is a former health professional who now works in the voluntary sector. She was prescribed psychiatric medication for over 15 years before successfully withdrawing from medication in 2007, since when she has been drug free.

ZOUNISH RAFIQUE works as a clinical psychologist in South Staffordshire and Shropshire NHS Foundation Trust. She is interested in exploring the applicability of Western understandings of psychological distress across cultures and using approaches that draw upon many different cultural beliefs when trying to provide help that is both respectful and appropriate.

CAROLE STONE is a former primary school teacher who left work due to her mental health problems. Since recovering from these problems she has worked as a volunteer within mental health, recently started paid work and is now considering returning to her career within education.

JOHN UPTON, during the past 25 years, has seen different psychotherapists on a one-to-one basis and been admitted to the local psychiatric hospital three times in the past decade. From his observations he is appalled by the dependency on prescription drugs rather than pursuing a course of psychotherapy. From his experience he is appalled by the lack of psychotherapy available through the National Health Service.

ELISABETH X has experienced good and bad traditional CMHT interventions. Both continue to have an impact. As well as having received services she also works in the NHS.

INDEX

STRAIGHT TALKING INTRODUCTIONS TO MENTAL HEALTH PROBLEMS
series edited by Richard Bentall & Pete Sanders
published throughout 2009

A STRAIGHT TALKING INTRODUCTION TO

Psychiatric Drugs   *Joanna Moncrieff*

Children's Mental Health Problems   *Sami Timimi*

Psychological Treatments for Mental Health Problems   *David Pilgrim*

Caring for Someone with Mental Health Problems   *Jen Kilyon & Theresa Smith*

Being a User of Psychiatric Services   *Peter Beresford*

The Causes of Mental Health Problems   *John Read & Pete Sanders*

Psychiatric Diagnosis   *Richard Bentall*

Rather than accept that solutions to mental health problems are owned by the medical professions, these books look at alternatives and provide information so that the users of psychiatric services and their families and carers can make more decisions about their own lives. Becoming more active in mental health issues requires knowledge — this series of books is a starting point for anyone who wants to know more about mental health problems.

These books also introduce ways of working collaboratively with doctors, psychiatrists and counsellors, and offer a better chance of building a constructive life with hope for the future.

For users of psychiatric services, carers, counsellors
support workers, volunteers and all in the helping professions

pocket sized and user friendly

www.pccs-books.co.uk   permanent discounts, free UK p+p